E-Commerce User Experience

International Standard Book Number: 0-9706072-0-2

Printed in the United States of America

First Printing: June 2001

04   03   02   01   5   4   3   2   1

Interpretation of the printing code: The rightmost double-digit number is the year of the book's printing; the rightmost single-digit number is the number of the book's printing.

Trademarks

Warning and Disclaimer

Publisher
Nielsen Norman Group
48921 Warm Springs Blvd.
Fremont, CA 94539-7767
USA
Email: info@nngroup.com
Website: www.nngroup.com

Home page for this report series:
www.nngroup.com/reports/ecommerce

Book Designer
Steven Thomas

Contents at a Glance

Table of Contents

Preface

As I am writing this preface, in the spring of 2001, the e-commerce field seems to have been thrown into a dark pit filled with bears that are busily devouring even the best sites. By the time you read these words, I hope the market is brighter. In any case, redesigning your site to match users' needs and follow the usability guidelines is good practice in any market, but usability is even more important when competitive advantage counts most.

I remain an optimist for the long-term future of e-commerce for one simple reason: we have empirical proof that mail order can be made to work and be very profitable. Many traditional catalog companies have prospered for decades. Also, over the years, many promising new mail-order companies have failed. Why should e-commerce be any different? Most new companies fail. That statistic doesn't invalidate entire industry segments. Our only problem is that during 1999 and 2000, the prevailing attitude was that anybody could start an e-commerce company and expect to be worth billions simply by being first-to-market, even if they were selling items that do not make sense for mail order.

It doesn't matter whether the market is up or down with respect to the usability guidelines contained in this report. It doesn't matter whether the hot segment is B2C, B2B, extranets, marketplace exchanges, inverse auctions, or something else. I safely predict that the analysts will be all abuzz about some new cliché no matter when you read this report. Well, industry buzzwords come and go, but human behavior remains constant. If you want to sell on the Web, you've got to make it easy to buy. Follow usability guidelines and you will do better than if you violate the usability guidelines. It's that simple.

At the time of this writing, an e-commerce site would gain a substantial competitive advantage by implementing a design that complies with most of the usability guidelines. Current e-commerce sites generally follow only about one-third of the guidelines, leaving vast room for improvement. In the future, I expect e-commerce sites to focus more on user experience and achieve higher compliance scores. Once that happy day arrives, the guidelines will still be valuable, because they will form a baseline for user expectations: in the future, sites that violate too many usability guidelines will simply not get any traffic because users will be expecting a consistently pleasant user experience. Even today, we often hear comments during user testing like, *"Why can't this site be as easy to use as Amazon.com?"* (Of those we scored, Amazon ranked the highest in terms of guideline compliance in 2001.)

The guidelines will remain in force for years to come because they are based on human behavior. Face it, we are not getting any smarter or more patient. In fact, people grow more impatient with difficult websites as the Web expands and matures, so demands for usability keep increasing.

I would like to take this opportunity to thank the many people who helped on this project. My co-authors, Susan Farrell, Rolf Molich, and Carolyn Snyder, obviously pulled the heaviest load, as did Sofie Scheutz, who conducted many of the overseas tests. We also got substantial help, input, and support from Tom Durkin , Shuli Gilutz, Luice Hwang, Hannah Kain, Donald A. Norman, Brenda Rexroth, Marie Tahir, and Steven Thomas.

Jakob Nielsen
Mountain View, California – April 2001

Acknowledgements

In addition to the authors, the following people worked on the project:

Sofie Scheutz: User testing

Tom Durkin: Editorial assistance

Steven Thomas: Design

Shuli Gilutz and Marie Tahir: Additional research and scorecard analysis

Joel Angiolillo, Douglas Chavez, Florian Egger, and Fran Rivkin: Review

Brenda Rexroth: Finance.

Introduction

This book is the collection of nine reports. This section presents information about the study and the executive summaries for each report.

About the Study – Overview of Method

In 2000, an international team of five usability experts led by Jakob Nielsen conducted usability tests of 20 business-to-consumer e-commerce websites. A total of 64 users participated: 39 from the United States and 25 from Denmark, giving us data about both domestic users (19 of 20 sites were American) and overseas users. Users ranged in age from their twenties to their fifties. All users had previously shopped online and most had made purchases; however, we screened out participants who had technical knowledge of the Web.

The typical user tested three of our 20 selected sites in a test session lasting two hours. Each site was tested by a minimum of nine users, six from the US and three from Denmark. We chose sites in seven different industries (such as clothing and toys) so that within each industry we had two or three sites for comparison.

Each user spent about 40 minutes on each site. We supplied the tasks, which were modeled on common goals of users during online shopping. Most tasks either asked the user to find a specific item that we knew existed on the site or were more open-ended, allowing users freedom to shop according to their own preferences. In most cases, we stopped the users before they entered a credit card number, so they did not actually complete the purchase. We also had a short task for each site where we asked users to find customer service information, such as how to cancel an order or return an item.

A highly experienced facilitator sat in the same room with the user, providing instructions to the user and taking notes. We asked users to think aloud as they worked.

The Methodology chapter provides greater detail about how we conducted this study, including copies of all the tasks.

Sites We Tested

Category	Site name	Main products offered
Clothing	Boo (www.boo.com)	Fashion and sportswear for men and women
	Jcrew (www.jcrew.com)	Clothing for men and women
	NorwaySweaters (www.norwaysweaters.com)	Sweaters in traditional Norwegian patterns
Department Stores	Nordstrom (www.nordstrom.com)	Apparel, shoes and accessories for men, women
	Sears (www.sears.com)	Tools, appliances, and home services
	Wal-Mart (www.walmart.com)	Discount department store
Flowers	1800flowers (www.1800flowers.com)	Flowers, gourmet foods, candies and gift baskets
	Iflorist (www.iflorist.com)	Flowers and plants
Food Novelties	BasketHaus (www.baskethaus.com)	Custom gift baskets that include foods and novelties
	Gevalia (www.gevalia.com)	Specialty coffee, tea, brewing equipment, desserts, and glassware
	Peet's (www.peets.com)	Freshly roasted whole bean specialty coffee
Furniture	Furniture (www.furniture.com)	Furniture and accessories for the home
	HermanMiller (www.hermanmiller.com)	Office, healthcare, and residential furniture
	Living (www.living.com)	Furniture and accessories for the home
Entertainment Media	CustomDisc (www.customdisc.com)	Custom music CDs containing songs chosen by the user
	Reel (www.reel.com)	Videos and DVDs
	TowerRecords (www.towerrecords.com)	Music CDs, videos and DVDs
Toys	Disney (www.disney.com)	Clothing, toys, collectibles, etc. featuring Walt Disney characters
	eToys (www.etoys.com)	Toys, books, software, videos and games for children
	SmarterKids (www.smarterkids.com)	Educational toys, books, software, videos and games for children

High-Level Strategy: Executive Summary

Page 1

Usability is a prerequisite for e-commerce success. If people cannot shop, then the site won't sell a thing. It doesn't matter how cheap the products are if people can't find them or if they get stuck on a step in the checkout process.

True, usability does not guarantee success for an e-commerce site. If prices are too high, people won't buy even if it is easy to navigate the site. But usability is one of the most important determinants for the success of an e-commerce site, especially considering how cheap it is to include basic usability methods in a project.

This chapter presents general findings regarding the relation between usability and e-commerce, including the following issues:

- **Why people abandon e-commerce sites.** People often feel powerless or overwhelmed while they are visiting a site, and other sites are just a click away.

- **The success rate for online shopping tasks.** The results of our own usability studies compared with those presented in several other reports.

- **Domestic versus international success rates.** Sites are so difficult to use for non-native speakers that improvements in international usability count as one of the greatest opportunities for increasing e-commerce sales. An entire chapter (International Users) is devoted to international usability issues.

- **Scorecard for compliance with our design guidelines.** Amazon.com follows 72% of the 207 guidelines we have documented. Other big sites' scores are lower, and smaller sites have horrible usability.

- **Different types of usability guidelines.** How to develop your own domain-specific guidelines.

- **Budgets for usability in Web projects.** What other companies spend, and how best to apply your usability budget to increase sales and user loyalty.

Selling Strategies: Executive Summary

All e-commerce websites share the goal of selling products to satisfied customers. Success on the Web requires intelligent usability engineering so users can find what they're looking for and buy it. Even if a website has perfect usability, however, the business will still lose sales if it has unrealistic prices or unfriendly policies.

Sales and marketing specialists, as well as site designers, can learn from this report. It reaches beyond classic usability concerns to discuss online selling issues such as pricing, selection, cross-selling, promotions, return policy, customer service, shipping and delivery. If your job involves marketing or sales, read this chapter to understand how certain policies and practices might cause you to lose customers. If your job involves site design, read this report to learn how best to support the sales and marketing strategies of your website.

The first part of this report covers e-commerce essentials: the precepts of online sales that websites must get right or risk losing customers. Our study shows that successful e-commerce sites must have:

- Fair prices, in line with the value customers perceive for the product.
- Reasonable shipping charges, revealed before the customer must enter any personal information.
- A wide selection of merchandise.
- Adequate inventory, with a minimum of out-of-stock items.
- Delivery that meets customers' expectations.
- Clear customer satisfaction policies.
- Specific information about returns.

Although the above points may sound self-evident, we found violations of all of them in this study. Some of these transgressions were so unacceptable that our users couldn't complete a purchase or said they would leave the site. We call such problems "sales catastrophes," because they represent not just lost sales, but lost customers as well.

In the second part of this chapter, you will learn tactics for supporting the sales process. These methods assist shoppers and might encourage them to buy more items:

- Give customers a visible means of buying promoted products.
- Suggest additional purchases on product pages, not during checkout.
- Always use an opt-in approach when suggesting additional purchases.
- Present recommendations and ratings that are relevant to your customers' needs.
- Provide expert help through online chat and toll-free phone numbers.
- Support gift buying and provide gift-related options.

The final part of this report addresses special considerations for "hybrid" stores — companies that have physical retail stores as well as a Web store. Our evidence shows that users expect consistent pricing and policies between real and virtual stores. We also found there are synergistic opportunities for hybrid enterprises whose online and offline operations collaborate.

Trust: Executive Summary

Page 77

Trust is hard to build — and easy to lose. A single violation of trust can destroy years of slowly accumulated credibility.

This chapter gives a broad overview of the trust-related issues that our 64 users brought up when we asked them to carry out basic shopping tasks on 20 US e-commerce websites.

Here, "trust" means the person's willingness to invest time, money, and personal data in an e-commerce site in return for goods and services that meet certain expectations. The more a person trusts a website, the larger the risk he or she is willing to take when dealing with the website. If a shopper doesn't trust a website, a "sales catastrophe" occurs. A sales catastrophe is an issue that is sufficiently important to either prevent a sale, or to discourage the person from returning to the site.

Trust is fragile. It is helped or hurt on every page of a website. Many of our users had little trust even in renowned online shopping websites. They said they wanted websites to win their trust by providing:

Succinct and readily accessible information about the company. Our users asked "Who are these guys?" They wanted the website to convey a real-world presence.

Fair pricing, fully revealed. Our users wanted visible prices, including taxes, shipping charges, and fees displayed right up front.

Sufficient and balanced product information. Our users wanted short but sufficient and accurate information about products. They wanted to see exactly what they'd get.

Correct, timely, professional site design. Our users made sarcastic remarks or even left the website in disdain when they encountered outdated content, spelling errors, bugs, unreasonable response times, or inhuman error messages.

Clear and customer-friendly policies. Our users appreciated privacy and return policies written in no-nonsense language.

Appropriate use of personal information. Our users were reluctant to provide personal information such as e-mail addresses and phone numbers. They wanted to shop without being forced to register.

Trustworthy security. Our users looked for secure servers. When security appeared doubtful, they wanted an alternative means of ordering, for example by phone or fax.

Access to helpful people. Our users said that providing access to helpful people through e-mail or online chat increases their trust. Curt and nameless contact can reduce trust.

This chapter discusses each of these issues in detail. To learn more about this study and the sites we tested, please refer to the Methodology chapter.

Category Pages: Executive Summary

Page 111

Category pages are those mid-level pages in an e-commerce website that help customers find the product listing pages — and thus, the products they want to buy. Category pages are critical-path elements in e-commerce transactions. Inability to find an item was the most common reason for task failure in our study, accounting for 27% of sales catastrophes in our study. A "sales catastrophe" is an issue that was sufficiently important either to prevent a sale or to discourage the customer from returning to the site.

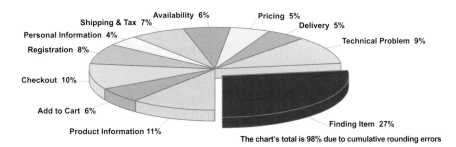

The chart's total is 98% due to cumulative rounding errors

Here are our most important findings about what works — and doesn't work — on category pages:

- **Home pages.** In one sense, a home page is a special type of category page. The home page must make it clear to users what products they can buy from the site. On a few sites we tested, users couldn't tell what the site sold even after exploring it for several minutes.

- **Classification.** Classification is vital: navigational links work better when users grasp how the site's offerings are organized. A good category page uses a classification scheme that users understand. Links should be sufficiently descriptive so that users can correctly choose which one leads to their goal. On some sites, it's necessary to provide multiple classifications and cross-references.

- **Product listing pages.** Category pages must deliver usable lists of product pages. If customers know what they're looking for, they should be able to recognize the product when they find it from the text or graphics on its product listing page. If customers aren't sure of what they want, the product list should supply enough information for them to decide which items to look at more closely.

- **Winnowing tools.** Originally, "to winnow" meant to separate the wheat from the chaff. On the Web, winnowing tools allow customers to choose specific filters to sift through a large number of products to locate the ones they are looking for. Some of our test sites provided page after page of product listings with no way to further reduce the number of choices. Few users looked past the second page. Several of our test sites provided winnowing tools, and we observed that a winnowing tool can be quite helpful — if it works well.

- **Comparison tools.** If the product selection is complex, the site should provide a means for the customer to compare similar items. As with winnowing, the selection criteria should be user-defined.

Search: Executive Summary

Page 153

You cannot sell a product if your customers cannot find it. In our usability study of 20 US e-commerce websites, our users had a success rate of only 64% in searching for — and finding — what they wanted. Given this low rate, Web designers and developers must treat the search function as a critical element of building a profitable e-commerce site. In our study, 27% of the sales catastrophes were caused by failure to find an item This figure includes both browsing and searching behavior.

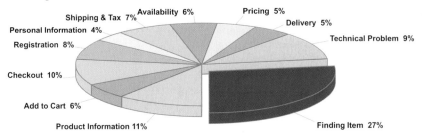

The chart's total is 98% due to cumulative rounding errors

Of the 20 websites we tested, 16 offered text search functionality. On those 16 searchable sites, our 64 US and Danish users attempted 344 tasks. Of those tasks, 95 involved search activity. We observed 52 of our users (81%) try the search function on one or more sites. The other 12 users (19%) did not choose to search.

The low success rate (64%) for search in our study showed that search functionality on many websites was inadequate. Simply indexing all the words used on your website is not enough.

Although 64% of our users' searches were successful, some of those successful users ultimately failed to complete their assigned tasks. Conversely, even though 36% of our users' searches ended in failure, some of those users found other ways to achieve task success.

With that said, this chapter focuses only on whether the searches were successful in yielding results that allowed our users to proceed to the next step in their assigned tasks. What happened after search success — or failure — is the subject of other chapters in this book.

Without exception, all of the search queries our users made were reasonable. Any human sales clerk would have immediately understood what the users wanted.

In analyzing our data, we identified the following aspects of a successful search:

- The user notices the website supports search.
- The user formulates a wish or a question and expresses it as a search query string.
- The user enters the search string and submits the query.
- The user interprets the search results.

Our data also showed that each search aspect is vulnerable in its own particular way. In this report, we discuss in depth how you can make the search facility of your website more customer-friendly — and less vulnerable to sales catastrophes.

The report concludes with a statistical analysis of our data. The analysis reveals a remarkable finding: If our users didn't find what they were looking for on their first search attempt, the odds *decreased* with each subsequent attempt that they would ever succeed in their search.

Put another way, site designers must create sophisticated search engines with a simple user interface capable of delivering the goods on the user's first search query.

Product Pages: Executive Summary

Page 193

A product page is one that is primarily devoted to presenting the details about a single product, including descriptive text, images, and purchasing information, such as availability and price. A product page also includes some mechanism for acquiring the item, such as a Buy button. Well-designed product pages are essential. Customers need sufficient information about an item in order to make informed purchase decisions.

In this study, 11% of sales catastrophes were caused by the user having insufficient information to feel comfortable about buying the product. An additional 6% were caused by the user's inability to get the chosen item into the shopping cart.

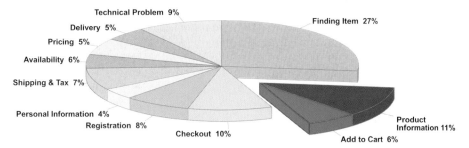

Technical Problem 9%
Delivery 5%
Pricing 5%
Availability 6%
Shipping & Tax 7%
Personal Information 4%
Registration 8%
Checkout 10%
Finding Item 27%
Product Information 11%
Add to Cart 6%

The chart's total is 98% due to cumulative rounding errors

None of the product pages we tested were perfect, although some were pretty good. As described in this report, we believe that a good product page has the following characteristics:

- Product has descriptive name, usually accompanied by a recognizable image.
- Product description includes all the factors customers care about.
- Page shows total cost, including price, delivery/shipping charges, and tax.
- Page states availability of product and shipping time.
- Page has links to manufacturer's warranty and site's guarantee or return policy.
- Page presents a highly visible means of putting items into the shopping cart.

Depending on the product, it may also be important for the product page to:

- Offer customer opinions and/or expert ratings.
- Have the capability to enlarge the product image to see details, including showing rotated or alternative views.
- Provide a means to specify — and view as specified — product options, such as color and finish.

Checkout & Registration: Executive Summary

Page 237

In order to buy things from a site on the Web today, a customer must generally put items in the shopping cart, select gift options and shipping method, enter shipping and billing addresses, review the order, provide payment information, confirm the sale, and perhaps save information for future convenience when shopping at that site in the future.

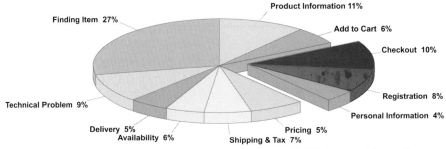

Product Information 11%
Finding Item 27%
Add to Cart 6%
Checkout 10%
Registration 8%
Personal Information 4%
Technical Problem 9%
Delivery 5%
Availability 6%
Pricing 5%
Shipping & Tax 7%

The chart's total is 98% due to cumulative rounding errors

Issues that arose during checkout and registration caused 22% of the sales catastrophies in this study.

When your customer is unable or unwilling to complete an online order after finding a desired product, it is a disaster for your site. Not only do you lose that sale, but often you lose the customer as well.

After deciding what to buy, the customer's next goal is to complete the purchase quickly. Confusion and unanswered questions slow people down, so one of the best strategies for streamlining checkout is to make it match the customer's expectations as closely as possible. We recommend the following model for the checkout and registration process:

1. **The shopping cart displays each line item, all additional charges, and the total based on the cheapest shipping method.** Shoppers want to know the bottom line before investing much time, because shipping charges help them decide whether to buy at all. The shopping cart page should also provide links to the return policy and any guarantees.

2. **Customer chooses gift options, if any.** People expect to specify any gift options such as a card message or gift wrap before entering their own information.

3. **Customer selects shipping method.** People want to compare the prices of various shipping options.

4. **Customer enters shipping address, then billing address.** Ask for only the information needed to fulfill the order and auto-fill forms whenever required information is already in the system. Some people leave a site if too much personal information is required. Providing error-recovery information is crucial to customer success.

5. **Customer reviews the entire order and provides payment information.** Some people are uncomfortable providing a credit card number online. Others are unable to complete the shopping process for some reason. Offer toll-free telephone ordering to avoid losing those sales.

6. **Site displays a confirmation page and gives customers the option to register.** Requiring registration before or during a purchase drives away business — many of the users in our study refused or were unable to register. Registration should always be optional. Customers must first perceive benefits to themselves and then get help from the site when choosing a user name and password.

International Users: Executive Summary

They don't call it the *World* Wide Web for nothing. A single click can take you to a site on another continent, and a business can attract customers from many countries. The unprecedented international exposure afforded by the Web increases the site designer's responsibility for ensuring international usability. International use is not a new phenomenon: Most computer companies and many large corporations have a significant percentage of their sales overseas.

The World Wide Web presents a unique opportunity for small, local companies. The websites of such local companies can provide fierce competition to foreign websites. Local companies have the tremendous advantage of knowing their local customers better than any foreign company can. In several cases, our Danish users compared the US websites we tested to similar Danish websites. Their message was that the US websites were just not getting it right. As far as we could see, the problems were indeed irritating but quite simple to correct.

Were the Danish participants able to use these e-commerce sites designed by and for North Americans? To answer this question we ran three to five usability tests with Danish users for each of the 20 US e-commerce websites we tested. We then systematically examined the main findings from an international perspective.

Our users helped us to find a wide assortment of international usability issues that arose from differences in language, dates, addresses, pricing, and delivery options. US site designers would do well to learn how to design for an international audience. However, when it comes to online shopping online in general, American and Danish users are more alike than different. We did not find that Danish users navigate, investigate products, or make their decisions in any fundamentally different way than their US counterparts. Sure, we saw problems unique to Danish users, but largely the same set of usability problems showed up on both sides of the Atlantic.

This similarity in behavior implies that it's unnecessary to design US websites differently for other countries, in particular, European countries. Of course, site designers must consider the issues of language, dates, addresses, and other foreign conventions, which are big enough challenges in themselves. But ultimately, the best way to improve your site's international usability is to make it more usable in its native country.

Denmark and the United States have a great deal of cultural similarity. Both nations are affluent, literate, and socially progressive compared to other parts of the world. Also, intense cultural exchange between Europe and America has existed for several centuries. Therefore, we would expect usability studies to find greater differences than reported here when testing US sites with Asian users, for example.

Are approximately 70 usability tests with 25 Danish users representative enough to draw conclusions for the very heterogeneous mass of non-US users in the world? We don't know for sure, because we haven't conducted similar usability testing in Southern Europe, Australia, Mexico, Russia, Asia, Africa, and lands beyond, yet. We do know, however, that our study has replicated most of the specific results reported by other sources. In addition, we believe we have discovered several other important findings we have not seen reported elsewhere.

Methodology: Executive Summary

Page 327

This chapter describes the methods we used to test the usability of 20 US business-to-consumer e-commerce websites. In this study we examined seven aspects of website design, such as search functionality and product pages presentation, by watching people shop. This book describes how users reacted to these sites and recommends specific design choices you can use to improve usability on the sites you develop.

We wrote this chapter for two intended audiences:

1. Those who want more information about our methodology as an aid to interpreting the results of our study.

2. Those who want to learn more about the practical aspects of website usability testing. For the benefit of this audience, we've included discussions on why we chose certain methods and implemented them in particular ways.

DialogDesign of Copenhagen, Denmark, created and distributed a survey to 13 people who work in the areas of website design or usability. We asked them which design factors we should write about. They urged us to include information about the methodology of the study itself, so readers can better understand how to interpret the results.

Reports about website design based on usability studies are increasingly common. More now than ever, website designers, usability professionals, and those responsible for the business aspects of retail websites recognize the value of usability data in building profitable sites.

The demand for information about what really works and what doesn't is so great that anyone with a usability lab and a little time can conduct a study and publish a report. We can expect to see not only an increase in the number of usability studies but also greater variations in their quality. Ultimately, the recommendations arising from any usability study can only be as good as the information on which they're based. The quality of this information depends on the methods used to collect the data.

Our goal in writing the Methodology chapter was to expose the inner workings of our e-commerce usability study: the hows and whys of our methods. We want to establish a standard against which other studies can be measured. Our hope is to discourage poor-quality imitators while helping our peers (and ourselves) produce work of even higher quality in the future.

Collectively, the five of us have more than 50 years of experience in usability in general and 22 years of experience in Web usability in particular. Although all of us have extensive experience in planning and conducting website usability studies, this project was especially challenging because of the large number of sites, short time frame (we completed all testing within a month), and the geographic separation of the five primary team members. We had many in-depth and fascinating e-mail discussions about our methods, which we have summarized in this chapter. We learned from each other, and we hope you can learn from us.

High-Level Strategy

" *Usability is a prerequisite for e-commerce success.*
... It doesn't matter how cheap the products are if
people can't find them or if they get stuck on a step
in the checkout process."

Usability and E-Commerce

Usability is one of the most important determinants for the success of an e-commerce site. The first law of e-commerce states: "if the customer cannot *find* the product, the customer cannot *buy* the product." In fact, as discussed in this chapter, there are many additional usability concerns in e-commerce beyond the simple ability to locate a desired product. Each and every usability deficiency in a design becomes an obstacle to the shopper's ability and willingness to buy. Low usability equals lost sales. It's as simple as that.

In simple terms, the success of an e-commerce site can be described with the following formula:

Unique_Visitors x Conversion_Rate = Sales

Increasing the first number is the goal of your advertising budget. Increasing the second number is the goal of your usability budget. In almost all e-commerce companies, the relative size of the two budgets is such that the greatest increases in sales will come from increasing the investment in usability. After all, to increase the desired outcome by a certain percentage, you can increase either of the two deciding parameters by that percentage. To increase visits by 10% usually requires an increase of much more than 10% in an already-large advertising budget. But the conversion rate can be increased by 10% through even the smallest usability project, if the site has never been subjected to systematic usability evaluation.

For the first few years of e-business, much attention was focused on the number of unique visitors to a site. Companies were sometimes valued based on this number instead of their real business models or ability to derive revenues and profits from the visitors. Getting people to your site certainly still matters: having the best site does no good if nobody knows about it. But it is at least as important to make sure visitors are satisfied and turn into customers. This second problem is the focus of usability and the goal of our design guidelines.

Of course, reality is more complex. It also matters how much each customer buys and whether people become loyal customers. These parameters are also highly affected by usability. The more pleasant and trustworthy a site seems, the more likely people are to return. The easier it is for shoppers to find what they are looking for, the more they buy. And the more that product descriptions and other content satisfy customers' needs, the more likely they are to spring for high-ticket items.

Why People Abandon E-Commerce Sites

Is the Web really the ultimate customer-empowering environment? The Web as a whole *is* empowering, because consumers have the power to click over to the competition at the slightest whim. Why then do websites so often leave people feeling powerless? The Web increases accessibility and defies geographical barriers. But e-commerce websites often decrease accessibility and make it easier just to go to the nearest store.

The Web as a whole is all about choice. The range of places available for people to do business is astounding, the options almost endless. Individual websites, however, often don't give people the flexibility that a physical store provides. Shoppers in physical stores have more power than those on e-commerce websites. Shoppers in physical stores can approach an expert (a salesperson or even a fellow shopper), to ask questions, explain their problems, and get recommendations. If shoppers want to compare similar items in a store, they can usually view the items side by side.

One of the oldest guidelines for usable interaction design is to increase the users' sense of control and freedom. It feels *good* to be in control. It feels *bad* to be dominated by a machine. There are a few exceptions to this rule, such as operations that happen only once and when it may be better to abandon responsibility and let the system take over. The wizard used to install Microsoft Office is a great example of an oppressive interface that is probably acceptable to most Office users.

Viewed overall, the Web encourages unparalleled user freedom with its millions of sites to choose from. In recent user studies, we found that people sometimes browse several sites in parallel, which gives them even more control over where they shop and when they leave a site that is too difficult to use. In contrast, users are often completely powerless over the details of their destiny on individual sites. They can leave at any time, but if they stay, they are locked into the site's way of doing things.

The contrast with physical stores is great: stores empower shoppers by allowing them to change tactics if something isn't working for them. If you get a lousy salesperson in a large store, you can look for a different one. If the store map doesn't help you find the department you need, you can ask a salesperson or a fellow customer for help. If the item that you need is not available, good salespeople will help you to locate items in other departments or at other locations and have the items sent to you directly. Good stores know that it's not enough for the store to *look* nice, it must *act* nice as well. They support the customer's total experience, including location, staffing, returns, payments, sales and so on. Too often e-commerce sites focus on looking attractive or cool, without investing in the underlying needs of their customers.

A superior e-commerce site would put its customers in control of shopping again, by offering the best of both worlds: convenience, good product selections, price and feature comparisons, flexible strategies for locating products, and helpful customer service. Whenever people have the options they want, they feel powerful and in control. Unfortunately, most websites don't provide a user experience that feels like *shopping* — instead the experience feels like *searching*, which is not the shopper's goal. People want to shop (or *find*) in a way that seems natural to them, not to search or struggle using Web tools and features that offer inflexible ways to do things. Worse, these tools and features are often built without any regard for how real users think, group things, name things, or approach their problems.

Physical stores aren't perfect — far from it. Frustration abounds in traditional shopping, caused by lack of parking, crowds, annoying salespeople, better prices for the same goods in other stores, and products being out of stock. It is harder to abandon a store and shop at a different one instead. Sure, you can walk out of one store and drive to another, but it's a hassle. And would the next store be any better, or might you have to drive to the next town if you're still not satisfied? So in the physical world, people have a great incentive to shop where they are.

When shoppers don't get what they want, they leave the store, online or not. But they leave more readily on the Web. Considering the usability findings presented in this chapter, it is no surprise that the Web is littered with abandoned shopping carts:

- In the physical world it is fairly difficult to get to another store but very easy to try alternative ways of getting what you want in the current store.
- In the online world, it is extremely easy to visit another e-commerce site but very painful to stay and attempt to get the current site to satisfy your needs.

Usability is the answer to this dilemma. Help your visitors get what they want. Make your site easy, fast, smooth, and pleasant. Watch people stay; watch sales increase.

Usability Increases Sales

E-Commerce companies closely guard their sales numbers, so there is not much publicly known about increased usability's effect on sales. In many cases, however, we know that sales increased by 100% to 400% when an e-commerce site launched an improved user interface. We know of one company that even increased sales by 2,300%, but this particular site was probably an exceptional case. Based on our experience, having sales more than double is not at all an unrealistic goal for a site that had ignored usability in the past but decided to embrace it for the next design.

Exactly how much do different degrees of usability impact sales? We don't know for sure. All our research proves is which design elements work, which designs are too difficult to use, and that poor usability can prevent a large proportion of users from being able to shop on a site. If a site follows more of the usability guidelines, it is natural to expect sales to increase, but usability cannot scientifically predict how much sales will grow.

We can speculate about the causes of the huge sales increases we often see. It appears that given two sites with the same merchandise and prices, people tend to choose the site that's easiest to use; and ease of use is perceived as a sign of trustworthiness.

One of the most likely explanations for the growth in sales that results from improved usability is that people recognize and prefer good service and high-quality websites. As a simplified example, let us consider a world with only two websites that sell a certain item. Let us furthermore assume that Site A is 10% easier to shop at than Site B. If a person finds both sites in a search engine, then where will that person end up buying? Site A will probably win in many more than 10% of the cases. Further, let's say that some shoppers make an initial purchase from both sites. Where will these customers turn for their next purchase? People will be more likely to choose Site A because it is easier to use. Quite likely, Site A could sell 100% more than Site B, even though it was only 10% easier to use.

Although we don't have formal data to prove this hypothesis, the popularity of Amazon.com does tend to support our analysis: once people have experienced how easy it is to shop at Amazon, they are unlikely to buy books and CDs anywhere else. In fact, our own website supplies proof of this statement: the Web page for Jakob Nielsen's book *Designing Web Usability: The Practice of Simplicity* provides links to two online bookstores where people can buy the book: Amazon and Fatbrain. For several months, the book sold at a 20% discount at Amazon and a 30% discount at Fatbrain. Even though these two discount levels were clearly listed on the page where the links appeared, the vast majority of people chose to follow the link to Amazon and buy the book there. It was not worth their time as busy Internet professionals to figure out a different user interface simply to save $4.50.

A second explanation for why usability increases sales is related to trust. A site that is easier to use sends the message that the company behind the site cares about its customers and has a commitment to good customer service. If it is easy to find the product the shopper wants to buy, and if the product description is easy to understand and answers all the person's questions, then he or she may believe that the company is likely to deliver the goods as promised and that the shipment will be in good shape and arrive on time. People may also assume that the ease of shopping indicates that getting support or other help would be easy too. Such user predictions are more emotional than logical, because there is no reason to expect that a company that has a high-quality Web design should necessarily have a high-quality fulfillment department or a responsive support center. But people are quite likely to transfer their impression of the quality of the user experience onto their expectations for other aspects of the customer relationship.

Results of Our Usability Study of E-Commerce Sites

We have derived a set of 207 design guidelines for creating a good e-commerce user experience. These guidelines are based on our empirical observations of 64 users shopping on 20 e-commerce sites chosen to represent a wide variety of product categories. We started out observing which elements of the various sites worked and which caused usability problems. Often parts of the designs were so bad that they completely prevented users from being able to complete purchases. We then generalized our findings into recommendations that apply to all e-commerce sites and not just the specific sites where we observed the individual interaction episodes.

The standard approach to developing user interface design guidelines is: first test a range of designs and then generalize the findings. You can use the same approach to develop more detailed design guidelines for your own site or even to perform a competitive analysis with a group of sites that sell a certain type of products or services to find the best-of-breed features. See "Developing Internal Design Guidelines" later in this chapter.

Success Rates

Across all the tests we conducted for this project, we observed a total of 496 attempts by users to perform tasks on e-commerce sites. The users succeeded in accomplishing the tasks in 278 cases, for a success rate of 56%.

The tasks involved three different activities related to shopping on the Web:

1. Finding and buying a specific product
2. Finding and buying a product that solved a stated need (leaving the choice of the specific product up to the user)
3. Getting customer service.

Thus, our definition of shopping includes:

- Product research
- The process of looking for products
- The actual buying procedures (typically performed through a checkout process)
- Customer service related to the fulfillment of the sale.

We did not study post-sales customer support, such as helping a customer operate a malfunctioning product. For a complete list of the tasks in our study, see the Methodology chapter.

Success rates are the simplest of all usability metrics and simply indicate the proportion of times users were successful in completing the task they were trying to perform. For more information about success rates, see Nielsen's February 2001 *Alertbox* column on the topic, listed in the References section.

There are several ways of analyzing a success rate of 56%. At first, it may seem rather depressing that users were successful only slightly more than half the time. True, this means that the e-commerce sites we tested lost a huge amount of sales simply because it was impossible for users to shop. Because Web shoppers are not a captive audience (unlike the users in our test), this lack of usability would likely cause more lost sales than the 44% failure rate implies, because real shoppers would be much more likely to leave a difficult site. Many users would abandon a site early just because it was too unpleasant to stay. Many other users, however, would choose to shop on sites that were more familiar or easier to use.

It is sad to report this, but a 56% success rate is actually one of the better outcomes ever seen in a major usability study of the Web. Most other studies find success rates of less than 50%. In other words, on average, people fail when attempting to do something new on the Web. The only reason the Web survives despite this dismal statistic is that people do *not* spend most of their time attempting new tasks on new sites. People are quite aware of the difficulty of using new sites, so they spend most of their time on sites that have above-average usability and where they have been successful in the past. Because of this behavior, having great usability is one of the best ways to attract and keep a loyal customer base.

Why do e-commerce sites have better usability than most other websites? We believe that the answer lies in the accountability for the design: for most non-commerce sites, top management has no way of knowing that their design is a failure. Thus, design teams are often rewarded for glamorous designs that do not work but that look great in demos. In contrast, e-commerce sites live and die by a very simple metric: how much did we sell today? If you add a splash page to the site and sales go down, you immediately know that was a bad idea. Improve the search engine and watch sales go up. (If sales decline, then the "improved" search is no good and has to go — but a non-commerce site rarely makes such tough calls after spending a fortune on new technology.)

Comparison With Other E-Commerce Studies

We know of three other studies of e-commerce sites that were also carried out in 2000. Here is a comparison of the success rates measured in the various studies (each of which is cited in our Reference section):

Success Rates by Study	
Studies Conducted in 2000	**Success Rate**
Marty Jerome	67%
Aamir Rehman	57%
Nielsen Norman Group	56%
Randy K. Souza:	35%
Average Rate:	**54%**

The two most likely explanations for the difference in success rates are that each study tested different sites and asked users to perform different tasks. Naturally, the more elaborate the task, the less likely users are to succeed (not because users are stupid, but because complex tasks tend to increase complexity in the interface). It will almost always be easier to buy the latest Steven King novel than to buy a set of dining room furniture.

Marty Jerome mainly tested the biggest and most accomplished e-commerce sites, and as noted in the "Scorecard" section below, best-selling websites tend to follow more of our design guidelines than sites that sell less. So there is a selection bias inherent in studies of big sites: they tend to get high usability scores, because having good usability is the way the sites got to be big in the first place. This selection bias is understandable and acceptable in the case of Jerome's project, which was aimed at providing shopping advice to consumers. Of course, consumers prefer to shop at the best sites, so those sites are the ones to include in this type of study.

The study described by Souza has a methodological oddity that may explain its relatively low success rate. In that study, users were handed a certain amount of money and told that they could keep all the money that they did not spend while shopping on the e-commerce sites being tested. In one way, this approach could be said to simulate real shopping, when people certainly get to keep any money they don't spend. But in terms of usability testing, the potential for an unexpected windfall of cash probably serves as a powerful deterrent to buying and could be the cause of the particularly low success rate in the study.

Because success rates depend on the chosen sites and the chosen tasks, there is no way for us to determine the true average success rate for all e-shopping unless we measured all sites on the Internet using the same methodology. Based on the above table, however, it seems fair to conclude that the success rate for e-commerce is probably slightly higher than 50%. As long as we are interested in measuring relative improvements in usability, we believe that a success rate of 54% is a reasonable baseline from which to start.

Usability Success Rates and Abandoned Shopping Carts

Estimates of abandoned shopping carts on e-commerce sites ranged from 65% to 80% in year 2000. In other words, people complete purchases only between 20% and 35% of the time, even after they have placed something in their shopping carts. How do these low numbers compare with our estimates of usability success rates of somewhat more than 50%?

Both statistics can be true. The success rate indicates users' *ability* to buy, not whether they will actually end up doing so on any individual website. In fact, people often shop on multiple sites simultaneously. Assuming that several of these sites have decent usability, shoppers will succeed in finding a product that satisfies their need on more than one site. Ultimately, however, most people will buy only one of those products. So several sites can count a product placed in the shopping cart even though only one site ends up closing the sale. Because of this behavior, we will probably always see a small percentage of abandoned shopping carts, even on sites that have maximized their usability. In the short term, however, sites have many opportunities to make this metric go down, and it's definitely a danger sign if the number of abandoned carts goes up.

There are several reasons people place items in a shopping cart without buying:

- As just noted, people often do comparison shopping.

- Even while people are shopping on a single site, they often use the shopping cart as a glorified bookmark mechanism simply to gather products they are contemplating buying. People know that most sites are hard to navigate, so they fear that they will not be able to find their way back to a potential purchase unless they capture it in the shopping cart.

- Most sites have very poor support for comparison shopping: to compensate, shoppers often employ the strategy of placing multiple products in the shopping cart in order to compare them there.

- On sites that make it hard to discover shipping and handling costs, users often place items in the shopping cart simply to find out how much they will have to pay.

- The shopping cart may become abandoned because a site with bleeding-edge features crashes the user's browser or because the user is interrupted during shopping.

Several factors affect whether a shopper will buy from a specific e-commerce site:

1. The site's usability failure rate provides the first hurdle: if someone can't find the product, or if the product description does not answer that person's questions, then they definitely will not buy on that site.

2. Price and the site's credibility and brand reputation form the second hurdle: if multiple sites can supply the shopper's needs, he or she will prefer sites with cheaper products and sites that seem trustworthy enough to deliver the purchase and not cheat their customers.

3. Finally, many additional usability factors help determine which site gets the buyer's money in the end: Which site has the easiest checkout process? Which site has a trustworthy design that makes people feel comfortable entering their credit card number?

International Success Rates

All 20 e-commerce sites in our study were English-language sites. The majority of the sites were based in the United States; one site was based in the United Kingdom. So it should come as no surprise that European test users encountered substantially more usability problems than our American test users. The success rates were as follows:

Comparative Success Rates	
US users:	61%
European users:	47%
(These rates were observed in this study.)	

The 14% lower success rates for European users occurred even though we recruited only test users who could read English. If we had tested people with lesser English-language skills, the results would have been abysmal.

It is very common in usability studies to see lower success rates for international users, that is, users who are from a different country than the one where the website was designed. In early 2001, Nua Internet Surveys (www.nua.ie) estimated that the total number of Internet users in the world was 407 million, of which 167 million were in the United States and Canada. Thus, 59% of the potential users are "international" as far as US websites are concerned. (This analysis assumes that Canadians don't have any special problems shopping on American sites; something that is not completely true.) Websites based in other parts of the world have an even greater proportion of their potential customers based outside their own country.

In a recently completed Nielsen Norman Group competitive website study of three content sites, the effect of a foreign-language interface was clearly found to be detrimental. We tested three different US-based content sites in the United States, Germany, and France. Interestingly, all three companies had made some attempt at localization, so the designs tested in Germany and France were partly translated into the appropriate local language. Averaged across the three sites, the success rates in the study were as follows:

Success Rates by Country	
United States	42%
Germany	15%
France	14%
(These rates were observed in a different Nielsen Norman Group study.)	

International users have much greater difficulty with websites than domestic users for several reasons:

1. **Translation is extra work for the user.** Using a foreign language imposes an added cognitive burden that distracts users from devoting their full attention to problem solving.

2. **Translated sites are not necessarily intelligible.** Even when a site has been localized, the translation is often done poorly and without understanding of the usability issues inherent in choosing vocabulary for an interactive environment, as opposed to a printed publication. For example, in our e-commerce user experience study, Danish users did not understand phrases like "Under the hood" and "Around the house" used to designate navigation elements for automotive and home products on the Sears website.

3. **Localization is not all about language.** Cultural differences and other differences in the way people approach a given problem make it harder for non-native users to match the interface to their needs.

4. **Forms can work against users in other countries.** Websites often blatantly ignore international users; for example, it is common for forms to refuse a mailing address that does not include a state.

E-Commerce sites are losing many local potential customers because of bad usability, but usability problems hurt sites much more in terms of lost international sales. The effect of international usability issues probably isn't fully felt on most sites yet, because they still spend relatively little to attract those foreign visitors. Companies would be well advised to fix those problems before spending that advertising money, however.

The Web is getting progressively more world wide every year, so the issues relating to international usability will only grow more serious unless Web developers start planning for international users and conducting international usability studies.

E-Commerce Design Guidelines: Some Examples

We have derived a set of guidelines for making the e-commerce user experience more usable. (See "Summary of Recommendations for Designers" starting on page 374.) During a design project, it would be best to read all the guidelines and use the complete list as a checklist for the quality of the site. To give you an idea of the type of advice contained in the guidelines, here is a short discussion of a few of them.

Search

Search is an area of e-commerce design that ideally could exceed the capabilities of real people in physical stores, in terms of speed, accessibility, and comprehensiveness. In reality, search is one of the most common and least successful ways that people look for things on the Web. Search is often as bad as the worst salesperson or customer service representative. Unfortunately, shoppers can't ask to speak to search's manager, although we've often seen users go to outside search engines such as Google when they aren't successful using a site's own search engine. From previous experience, people know that Google works and finds good answers, so they waste no time in struggling with an internal search engine that returns junk hits. Of course, as soon as visitors leave for Google, they may also decide to take their shopping elsewhere. (Disclosure: Jakob Nielsen serves on Google's advisory board.)

Design Guideline: *Support search for non-product terms.*

Make sure your search engine can address non-product needs that shoppers have, such as customer service topics. In physical stores, good customer service representatives and salespeople can easily help people find the gift registry and help them return items or make payments. In contrast, none of the websites we tested appeared to support non-product searches for items like "payment," "price protection," and "returns." This lack was more than an annoyance; the user who entered "payment" had selected an item and couldn't get past the product page to check out. The search engine returned a "No products found" message. It's hard to imagine how a store could be so bad that a salesperson would tell a customer looking for the checkout counter: "Sorry, we don't carry checkout counters."

Design Guideline: *Tell customers what you don't have.*

A salesperson in a store generally tells you if the store doesn't carry something you're looking for. Web search engines unfortunately often tell you nothing in this situation. When a search returns no hits, people struggle to understand what that non-result means. Does the site really not have the item? Do they call it something else? Did I misspell the name?

Very few websites tell you when they *don't* carry an item. But is very common to see users work hard to interpret empty search results. On CustomDisc, one user searched for "elvis" and got a hit on "Melvis / The Megatones." The user typed "presley" and got a hit on a band named Presley. The user typed "elvis presley" and didn't get any hits. At this point, the user gave up. What the user didn't know — and the search results didn't explain — was that copyright restrictions prevented CustomDisc from selling Elvis Presley songs. Although CustomDisc explained these restrictions in Help, a better place to provide this information would have been on the no-results page, shown whenever search found nothing that matched the user's query.

Can't Find a Song?

Most songs are owned by an artist or record label. If they choose not to participate in our CustomDisc service, then we cannot legally sell their music. However, we're constantly expanding our roster of artists and record labels, so you may want to subscribe to **our newsletter** for updates on new music.

You may not find every song you want. But you'll probably find more than you planned. With over 200,000 songs available for your disc, browsing CustomDisc is your best bet.

Back to the Help Index

CustomDisc showed the right information in the wrong place. This message (or something shorter) should have been shown whenever searches for songs and artists failed. H1

Side-by-Side Comparisons

People like to comparison shop. Nothing excites shoppers more than getting the best deal, whether they've got $10 or $10,000 to spend. In many studies, again and again we've heard users ask for ways to compare items side by side. Without comparison tools on websites, users must drill down to get information on a product, grasp the most important details and either remember them or print them out; back up, find another item, and start the process again. Often users can't remember key features of one product once they've gotten to another, so they're forced to compare based only on what they do remember.

Advanced Web users create their own solutions. We've seen these users open multiple browser windows and tile them so they can see more than one product at once. This window jockeying wasn't enjoyable for these users, however, and it can lead to closing the window that controls the shopping cart accidentally. Users resented having to invent their own comparison solutions and instead wanted the site to support what they wanted to do. The most successful sites we've seen provide tools to compare products.

Design Guideline: Design comparison tables to highlight differences.

Comparison tables work best when they offer a snapshot view that clearly shows what's different about the products being compared. "Snapshot" implies that you can see the maximum amount of information at once, without a great deal of scrolling. Image H2 shows a comparison table that users generally liked at HermanMiller.

We've got chairs for every size, every budget, all at extremely reasonable prices, and all ergonomically designed for healthful support.

And when you buy any chair between now and January 31, you're automatically entered in our **Office for the New Millennium Giveaway!**

Every chair in our "Office Chairs" section is eligible. Your chair order enters your name in our random drawing (one entry per person, please). You could win sleek, mobile, **high-tech office furniture** that's valued at $7,000! And since it's one of those no-purchase-necessary, void-where-prohibited deals, you can drop us a **note** with the subject "Enter The Office Of The New Millennium Giveaway" to enter, too.

Everybody deserves a good seat, and when you buy yours don't forget to choose either our UPS/RPS or standard freight carrier delivery option, and we'll ship your chair FREE OF CHARGE anywhere in the continental USA. Shop from anywhere on our site, or check out the convenient list below. And take comfort!

Work Chairs

	Aeron	Equa 2	Ergon 3	Equa 1	Ambi	Reaction	Avian
Base Price	$749.00	$479.00	$449.00	$364.00	$349.00	$363.30	$225.00
Adj. Arms	Yes	Available	Available	No	Available	Available	No
Adj. Back Height	No	No	Yes	No	Yes	Yes	No
Adj. Lumbar Support	Yes	Yes	No	No	No	No	No
Adj. Seat Depth	No	No	No	No	No	Yes	No
Adj. Tilt Tension	Yes	Yes	Yes	Yes	Yes	Yes	Yes
Forward Tilt Angle	Yes	No	No	No	No	Available	No
Tilt Lock	Yes	No	Yes	No	Yes	Yes	No
Pneumatic Lift	Yes	Yes	Yes	Yes	Yes	Yes	Yes
12 Year Warranty	Yes	Yes	Yes	Yes	Yes	Yes	Yes

Users liked the concept of this table but didn't like the horizontal scrolling or the table wasting row space on a feature all chairs had. H2

This table has two main drawbacks: in several rows, every chair has that feature marked "yes." Seeing that all HermanMiller chairs have a certain feature does not help users assess what's different about a particular chair in order to choose one. Users liked seeing all the chairs in one place but disliked scrolling horizontally, because then they could no longer see the row headings. In general, users have difficulty with horizontal scrolling, so it's best to design pages no wider than a monitor set to 800 x 600 resolution can display.

The type and format of the feature information among products in a comparison tool needs to be the same, or it's meaningless to compare. We found that users need to be able to determine whether a feature listed in one product exists in another, or else they're left wondering whether it doesn't exist or just wasn't mentioned in the feature list.

Winnowing

Although abundant selection makes Web users feel powerful and in control, filtering through the good and the bad can overwhelm them if they don't get any help from the website. In physical stores, good salespeople listen to what their customers need and then show a selection of the stock that meets the criteria. Similarly, when you have a lot of products or content on your website, you need to provide ways for your customers to narrow down the choices. We saw an interesting behavior in our study: no matter how websites displayed their product listings — with small, big, or no graphics, short, long or no descriptions — users stopped looking at product listings after two or three pages, and sometimes they didn't even look past the first page. So if you have a large number of products, you need to help your customers narrow the selection to a list that fits on two or three pages. We use the ancient term "winnowing," which originally meant to separate wheat from the chaff, to refer to this filtering process.

Design Guideline: Allow winnowing by the most useful differentiating factors for that type of product.

In order to make winnowing tools that work, you must understand how your users want to see subsets of your product. For example, many people in our study who had to buy toys for children wanted to search by age of the child. Winnowing tools that narrowed toys down by school year or groupings like "infant" or "youth" were perplexing for people who didn't know which ages those terms refer to. Some specific examples of most useful differentiating factors for winnowing are filtering toys by age of child and clothing by size (showing only what's in stock for your size, because you wouldn't change sizes to get an in-stock item).

Design Guideline: Pick winnowing criteria your customers understand.

Peet's, a coffee and tea site, offers a winnowing tool that asks shoppers five questions and then recommends a coffee for them. Unfortunately, our test users didn't understand the flavors questions. If preferred flavors are indeed highly relevant to coffee preference, Peet's should explain the questions and answers in more detail or give examples of foods with those flavors.

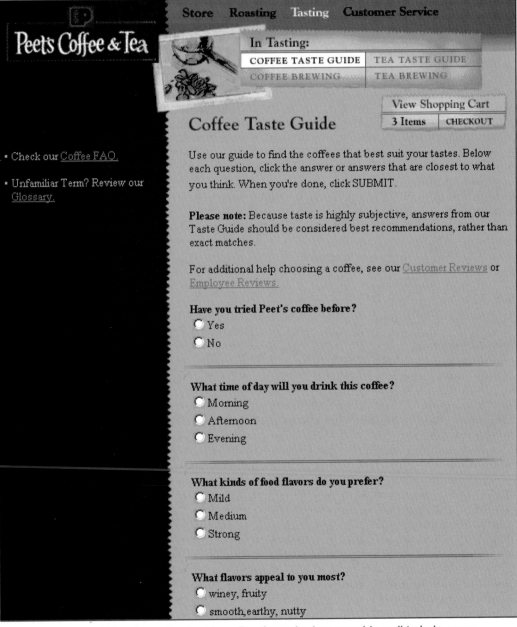

This winnowing tool from Peet's worked reasonably well to help users choose the type of coffee they might like. They were confused, however, by the questions about flavors. H3

In addition to being able to narrow a set of choices, an optimal design would also allow users to broaden their choices in desired directions. Selective broadening is particularly important when the user has narrowed the choices too much. It is very frustrating to go directly from 100 choices to one or two (or none!) without an opportunity to back up a little and get, maybe, 10 choices.

Help Users Feel in Control

Here is the most important design principle of them all: if you increase the users' sense of being in control while they are visiting your site, they will feel good about your site and will enjoy their visits. Even better, you will enhance users' control of their overall Web experience, because they will likely abandon your competitors' sites where they feel powerless in contrast with your more supportive and flexible site.

Scorecard: How Sites Comply With Usability Guidelines

After we developed the design guidelines for e-commerce user experience, we scored 20 e-commerce sites for their degree of compliance with the guidelines. These other 20 sites were different than the 20 sites we tested in the original usability study, because of course if we had scored the same sites as we had used to derive the guidelines, we would have been pursuing a circular argument.

We chose these other 20 sites to include 10 best-selling e-commerce sites and 10 medium-selling sites in the same businesses as the 10 big sites. The 10 best-selling websites were chosen from a list of the 20 best-selling sites among American home users. We avoided sites that were included in our original usability study and limited the choice to only two from any given product category. For the purpose of this scorecard comparison, we decided to treat Amazon as a general store and not as a bookseller. Thus, we paired Amazon (big seller) with Kmart (medium seller, as far as Web sales in 2000 were concerned). We did not score any small e-commerce sites, although we included some in our usability study.

The results of the scorecard are shown in the tables below. The easy first conclusion is that Amazon.com is indeed the best e-commerce site: at 72%, it scores much higher than any of the other sites we analyzed. In other words, Amazon has reached its stature as the Web's leading retailer, not because it is named after a river, but because it is the easiest place to shop.

Second, even Amazon does not have perfect usability, but it does come pretty close. Following 72% of our guidelines is almost as good as most sites need to be. Optimal usability would typically be reached by complying with about 90% of the guidelines, because any given website will have good reasons to deviate from a few of the guidelines. All of the guidelines are good advice in general, but in specific instances some of them may not apply, and a site may be better off with a design that accommodates the special needs of its users and their tasks. We do recommend, however, that a site deviate from a guideline only after a user test confirms that a deviant design does indeed provide better usability under that site's own special circumstances (users, tasks, and product categories).

Big Sites' Guideline Compliance	
Amazon	72%
MotherNature	60%
CDNOW	60%
Barnes&Noble (bn.com)	55%
Gateway	51%
Pets	49%
drugstore	48%
VictoriasSecret	47%
PlanetRx	45%
ticketmaster	39%
Average	**53%**

Medium Sites' Guideline Compliance	
AlphaCraze	45%
HardwareStreet	41%
Kmart (bluelight.com)	41%
Healthshop	41%
CDconnection	40%
PetfoodExpress	39%
Sav-OnDrugs	38%
VermontLingerie	34%
TicketWeb	26%
MediChest	25%
Average	**37%**

It is clear from these scores that the big sites have substantially better usability than the medium-sized sites. This difference is a great indication of the value of usability to drive sales.

Of course, having good usability and a famous name will not save an e-commerce site if it does not have a sustainable business model. Pets.com is a good example of this problem: it got a fairly good rating in our scorecard analysis and the company still died a few days after we had collected the data. All usability can do is to increase the sales of a site. If the site loses money on every sale, then even the best usability will do it no good.

These scores also show that the state of usability in e-commerce is appalling. Setting aside Amazon, we see that even big and famous sites follow only half of the usability guidelines. Medium-sized sites follow only a third of the guidelines. We have not dared score small-business sites, but they would probably get an even lower score.

Three conclusions:

- **Common sense is not yet common practice.** Even though many of the design guidelines might seem obvious to some, we still have a long way to go before good usability is truly the state-of-the-art on the Internet. Our guidelines may describe *best* practices, but they don't describe *common* practices, because most sites don't follow most of the guidelines.

- **The degrees of compliance and rates of success are suspiciously similar.** The low average rate of compliance with the design guidelines goes a long way toward explaining why usability studies of e-commerce sites usually find a success rate of around 50%. Any way you look at it, people are incapable of buying what they came for about half of the time.

- **Becoming one of the most usable sites on the net is still pretty easy.** Following only half of our guidelines would be sufficient to place a site in very good company and make it one of the best on the Internet. Following three-fourths of the guidelines would make a site a true top scorer.

The next table looks at the compliance scores for each of the different design topics covered in our project. The table is sorted by the difference in scores between the big sites and the medium sites. In other words, the first entries in the table indicate the biggest differentiators — areas in which the big sites perform substantially better than the medium sites.

Compliance with Usability Guidelines by Design Aspect

Aspect of Site	Big Sites	Small Sites	Difference
Category Pages	51%	28%	23%
Selling Strategies	63%	44%	19%
Product Pages	63%	45%	18%
Search	42%	27%	16%
International Users	30%	15%	15%
Trust	61%	50%	11%
Checkout & Registration	59%	51%	8%

It is interesting to note from the table that all the sites score relatively well on the Checkout & Registration guidelines. Most likely, the intense scrutiny of shopping cart design in the trade press during 1999–2000 (when the "abandoned shopping cart" problem was seen as the most prominent indicator of e-commerce trouble) accounts for this similarity in scores. Another possible explanation is that the shopping cart is the easiest part of an e-commerce site to get from somewhere else and have it still work on your site.

It is also clear from the table that international users are neglected on virtually all sites, even the biggest ones. Again, increasing website usability for people who don't speak your site's language natively is one of the greatest opportunities for e-commerce sites to increase their sales.

Another big opportunity to improve sales is in helping people quickly find what they want in the online catalog. The biggest differentiator between sites that sell a lot and sites that sell less turns out to be the usability of their category pages. Category pages are mid-level pages in an e-commerce website that help customers find the product listing pages — and thus, the products they want to buy. See the Category Pages chapter for in-depth information about these critical-path elements in e-commerce transactions. This area of e-commerce usability is closely related to the site's ability to help users locate the products they want, both in terms of facilitating navigation and in terms of differentiating the products and allowing users to target a small number of promising offers. One of the main reasons users are less attracted by the medium-selling sites could well be that those sites seem more confusing and overwhelming, whereas the big sites seem more helpful because of their better category pages.

Nielsen Norman Group can deliver a scorecard that measures your sites' compliance with the e-commerce design guidelines, both as an overall metric and relative to each of the usability aspects covered by the guidelines. For more information, please see www.nngroup.com/services/scorecard

Using Guidelines to Improve Design

As you read the findings from our usability tests of 20 different e-commerce sites, you will probably often say, "but that's common sense." Well, common sense seems to be less common than one might think, because every single design blooper that we found was on a professional website designed by people who wanted to sell. You can be sure that the designers were not interested in being featured in a usability report as examples of bad Web design.

We agree that many usability problems represent violations of simple principles like our design guidelines. Many of the worst types of problems could be prevented by a guidelines review in which the designer looks through the checklist of usability guidelines to see whether the design complies or not.

Usually, the designers themselves perform guidelines reviews, and a design certainly benefits if all designers familiarize themselves with the usability guidelines before starting an e-commerce project. It is best to have at least one review performed by somebody who is not connected with the project, however. Most usability methods work better if they are tightly integrated with the design project and performed by the company's own staff. After all, your own people know your business, your product line, and (you hope) your customers better than anybody else. Usability reviews, however, benefit from an independent approach by somebody who does not know that "this is how it's always done around here."

Multiple Levels of Guidelines

In designing your own website, you should follow three levels of guidelines:

1. General usability guidelines that would apply to any design.
2. Domain-specific usability guidelines that apply to the type of site you are designing.
3. Company-specific usability guidelines that apply to your individual site and depend on the exact products and services you offer.

General usability guidelines can be found in many other publications. For Web design, we recommend *Designing Web Usability: The Practice of Simplicity*, by Jakob Nielsen, but there are many others (see the References section).

This series of e-commerce design guidelines is intended to supply the middle set of guidelines. Even though some of the guidelines apply to other forms of sites, one would need a different set of domain-specific guidelines for the design of, say, a newspaper site, a government site, or a big-company intranet. The present guidelines apply to sites that are mainly intended as online retailers. Other forms of Internet-based sales may be sufficiently similar to online retailers that they can use many of the guidelines. For example, we have been engaged in usability projects for online wholesalers, online leasing companies, and financial services companies, and we found that their sites do benefit from many, although not all, of these guidelines.

B2B Guidelines

Design guidelines written by others will take you part of the way. To truly empower your specific customers requires a deep understanding of their needs and behavior, which differ from industry to industry. Even so, we have found a surprising amount of overlap between very different types of users, whether business professionals shopping for highly complex B2B (Business to Business) products or consumers shopping for mass-market B2C (Business to Consumer) products.

This set of e-commerce user experience guidelines is most comprehensive for B2C sites because those were the ones we tested when developing the guidelines. Most of the guidelines also apply to B2B sites, partly because the users and their general behavior are highly overlapping: often the same person is a "B" from 9–5 and a "C" in the evening. Because business users often have tried shopping at the best consumer sites, their expectations for e-commerce usability have been set based on their user experience at those sites.

Indeed, when testing B2B sites, we often hear complaints such as: "If I can get this good service from Amazon.com when buying a $5 paperback, then why can't I get equally good service when buying $50,000 worth of stainless steel valves?"

On today's Internet, the bar for usability is not being set by your immediate competitors in your own industry but by the very best sites on the entire Web. This comparison may seem unfair, but it's the truth. Thus, B2B sites are strongly advised to consider all of the B2C design guidelines and implement them to the extent that they apply to their sites.

B2B sites require additional usability effort in order to support complex products and group purchasing processes. On a B2C site, it is usually the same person who is using the site, deciding on the purchase, approving the expense, and arranging for payment. In a B2B scenario, several employees at various levels of the organization (and working in different departments) may be involved in a single purchase. Many B2B sites currently provide much too little support for this multi-user process.

Because B2B products and services can be highly complex and often are very expensive, it is also often necessary for a B2B site to provide much more substantial product information than a typical B2C site offers. Customer support and service also become much more important. The specific requirements for these elements often differ among industries, so we recommend that you develop your own internal usability guidelines for the best way of presenting your type of products in an interactive selling environment.

Developing Internal Design Guidelines

To develop your own company-specific guidelines, you can use a variant of the approach we used to develop the general e-commerce guidelines, as documented in the Methodology chapter. Select a number of e-commerce sites that sell the same type of product as you do and test a number of your customers as they shop on those sites. You should include your own site in this study. During the tests, note which elements of the various sites help or hinder users and then generalize these observations to form the guidelines.

In selecting test users, decide whether to test only current customers or to include potential new customers. We usually favor including some people in the test who have never done business with the company. Testing with only current customers often shows a bias in favor of the site that would mask some of the important barriers to becoming a customer in the first place. Many websites are incredibly opaque to new visitors who don't know anything about the company or its products.

It cost Nielsen Norman Group a quarter million dollars to develop and publish the design guidelines for *E-Commerce User Experience*. Some guidelines projects are even more expensive: it is not publicly known how much Apple Computer spent developing the *Macintosh Human Interface Guidelines*, but we would estimate the cost at several million dollars spent over many years and several editions. The same would be true for the *Microsoft Windows User Experience* guidelines.

Most companies can develop their own guidelines on a much smaller budget. Company-specific guidelines should be incremental rather than comprehensive. There is no need for you to replicate the research to develop general usability guidelines for e-commerce user experience design. Instead, you can just incorporate our design guidelines into your own by reference. Basically, you say that your designers should follow the general guidelines plus a smaller number of industry-specific guidelines in your own document.

Here are several other ways your guidelines project can be cheaper than ours:

- **Use fewer sites.** It is not necessary for you to test 20 websites. Instead pick 3–5 sites in your own industry to get sufficient coverage of the main issues.

- **Test locally.** Even though it is always best to consider international users, it is often possible to get most of the industry-specific findings from a domestic study, thus saving the cost of running tests in other countries.

- **Use fewer experts.** Our team has more than 50 years' combined experience in the usability field and 22 years' combined experience with Web usability. This level of expertise may be necessary to derive the deep insights one wants for a general set of design guidelines, but it is somewhat easier to derive more specific guidelines; thus a smaller and less senior staff will often suffice. It is usually important to include a person with substantial domain expertise in the guidelines team, so that is one area in which domain-specific teams will face a small added expense.

- **Take less time.** Because our guidelines are intended as the foundation for all e-commerce designs in the future, we were very thorough in developing the guidelines and in making sure that our analysis would hold up. Each guideline was subjected to extensive analysis by a large team of senior usability authorities. Of course you also want your own set of guidelines to be correct, but it is possible to move faster with an internal set of guidelines, because it is easier to correct any mistakes that may be discovered after the initial release of the draft guidelines to your design teams.

- **Be more concise.** Our final guidelines span about 400 pages of content, including extensive examples, commentary, and methodology reporting. We constantly attempted to reduce the material, but we wanted to cover the entire field of e-commerce design, so we needed to be comprehensive. Specific guidelines for use inside your own company should be written much more tightly: 50 pages would be a good limit.

- **Use less polish.** Our reports went through several rounds of editing and graphic design to improve the language and appearance for professional publication. Internal reports can cut some corners there, even though any publication should have one round of editing.

You can develop your own guidelines using the approach described here and in the Methodology chapter. It is possible to get assistance from an outside firm to develop domain-specific or company-specific design guidelines. The most cost-effective approach is for the consultant to review a draft of the guidelines after you have developed them yourselves, but you can also outsource all or part of the complete process, including the initial competitive usability study of multiple sites in your industry.

Cost of Usability

Given that improved usability can often double the sales of an e-commerce site, how much does it cost to make a website easier to use? There is no simple answer, but here are some ways of assessing the cost of usability.

Today's Best Practices

In late 2000 and early 2001, Nielsen Norman Group collected information on the usability budgets for approximately 1000 companies that participated in our usability conferences. The sample was obviously biased, because only companies with a significant interest in usability would invest in sending staff to a high-level usability conference. However, exactly *because* we had a biased sample, our survey represents current best practices in the field of usability.

According to our survey respondents, companies spent an average of 10% of their design and development budgets on usability. Obviously, the average investment in usability across all Web design projects in the world would be much lower, because the vast majority of projects currently have no usability at all, but place their faith in the designers' best guesses as to what users need. For well-run design projects with a commitment to usability, however, 10% of the budget is a reasonable goal in 2001.

Past and Future Expenditures

The outcome of our 2001 survey can be compared with a similar survey Jakob Nielsen conducted in early 1993 of leading software development companies and their usability practices (see the References section). That survey, which also used a biased sample of companies with a high commitment to interface quality, found that the average project allocated 6% of its budget to usability. So the change from software design to Web design and the increased demand for interface quality over the last eight years has increased the recommended proportion of project costs that goes to usability from 6% to 10%.

We predict that investments in usability will continue to increase for four reasons:

- **Competition.** Increased competition on the Internet will lead to increased requirements for usability: people will simply refuse to use any sites that are not as easy as the very best sites on the Web.

- **Return on investment.** It will become more widely recognized that the return on investment from usability is much bigger than for almost any other investments that can be made in Internet projects. We are nowhere near the point of diminishing returns, so sites that invest more in usability will become easier to use and will sell more.

- **Changing audience.** As the Internet continues to grow, it will reach many more users, and these users will have less computer and Web experience than today's users do. The early adopters were technically savvy; the late adopters will need dramatically improved usability or they will not be able to use the Web at all.

- **Internationalization.** The Web will also become increasingly multilingual, with a majority of users who do not speak English, leading to an increased demand for international usability assessment.

The cost of individual usability activities varies widely, from a few thousand dollars for a fast test carried out by your own staff to a million dollars or more for big studies with multiple rounds of testing carried out in many countries on several continents.

In the long run, the most economical way to integrate usability into your company is to train your own staff in usability methodology. Luckily, the simplest usability methods are very easy to learn. For example, we run a three-day course called "Learning-by-Doing" that teaches user testing in the context of using the seminar sponsor's own Web project as the case study for a complete usability study: Day 1 is spent planning the test; on Day 2 we test the site with several test users; Day 3 is devoted to analyzing the data and recommending changes to the site. Incidentally, the fact that this three-day seminar includes a complete user test is proof that it is possible to run a test in that amount of time and get good data that will lead to many improvements in a design.

So, there is no excuse for not testing the design before releasing an e-commerce site. It can be done in three days. Even the wildest rush to market can wait that long in order to launch a high-quality site.

Even the simplest usability test uncovers a large number of usability deficiencies in a design. Some companies might avoid testing because they feel an obligation to fix every problem found, which usually isn't possible in the available time. A more fruitful approach is to proceed with usability testing, while acknowledging that some problems may be too time consuming to fix within the current project. It is still better to know about such issues, because they can be placed on the agenda for the next release. Also, it is better to manage the project based on knowledge of the real situation. It may be a tough call to release a design that contains known weaknesses; still, it's better to know about these weaknesses and their usability impact in advance. One of the outcomes of a usability study is insight into the severity of each of the usability problems, which allows project management to make the necessary trade-offs and fix most of the worst issues while deferring less serious issues for a later release.

There are many usability methods besides user testing, including field studies and expert reviews. Field studies should be done early in the project to collect data about users' natural behavior and allow the design to be based on real user needs. Expert reviews can be conducted at any stage. Expert reviews provide an independent, outside assessment of the project and its design as well as a strategic analysis of the site's usability directions. These more advanced methods can be more expensive than simple user testing, but the best projects use a combination of several methods.

Not all projects need to make use of the full range of usability methods. Some projects have budget for only a few cheap tests. The important thing is that a design informed by usability testing will always be better than a design with no usability influence at all.

Selling
Strategies

*" You can't sell anything to a customer
who has left the store."*

E-Commerce Essentials

Introduction

You can't sell anything to a customer who has left the store. In this study, we introduce the concept of a "sales catastrophe," which is any issue that prevents a sale, or discourages a customer from returning to the site. In some cases, users successfully completed the tasks, but afterward explained why they wouldn't buy from the site on their own.

For example, one coffee-drinker said she wouldn't return to Peet's, because, "It was pricey, four times what I'd pay in the grocery store." Although we counted this task as successful from a usability perspective (in terms of the user's ability to select and purchase an item), it's hard to consider it a success from an e-commerce perspective.

The chart shows the four types of sales catastrophes we consider related to selling strategies, which total 23% of the failures.

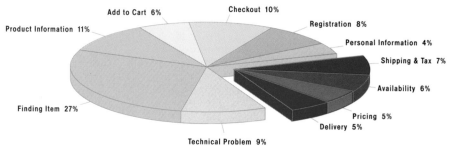

The chart's total is 98% due to cumulative rounding errors

- **Pricing:** Users did not perceive sufficient value in the merchandise to justify its price, prices were not shown, or users believed the site was trying to cheat people.
- **Shipping and Tax:** Users believed that shipping costs (or tax) were unreasonable.
- **Availability:** Users could see an item but could not purchase it. About two thirds of the incidents in this category came from Danish users who were confused or mistaken about whether a site would ship to Denmark.
- **Delivery:** Users had concerns about getting what they wanted, when they wanted it.

In this section, we also discuss the importance of good customer service. Users wanted clear explanations of guarantees and return policies.

A Note Regarding International Sales

We discovered many usability issues just by testing US sites with US users. These problems were magnified when we tested US sites with Danish users. All 20 test sites in this study were US-based. About two thirds of our data came from US tests, and the remaining third came from tests in Denmark. Because the entire International Users chapter addresses the challenges faced by e-commerce sites in the global marketplace, this chapter will only briefly mention factors that affected sales to Danish users.

Pricing

Pricing issues caused 5% of the sales catastrophes in this study. Typically, users successfully completed a task, but said they wouldn't return to the site because of high prices.

Although 5% is not a large percentage, its significance increases when you consider that our users weren't spending their own money in these tests. Also, we didn't ask them anything about pricing, but they made many spontaneous comments. If they had been spending their own money, we believe that pricing issues would have caused a larger percentage of sales catastrophes.

To interpret users' reactions to pricing issues, it helps to know their economic background. We did not ask our study participants to tell us their income, but we can characterize them as middle-class consumers. The US users lived in southern New Hampshire, roughly 30–50 miles north of Boston, Massachusetts. According to 1998 US Census data, the median income for New Hampshire was about 12% higher than the national average. The Danish users lived in the greater Copenhagen area and were middle-class consumers too. More than 90% of our study participants worked full-time.

▶ *Communicate the value of the merchandise.*

The necessity to communicate value during the sales process is certainly not new, but it's especially difficult to do online. Customers can experience the merchandise in an environment that engages, at most, only two (vision and hearing) of their five senses. We found many cases in which users did not appreciate the value of the merchandise in relation to its price. Compare these users who voiced their impressions of HermanMiller's office chairs:

- Did not perceive value: One user laughed out loud upon seeing a price of $393 for an ergonomically designed office chair.

- Perceived value: Another user said, "The pricing of the items I saw seemed reasonable for the quality of the product. ... I'm kind of familiar with office furniture."

- Wondered about value: A third user asked, "Why should I be spending hundreds of bucks? What benefit is it to me?"

Although HermanMiller provided detailed information about the specifications and operation of its chairs, the third user pinpointed the issue: HermanMiller did not communicate the *benefits* of the merchandise to the users (except to those who already knew something about office furniture).

In fairness to HermanMiller, if their primary clientele is corporate furniture buyers rather than middle-class consumers, their site might do an adequate job of communicating value. And users had problems understanding why products were so expensive on most of the sites in our study:

- Boo: "I'm seeing some really expensive pants ($200), and I don't understand why. ... Their prices definitely aren't cheap."

- Iflorist (Internet Florist): The product pages for rose arrangements noted that their prices were higher just before Valentine's Day. Some users accepted this price shift, but others didn't. One user said this policy would deter her from doing business with Iflorist.

- NorwaySweaters: One user was not likely to return to the site because, "I wouldn't pay that kind of money for a sweater." (Sweater prices ranged from $130–150.)

- Reel: One user found a movie she wanted but when she discovered that the VHS videotape price was $90, she said she'd leave the site. "This is where I'd say this is a pain in the neck. I don't understand why these two VHS ones are so expensive." (The price for the DVD version of the movie was only $18, and the two prices appeared on the same page.)

Although some users found prices they thought were reasonable or even good, the ratio of negative to positive comments was about two to one. What we found especially interesting were the statements of a few users who said they would *leave the site* after encountering a price they thought was too high. (During the pre-test briefing, we asked users to tell us if they encountered a situation that would cause them to leave the site. We did not repeat this instruction as we watched them shop.) When users declare they would leave a site during a study in which they are being paid to use the site, we believe their remarks indicate a significant problem. We don't know, however, to what extent this behavior is representative of the consumer population online.

We are not suggesting that e-commerce sites should compete solely on price. But, sites will not thrive if they take the attitude that e-commerce is trendy and exclusive, so prices can be correspondingly high. We did not find any evidence that middle-class consumers think they should pay more for products just because they are sold on the Web.

In fact, some consumers are knowledgeable enough to realize that e-commerce relieves merchants of the expensive overhead of physical stores and individual customer service. People might reasonably expect online prices to be the same or even lower than they are in physical stores. Thus, websites must pay at least as much attention to pricing as offline merchants do.

Large, high-quality images help the merchandise sell itself. SS1

Tip: Explain the benefits, not just the features, of your merchandise. It's especially important to explain benefits whenever customers might not be familiar with the product line. For example, HermanMiller could cite studies of medical problems and lost productivity attributable to poor-quality office furniture. Or they could offer a short quiz to help people become aware of how uncomfortable their current chairs may be.

Tip: Provide high-quality images. For clothing, furniture, or other items in which texture or comfort are important, show the product from different angles or provide close-ups of material texture and details of the product construction. (See the Product Pages chapter for more information about successful product descriptions and images.)

Tip: Show the production process. If your product is manufactured to high standards, is environmentally friendly, or is in any other way exceptional, show that. Although some of our users were more accepting of NorwaySweaters' prices when they learned the sweaters are handmade, others were suspicious of what "handmade" actually means. NorwaySweaters could show people knitting the sweaters.

Tip: Provide human sales assistance online. As described in the "Sales Assistance" section of this chapter, sites that sell expensive items like furniture might make more sales if they keep human beings involved in the sales process.

➡ *Don't hide product prices.*

Our users expected to see a price along with the first mention of an item. Most of the sites in our study met users' expectations in this regard. One site broke this pricing rule, and it evoked strong negative reactions.

Requesting prices by e-mail was unacceptable to users shopping on Living. SS2

Some of the furniture items pictured on Living carried the instruction, "Click for price." This link opened a second window that asked the user to enter an e-mail address. Living then e-mailed the price to the user. Having to request a price by e-mail evoked negative reactions from our users:

- "Click for price, that's not good. Must be more than I can afford," said one user. This tactic reminded her of what fancy restaurants do. Because the food is so expensive, only the person paying for the meal sees a menu that includes prices. This user said she would not enter her e-mail address to get a price, despite the fact that the "click for price" rocking chair was the only one of the three chairs that she liked.

- "I wouldn't order this chair online if I had to go through this. I want to know what the price is right then and there," asserted a user. "I think if the [manufacturing] company's too snobby to give me their prices, they don't deserve to have me buy from them. I wouldn't buy that chair, just for that reason," he stated. This user blamed the chair manufacturer, not Living, for withholding the price. Not all users were so discerning in their criticism.

- "They are doing this only because they want to abuse my e-mail address for marketing purposes," complained another user.

Only two users of nine actually requested a price via e-mail. One received a response within a few minutes, and he was satisfied with the response. The other user did not receive a reply before the test was over. Ultimately, none of the nine users chose an item on Living that had a hidden price.

We recognize that the policy of having to request a price by e-mail probably originated from Living's vendors rather than from the designers of the website. Our findings, however, clearly indicate that a site that tolerates hidden prices from some vendors risks losing business site-wide. Customers tend to form a negative impression of the entire site, not just of the price-withholding vendor. Most of our users didn't stop to wonder why some items on Living showed prices and others didn't. They just knew they didn't like this tactic.

Shipping and Tax

All the users in our study had previously shopped online and most had also purchased from e-commerce sites. Even users with limited online experience were aware that shipping and handling could add a substantial amount to the cost of the purchase. We traced 7% of the sales catastrophes to users who found shipping costs (and in one case, tax) to be unreasonable.

➡️ *Make it easy to see the total.*

Users in our study wanted to know the total amount of their purchase, not just the subtotal. On the sites we tested, users had to begin checkout and type in their shipping address before seeing the total for their purchase, which was a lot of work just to discover how much money they would actually be spending.

As one user commented: "I want to know details about what I'm getting into. I'm interested in shipping and handling. That makes a difference as to whether I want it." Another user concurred, "If I'm on the phone, they say, 'Your total will be … .' Shipping [charge] needs to be clearer."

Of the 20 sites we tested, only CustomDisc displayed a running subtotal in a fixed location on the page. This approach worked fairly well, but we recommend showing an estimate of shipping cost with the subtotal.

➡ *Show shipping charges before asking for personal information.*

On most of the sites we tested, users could not find out the shipping cost until they revealed their shipping address. (The only exceptions were the sites that offered free shipping.) Users wanted to see shipping costs *before* they released personal information.

One user explained why she balked: "I found it difficult that I had to [enter personal information] to get any information about billing or delivery. ... It's like leaving my credit card at the front desk when I walk into Wal-Mart. I like to be able to go in and look and know exactly what I get before I commit myself to buy it."

Our users appreciated having access to the shipping cost for an item, before they put it in the shopping cart. Iflorist was the only site that showed the delivery charge right on the product page.

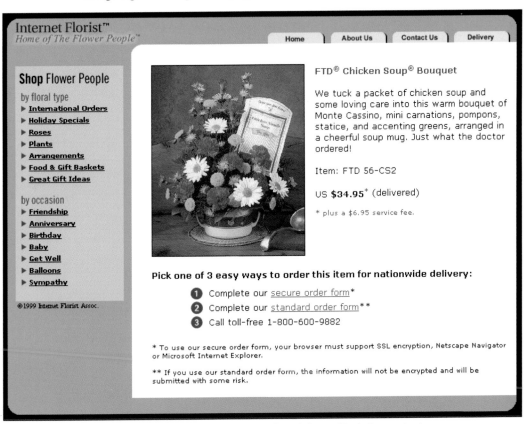

Users liked seeing the delivery fee right on Iflorist's product page. (They didn't necessarily like the fee, but they liked the fact that it wasn't hidden.) SS3

Of course, the difficulty for the site designer is that shipping and tax usually depend on where the item is to be shipped, which can't be determined until the customer provides an address. One user suggested adding a form field on the product page where she could put in a postal code so the site would calculate shipping cost. This suggestion seems reasonable, but we didn't test any sites that calculated shipping costs on the product page.

Allowing users to enter a postal code would also catch the "We do not ship outside the Continental USA" problem early. Danish users, who tried to order from some US-based sites, encountered this message, but usually not until they'd wasted quite a bit of time shopping for items they couldn't buy.

Tip: Provide a link to shipping information on the home page. If customers have encountered high shipping charges on other sites, they may look for information about shipping costs even before they begin shopping, as several of our users did. It might help to put a link on the home page that leads to an explanation of shipping charges and delivery area. As described in the International Users chapter, Danish users looked for a such a link.

➡ *Keep shipping charges within reason.*

Shipping charges were acceptable to most users, as long as they perceived the costs as reasonable. Our users thought these shipping charges were reasonable:

- eToys: A charge of $4 to ship a $29.95 Barbie doll seemed "typical" to one user.
- Iflorist: "It's really a convenience charge [$6.95], no different than if you call a florist and send FTD. ... I personally don't have a problem with that. I'm paying for the convenience of having it online." This user was atypical. Most of our users did not express a willingness to pay for convenience.
- Sears: Reading about basic delivery cost for appliances, one user said: "They charge you 10% of the cost of the item. A minimum of $5, max of $30. Not that much out of line."

City:* [   ] State:* [▼] Zip:* [   ]

Daytime Phone:* [   ]   Evening Phone: [   ]

Shipping Options

How would you like to ship your order? Choose one of the following:

⦿ **Standard** (5-8 business days) $4.00 + $0.97 per item

○ **Premium** (3-5 business days) $6.00 + $2.47 per item

○ **Express** (2-3 business days) $12.00 + $5.97 per item

*Shipping information applies to merchandise shipping within the Continental U.S.

*required fields

FIXED SHIPPING
Due to size and weight, some of our merchandise may have a Fixed Shipping charge. These items will be shipped Standard delivery time, and you won't be charged any additional shipping fees.

SHIPPING INFO
As soon as we receive your order

One user calculated that a $6 item from Wal-Mart would cost her almost $5 in shipping. She removed it from her shopping cart. SS4

Other sites had shipping charges our users found unacceptable:

- Wal-Mart's shipping charges were rather complicated and required users to perform calculations. One user discovered an unreasonable shipping charge for one of her items: "The [shipping cost for] the Pooh sunshade is $4 plus $0.97. I wouldn't pay $5 for a $6 item. I would go back and get rid of the Pooh." Even though the user wasn't actually completing the purchase in our test, she felt strongly enough about the shipping cost that she used her browser's Back button to remove the sunshade from her shopping cart.
- Jcrew: "Whoa! $11.95! That seems like a hefty shipping and handling charge." (The pair of boots cost $128.)

- NorwaySweaters: The user noticed the shipping charge late in the ordering process. "Oh, I had not considered that it would cost me $15 to have it shipped. That's quite a lot."

Very few of our users expressed a willingness to pay for the convenience of shopping online. In fact, several users commented that they saw no reason why they should pay shipping charges if they could purchase the same item at a local store.

➡ Consider making shipping "free."

Our users liked free shipping. The furniture sites, which carried high-ticket items, all had free shipping. Of course, free shipping isn't really free, and our users realized that. As one user said, "Even though it's added into the cost of the products, it just makes me feel better." Thus, it might be a good sales strategy to build shipping costs into the product price and then offer "free" shipping.

Boo tried to tell users that shipping was free, but showing a cost of $0.00 didn't make this clear enough. ss5

A site that offers free shipping must work to get the message across to users. Boo had free shipping. It said so on the home page and at the bottom of every page of the shopping cart. Still, some users didn't believe the order confirmation page that showed shipping was free:

- Said one user: "Shipping and handling is zero? I don't think so." Later, while looking at the home page, she discovered it did indeed say free shipping and free returns: "That's nice. It did sound too good to be true, but I guess they make up for it in the price of their pants."

- "There's no shipping and handling," another user commented. She expected a charge for shipping and handling, so it was not clear to her why those amounts were shown as "$0.00."

Tip: Display "free" instead of "$0.00" when shipping is free. The $0.00 implies that a different cost might be inserted later. The word "free" is unambiguous.

Tip: Make "free shipping" a link. A couple of users tried to click on the words "free shipping" on Boo's home page to find out more about free shipping. They wanted to know, for example, whether there was a required minimum purchase amount to qualify for free shipping.

➡ *Consider explaining taxes.*

Sales tax is a complicated issue, with a great deal of uncertainty. In the year 2000, lawmakers debated how to tax Internet sales. The taxation issue is far from being resolved. Within the United States, some states charge sales tax and others do not. The amount of tax can depend on the company's physical location (even for Web-only enterprises) as well as the location of the purchaser.

The state of New Hampshire does not charge sales tax on items purchased at physical stores within the state. In a few instances, users living in New Hampshire provided a shipping address in another state and saw a tax charge appear on the website's order form. Some users weren't bothered by seeing a tax charge, but others wanted an explanation. One user would not have proceeded with his order, because he believed the sales tax was applied to his purchase in error.

- Jcrew: Looking over an order summary, one user said, "And tax. Jeez. We live in New Hampshire; shouldn't be tax. I don't know if Illinois [where he was shipping the boots] has sales tax." (It does.)
- Similarly, another Jcrew user stopped when he saw an estimated tax for a New Hampshire billing address: "At this point I wouldn't go through with the order. … Why would there be tax for a billing address in New Hampshire?"
- NorwaySweaters: "Shipping and tax may be added to your order. … It shouldn't say 'may,' " commented one user. He went to the Information page (where company contact instructions were located). He expected to find "tax rates to other parts of the world." He looked on a few other pages and then concluded, "I don't know where you'd find out what the tax is."

These observations suggest that a site might not only have to comply with the tax laws, but might also have to *explain* them in terms typical consumers can understand. We did not test any sites that attempted to explain sales tax.

Selection, Availability, and Delivery Time

- **Selection** is the range of items offered. Seasonal items or items not always in stock are still considered part of the site's selection of merchandise.
- **Availability** is the ability to purchase an item that is shown on the site.
- **Delivery time** is the difference between when the customer places the order and when the customer (or gift recipient) receives the shipment. Delivery time can include the time to produce the item, process the order, ship, and deliver it.

For example, for some items such as pre-release movies or made-to-order furniture, a site can offer the merchandise (selection) now. The customer can buy the merchandise today (availability). The merchandise itself, however, may not arrive for several weeks (delivery time). (Availability and delivery time are covered in the next two sections of this chapter.)

Selection of Merchandise

We didn't set out to study the effects of merchandise selection on e-commerce sites, but we did get insights into how users perceived the variety of products available on the sites we tested. None of the issues mentioned in this section was serious enough to cause a sales catastrophe during our study. Keep in mind, though, that many of our tasks asked the users to buy an item that we knew was available on the site. When people are pursuing their own goals, they are likely to be even more aware of selection than the users were during our study.

➡ *Provide a wide selection of merchandise.*

Sites that drew positive comments from users about their broad selections included Reel, 1800flowers, and TowerRecords. Our users expected a broad selection of products from all but the small specialty sites. They wanted at least as good a selection as they would find in a comparable local store.

- After finding six options for baby car seats (half of which weren't even car seats but infant carriers), one user's reaction to Wal-Mart was: "Not much selection. A little disappointed with that … kinda like more to choose from. … That's one of the things you kind of just expect these days."

- Users who tested both Iflorist and 1800flowers commented on 1800flowers greater selection. In the words of one user: "Seemed like [Iflorist] didn't have as much to offer for roses. The other [1800flowers] had 38. This one had 15, not as much selection. You'd think they have more arrangements for roses than 15."

It's possible that a limited selection may be less of a drawback for online merchants if users know the site is a small business. NorwaySweaters offered only six styles for sale. BasketHaus pictured just 14 gift baskets on their site and took custom orders over the phone. Although users did wish for a greater selection on these sites, they didn't have the same expectations as they did of retail giants like Wal-Mart. Regarding NorwaySweaters, one user said: "I was surprised to see there weren't more choices of colors. There seems to be pretty much two sizes available. I'd say limited selection. But in all fairness, in reading they're handmade, I can see where they'd be limited."

Part of the burden of having a wide selection means maintaining an inventory with a variety of product options such as colors and styles. Users remarked on the lack of selection on Boo after finding a jacket that came in only one color or gloves that were not available in medium.

1-800-flowers.com.
FLOWERS ARE JUST THE BEGINNING...

Your Account · Customer Service | Return Home · Shopping Basket

welcome | greetings | flowers | plants | gift baskets | gourmet treats | unique gifts | garden works

Gift Center | Best Sellers | Magazine | Contests & Promotions | What's New

Search by:
all channels
and keyword:
go

Important Delivery Information!

eQ&A
Online Customer Service

Get Well Bouquet
Product Code: 9011
When you want to send a special "Get Well" gift, send the Get Well Bouquet! Our most popular arrangement will arrive with a cheery Get Well mylar balloon that will perfectly express your sincere wishes. The lovely floral arrangement will brighten someone's home with spring's breathtaking blooms, while the balloon will certainly pick "up" someone's spirits. *Balloon may vary.*

ITEM	PRICE
○ Small	$34.99
◉ Medium (as shown)	$39.99
○ Large	$44.99

add to basket ▶

▶ checkout now

Delivery Information
This product can be delivered the same day during non-holiday periods if placed before 1pm in the recipient's time zone. Delivery hours are between 9am and 7pm. All other orders will be delivered the next day unless otherwise specified.

Users liked the size options on 1800flowers, even though there weren't any images showing what the various sizes would look like. SS6

One user appreciated that 1800flowers offered the Get Well Bouquet in small, medium, and large sizes (in $5 increments). Another made a similar comment about BasketHaus, which offered most of its gift baskets in two or three sizes. Our users wanted to know exactly what they would get for the different amounts of money, but neither BasketHaus nor 1800flowers offered that information.

Our observations do not necessarily suggest that people will like your site better if you add a multitude of options. The users in our study responded well when a site offered them what they cared most about: choices of size, color, and price.

A broad selection of merchandise means that it is difficult for the customer to see everything. In their FAQ, Furniture claimed they don't have a paper catalog because it would require more than 50,000 pages. To serve people who say they want to see everything (as some of our users did, not realizing that they'd be there for days), sites must have a good strategy for organizing and presenting their products and help users find what they're looking for. The Category Pages chapter explains in depth the strategy we call "winnowing."

➡ Improve site navigation to enhance customers' perception of your merchandise selection.

There is a difference between the selection an e-commerce site offers and the selection users *perceive* that it offers. Inability to find an item is a classic website usability problem. Indeed, it caused 27% of the sales catastrophes in our study of the sales catastrophes in our study. The "Finding Item" category includes both unsuccessful searches and difficulty getting to an item via links.

The ultimate effect of navigation problems may be even worse than the 27% suggests. If people fail to find an item once, they may never look for it or similar items on your site again. Poor navigation can cause customers to form negative perceptions of a site's selection. We saw users who were unable to locate specific items draw false conclusions about what the entire site actually had to offer.

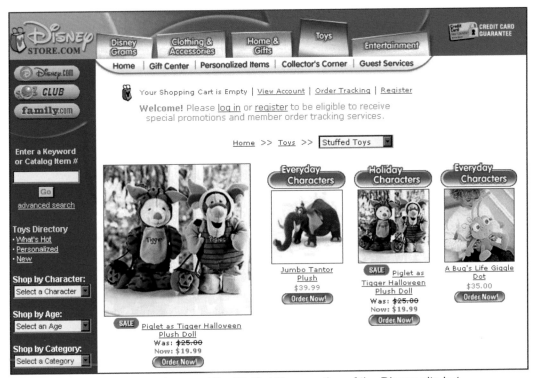

One user browsed the Stuffed Toys section of the Disney site but didn't see Winnie the Pooh, so he mistakenly concluded that the Disney site didn't offer stuffed Pooh bears. SS7

For example, a user on Disney looked for a Winnie the Pooh stuffed animal. He clicked the Stuffed Toys button but saw nothing related to Pooh. "I'm thinking there's only four things shown here. I'm surprised they don't have a 'Pooh Corner.' It doesn't look like they have a lot of stuffed animals online." He eventually gave up. Later, he commented, "It really didn't seem like as many products as I expected."

Of course, the online Disney Store did have a large selection of products, including several stuffed Pooh bears. Although this user was the only one who voiced his belief that the Disney site didn't carry stuffed Poohs, he was not the only one who failed to find them.

In addition to Disney, we saw evidence on Nordstrom, Living, and Furniture that users may form mistaken impressions of a site's offerings based on their failure to find one item. The Search and Category Pages chapters discuss why users had difficulty finding appropriate items.

➡ *If customers look for items you don't sell, either stock those items or make it clear that you don't carry them.*

People's expectations of a site's selection are shaped by their experiences with other stores (both online and offline). Specialty sites in particular run the risk of having customers look for items they don't carry. In our study, users sometimes looked for an item that wasn't offered, especially on Peet's and CustomDisc.

For example, one user looked eagerly on Peet's for flavored coffees, which she loved. When she failed to find them, it wasn't clear to her whether the site didn't offer flavored coffees or they were hidden someplace she hadn't looked. Her biggest unanswered question for this site was: "Where's the flavored coffees? I want them!" As far as we could determine, Peet's did not sell flavored coffee. Flavored coffees, however, are offered on other coffee sites and at the local grocery store. If many of Peet's customers want flavored coffees, Peet's should explain why their site doesn't sell them.

Can't Find a Song?

Most songs are owned by an artist or record label. If they choose not to participate in our CustomDisc service, then we cannot legally sell their music. However, we're constantly expanding our roster of artists and record labels, so you may want to subscribe to **our newsletter** for updates on new music.

You may not find every song you want. But you'll probably find more than you planned. With over 200,000 songs available for your disc, browsing CustomDisc is your best bet.

Back to the Help Index

This section of CustomDisc's Help page should have been shown on the search results page whenever a search returned no hits. SS8

Although CustomDisc offered more than 200,000 songs, conventional CD retailers offer a much larger selection. CustomDisc tried to explain why they have a limited selection of songs compared to other music sites, but most of our users didn't find the explanation. Only one user of 10 saw the explanation and accepted the reason for the site's seemingly sparse selection. Most of the other users in our study searched in vain for songs by well-known artists (like Elvis Presley) and didn't know why they couldn't find the songs.

The main problem with CustomDisc's explanation was that it was in the wrong place. When users typed an artist or song title into the search field, the "No Hits" search results page didn't say anything about why the user's search might have failed. CustomDisc should have moved their explanation from the help topics to the search results page.

Of course, it's not practical to list all the items that a site doesn't sell, so the key strategy is to look for *patterns* in what users search for. (The Search chapter describes how to identify these patterns.) If many customers are interested in a particular type of merchandise, the site should either offer it or explain why it doesn't.

Tip: Review competing sites and physical stores to identify the merchandise that they carry that you don't.

Tip: Review your website search logs to identify searched-for items that your site doesn't carry.

Tip: Provide a feedback form. Let users tell you which merchandise they'd like you to carry. The "no results" search page might be one good place to put a link to the feedback form. Accept, however, that most people won't bother to fill out the form. The user who wanted flavored coffees on Peet's found the feedback form, but she didn't fill it out, saying she doubted that they'd do anything about her request.

Tip: Run usability tests and ask users what they expect from the site.

Tip: Talk to your customer service representatives to find out what customers ask for when they call.

Availability

Our January 2000 study followed the record-breaking 1999 e-commerce holiday season. It was also a time of year when clothing merchants try to get rid of their winter stock by holding clearance sales. Although we weren't surprised to see out-of-stock items, our users were.

Availability issues accounted for 6% of the sales catastrophes in this study. Two thirds of these cases involved Danish users, who were confused or mistaken about whether the site would ship to Denmark. Several of the sites we tested would not ship to Denmark at all, but our users had difficulty determining that. Users were frustrated when they could see an item on the site but could not find out whether they could actually buy it. Clearly, availability is an issue for websites that want a strong international presence. (See the International Users chapter for more information on global e-commerce.)

Availability was an important issue for US users as well. The US availability sales catastrophes happened on Jcrew, Disney, Nordstrom, Reel, and TowerRecords. Users could see out-of-stock products on the site but were unable to buy them. Disney had an especially high number of unavailable items. For some tests, as many as half the items that users searched for were out of stock.

Many of our tasks asked users to purchase items that we knew were available on the test site. Our testing methodology may have caused the percentage of availability catastrophes to be artificially low compared to availability problems consumers encounter when shopping on their own.

➡ *Don't show products that customers can't buy.*

Our users were frustrated when they could see an item they wanted but they couldn't buy it. Even when shopping for clearance merchandise, when it's reasonable to expect that stock will run out and not be replaced, our users were irritated. The sites gave no indication when (or if) the item would become available in the future. "Not available" messages elicited some choice remarks:

- "I finally find something [that I want], and they don't have it."
- "You dumb people, why do you have them there then?"
- "Bummer. It gets you that close, but you can't do nothing with it."
- "I'm thinking they shouldn't have had it in there if it was sold out."
- "Then take it off your site. … This site is so annoying."
- Upon encountering her second sold-out clearance item, one user said, "About now I'd be saying this isn't worth the hassle." She said she'd leave the site.

➡ *Show availability information as soon as possible.*

Users wanted to know if they could buy a product before they expended a lot of effort investigating it. eToys showed availability ("In Stock") right on both the category pages and the product pages. We recommend that sites use a clear and visible availability indicator like eToys and Reel did.

eToys clearly showed "In Stock" on its category pages. Users liked having this information available at the start. SS9

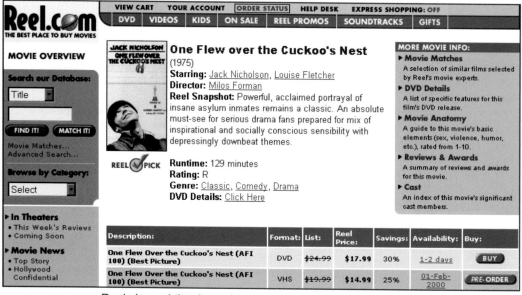

Reel showed the date when a video would become available. SS10

All items we saw on eToys were apparently in stock. We don't know how eToys handled out-of-stock items. Sales fulfillment must match the customer's expectations, which are set by the availability information provided on the site, however. It would be very bad if a site were to show "in stock" for everything and tell customers later that their purchases had been back-ordered.

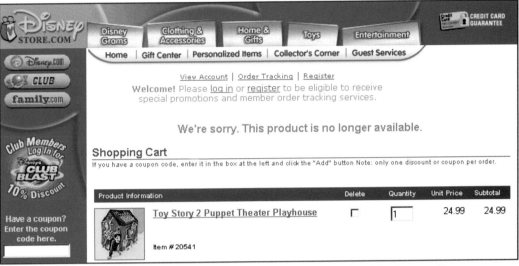

On Disney, all items were shown with "Order Now!" buttons on the category pages even when the items were not available, so users put products in the shopping cart before they were told the items could not be purchased. SS11

In contrast to eToys, Disney hid availability information from users. The product pages showed "Order Now!" buttons for all items. When users clicked "Order Now," however, the shopping cart appeared with a message stating that the item wasn't available. Users who looked carefully at the product page before attempting to order eventually noticed the tiny words "this item is currently not available." Users discovered this message only after studying the item and deciding they wanted it, so they were confused and frustrated.

Nordstrom deserves credit for trying to show availability information on the product page, but they used the wrong mechanism to do it. The user chose size and color through a set of hierarchical, lateral menus. Unavailable combinations were grayed-out. Users quickly figured out what gray meant. The mechanics of traversing the lateral selection menus, however, proved to be a significant usability hurdle. As we have seen in other usability studies, some users didn't realize that they had to make two mouse movements at right angles, rather than taking the direct, diagonal route. A diagonal move caused the menus to disappear.

Nordstrom's method of showing availability worked conceptually, but the hard part was traversing the menus. In this example, when a user tried to move the mouse diagonally from the Color menu to "MEDIUM" on the size menu, the menus disappeared. SS12

▶ **For items not in stock, show the date when the item will be shipped.**

Movies in the United States are first shown in theaters only and may not be released for home use until several months after they leave the theater. Reel and TowerRecords usefully showed availability dates for videos that had not yet been released. Customers could buy the videos in advance by pressing a "Pre-Order" button. Not all users understood what "pre-order" meant, however.

In contrast, Disney did not show availability dates. One user ordered an *Aristocats* DVD from Disney on January 17. The order confirmation did not contain an estimated delivery date, and the user was unable to figure out how the online order-tracking system worked. On February 1, he contacted Disney to determine when the item would be shipped. Disney said that the release date for the *Aristocats* DVD was April 4, 2000, and that the video would not be shipped until then. In response, he cancelled the order.

Lengthy delays can be a problem for seasonal items. Showing the availability date didn't work very well for clothing on Jcrew. During our January test, one New Hampshire resident laughed at the idea of waiting until April for wool pants. Jcrew does deserve credit for showing the availability date instead of the less informative "not available" message encountered by users looking for other items. Even so, the three-month delay resulted in an absurd delivery date for a seasonal item. Jcrew might have fared better if they had recast the delay as an opportunity to order early for next winter.

▶ **Don't automatically substitute items.**

If a product isn't available, a customer might be willing to consider a similar but available item. Don't automatically substitute a comparable item, though, because some customers might feel pushed into buying something they don't want. First tell the customer the chosen item is not in stock, then allow the customer to choose among substitutes.

For example, Jcrew's product pages didn't show that an item was sold out in a particular color. When a user put the item in the shopping cart, the item (in the chosen size) was shown along with the list of available colors, with one color selected as the default. Although Jcrew's approach seemed well intentioned, their implementation was too subtle, because it allowed customers to complete purchases without explicitly acknowledging that they had accepted a substitution.

One of our users would have ordered the wrong color because he didn't notice that the color he selected had been changed. He said that once he saw the words "in stock," he thought everything was fine: He could order the blue shirt he wanted, and he didn't have to bother reading the rest of the page. When we pointed out that Jcrew had substituted a green shirt, he said that he would have been very unhappy if he'd received a green shirt instead of the blue one he thought he had ordered.

One of our users didn't realize that this page was telling him that his choice of a Navy blue shirt was sold out. By clicking OK, he inadvertently ordered a shirt in a color called Surplus (olive green). SS13

Tip: Consider showing similar items on the product page. Show the customer an item similar to the one that is out-of-stock, perhaps on the same product page as the out-of-stock item. Don't wait to show substitutes in the shopping cart.

Delivery Time

In our study, concerns about delivery time (the length of time it would take to receive purchased items) caused 5% of the sales catastrophes. Even though we did not ask users to complete purchases for most tasks, many users wondered when an item would be delivered. They were not always satisfied with the answer.

We believe they would have been even more concerned about delivery times if they had really been buying for a holiday or birthday instead of participating in a study. The highly publicized failure of many e-commerce sites to deliver items on time during the 1999 holiday season underscores the need for improvement in meeting customers' expectations for delivery time.

▶ *Deliver in-stock items within a few days.*

In our study, most users accepted that it might take up to a week for them to receive items like toys and clothing. Users were pleasantly surprised when a site promised to ship items the next day, as NorwaySweaters did. The flower sites offered very prompt delivery, sometimes even on the same day.

In contrast, the time to produce made-to-order items was a sales deterrent. Buying furniture on the sites we tested could result in delays of 6–12 weeks for manufacture and delivery. One user would have left HermanMiller because of that delay: "When I make up my mind to buy something, I want it then, not six weeks from now. … When I do online shopping, it's because I know I can get it right away." Although this user didn't mention a specific site, some sites do offer next-day delivery of standard office furniture.

Our recommendation to deliver in-stock items within a few days is a generalization that depends on customers' expectations. Factors that affect customers' expectations and willingness to wait include:

- **Delivery times for local stores.** For example, Danish customers are accustomed to waiting 1–2 months for new furniture purchased at their local store, so they would likely accept a similar delay online. However, many US furniture stores have local warehouses and can deliver furniture in a matter of days, so US customers may not be as tolerant of long delivery times.

- **Delivery times for other online merchants, even if they offer a different type of merchandise.** For example, a customer who can get a book in one day might wonder why it takes a week to receive a sweater.

- **The ease of finding the same or comparable merchandise elsewhere.**

➡ *Estimate the number of days until delivery.*

Although the online merchant may not have direct control over shipping, users liked seeing an estimate of the number of days it would take to receive their purchases. Nordstrom and Reel both estimated delivery dates.

PLEASE CHECK YOUR ORDER

STEP ①②③④⑤⑥

Below are the items that you added to your shopping bag. At this time, you can remove any item, cancel your order, return to shopping or continue to check out. Become a member and save time on future purchases!

Questions? Email: orders@nordstrom.com or call 1 - 888 - 282 - 6060

Please Note: We will be conducting our annual physical inventory and cannot offer Two Business-Day Delivery, Next Business-Day Delivery, or Saturday Delivery on orders placed after 1 pm PST, Thursday, January 20, through Monday, January 24, 2000.

Item	Unit Price	Qty	Price	
#22361 BLK Medium Wrought-Iron Candleholder Usually ships in 1-2 business days and arrives within 3-6 business days.	$25.00	1	$25.00	Remove
#S00868 200 10 M Monet Usually ships in 3-5 business days and arrives within 6-10 business days.	$79.95	1	$79.95	Remove
#18044 RED 12 Paisley Cap-sleeved Peasant Dress Usually ships in 1-2 business days and arrives within 3-6 business days.	$79.90	1	$79.90	Remove
		Subtotal	$184.85	

🔘 **Return and Exchange Policy**

Users liked seeing the estimated shipping time on this Nordstrom order confirmation page, but not all users understood the definition of "business days." SS14

Tip: Show a specific date rather than a number of business days. Two Danish users were confused about the meaning of "3 business days" to ship international orders on 1800flowers. Because it was not clear to them that business days excluded weekends, they formed incorrect expectations of when their orders would be delivered. For US deliveries, both florist sites showed exact delivery dates, so US users avoided this confusion.

➡ *Provide a choice of shipping methods, and list the carriers.*

Our users paid a surprising amount of attention to the shipping options, though there was nothing in our tasks or instructions that would have focused their attention on shipping methods. Nearly a third of the 39 US users made a spontaneous comment about shipping method. Their comments indicated that they recognized trade-offs among cost, speed, and service. They also said that they wanted control of these trade-offs:

- **Delivery destination:** "If it was being shipped someplace when someone might not be home, then I'd rather have the post office than UPS [United Parcel Service] leaving it under the porch," said one user. "On the other hand, during regular business hours, UPS works fine."

- **Ability to track a package:** One user chose UPS, "because if something gets lost, you know where the delivery is. UPS has a 24-hour tracking system. Postal service … kind of 'good luck.' "

- **Faster delivery:** "Didn't tell you who it's shipped by," complained a user. "Depends on how fast I want it. Didn't see any options for UPS or overnight."

Sites with only one shipping method seemed odd or restrictive to some users. (NorwaySweaters, Iflorist, and 1800flowers offered only FedEx for some items.) Despite users' reservations about having no choice of shipper, they seemed willing to proceed with the order.

Our Danish users didn't comment on shipping methods. In many cases, there was only one option available for international deliveries. Danish users were primarily concerned about whether the site would ship to Denmark at all. This question might have overshadowed any other concerns they had about shipping carriers.

➡ *Provide additional delivery information, when necessary.*

Some items are more complicated to deliver than others. For perishable items like flowers, our users wanted to know what happens when the recipient is not at home. For bulky items like furniture, the users wanted to know how large and heavy the box would be and how much assembly would be required. Living explained specialized delivery well.

Some users liked this level of detail about furniture delivery from Living. SS15

Customer Satisfaction Policies

➧ *Make links to guarantees and policies prominent throughout the site.*

Readily visible guarantees made a positive impression on our users. In some tasks, we specifically asked the users a question involving the return of an item. We also observed a number of users checking out return policies on their own. This voluntary behavior illustrates the importance of guarantees and policies to customers.

There was no one place on a website where users looked for policies or guarantees. Questions about policy arose while users looked at products or when they saw the first page of the shopping cart. We recommend that return policies and guarantees be visible on the home page, product pages, and throughout checkout. Some sample user comments:

- Sears: A user liked that links to the guarantee and privacy policy were at the bottom of every page, as opposed to "something I had to go search for."

- Living: A user on the sign-in page, commented, "I would want to know what their return and exchange policy was before I went any further. It's good they've got that right there. That's a definite plus." She looked at it and was satisfied with the information in it.

- Wal-Mart: A user found the return policy in the shopping cart and remarked, "Good return policy."

Wal-Mart displayed their return policy in the shopping cart, which is a good place to put the return policy, but it is not the only place to present policies and guarantees. ss16

➡ Explain the return policy and process.

Our users understood and were satisfied with most of the return policies on the sites we tested. Sometimes, though, it was hard for our users to determine under which conditions they could return an item, whether they would get their money back, or what the return procedure was.

On NorwaySweaters, it wasn't clear what constituted an acceptable reason to return a sweater. The page said, "Every item that we sell is guaranteed unconditionally for its normal life under standard use." One user interpreted the guarantee to mean that she could return the sweater only if she found a problem with its quality. She assumed that if she bought the wrong size, she would be out of luck. The guarantee page also did not explain how to return the sweater, for example whether there was a form that must be filled out, and who would pay for shipping.

return or exchange online purchase

Return postage labels are included with every purchase from the Online Store in the event you need to return an item. If your order was purchased with your Nordstrom Card or Nordstrom Visa, your return shipping is free (USA only). If you used another method of payment, $3.95 for return postage will be deducted from your order refund. You may also return any online purchase at the Nordstrom Store nearest you.

If you need to exchange an item purchased in the Online Store, please e-mail us at orders@nordstrom.com or call 1-888-282-6060 with the following information:

• your original order number (from your e-mail confirmation)
• your name and address
• list the items being returned:
 - item number and description
 - color
 - size

• list the new item you would like sent:
 - item number and description
 - color
 - size

You can return your item to be exchanged using the pre-paid return postage label included with your Online Store purchase. You will be credited for the item (excluding shipping charges) upon our receipt of the item. The new item you have selected will be sent to you at no additional shipping charge.

On Nordstrom, the return policy was also confusing. Although it stated, "You will be credited for the item," two users were not confident that this meant they would get their money back. SS17

Peet's Coffee & Tea

Store   Roasting   Tasting   Customer Service

In Customer Service

HOW TO ORDER   BUSINESS ACCOUNTS
RETURN POLICY   PROFILE MANAGEMENT

View Shopping Cart
1 Items   CHECKOUT

• Check our Customer Service FAQ

Return Policy

100% Guaranteed
If any Peet's product fails to meet your expectations, we will replace it or refund the full cost of the product, no questions asked. Just call us at 800-999-2132, and we will do whatever we can to ensure that you're satisfied.

Peet's return policy was clear. Users had no problems understanding phrases like "100% guarantee," "full refund," and "no questions asked." SS18

> *Offer free returns and clearly state that returns are free.*

Most users assumed they would have to pay the shipping cost to return an item, but when actually confronted with just such a policy on Nordstrom, they balked. A close reading of Nordstrom's return policy revealed that Nordstrom included "return postage labels" with every order. An even closer reading, however, divulged that "$3.95 for return postage will be deducted from your order refund" — unless the item was purchased with a Nordstrom credit card. Our users (none of whom had Nordstrom cards) didn't like the idea of being charged for returning an item.

One user was so annoyed by this return postage fee that she said she would have left the site: "It's a complicated process, their returns. … I wouldn't order from them, because return postage is 'free,' but then they take it out of your order refund. And they automatically do $3.95. I could probably mail it back for less than that." She said that this issue alone would prevent her from shopping at this site.

When users realized that a site actually offered free returns, they were pleasantly surprised. But even on a few of the free-return test sites, some users just didn't get the message:

- HermanMiller: "I'm comfortable I could get my money back, except for the shipping and handling. You never get that back," grumbled one user. On this site, return shipping really was free, but the user never realized that, even though she was on the page that explained free shipping.

- Living: "Money-back guarantee isn't bad. Of course, they probably won't ship it back for free," said another user. Living did offer free return shipping, but this user didn't realize it.

Boo was one site that promoted its policy of free returns well. The words "free returns" were visible on most pages. The words "free returns" should have been a link to the actual return policy, though, because some of our users clicked on the words, but nothing happened.

Payment Options

We didn't ask users to complete purchases during most of our tests. Despite that, six users looked on their own to find out which forms of payment were accepted.

➡ *Accept a variety of credit cards.*

Two users noticed sites that didn't accept the Discover card, because they usually shopped with that card. Typically, our users couldn't find out which credit cards a site accepted until late in the checkout process. One user said he wanted to find this information on the home page, explaining, "If I go to a brick-and-mortar shop, I can see it on the front door." Another user commented that seeing the Visa logo on CustomDisc's home page communicated to her right away that the site sold something. Ironically, the logo she referred to was a banner ad.

Tip: Consider showing credit card symbols on your home page. Although we heard comments from only two of the 64 users in our study about wanting to see credit cards on the home page, we believe that people who use less common credit cards want to know in advance whether a site accepts their cards. We don't necessarily recommend that sites provide a list of credit cards on the home page (unless it can be done without taking up too much space), but it might be good to provide at least a link on the home page to credit card information.

➡ *Consider providing payment alternatives.*

One user, who was concerned about managing his debt, told us that he tried to avoid using his credit cards. He wanted more sites to offer alternative methods of payment, such as an electronic withdrawal from his checking account. He did not recognize that a "check card" or "debit card" (offered by most banks in the US with every checking account) can be used to do just that.

Wal-Mart was the only site we tested that offered the option to pay by mailing in a check. Although users said this option was interesting, most still preferred to pay with a credit card. They knew their check would have to clear the bank before the retailer would ship the purchase, resulting in a likely delay. Some people who don't have credit cards would probably appreciate the option to pay by check or money order, however. The percentage of consumers who use credit cards online varies by country.

Supporting the Sales Process

Some sites we tested employed various strategies to help customers complete a purchase or to encourage them to buy additional items. Although this section does not attempt to provide a comprehensive survey of selling tactics, we did gain some insights about the effectiveness of the methods we saw.

Promoting Products

➡️ *Provide a visible means of buying from promotional pages.*

Most of sites we tested devoted some space to promoting certain products. In a few cases, our users were interested in a promoted item but couldn't figure out how to buy it, because the page describing the product lacked a readily visible means (or just lacked a means, visible or not) to purchase the item.

- Gevalia: On the Coffee 101 page (which described methods for brewing coffee), two users found a description of a plunger pot (also known as a coffee press), the type of coffee maker we'd asked them to find. One user tried to click on the word "plunger," saying: "This seems to be the thing we're looking for, but they won't let me click on it. I would have wanted to pull it up, [so] it would tell me how to get one."

- Iflorist: When looking for roses, two users clicked a link on the home page that said "Everything's coming up roses." As one commented, "I assume that's where you go to find roses." It wasn't. It was only a page of interesting facts about roses. "Just tells me about them. Doesn't give me any options to buy." Both users ignored the Roses link, which appeared in the left navigation panel of every page on the website. They both focused their attention on the central part of each page.

- Reel: One user decided she wanted to buy *The Thomas Crown Affair* video after reading a promotional page about it, but she couldn't figure out how to buy it from there. It didn't occur to her to click on <u>The Thomas Crown Affair</u> link within the text, which would have taken her to the product page. Ultimately, she selected a different video. As we explain in the Product Pages chapter, we recommend using a simple but distinctive Buy button. The idea is to make the purchase option as noticeable and easy as possible. The subtle text link on Reel just wasn't enough to attract users' attention.

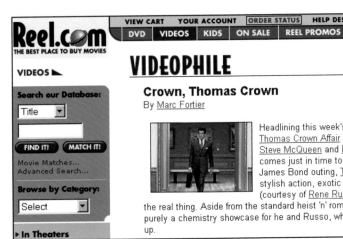

VIDEOPHILE

Crown, Thomas Crown
By Marc Fortier

Headlining this week's slim slate of new renters, John McTiernan's Thomas Crown Affair is a stylish remake of the 1968 film starring Steve McQueen and Faye Dunaway. Ironically, the video release comes just in time to cover up star Pierce Brosnan's decidedly weak James Bond outing, The World Is Not Enough. Considering *Crown*'s stylish action, exotic locales, and sexy, sophisticated female factor (courtesy of Rene Russo), this thriller is arguably more "Bond" than the real thing. Aside from the standard heist 'n' romance plot line, the Brosnan-produced *Crown* is purely a chemistry showcase for he and Russo, who spend the majority of screen time heating it up.

One user decided she wanted to get "The Thomas Crown Affair," but she couldn't find a way to buy it from this page and eventually gave up. SS19

► *On "What's New" pages, emphasize new products rather than site updates.*

When people click a link that says, "What's New" (or something similar) on an e-commerce site, they expect to find information on new *products* (the customer's point of view). They do not expect to find a description of recent changes on the *website* (the designer's point of view).

Of the sites we tested, only Gevalia and Peet's had What's New links. Only five users clicked the links. They all expected to find information about new product offerings. The "New at Peet's" page met their expectations. Gevalia's What's New page did not, because it mainly described updates to the website.

GEVALIA KAFFE
FINE COFFEES OF EUROPE

WHAT'S NEW

It's been a hot, dry Summer, so it seems only natural that as it comes to an end your thoughts start wandering to...Christmas? Well, maybe not snow and stuff, but it isn't too early to start thinking about Holiday entertaining, perhaps a nice Autumn brunch, watching the leaves changing color...and don't forget Gevalia coffee and tea!

The **1999 Holiday Catalog** is online today. This latest edition of our catalog is filled with great ideas for Holiday entertaining and gift giving. While you're browsing through our new catalog, set up your Preferred Shopper Profile. We'll save all of your info in our database so you don't have to enter it again, making your shopping really easy and convenient.

Our new Preferred Shopper program has some other features as well, including an online address book and your order history, available for review.

We're excited to be introducing Gevalia Select Green Tea. Four exciting, new flavors to introduce you to the healthful benefits of drinking green tea.

If you're new to Gevalia, you'll want to check out **Online Customer Service**. Just register (you'll need your account number) to set up your ID and password, and then manage your account online.

Online Customer Service continues to be updated. It doesn't matter if you are a Gevalia member, belong to the European

Gevalia's What's New page did not fulfill our users' expectations that it would show new products. SS20

In our study we looked at first-time use rather than repeat visits to the test sites, so information about recent site changes was not relevant to our users. It's possible that this guideline would not apply as stringently to sites that people visit frequently, where an explanation of recent site changes might be helpful to them.

➡ *Provide a Sale section.*

We gave users a few minutes to look around each site before giving them their first task there. Many clicked on links that said "sale" or "clearance" (although the term "clearance" was not as familiar to Danish users). They also often explored sale links during free-form tasks when they were allowed to look for items of interest to them. Some sample comments:

- Nordstrom: "If *I* were doing this [shopping on her own], I'd be over here in sale."
- SmarterKids: "I did check with the specials first. That's how I do my shopping."
- Jcrew: "I love to go to clearance."

➡ *Consider offering samples.*

Giving away samples might encourage sales of certain kinds of merchandise, by helping customers gain a better understanding of the product. Offering samples makes the most sense when the cost of offering a sample is low (for example, downloading a file) or the value of the product is high (for instance, a fabric swatch from a sofa).

CustomDisc provided free samples of music. One might also imagine video sites offering video clips, but neither of the sites we tested did so.

CustomDisc's samples were quite effective in the six US tests. After listening to song excerpts at the click of a button, all six US users said they could decide with confidence whether a particular song was one they wanted.

The samples were useless in the three Danish tests, however, because the test computer did not have the required audio software installed. All three Danish users gave up immediately when the Listen button didn't work.

On the coffee sites, a couple of people wanted sample packs of coffee. Gevalia had a sampler pack for sale, but Peet's did not. One user looked for a way to get a free coffee sample from Gevalia, saying he wanted to do this before he ordered a large quantity. (We don't know whether a free sample would have actually encouraged him to buy coffee.)

Living offered free furniture fabric samples, which one user appreciated. None of the other users came across this option. Free samples were not available for all products.

➡ *Don't make important page elements look like ads.*

In a website phenomenon called "ad blindness," people tend to ignore site content that looks like an advertisement. All of us involved with this study have observed this phenomenon in other studies. We believe people have learned to screen out distractions while they are looking for something in particular. Ironically, ad blindness is even worse for animated ads, because people have apparently decided subconsciously that if something is moving, it's useless.

We saw two instances of ad blindness in this study, both from 1800flowers. Unfortunately, what the users ignored were links to content that they needed, because these links looked like ads.

- One of our tasks specifically asked about order lead-time for Valentine's Day. (We conducted our tests in January, when such a question was relevant for the February 14 holiday.) All the users ignored an animated truck bearing the message "Important Delivery Information." On many of the pages, the truck constantly "drove" across a graphic element in the left margin that looked like an ad. In the last two tests, we asked the users at the end of the test whether they'd noticed the truck. They said no.

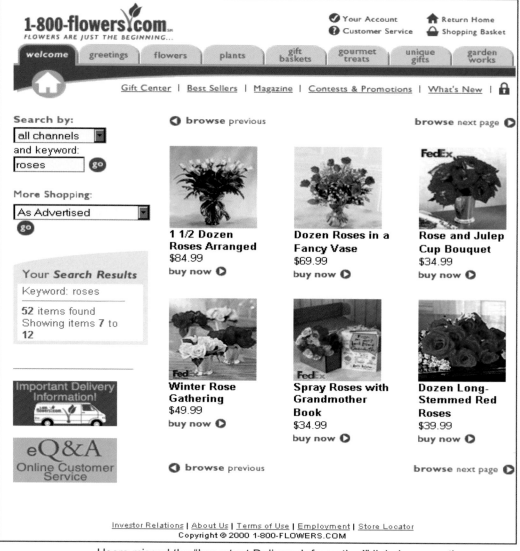

Users missed the "Important Delivery Information!" link, because the animated truck made the link look like an ad. SS21

- Users skipped over a link on the First-Time Visitors page because it looked like a banner ad. Actually, it was a link to a page containing information that some users said they wanted about the site's features.

The apparent banner ad near the top of the First-Time Visitors page was actually a link to information first-time visitors might want. Our users, who were looking for that information, didn't respond to the link. SS22

We aren't saying that sites should never display ads, but if you want your customers to notice important products and information, provide links to it in the same manner that you link to other essential content on the site.

Encouraging Additional Sales

Anyone who has ever visited a fast food restaurant has probably heard a question like, "You want fries with that?" At least in the United States, people have been conditioned to expect this sales tactic (called "cross-selling" or "up-selling") to encourage additional purchases. Many of the sites we tested suggested additional items on their product pages. Our users' reactions ranged from very negative to mildly positive, depending on how sites presented their add-on suggestions.

➡️ *Suggest additional items, but don't put obstacles before the cash register.*

Although there was nothing in our tasks that required it, several of our US users opted to add suggested items to their shopping carts on various sites.

- Wal-Mart: A user decided on her own that she wanted the Winnie the Pooh sunshade that was shown on the Car Seat product page.

- Iflorist: Upon seeing the option to add a balloon, a user commented, "If she [the hypothetical gift recipient] was in the hospital, I might have put a balloon in there." In the next task, which did involve getting something to cheer up a sick neighbor, this user added a balloon.

- eToys: "With the money you save, you could even buy an accessory pack," said one user, who added an accessory pack to her order.

We don't know whether they would have chosen the add-ons had they been spending their own money, because in this study they were either not actually making purchases or were being reimbursed for them. Interestingly, none of the Danish users chose to add suggested items. We don't know why they didn't, but perhaps the difficulty of shopping on a foreign language site made them less inclined to further complicate the task.

eToys offered additional items on the product page. This approach, used by several of the sites we tested, seemed to be acceptable to our users. SS23

The sites we tested used several ways to suggest additional items.

Acceptable approach: Make additional items available on the product page.
Several sites presented additional items on the product page. No one made any negative comments about this approach. A few users decided on their own that they would get one of the suggested items even though there was no requirement in our tasks to do so.

Bad approach: Suggest additional items during the checkout process.
1800flowers created an obstacle by inserting an additional gift suggestion page into the checkout process.

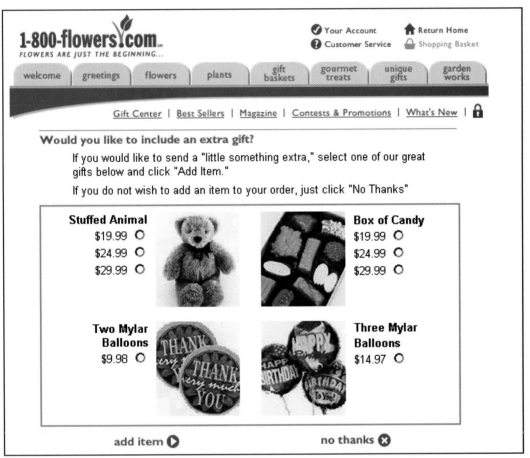

This intrusive gift suggestion page used by 1800flowers interfered with the checkout process. This add-on sales approach confused some users and annoyed others. SS24

After clicking "Add to Basket," the user was presented with a page that suggested including an extra gift, such as balloons or teddy bears. This approach confused and annoyed our users:

- One user clicked her browser's Back button to get off the gift suggestion page, because she thought it was a customization option instead of the shopping cart. Then she was unable to figure out how to complete the purchase. Another user was similarly confused but managed to figure it out.

- Another user said: "Now they're just trying to get me to buy more. … That would irritate the crap out of me. I'd go to Jackson & Perkins [another flower and garden site]."

By introducing an extra step into the checkout process, 1800flowers forced users to take an overt action to refuse to make an additional purchase before they could proceed to checkout. Customers may or may not mind when a human sales clerk makes an additional purchase suggestion, but this same tactic is less tolerable on a website.

Interestingly, Iflorist used a variation of this tactic that users didn't seem to mind. In Iflorist's implementation, the image and description of the product the user had selected appeared at the top of the order form. If there were any suggested add-on items, Iflorist presented them below the selected product. The add-ons consisted of a short suggestion (for example, "Add a Teddy Bear"), the price, and an opt-in check box. Not all products came with suggested add-ons, so we saw this sales tactic only a few times.

Compare 1800flowers' approach with that of Iflorist. Both wanted to entice users into buying additional items. The 1800flowers tactic actually interfered with the buying process, though. Users couldn't see what they were trying to purchase until they got past the gift suggestion page. In contrast, the Iflorist sales method first confirmed (with picture and description) the item the user wanted to buy, then it offered gift suggestions below.

Unlike 1800flowers, the Iflorist approach didn't seem to trouble users. If they weren't interested, they simply scrolled past the items without complaining. Even so, we hesitate to recommend soliciting add-on purchases during checkout. Potentially, the add-ons could distract the user from completing the primary purchase. We suggest conducting usability tests before adopting this sales method.

Iflorist's order form first showed a description and image of the item the user had selected, and then offered add-ons. In contrast to 1800flowers' approach, users didn't seem to mind the suggested items on Iflorist. SS25

Tip: You don't have to suggest additional items on all pages. We did not find any evidence that a site must offer additional items on all product pages for the sake of consistency. The sites we tested sometimes had additional items and sometimes didn't. None of our users commented on this inconsistency. Thus, we would encourage site designers to experiment with adding suggested items to specific product pages. Then track sales of those items as a measure of success.

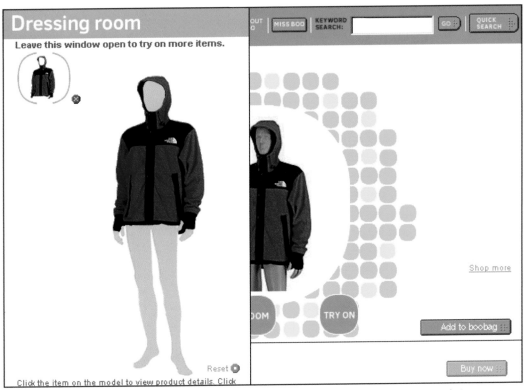

Boo's "Try On" Dressing room feature was an intriguing approach to encouraging additional sales, but it didn't work. SS26

Boo's Dressing room "Try On" feature was an add-on sales tactic that employed a virtual mannequin. It was an intriguing idea in theory that just didn't quite work in practice. The feature allowed shoppers to find out how different articles of clothing would look when worn together, encouraging users to buy entire outfits at once.

The main problem with Boo's Try-On feature was that users saw it at the wrong time. The Try-On feature was useful only *after* the user had chosen one item and was considering complementary articles of clothing. Unfortunately, users investigated the Try-On feature with their first item. They couldn't understand what its purpose was. The mannequin, now wearing one item of clothing, looked essentially the same as the product page. No users came back to the dressing room, not even those who selected multiple items.

The Try-On feature might have been more successful if it had appeared after a user added the first item to the "boobag" (shopping cart). It might have been even more helpful if the Try-On feature included instructions on how to use it.

➡ *Use opt-in, not opt-out, for items the customer hasn't specifically selected.*

Websites can suggest additional purchases to users in two ways. One works better than the other.

- Opt-in: The item is shown, but not included, unless the user consciously chooses it.
- Opt-out: The item is automatically included in the order unless the user notices it and deselects it.

We recommend the opt-in approach. With opt-out, you risk losing customers. It can cause a sales catastrophe if a site automatically includes extra items, forcing the user to deselect them manually, or worse yet, to purchase the items unintentionally. As discussed in the Trust chapter, the principle of opt-in rather than opt-out also applies to e-mail newsletters.

Of all the sites we tested, Furniture's opt-out selling strategy antagonized our users the most. If a user specified a piece of furniture (say, a table), most of the images returned by the site showed complete sets of furniture. If a user clicked on one of those images to go to the product page, that page typically had all the items in the set selected by default. To avoid getting the entire set, users had to deselect the other items in the set. Also, there was no way to view images of each item separately.

Our users were upset because they asked for a table, not an entire dining room set. One user felt so manipulated by Furniture's opt-out approach that he would have left the site. It didn't bother users that the site initially showed complete sets of furniture, but the assumption that the user was buying a complete set did bother them.

eToys used an opt-out approach for batteries. When the user selected a toy that ran on batteries, the site recommended the necessary sizes and types of batteries. That much was fine, but the default option was set to: "I would like batteries included with my order." As she checked the "No" option, one user muttered about "the hidden cost of these toys." She explained that she bought batteries in bulk at discount stores.

Delivery and Service Preferences

1 Please Note: We ship to the 48 continental United States only. If you live outside the continental U.S., please click "contact us" above and use the store locator to see if there is a Sears store near you.

2 Your product can be protected by a Sears Maintenance Agreement.

- Professional service provided by the trained repair specialists at Sears HomeCentral®
- Complete parts and labor for all covered repairs.
- Unlimited service calls on covered repairs at no extra charge.
- A free annual preventive maintenance check, at your request.

○ $19.99 for 2YR In-Shop Maintenance Agreement.
   Only $ 1 per month on Sears Charge Plus.*
○ $29.99 for 3YR In-Shop Maintenance Agreement.
   Only $ 1 per month on Sears Charge Plus.*
○ $49.99 for 2YR In-Home Maintenance Agreement.
   Only $ 1 per month on Sears Charge Plus.*
○ $69.99 for 3YR In-Home Maintenance Agreement.
   Only $ 2 per month on Sears Charge Plus.*
◉ No thank you

Continue

Users didn't mind this opt-in approach to Sears' maintenance agreements. SS27

In contrast, some sites used an opt-in approach. Sears had an opt-in choice for maintenance agreements on appliances. Furniture offered an opt-in choice for in-home protection plans. Our users made no negative comments about either of these approaches.

While we were testing Sears with US users, we asked them whether they normally chose a maintenance agreement when purchasing appliances in physical stores. Those users who said yes confirmed they would also buy an agreement from the website.

Providing Sales Assistance

▶ *Consider creating a first-time visitors page.*

A few of the test sites had orientation pages intended for new users. We observed that some users actually do visit these pages.

One user said he would take the Boo tour if he were exploring the site on his own. (Our test computers had 56k modem connections, which were too slow to spend the limited test time on Boo's high-bandwidth features.) Another user took the tour on eToys while she was trying to find the gift registry.

On 1800 flowers, seven of the 10 users were attracted by the first-time visitors page (Image SS22). Regrettably, all seven users decided that the first-time visitors page had wasted their time. One user was sharply critical: "That's a waste. I don't care why he's in business. I'm here to get flowers."

The 1800flowers First-Time Visitors page didn't contain anything that our users actually found helpful. They said they expected "information about their flowers, house plants," or information about how to find things on the site. The only page on 1800flowers that could meet those expectations was linked from the First-Time Visitors page by an image that looked like a banner ad. As previously discussed, our users suffered from "ad blindness" and thus, never explored that link.

Tip: A first-time visitors page should contain some combination of the following:

- An overview of the site's products
- An explanation of the site's organization
- A directory of assistance (online chat, toll-free phone number, FAQs)
- Links to important policy information (guarantees, privacy, security, returns).

➡️ *Make sure that recommendations are relevant to what the customer wants.*

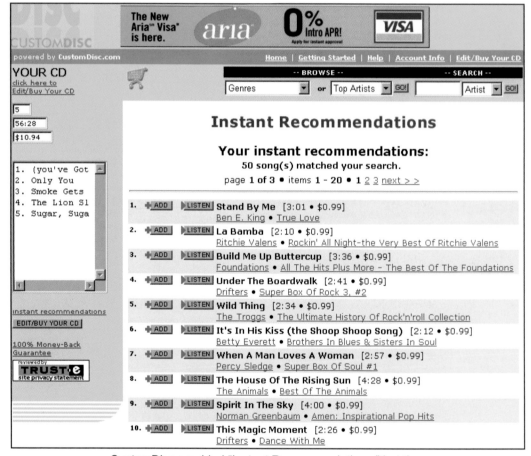

CustomDisc provided "Instant Recommendations," but there was no way to tell why it returned the songs it did. SS28

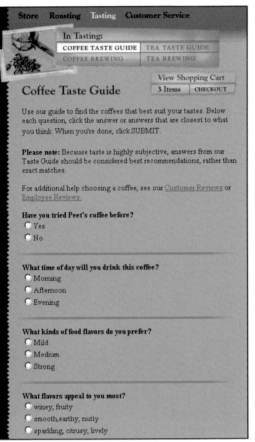

Peet's Taste Guide returned a small set of recommendations based on a user's preferences. SS29

CustomDisc had an "Instant Recommendations" feature that two of our users tried. One user said she liked this feature, but she didn't actually listen to any of the songs it returned. The other user wasn't sure what it did: "It looks like it just gave me more songs." He also didn't explore any of the recommendations.

CustomDisc did not make clear which criteria they used for their recommendations: for instance, the type of artist, the year the song came out, or the purchases made by other customers. It was hard for users to understand how the selections were relevant to the music they'd already chosen.

Peet's tried something a little more successful at making relevant recommendations to their customers. The coffee merchant had a five-question Taste Guide quiz that asked users about their coffee preferences. Based on a user's input, Peet's returned a handful of suggested coffees.

Out of nine users, three tried the Taste Guide. One ignored the results, a another chose one of its recommendations, and the third liked the idea of the Taste Guide but was disappointed when it didn't offer a sample pack of flavored coffees. We have seen from other tests that people appreciate quizzes of this kind, provided they perceive (as our users did) that the quiz is for their benefit, not just the site's.

➡ *Don't substitute cleverness for helpfulness.*

Microsoft learned a lesson about overly clever assistants with the infamous Office paperclip: People loathed it.

Boo reincarnated the concept of an animated assistant with Miss Boo, who introduced herself as "your virtual personal shopper and futuristic fashion guru." As users viewed products and completed order forms, Miss Boo offered comments ranging from frivolous to helpful to obnoxious. She blinked, gestured, and tossed her pony-tailed head flirtatiously. For example, when a user omitted the phone number on the order form, Miss Boo asked, "Hey, you're cute. Can I get your phone number?"

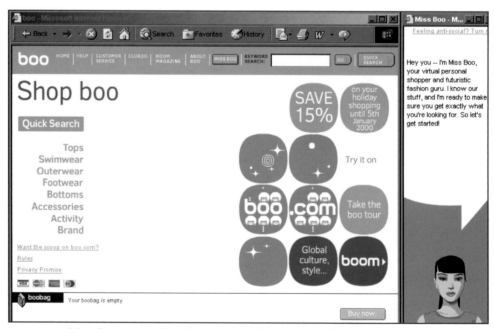

Miss Boo was neither fun nor useful. During the US tests, she kept reappearing after users closed her window. SS30

Our users perceived Miss Boo as neither fun nor useful. On a 56K connection, Miss Boo couldn't keep up with the action. (Her response time seemed acceptable to us over a much faster cable connection, however.) Users weren't amused by her, except initially, and their amusement quickly turned to annoyance.

When one of our users tried to register on Boo, he typed his full name as a username. His name contained more characters than the site would accept. Miss Boo scolded him: "Hey you! Take a break. We're not asking you to write a book. Try a name of 4 to 10 characters." The user didn't understand which field on the registration form was causing the problem, so he was unable to fix it.

If Miss Boo had been truly interactive instead of just displaying canned responses, users' reactions might have been different. One user who was having trouble finding warm gloves mused: "I wonder how personal shopper works. ... If she talked to me, I'd ask her, 'All right, Personal Shopper, which ones are the warmest ones?' " But until computer software can reliably offer this level of sophisticated interaction with people, we believe it's better to leave out the Miss Boo approach, which fell far short of the mark.

Although it was possible to turn off Miss Boo, she didn't stay away. She kept coming back as soon as the user went to another page. (This may have been a bug, because it happened on the US version of Boo's site but not on its Danish counterpart.) Only one user out of nine had any kind of positive reaction to Miss Boo: "That personal shopper doesn't have too much to say, but I thought it was kind of fun." The most extreme negative reaction was: "Miss Boo should be shot!"

➧ Consider the ultimate online sales assistant: a person.

Furniture, 1800flowers, and Reel offered a live chat feature with a customer service representative. (Reel's chat was so well hidden that none of our users found it.) Only three of our users tried online chat: two on Furniture, one on 1800flowers.

Furniture's Live Chat was a complete success with the two users who tried it. They appreciated getting help from a real human being. SS31

The user responses to Furniture's chat showed how a human sales assistant could have a positive effect on users. Two users successfully used live chat to locate wine racks, which were difficult to find on the site. They raved about how great the chat facility was. Despite connection problems and delays of up to a minute between responses, the users received the assistance they wanted. They were particularly impressed when the customer service representative made a page containing the wine racks appear.

- "Seeing that was just like, *Wow!* Having an online chat is a beautiful thing. Very helpful. Some of the other sites, it's kind of like, 'good luck to you.' [But here] you have someone like in any store, able to help you. … There's someone behind the company, not an automated warehouse that's completely mechanized."

- "They've got someone sitting there live, an expert sitting there who will help me. That's great, an IM [instant message] from their website. I like that. She gave me three choices. I would have bought it."

Just as they would have in a voice conversation with a customer service representative, our users noticed mediocre service in chat. The representatives on 1800flowers and Reel offered nothing more than the same information already available on the sites. In neither case did the representatives try to provide additional assistance.

- On 1800flowers, the representative did not provide any suggestions for the user who asked about morning delivery. The representative simply told her that they could not guarantee morning delivery. He did not attempt to help her identify a delivery alternative, such as asking whether a neighbor was home during the day, or if the delivery could go to the recipient's workplace.

- One of our facilitators described his experience chatting on Reel: "I got the impression that I did not have his full attention, perhaps because he was chatting with several customers simultaneously. … I received only answers that were apparent from the website. Although there was nothing specific to blame him for, I had the impression that his goal was to get rid of me as soon as possible. He succeeded."

It's not always possible to replace the human touch. One user told a poignant story about ordering flowers right before Valentine's Day. The flowers were not for a sweetheart, but for her father's funeral. When she called her local florist on Feb. 12, she was first told they wouldn't guarantee delivery. When she explained that the arrangement was for her father's funeral, the florist responded, "No problem. We'll take care of it." The flowers were delivered on time. The user was skeptical that an online florist would provide this degree of personal service.

➡ *Provide a toll-free phone number.*

About 20% of the US users commented on the presence (or absence) of a toll-free phone number. For some users, their comfort level in completing an order online depended on how familiar they were with the store. One user remarked on the absence of any phone number, toll free or otherwise, on NorwaySweaters: "Not having a phone number is a pretty negative thing, especially for a small unknown site."

jcrew.com is secure The Secure Socket Layer Protocol is used to ensure that your information is sent directly to J.Crew, and that only J.Crew can decode it. If you prefer, click here for a printable form to phone, fax, or mail in your order.

Ordered by billing address

Ship to address if different

> Jcrew's alternatives to online ordering were reassuring to those users who had security concerns about providing their credit card number over the Web. SS32

Users liked Jcrew's clearly presented alternative methods for ordering, which reassured those who were not completely comfortable ordering online:

- "This asks you if you want to phone or mail your order, instead of [ordering] online. If you didn't want to give your credit number over the computer, you wouldn't have to."

- "At home, I would be tempted to hit that [where it said click for a printable form], and phone in or mail my order."

Having a toll-free number wasn't just useful to allay concerns about credit cards. Other users said they wanted a toll-free number for customer service in case they had questions about the product or a problem with an order.

Supporting Gift Buying

In about one-fourth of our shopping tasks, we asked users to get an item as a gift for someone else: for example, something to cheer up a sick aunt, boots for a brother's birthday, or educational software for a niece. In other cases, users themselves raised questions about what they would do if they were buying for someone else. They wanted to know if the site would let them ship an order to multiple addresses or how the recipient could return an item.

➡ *Consider selling gift certificates or providing a gift registry.*

For some sites we tested, gifts probably represented a significant percentage of sales. For example, it is much easier to imagine giving toys or flowers as gifts than giving office furniture. Our users responded positively to sites that offered options related to gifts.

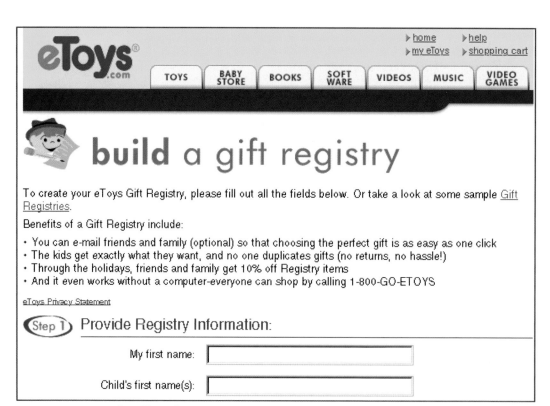

On eToys, American users liked the gift registry, even though they weren't quite sure how it worked. SS33

eToys had the most sophisticated functionality for buying gifts, including both a gift registry and a wish list. Two users were confused about the difference between the gift registry and the wish list. The wish list was intended for the child. It could be converted into a gift registry, so that adults could keep track of the items that had been purchased.

Cultural factors play a role in deciding whether it's appropriate to have a gift registry. Danish stores do not have gift registries. Two Danish users thought the concept was so ridiculous that they refused to continue with the task.

▶ *Assume that some gifts will be shipped to the sender.*

We were surprised by how many users said they prefer to have gifts shipped to themselves rather than to the gift recipients. Buying a gift does not always mean having separate billing and shipping addresses. The reasons the users gave for having the gift shipped to themselves included:

- **Making sure the item was acceptable.** One user recalled receiving a single coffee mug from a friend who had meant to send a set of six. Another user commented that it was impossible to inspect a gift that was already gift-wrapped.

- **Avoiding annoyance for the recipient.** One Danish user had previously bought toys for himself and had received a call from the customs authorities demanding he pay duty for the items. He did not want his gift recipient to suffer the same annoyance.

- **Gift-wrapping it personally.** Some users were not willing to pay very much for gift wrap. Others believed they could do a nicer job themselves.
- **Hand-delivering the gift.** Some users said they like to deliver gifts in person when the recipient is nearby.

Let the giver include a personal message.

Even when an item isn't going directly to the recipient, there are other gift-related services that a website can offer. Several sites include a gift card and message to the recipient. Users liked these options, and many of them took the time to enter a message even though they were working on a fictitious task. Most of the sites didn't remind users to sign their name. One user remarked: "I guess I would put 'Love, Paula' on the card. I wouldn't expect them to do that."

Provide options to suppress price and billing information.

Users liked knowing that NorwaySweaters and Jcrew omitted prices and included gift messages, but they didn't like Jcrew's all-or-nothing implementation. When there was no gift box available (as users discovered when they tried to send a pair of boots), the site wouldn't let them proceed until they unchecked the "Send as a gift" option. Users still wanted to have a gift card included and the price removed. They didn't understand why Jcrew wouldn't perform those services.

Day phone [ ]	☐ **Send as a gift** we'll omit prices
Evening [ ]	
Email [ ]	Gift boxing available for an additional $5 per box and includes tissue wrap, ribbon and a gift card with your message. Type message below:
☑ Email me special promotions	[ ]
	[ ]
Shipping method	[ ]
For overnight delivery, orders must be submitted Monday through Friday by 11 AM EST (orders submitted before 11 AM EST Friday will ship Friday and arrive Monday; orders submitted after 11 AM EST Friday will ship Monday and arrive Tuesday)... **no express delivery to Canada, Alaska, Hawaii, Puerto Rico, Guam, Virgin Islands, APO/FPO or P.O. boxes.**	[ ]
	Redeem Coupon
Regular Shipping ▼	[ ]

Gifts on Jcrew included a gift card, tissue wrap, ribbon and hidden prices. Unfortunately when a gift box was not available, neither were the other things. SS34

If you offer gift wrapping, keep the price low.

As much as they liked options to select a gift box (or gift wrap), users weren't willing to pay much for them. Here are some typical comments:

- Commenting on Disney's $4.95 gift boxes, one user said, "I probably wouldn't buy them." If, however, the boxes cost just "a couple bucks," he said he would buy them.
- Another Disney user laughed at $4.95 for a gift box, adding, "and you can only put one item in a box."

- A user on eToys liked the gift-wrap service but had some reservations: "Really cool. ... I can have each box wrapped in a different paper." The $3.96 charge per item seemed "a little steep," so the user didn't choose gift-wrapping.

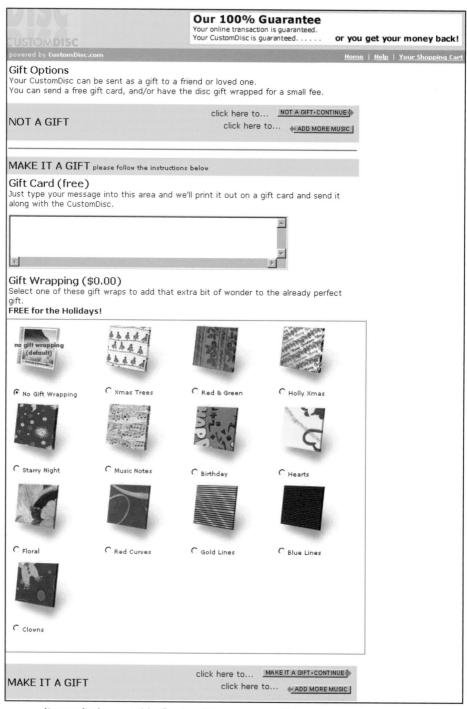

It wasn't clear on this CustomDisc page whether gift-wrapping was free or not. SS35

Although users liked CustomDisc's options for gift-wrapping, the Gift Options page was confusing. A "small fee" for gift-wrapping was mentioned on one part of the page, but the same page also showed the fee as "$0.00." (Maybe CustomDisc offered free gift-wrapping for the holidays, but forgot to remove the "small fee" text.) This price confusion was enough to deter two users who weren't sure what the real cost would be.

➧ *Provide follow-up delivery information to the sender.*

Without any prompting, two users wondered how they would know that a gift had actually been delivered. Although this question was outside the scope of our study, what they said is worth noting:

- "Knowing the delivery actually occurred ... doing something over the Internet. I would appreciate at least an e-mail."

- "I don't know if it's possible, but it might be nice if they could send me an e-mail that it was delivered, to let me know."

In our study, some users were reluctant to provide their e-mail address along with the rest of their billing information. Thus, the site must clearly state that the e-mail address would be used only to communicate with the sender about the order.

Hybrid Stores

Businesses that have both physical and virtual stores face additional challenges in coordinating these similar-but-different enterprises. The results of this study suggest that users expect a high degree of consistency, especially in pricing and policy, between how "Store X" and "storex.com" conduct their business. Although we did not study shopping in traditional stores, some of our findings point to important sales strategy questions that hybrid businesses should consider.

➧ *Consider consistent pricing — and policies — for Store X and storex.com.*

Users had mixed expectations as to whether merchandise would be cheaper online or in a physical store. As with merchandise selection, the users believed they would have to check both places to get the best deal. At the time of this study, some hybrid enterprises did indeed have different pricing online and offline.

A few users said they expected consistent pricing and policies between the physical and virtual stores. For example, three users commented on Wal-Mart's price matching guarantee. Two users said they would call or e-mail the store to see if they could convince Wal-Mart to extend this policy to physical stores. The third user planned to show up in person: "That's for Internet sites, that lower price. But if they do it for Internet sites, I'm assuming they'll do it for brick-and-mortar. Go [to the local store] with the ad and receipt and product. From the sound of it, they'd take care of you."

➧ *Provide a store locator.*

A few of the sites — Peet's, Jcrew, Nordstrom, and Sears — provided a way to find the closest store. On Jcrew, we had a task in which we actually asked users to find the closest store. On Peet's and Nordstrom, users discovered the store-locator feature on their own. They liked knowing where the physical stores were located.

Customer Service

- How to Shop
- How to Buy
- How to Return
- Secure Shopping
- Pricing Policy
- My Wal-Mart
- Registration
- Passwords &
  User Names
- What Wal-Mart
  Offers
- Contact Wal-Mart
- FAQs

Wal-Mart's Always Low Prices

Jeremi,
Associate

Wal-Mart believes in *always* giving our customers the best value for their money, whether you're in our stores or online. Here are some key ways we do this ...

We're here to serve you

Travel
Customer Service

Photo Center
Customer Service

Every Day Low Pricing + Price Matching = Great Value

You work hard for your money, and Wal-Mart wants to see your dollars go far. This is why we guarantee our low prices every day-on every item in the store! If within 8 business days of your purchase you find the exact same product from a verifiable Internet site at a lower price, we will credit you the difference (limit 1 per customer). Clearance, coupons, and % off do not apply. Just e-mail us with your name, e-mail address, order #, competitor's URL, and competitor's price. We will review your request and e-mail you the results. If you have any questions you can contact our customer service at 1-800-966-6546 between 7 a.m. and 11 p.m. CST, Monday through Saturday, or between 9

Maybe you have a question you think someone's asked before. Why not check out our FAQs, and see if we have your situation covered?

Want to know how

Wal-Mart's lowest-price guarantee applied only to its online competitors. Some users wanted the policy extended to include physical stores. SS36

➧ *Tell the customer whether the merchandise is available at the local store.*

We didn't ask users if they believed the online site offered exactly the same merchandise as the physical store. We did notice, however, that the US users on Sears formed the mistaken impression that the site offered everything the Sears retail stores did. Actually, Sears sold only tools, appliances, and a few other products online. Danish users, being unfamiliar with Sears' department stores, were even more confused about what the Sears site offered, especially when they saw "in-store" specials.

The reactions were mixed on Wal-Mart. One user, who found only one toaster, said he didn't believe the physical store would have more. Another user, who managed to find five toasters, believed the real store would have an even better selection.

We don't know who was right. None of our users could say with confidence that they had comparison-shopped. We suggest that hybrid websites explore ways of telling users which products are in stock at their particular local stores.

Real-time inventory control across the enterprise is quite a technical challenge, because it requires knowing exactly where all the inventory is, all the time. Still, it could be a competitive coup for a hybrid enterprise if a user could visit your website, find out if (or when) an item is available locally, make the purchase online, and then go to a local store to pick up the purchase.

In the absence of an integrated inventory control system, perhaps a human solution would be best. A user's request for merchandise availability could be received by a customer service representative who would check the local store's inventory. Users might be willing to reveal their postal or ZIP Code and wait a short time (a minute or two) if they knew they were waiting for a person instead of a machine. (We saw users accept similar delays during live chats with customer service representatives on Furniture.)

➡ *Clearly distinguish promotions for the physical stores from promotions on the website.*

The Sears site had links to "in-store" specials. It was not clear to users (or even to us at first) that these specials were available only in Sears' *retail* stores, not online.

WEEKLY IN-STORE SPECIALS
Weekly in-store specials, be sure to check back for new offers.

women's fashions
- Reebok® Fitness Glide
- save 30-50%

men's fashions
- Reebok® Fitness Glide
- save 30-50%

junior's fashions
Please check back next week.

kid's fashions
- save 30-50%

home fashions
- Matelasse coverlet
- New Traditions® handcrafted quilts

Sears promoted its "in-store" specials online. None of these links went to a page that let a user buy anything. SS37

Users who clicked on the in-store specials saw a brief description of the sale, but they saw no specific items and were provided no means to purchase anything online. Sears also didn't do a very good job of showing that its website contained only a subset of its product line, so most users thought that Sears' website had a much wider selection than it actually did.

➡ *Offer free shipping when one of your stores is located near the customer.*

Our users were even less willing to pay for shipping from a hybrid store than they were for an online-only enterprise when a physical retail store was nearby. The US tests were conducted in a geographic area where Wal-Mart stores are common. Here's what our users thought:

- "Shipping adds a significant cost. One of my pet peeves. Added 10% to the cost. And I can get the same price if I just go down [to the nearby Wal-Mart] and get it myself."
- "Go to the Web page and get shipping costs when I can drive down the street? I'm not sure."

➡ *Allow free returns to the local store.*

Paying to return merchandise was also less acceptable to users when buying from hybrid stores instead of online-only companies. One user was pleasantly surprised by Reel's free-return policy, because he expected that he would have to "eat the shipping and handling" fees if he needed to return a video. He predicted that more online video stores will have to offer free returns in the future "to remain competitive with the regular video store where you can just walk in and return it."

Users said they liked hybrid stores that allowed them to return items to the local store instead of shipping them back to the website's warehouse, because it was easier. One user related how she ordered a video online but then found it in a local store (not affiliated with the online store) before the online purchase arrived. She returned the video purchased online to the physical store. She said she did this because it was easier than mailing back the video.

Of the sites we tested, only Disney and Wal-Mart had return policies that explicitly stated that items could be returned to a local store. Disney's policy applied only to US orders. Users of each of these sites commented that they liked being able to return items to the local store.

Within the US, Disney allowed online purchases to be returned to The Disney Store. SS38

Conclusion

Creating a successful e-commerce site has many parallels with opening a physical store. It is essential to have a solid foundation:

- A good selection of merchandise.
- Prices that match the value customers perceive.
- Effective ways to find the merchandise.
- Sufficient information about your products to answer users' pre-purchase questions.
- Customer-friendly policies that encourage people to do business with you.
- Sales help and customer service provided by human beings.
- Ability to deliver what you have promised to the customer.

An e-commerce site must make every effort to build on this foundation by conducting usability tests to make sure the site can be used as planned.

Once the website is usable for most users, it may be appropriate to focus efforts on encouraging additional sales — through such tactics as advertising special promotions, suggesting additional purchases, and providing amenities for buying gifts.

Trust

" Trust is hard to build – and easy to lose.
A single violation of trust can destroy years
of slowly accumulated credibility."

Succinct and Readily Accessible Information About the Company

➡ *Show detailed company information.*

During our test sessions, several users looked for information about the company whose site they were browsing. They frequently asked, "Who are these guys?" Our users wanted to see:

Street address. They wanted to know if the company had a real-world presence, such as a physical address.

Contact information. They looked for phone and fax numbers and e-mail addresses. US residents appreciated toll-free phone numbers.

Physical presence. They wanted to see proof that the company exists. They wanted to see pictures of stores as well as the corporate headquarters and warehouses.

People. They wanted to see pictures and biographies of the founders and key players in the company.

Affiliation. They wanted to know if the company a part of a larger organization.

History. They wanted to find out how long the company has been in business, the number of employees, annual turnover, and so forth. Availability of annual reports and investor information went a long way toward establishing the credibility of an online business.

Reputation. They wondered if the company was recognized by an independent, reputable third party, like the Better Business Bureau (BBB).

Philanthropy and Social Consciousness. They liked reports on the company's social consciousness and philanthropy, such as aid to the community or environment.

Description of production facilities and quality standards. They wanted to see high quality standards, to know where the products come from and how they are made, and to be sure there is more substance to the business and products than marketing hype.

- A Boo user said: "I don't really know the origins [of the company]. I like to know where a company's headquarters are, where their foundation is. I didn't pick that up as I was going through it. As I'm putting in billing information, I start thinking about it."

- A NorwaySweaters user remarked: "I didn't learn a lot about the company. … I'm still somewhat hesitant when I stumble across websites I don't know very well. … If it's a little Web page. … This one at least is affiliated with Yahoo, which would give it stock in my mind. I look for how professional they've done things." Later, he commented, "Not having a phone number is a pretty negative thing, especially for a small, unknown site."

- A Peet's user said he liked their Philanthropy section. He was impressed that they made an effort to help the communities where their coffee is produced.

- Users of Reel, Boo, NorwaySweaters, and other sites complained that information about the companies was hard to find on their websites.

Company information should be easy to locate without scrolling, as it was on Peet's home page. Some of our users did not care about company information, but those who did appreciated that it was in "About Us" — right where they expected it to be. T1

Tip: Provide an "About Us" or "About (company name)" link on the home page. Show some humility. About Us should be the last navigation item, not the first one. This tip comes from observations in the current study and from card-sorting exercises carried out by the author in other studies.

| Home | About Us | Contact Us | Delivery |

Shop Flower People

by floral type
▸ **International Orders**
▸ **Holiday Specials**
▸ **Roses**
▸ **Plants**
▸ **Arrangements**
▸ **Food & Gift Baskets**
▸ **Great Gift Ideas**

by occasion
▸ **Friendship**
▸ **Anniversary**
▸ **Birthday**
▸ **Baby**
▸ **Get Well**
▸ **Balloons**
▸ **Sympathy**

©1999 Internet Florist Assoc.

About Flower People

Send A Free Virtual Flower Bouquet
Your Green Thumb
Everything's Coming Up Roses
The Meaning of Flowers

If you're looking for flowers, you've come to the right place. We offer the experience, selection and quality you deserve.

We're connected.
Internet Florist is an active member of FTD*, Teleflora and AFS - networks of over 25,000 florists in the United States and Canada.

We know the flower business.
With over 50 years' experience servicing wire orders, we have the qualifications to assure your total satisfaction. We offer flowers and plants for every occasion. Browse our selections, grouped by occasion for your convenience. If you don't find what you want, let us know by e-mail or call 1-800-600-9882 any time, day or night, to speak with a floral expert.

We're fast.
Same-day-delivery (excluding Sundays and Holidays) is available anywhere in the USA and Canada if your order is submitted by 11:00 a.m. in the time zone of the delivery.

We stand behind our product.
We guarantee that your floral arrangement will be fresh and of the highest quality or we will cheerfully have it replaced free of charge.

We protect your privacy.
We at Internet Florist are committed to protecting your privacy. We use the information we collect on site to properly process your order. We do not sell or trade the names, physical addresses or e-mail addresses of our site users and recipients to any other company.

If you have any other privacy concerns or questions that have not been addressed, please e-mail us with your questions at Florist@InternetFlorist.

We're secure.
We've taken the necessary steps to create a secure environment for credit card transactions. You'll find us registered as an authentic and secure site through VeriSign.

We're committed to your satisfaction.
You can independently verify that we are an established and reputable business by visiting the BBB Online, the Better Business Bureau's website.

* FTD selections ordered through Internet Florist are relayed by the Flower People located in Egan Minnesota. For more information, call 1-800-600-9882.

The About Flower People page on Iflorist provided much of the information that our users wanted to know before they were willing to do business with the company. T2

An Iflorist user said, "It would be nice to find out a little more about the site, who they are." The facilitator asked if the "About Flower People" information was useful. "Yes, you like to know they're affiliated with FTD [Florists' Transworld Delivery, Inc.]. Being an FTD florist, I can trust what they say. Right up front [they say] that they don't sell their lists." She cited this information as one of the main things she liked about the Iflorist site.

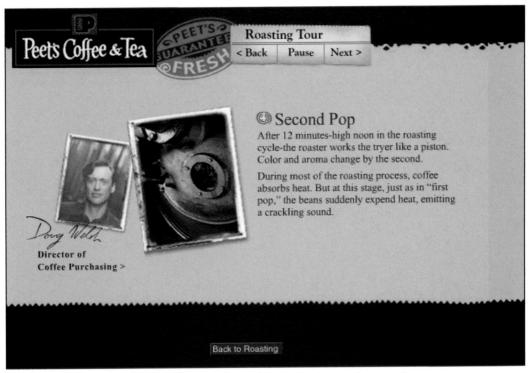

Peet's offered a virtual tour of its meticulous coffee-roasting process. One user commented, "When you sell consumables, you build trust by showing your production facilities." By showing — not just telling — what they do, Peet's justified the somewhat higher cost of their coffees. T3

Tip: Include "Seal of Approval" logos, but don't rely on them to establish trust. None of our users showed any interest in third-party trust logos, emblems, seals of approval, or similar brass, such as TrustE or BBB.

We recorded only a few comments on the presence or absence of such logos and seals, which is significant because users commented freely on many other aspects of the sites — both good and bad — without our asking them. We can interpret the users' silence to mean:

- They didn't notice, or they disregarded the emblems, considering them part of the common background noise on the website.

- They didn't care.

- They noticed, and the logos possibly conveyed positive third-party endorsements and so created an atmosphere of trust, even though most of our users didn't mention it. Maybe once shoppers have clicked on one of these emblems, they do not need to go back to see that information again. We did not, however, ask if our users already understood the logos from previous experience.

The study "Developing a Model of Trust for Electronic Commerce" reported by Egger and de Groot (see the References section) indicated that European users tended not to trust US, online-only seals of approval. When asked whether an emblem from their national consumers' association (for example, the Dutch consumentenbond) would be effective in certifying a site's trustworthiness, all reported that it would indeed help, because they are familiar with and respect their own reputable national institutions. We believe logos don't hurt — and might help — trust.

We recorded only a few comments on the presence or absence of third-party trust logos and seals of approval. T4

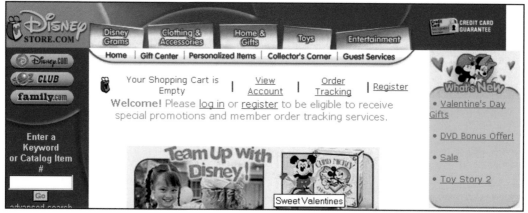

Only one user explicitly appreciated the credit card guarantee on top of Disney's home page. T5

➤ Build on the trust customers have for existing merchants and brands.

As consumers, we learn to trust certain brand names and certain merchants — a trust that translates into loyalty. Brand-name and merchant recognition often get confused in today's dot-com mania. Sears is a merchant. Craftsman and Kenmore are two of its brands. Some companies create separate brands to accomplish different purposes. For example, Craftsman tools carry a lifetime replacement guarantee, which Sears does not offer for most of its other merchandise. And Disney created Touchstone pictures so they could branch out into PG- and R-rated movies without tarnishing the wholesome Disney image.

Tip: Build on the trust customers have for existing merchants in the industry.
Building on existing merchant names is more effective than using a generic third-party symbol of trustworthiness such as Trust-e. Consider the following user comments:

- Wal-Mart: "I have a high level of trust because it is such an establishment."
- Disney: "I am sure that because it's Disney, it's going to be done right." (The user said this before the page even loaded.)

- Disney: A Danish user was purchasing a DVD (digital video disc), and while he was reading the order summary, he suddenly remembered that European DVD players are unable to play American DVDs. "I'll order it anyway. Disney has an office in Denmark. Also, Disney knows that I am ordering the product from Denmark [so they will send me a suitable DVD]." This user was purchasing the DVD with the facilitator's money. We are not sure he would have ordered the DVD if his own money had been at stake, but his trust in the brand name is certainly remarkable.

Tip: Carry familiar and trusted brands. Just as our users expressed confidence in high-profile merchants, they also trusted well-known brand names — and didn't trust unknown brands. For example:

- Sears: A user was shopping for a cordless drill. He chose Black & Decker because this was a brand name he knew. Another user recognized DeWalt tools as high-quality merchandise because her electrician husband used them.

- eToys: A Danish user complained that he had no idea of the quality of the toys [because he did not recognize the brand names]. He feared that the quality was "below the coupon booklet level." None of our US users voiced similar concerns, probably because they were more familiar with the brand names.

Tip: Display brand names. If you've got brand-name merchandise, say so. Failure to do so can cost you sales. Here's why:

- BasketHaus: A user said about the "Last Second Basket" (see Image T10 in this chapter), "they don't say what brand of cheese they have in the basket. They just say that it is 'gourmet' and 'scrumptious.' "

- TowerRecords: Two users searched for Disney's video *Fantasia*. Both of them refused to accept the search result *Fantasia* that appeared on the list. They insisted on finding a search result named *Disney's Fantasia*.

Note that product brand names may be especially important for sites like BasketHaus that don't have an established brand of their own.

➡ *Link to reputable, independent sources.*

We believe that a sign of trustworthiness is being connected to the rest of the Web with links both in and out. Not being afraid to link to other sites is a sign of confidence. Also, third-party sites are much more credible than anything you can say yourself about your website. Isolated sites give the impression that they have something to hide.

The Google search engine, which we did not test in this study, maintains a reputation rating for every site on the Web. It uses this reputation ranking to list the highest-quality websites first. Roughly speaking, Google derives its estimate of a website's quality from the number of other sites that link to it. In other words, Google measures connectedness, which is becoming an actual measure of confidence.

Tip: Make it easy for your customers to check your trustworthiness. Although none of the sites we tested displayed third-party endorsements, we recommend that if your business, products, or services receive a positive review or rating from reputable, independent sources — such as Consumer Reports or Underwriters Laboratories Inc. — you should place a prominent link to these sources on your site.

Several dozen third-party endorsers may be found on Yahoo! at: Home > Business and Economy > Electronic Commerce > Consumer Information.

One word of caution: Entities such as Consumer Reports and Underwriters Labs are very aggressive about protecting their names from unauthorized use. Be sure you review their policies and gain their permission before adding a link to their sites.

Tip: Provide relevant links only. External links should be provided only when they contribute something beneficial to the shopping experience, such as anticipating customers' information needs or showing that the company is an expert in a particular domain and, as such, presents a selection of recommended resources.

The one user who looked at the links to other sites on BasketHaus thought that they were kind of odd, especially the Shop New Hampshire Web Ring. This link had nothing to do with gift baskets. It was a distraction.

Word of Mouth

Trust is affected by external forces. People will accept and trust a friend's recommendation more than a brand name. For example, one of our users would enter her phone number on a site only after someone she knew had recommended the site.

Just as face-to-face, word-of-mouth advertising is highly effective, online communities can have a similar impact on improving — or damaging — the trust level of an e-business. How much of an impact they have, however, is beyond the scope of our study.

Fair Pricing, Fully Revealed

Trust is also related to pricing. High prices, shipping costs that appeared unreasonable, and hidden prices caused 5% of the sales catastrophes in this study. This section describes the pricing issues that affected trust. A more thorough discussion of pricing policies may be found in the Selling Strategies chapter.

▶ *Show total cost, including taxes, shipping and handling, as soon as possible.*

Our users commented negatively on hidden prices. They were unpleasantly surprised by high shipping costs that were not shown until after they had gone through a lot of effort to find suitable products.

- Recalling a bad experience from another e-commerce site (not one in our study), a user of Iflorist immediately clicked the Delivery button upon entering the website. She explained: "I wanted to see if they have a delivery charge. I look at everything else, before I order something — to make sure there won't be a big surprise at the end. My daughter went to order books. It had this big 'free delivery' when you got to the site, but we had a delivery charge. I found out it was free only for orders above a certain amount."

- A Danish user of Disney said that she would not buy the product because the shipping charges were too high: "That's outrageous. Thirty dollars to ship a product worth 40 dollars! I'm in a state of shock. It has taken me so long to find this item. Why haven't they told me before?" The user went back to the Shipping Summary page to see if she had overlooked the shipping cost information. She had not overlooked it — the information wasn't there.

- One of the most moving moments of the test series occurred at the end of a test of Disney when one user quietly remarked: "When shipping is so expensive I want to know right up front how much shipping will cost me. I hate to think that Emily [her five year old daughter] and I [could] sit at the computer and agree to buy something for her, and then it turns out much later that shipping is prohibitively expensive."

For these reasons and more, show the total product price — including shipping charges, taxes, duty, and any other fees — as soon as possible. Don't wait until after the customer has placed an order. Danish users in particular were unpleasantly surprised about the high shipping costs, which sometimes exceeded the value of the merchandise.

Tip: Allow customers to enter their ZIP or country codes early in the shopping process. Explain that entering the code enables the website to provide precise shipping costs as customers shop. This technique also allows the website to warn customers if one or more items cannot be shipped to the required address.

Also the billing address might be different than the shipping address. Make sure the customer understands that it is the shipping address — not the billing address — that determines the shipping cost.

If a customer does not provide a ZIP or country code, let the sale proceed anyway. Continue to discreetly display the offer. After a while, reticent shoppers may realize that the offer is to their advantage. We believe that showing shipping costs first prevents unpleasant surprises and sales catastrophes caused by high shipping costs.

None of the websites in our study used this approach so we have not tested this tip. Staples (a site not tested in this study) uses the ZIP-code approach to reveal full costs and availability. The Staples tactic is discussed in more detail in the Checkout & Registration chapter.

Tip: Never hide product prices. On Living.com users had to send an e-mail to obtain certain furniture prices. Our users complained about this policy. In particular, they had a deep mistrust of what additional use the website would make of their e-mail addresses. This tip is discussed in more detail in the Selling Strategies chapter.

➡️ *Justify prices that appear odd.*

Like shoppers everywhere, our users reacted adversely to prices that seemed higher than normal. Provide a good and easy-to-find explanation for items that seem unusually expensive. When prices are high, communicate value:

Build trust by explaining the outstanding, relevant features of the product:

- Present high-quality pictures of the product.
- Compare the product with cheaper products.
- Address the price / quality relationship openly.

Tip: Explain prices that seem particularly low. Would you trust a site that tells you it sells genuine new Rolex watches for $50? Address possible buyer concerns by explaining how the company manages to offer a highly competitive price for a given product or service. In this case, communicate the bargain:

- "By cutting out the middleman"
- "By fully automating the process"
- "By gaining revenues from advertisers."

For more advice on justifying prices, see the Selling Strategies chapter.

YOUR CD

click here to
Edit/Buy Your CD

`6` # songs selected

`54:18` time remaining

`$11.93` cost (explain)

track list

1. Allegheny M
2. Don't Forbi
3. Moonlight G
4. Boppin' The
5. Donna
6. Tom Dooley

How Is Your CD Cost Calculated?

An average CustomDisc costs about $20 US.

Price is determined by adding the cost of each song plus shipping and handling to our base manufacturing cost of $5.99.

But there are almost always free songs, specials or promotions to save you money! Some past specials include: Up to 10 songs for $12.99, Up to 12 songs for $15.99, etc. Look for featured specials or promotions on our home page and in your favorite lounges!

On CustomDisc, users noticed immediately that most songs cost $0.99 each. After selecting a few songs, they started to wonder how, for instance, six songs could amount to $11.93 as shown in the left example above. All users noticed the "explain" link, clicked it, and read the explanation shown on the right. All users, except one, understood the explanation, considered it reasonable, and continued shopping. One user, however, was completely confused and put off by the explanation. He truly didn't understand what it was trying to tell him. T6

Two users had negative responses to Iflorist's pre-Valentine's Day price increase. One said, "They give the little disclaimer to cover themselves, but I don't buy it." What should Iflorist have done? Our suggestion would have been to link to an independent, trusted source, for instance, a reputable newspaper that confirmed that prices are actually higher in certain high seasons in certain parts of the world. T7

Sufficient and Balanced Product Information

Lack of product information caused 12% of the sales catastrophes in our study. Consumers want succinct, sufficient, and accurate information about products. Few of our users, for example, felt comfortable buying from BasketHaus, because they couldn't tell what they would get. They wanted to know the brand, weight, and size of the cheese — and the size of the basket.

➡ *Provide honest information about products.*

Complete honesty builds trust. Online consumers want honest information about:

- The product itself, including images that show detail.
- Product availability. Trust is negatively affected by items that are advertised but not available. (See the section in this chapter "Correct, Timely, Professional Site Design.")
- Price, including hidden costs, such as taxes and shipping. (See the section in this chapter "Fair Pricing, Fully Revealed.")

You can read more about the need for good product information in the Product Pages and Selling Strategies chapters.

➡ *Provide balanced second opinions.*

Consumers appreciate second opinions. The moment your website starts providing opinions, however, you must be able to convince your customers that your judgments are trustworthy. Convincing them is difficult, because people naturally doubt the objectivity of judgments provided by a retailer.

For example, a user of Peet's clicked a link to read a coffee review, but as it was coming up, he commented sarcastically, "Like this isn't gonna be hype." He closed it without reading it.

Tip: Address the problem openly. Explain how you guarantee the independence of the reviewer. Suggested heading: "About our reviewers" or "About our review process."

Tip: Provide sufficient context for ratings. A user of SmarterKids who liked the ratings also commented. "Is this a rating system? It doesn't make sense if everything gets high ratings." To build trust in your rating system you must show how you use the rating scale. For example, "Our overall rating of this product is 4.0 (out of 5.0). The average overall rating for all our products is 4.4." Notice how the second sentence suddenly casts a different light on the first sentence.

Tip: Include both pros and cons in each review.

Tip: Humanize the reviewer. Provide a biography and the name and e-mail address of the reviewer. A photograph shows that a human being is putting his or her face — as well as reputation — at stake with these reviews.

Second opinions are not necessary for all types of products. We have a hard time, for instance, envisioning how a review of a rocking chair would help a purchase decision if a shopper's main concern is whether it would look good in the living room. Similarly, a rating or opinion of the rose arrangement a man is about to send to his mother would be meaningless — he cares only whether Mom likes the roses or not. An independent rating of the delivery punctuality and the roses' freshness would be relevant, however. Also, an online feedback form for Mom to respond to the sender — and possibly other customers — could provide credibility. Second opinions are helpful only to the extent that the shopper can relate this information to his or her own needs — and trust it.

Magic School Bus: Explore the Solar System
Grade: 1 to 3

Our Price: $17.95

Davidson
Prod. #05185

| Add to Cart | **View Cart** |

| Add to Gift Registry |

| Recommend to a Friend |

| Teacher Review | | Skills Addressed |
| Educational Approach |
| Software System Requirements |

Miss Frizzle, from the popular television series, takes her students on another adventure. This time they are travelling through the Solar System. Users will drive the famous bus to explore all of the nine planets. The program is filled with informative facts, and 3-D animation. One CD and travel passport included.

Overall Rating: ✓✓✓✓

Ratings   Learning Styles

How we rate products   ✓✓✓✓✓ = Highest Rating

Reviewer's Opinion: ✓✓✓✓

Ease of Use: ✓✓✓✓

Fun: ✓✓✓✓

Depth: ✓✓✓✓

- Linguistic
- Visual
- Musical

Teacher Review

by Diane Kendall
Children's Software Press

Ms. Frizzle and her class full of inquisitive youngsters are ready to embark on a trip to the planets and beyond. In this older title in the Magic School Bus series, players must travel through the solar system, stopping at the

Users appreciated the ratings and the teacher review on this product description from SmarterKids. One user noted appreciatively: "There is quite a lot of information here." The user believed that the review made the website appear trustworthy. Note that the reviewer's name and professional affiliation are given. What we see of the teacher review reads like a book report, however, not a review. Also, the constant four-check ratings do not build trust even though they might be fair. T8

The design of an e-commerce website communicates trustworthiness online, just as the appearance of a store and its sales staff do in the physical world. Professional appearance builds consumer confidence. Comprehensive, correct, and current product selections and site content convey quality.

Clear navigation also conveys respect for customers and an implied promise of good service. Typos or difficult navigation communicate just the opposite.

If a site has **product photos**, it should have good shots of all products. Haphazard content signals a lack of concern, professionalism, and credibility.

To ensure trust, you must take care to **eliminate even small errors**, like links that don't work or typographical errors. Would you trust a brick-and-mortar store with half-stocked shelves and sales people who don't know the products?

➡ *Remove outdated content immediately.*

Trust can be eroded by small things. Something as seemingly trivial as outdated information undermines trust. Here are some examples of outdated information, preferences, and graphics problems that elicited sarcastic remarks from our users:

- On Jan. 10, 2000: A user saw an item on Disney that said it would ship on December 7, 1999. The user joked, "they have a little Y2K problem."

- On Jan. 3, 2000: The cover art on CustomDisc was still in a Christmas motif. "That's a disgrace!" said one offended user. A little later, the same user noted: "Gift wrapping ... free for the holidays. ... They haven't discovered yet that Christmas is over!"

- On Jan. 6, 2000: TowerRecords' home page still displayed Christmas decorations, and the website suggested "[Click here if you] Need Gift Ideas." A user remarked that they ought to remove their Christmas decorations.

- On Jan. 17, 2000: A user commented scornfully that Iflorist promised it could deliver flowers in 1999.

Desired date of delivery

Next business day delivery is available to most areas for orders received by 11 AM CST. We can guarantee delivery dates for orders received three business days in advance.

Friday ▾	January ▾	21 ▾	2000 ▾
			1999
			2000

Payment Information

On Iflorist a user noticed that she could select 1999 as the year of delivery even though the test was conducted on Jan. 17, 2000. T9

➡ *Eradicate all typos.*

There were only a few misspellings on the websites we tested. But invariably, when there was a misspelling, we heard comments like, "How can they make baskets when they can't even spell?"

We saw typos even on professionally produced sites like Disney. Mistakes in grammar and spelling don't bother those who don't notice, but for people who do, it can make all the difference in where they spend their money. It's bad business to present unprofessional, mistake-laden Web pages.

The Last Second Basket
When your down to the last second for a gift, this is the life saver! This custom made basket has Gourmet Beef Sausage, Honey Roasted Nuts, Holiday Crackers, Gourmet Cheese, Yankee Chutney, Scrumptous Cookies, Almondina Truffles and Holiday Coffee! $55.

Even Danish users noticed spelling errors in this excerpt from a BasketHaus Product Page. The correct usage of "your" is "you're," and the correct spelling of "Scrumptous" is "Scrumptious." Similarly, "life saver" is one word, "custom made" should be hyphenated, and most of the words in the second sentence should not be capitalized. T10

▶ *Don't advertise items that are not available.*

Unavailable products were a big trust-breaker in our study. Trust was negatively affected by items that were advertised but not available. One user of 1800flowers said she was fond of tulips. When she clicked "Timeless Tulips," however, she got the message, "Sorry, product currently not available." She was clearly annoyed: "You dumb people, why do you have them there then?" We cover product availability more extensively in the Selling Strategies chapter.

▶ *Pursue technical problems vigilantly — and fix them.*

Technical problems accounted for 9% of the sales catastrophes in our study. Website technical problems can range from the absolutely critical trust issue of secure encryption for financial transactions to the exasperatingly slow download speeds of some multimedia product pages. People tend to trust a site more when it has a reliable and responsive server.

Our experience from other studies has been that when users encountered technical difficulties at a previously preferred site, their reactions were:

- Continued loyalty: User tries again later.
- Split loyalty: User finds a different site. Future use alternates between the original site and the new site.
- Lost loyalty: User abandons the site forever.

Most of our users had little technical knowledge of the Web. When they encountered a problem, they often couldn't diagnose the problem and work around it. In these situations, we often heard users say they would leave the site. We have no accurate way of predicting how many of those users would ever come back to the site to try again.

In general, the websites we tested worked reasonably well from a technical viewpoint. The main technical problems were: slow page loads, missing images, broken links and server errors, problems with the connection, and internal errors.

Slow Page Loads

Slowness was by far the most common technical problem we saw. All the tests in our study were done over a 56k modem, the most common connection speed in use at the time of our test. Lacking experience and technical understanding of the Web, many of our users were unsure how long to wait for a page to download. Often, it was not clear to the user whether a page was still loading or not. Most users didn't know about the Stop and Reload browser functions. Without our encouragement, some users would simply have given up and left the site.

- HermanMiller: Because of the way the page loaded, the first words one user saw when she entered the online store were "currently empty." This statement referred to the shopping cart, not the site, but it confused her for a moment: "Maybe they sold out of everything." This user did understand the loading progress indicator in the browser's status bar, but she didn't always look at it to see if a page had finished.

- Living: While the Chairs page slowly loaded, the user had time to look in the "Browse For" selection list. She accidentally clicked "Browse for Curios." The Chairs page appeared briefly, and then the Curios page started to load. She didn't understand what had happened. She had to select the Chairs page again — and once again incurred the same download delay that allowed her to be distracted in the first place.

Missing Images

We saw a few websites where images were just plain missing. On Iflorist, for example, a user was disconcerted that the picture of the chosen bouquet was missing in the upper left corner of the order form and the order review. Often, these problems were not reproduced when we looked at the page again later.

Broken Links and Server Errors

We saw few link problems. To us, this attention to detail is a healthy sign that the market is maturing. But on Jcrew, a user selected the Store Locator link on the home page, and gave up when the server crashed.

Problems with the Internet Connection

We saw few connectivity problems, although it was clear that most users didn't know how to distinguish a slow site from a slow connection and didn't understand the browser Stop and Refresh buttons, so they were unable to reload a failing page, which sometimes helps.

- Jcrew: A user went to check out and got a connection error message: "I would say God doesn't want me to buy this. I'm out of here." Facilitator's note: "I didn't get the impression she truly saw this as some sort of divine intervention, but she would have left the site."

- Disney: Three users experienced multiple error messages saying that the connection to the server had been broken but had been reestablished. These errors occurred during the checkout process. When they saw the error, all three users announced that they would leave the website. They continued only because the facilitator asked them to try again. In most cases, an additional click on the same button caused the desired action. In a few cases, every second click on any button on a page during the checkout process caused this message (and every alternating click caused the correct action).

Internal Errors, Coding Errors or Refusal of Service

Occasionally, our users encountered other messages about technical difficulties on a website. The typical user reaction was to leave the site immediately. Most of our users would not have given the website a second chance if we had not been there to encourage them.

- On CustomDisc, a Danish user correctly entered the billing country as "Denmark" during registration. When the website returned a page asking the user to confirm the billing address, the website had changed the country to "United States."

- On HermanMiller, two users encountered the message: "Closed temporarily for update." One saw the message after submitting shipping information, and the other saw it while selecting a chair. Both users were inclined to give up after seeing this message. It seemed that they interpreted the error to mean "We have technical problems. Go away!"

◆ *Phrase error messages constructively and politely.*

When your server encounters technical problems while processing an order, the professional thing to do is to provide a friendly and helpful error message, no matter whose fault it is.

Two of our users made input mistakes when purchasing items from eToys. They got an error message that read, "Whoops! It looks like you've sent an invalid request to our server." The tone was unnecessarily accusatory and technical. It was as if eToys were saying, "Shame on you! You're causing us trouble."

Fortunately for eToys, these were not sales catastrophes, because both users followed the instructions in the error message and were able to complete their purchases successfully. Even though our users did not comment on it, we believe such negative wording hurts trust.

Whoops! It looks like you've sent an invalid request to our server. Please click the "back to shopping cart" button below and continue with the normal checkout process.

> back to last page

Two of our users got this strange error message during checkout at eToys. Note that the button name and the instruction do not match. T11

Tip: Express yourself as you would in a face-to-face conversation. The customer may not always be right, but there is no profit in saying so.

Tip: Speak the user's language. Don't say, "You've sent an invalid request to our server." Odds are, the user won't even know — or care — what a server is.

Tip: Use apologetically worded messages. Say that you're sorry an unexpected technical problem has occurred, and that it is not the user's fault.

Tip: Place any internal codes that are required to trace the problem at the end of the message. Use a heading like this: "Technical Stuff — Please include the following information when you report this problem to us."

Tip: Explain how to recover or when to try again. "Click the Back button" or "Press the Reload or Refresh button" are helpful instructions for recovery. Don't say "Closed temporarily for update" or "Try again in an hour," but instead say something like "Try again after 3:00 p.m. EST."

Tip: Allow users to report technical problems. At least provide an e-mail address. A telephone number, too, would be even better.

Tip: Show your appreciation when anyone reports a technical problem. Respond immediately and politely. Provide a customer service representative's name in the answer so the person will feel that a human being cares — even if the message was generated by an autoresponder.

While researching for this Online Shopping study I (the author) ran into a technical problem with Customdisc.com. It suddenly refused to accept more than five songs on my custom disc. I reported the problem on a Sunday. On Monday afternoon Customdisc sent me the following exemplary reply:

Greetings and Happy New Year!

Thank you very much for bringing this problem to our attention. I am VERY sorry for the inconvenience you experienced with our site. Our technicians have fixed this error and you are free to return to our site and complete your CustomDisc.

As a token of our thanks for letting us know about this problem, please enjoy the following discount code and receive 50% off of your CustomDisc order. Discount code: CS00SB50

Simply provide the discount code when checking out your CustomDisc order!
This discount code will be valid until January 31, 2000.

If you have any more questions or comments, please let me know.

Cheers!

Mike Sullivan
Customer Loyalty Associate
Custom Revolutions, Inc.

This excellent customer appreciation message from CustomDisc was probably a form letter, but the point is that it didn't feel that way — and it rewarded the customer with a valuable discount. T12

➡ *Use form elements for user input on checkout pages.*

It is particularly important to present a professional image when conducting financial transactions with customers. Several of our users thought the BasketHaus Billing Information page was unprofessional and untrustworthy, because it provided a plain text box for credit card information instead of the specialized form elements they expected.

Some users were so suspicious of the ordinary text box that they experimented by entering meaningless information in the box and submitting their order. When the website replied, "Thank you for your basket order," users lost trust.

Tip: Use form elements for gathering billing information — and set up a transaction program that politely rejects bogus input.

your email address so we can email you back

Type credit card info below.
Mastercard, Visa or Discover. Expiration Date and the card number.

Type Credit Card Info here.

On BasketHaus, users were asked to enter their credit card information in an ordinary text box. Several users said that it was awkward to enter credit card number in the free-form fields, and it made them suspicious of the site. T13

➤ *Give users only what they ask for.*

When a search returns results, people expect those results to be what they asked for. If the search returns items that the user did not ask for, it can break trust. We asked some users to shop on Furniture.com for a dining room table that would suit their needs. One user entered the following selection criteria that expressed his desires:

- Select Piece = Dining Room Table
- Select Style = Country
- Select Finish = Birch
- Select Price Range = $0–$500.

The search returned 44 hits as shown in Image T14. The user thought he was shopping for rather special furniture, and he was a bit surprised to get so many results. When he started looking at specific products, he noted with growing dissatisfaction that the search had returned products that did not match his search criteria. "This is not what I asked for!" he exclaimed. For instance, there was a dark-colored table that cost more than $1,500. He said, "I don't want anything with laminate, and here are lots of laminated tables." He checked several other tables in the search results page and found that they did not meet his search criteria either.

As a result, he lost his faith in the value of the search. He didn't notice the message on the search results that warned: "No exact matches found. Results shown for: Dining Table > Country." Facilitator's note: "I didn't notice the warning during the test either. I only noted it when I analyzed the test results after the test was over."

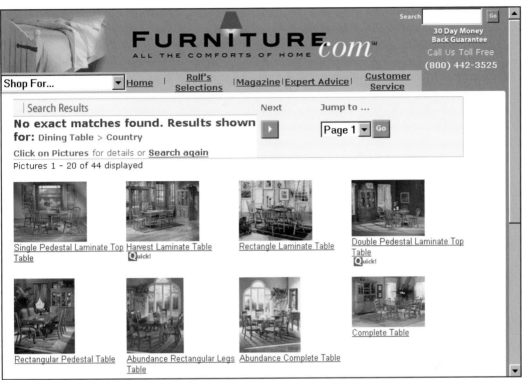

"This is not what I asked for!" A Furniture.com user asked for a birch dining room table in the price range of $0–$500. Instead of telling him that no such tables were available, the website disregarded his search criteria and presented results that were out of his price range and not in the finish he had specified. He did not notice the disclaimer at the top of the page. T14

Tip: Let the user broaden the search — don't let the system decide. Don't broaden a search automatically. When a search returns no results, provide a constructive message that tells the user how to broaden the search. Provide examples of what "broadening" means. We believe that people are much better than computers at broadening their own searches.

Tip: Make in-page warning messages more visible by using contrasting text and graphics. The most easily noticed contrast parameters are color and size.

Tip: Test with users to make sure they notice the no-results warning. Keep making the contrast more extreme until users get the message.

➡️ *Preserve information the user has entered.*

Users expect that any information they have already entered on a website to be preserved — even when they have clicked the Back button instead of submitting the information.

Tip: After displaying an error message or information page, always restore the data the user has already entered.

- Disney: "Didn't I already do this?" asked a frustrated user. Indeed, he had already filled out the billing information form, but he had also clicked the Back button before submitting the form. As a consequence, he lost all the information he had already entered.

- Living: When a user submitted her registration form and the server found errors, it returned her to the blank registration page. "What happened to all my stuff I had here?"

- CustomDisc: This site kept one user's information from a previous task even though she didn't complete the sale. She liked that.

- CustomDisc: Another user was not so lucky. After seeing that the website had blanked out all the billing information she had entered, she commented, "I have to be extremely motivated to continue after this." She continued only because we asked her to. It appears that CustomDisc preserves user input if the user submits it, even if the user doesn't complete a sale, but that it doesn't preserve user input when there is just a slight input error.

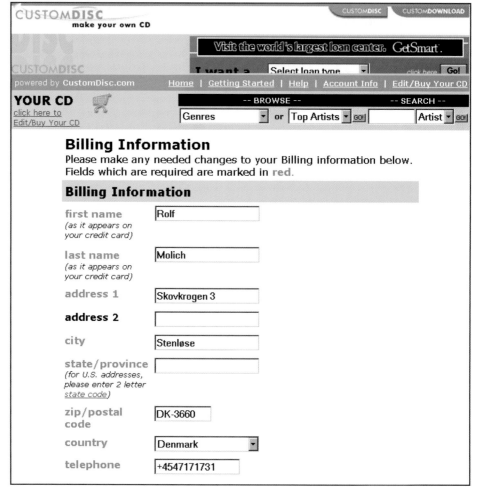

All Danish users initially had problems in filling out the CustomDisc Billing Information page, which is hard for non-American users to get right. After returning from an error message page ("State must be a two character code"), one user found that the website had blanked out the Billing Information page. (For more on information on the challenges faced by non-American users, see the International Users chapter. For more information on making good checkout forms, see the Checkout & Registration chapter.) T15

Clear and Customer-Friendly Policies

⬤ *Present policies and guarantees prominently.*

Our users expected guarantees and policies to be easy to find, easy to understand, and reasonable. By placing information about return policies in a prominent place, you can give your customers a pleasant surprise. When we asked a user of Reel to find out if he could return a video, his first reaction was, "They are probably not placing this kind of information [about return policy] right up front!" He was right.

We believe that placing a link to the return policy right on the home page will generate trust — even from those who do not need to return a product. It is not enough, however, to place the return policy prominently. It also has to be a good return policy.

⬤ *Offer free returns, and other sales inducements.*

A free-return policy is an especially strong sales inducement for big-ticket items with high shipping costs, like furniture. Both Furniture and Living featured prominent 30-day guarantees. Offer a good return policy. Nordstrom's return policy was a turn-off for some users. There was a $3.95 return charge — unless the item was bought with a Nordstrom credit card.

30-Day Money-Back Guarantee

Because Furniture.com wants you to love your new furniture, all products are backed with our 30-Day Money-Back Guarantee.

Furniture.com's 30-Day Money-Back Guarantee

Take an entire month to live with your purchase and decide if it's right for you. If you're unhappy for any reason, just let us know. We'll take your furniture back – and even pay the return shipping costs! We will have our Design Consultants assist you with making another selection or, if you prefer, we will issue a full refund.

Simply contact our Customer Care Department within 30 days of delivery to arrange for a replacement or to return the product for a full refund. You pay no restocking, handling or return charges.

Your 100% Satisfaction Guarantee

We believe in the high quality of our products, and our ability to ship and deliver these products to your home to your complete satisfaction. In fact, we guarantee your satisfaction.

If you decide to cancel an order, you may do so prior to receiving your shipment. There is no penalty and, if your order required a deposit, living.com will refund the full amount.

Once you've accepted delivery of your order, if you are dissatisfied with your purchase, you may return it within 30 days for a full refund - no questions asked. We will arrange and pay for shipping back to our warehouse.

Both Furniture.com and Living.com clearly stated they would pay shipping costs if the customer wanted to return the furniture within 30 days. Furniture.com said, "We want you to love your new furniture." T16

Tip: Consider offering free or discounted samples. Although not appropriate in all instances, free samples can be real trust-builders for long-term customer relationships. Samples can prevent problems — and preventive action is even better than a good return policy.

- Our users appreciated that they could have free fabric samples from Living.com.

- One of our users was in doubt about which coffees to choose on Gevalia. He wanted free samples or a discounted sampler pack before he ordered large quantities.

Note that we have only qualitative and no quantitative data about the effectiveness of offering free or discounted samples.

➡ *Test your policies to make sure your customers understand them and find them acceptable.*

Show your policies to typical customers. Ask them questions that can be answered only by reading and understanding your policies. Consider hiring an independent usability expert to carry out a usability test for you. You can learn more about how we conducted our usability tests in the Methodology chapter.

Appropriate Use of Personal Information

Our users' refusal to enter personal data in order to accomplish a purchase caused 4% of the sales catastrophes in this study. Many users entered something, but most clearly weren't happy about it.

➡ *Ask for sensitive information only if it is absolutely necessary to process the order.*

Many, but not all, users were reluctant to submit information that they considered sensitive. Some users entered personal information without hesitation. Others flatly refused and said that if the information was required, then they would not buy from the website.

Our US users were given the option of using a false identity for our test sessions. Even while entering false data, they expressed their concerns about what might happen to the information.

The users were reluctant to provide any information that they did not perceive as absolutely necessary to process and ship their orders. They did not object to entering their names and addresses for shipping and billing purposes, but they objected to providing:

- Social Security number
- Phone number
- E-mail address
- Someone else's personal information (a gift recipient's phone number, for instance).

➡ *Explain carefully why you need information that people consider sensitive.*

As politely as possible, state why you need sensitive information. Or even better: Say, inoffensively, what the consequences of not supplying the information might be. For example: "It is okay with us if you don't provide a telephone number. But if you don't, we can't contact you quickly if there is a problem with your order, which might delay delivery."

When a user skips a field with required, sensitive information, provide a constructive error message. For example: "Please enter your e-mail address. We need it to send you a confirmation and to verify your identity. If you don't have an e-mail address, click here. Example of an e-mail address: joe@aol.com." If the user enters "joe@aol.com," reply "Sorry, joe@aol.com is just an example — we need your personal e-mail address to verify your order, for your protection."

Tip: Give customers access to their profiles. If you require your customers to register with your site (something we don't recommend), giving them open access to the data stored about them may assuage their fears. Let them modify, update, or delete their profiles.

Social Security Number

Social Security numbers are the most sensitive information we saw any website ask for. Many people, both in the US and abroad, consider information of this kind sensitive, because it is sometimes used as a default account number or (often illegally) as verification of identity.

For example, a Massachusetts driver's license number used to be the Social Security number of the driver — although this is no longer considered good business practice because it led to identity theft. With a Social Security number and a little personal information, it is possible to obtain false IDs or to open fraudulent credit card accounts.

Only the Danish version of Boo asked for the user's civil registration number (the Danish equivalent of a Social Security number). Boo did not explain why they wanted the number or what they would use it for, but it was marked optional on the Billing Information page. Our users reacted strongly against this request: "What do they need that for?"

TowerRecords asked for the user's birthday, which also seemed odd to some users. Again, the information was optional, and there was no explanation of what TowerRecords would use the birthday information for.

Phone Number

Our users were reluctant to give out their phone numbers, primarily because they detest telemarketing.

- Iflorist: "Unless [both my daytime and evening phone number were] required, I wouldn't put either. It says this information will not be given to others. Maybe I would give my evening number." This user had no concerns about giving the recipient's phone number to 1800flowers (a site he also tested), because he understood it might be needed in case of delivery problems.

- HermanMiller: "They don't need my phone number," declared one user as she filled out an order form. She got an error message. " 'Phone number is not supplied.' Yeah, and you're not getting it either. … I don't want them to call me." She said she would supply a phone number if she were really buying something, however.

Tip: If providing a phone number would help the customer get the delivery on time, say so.

E-mail Address

Similarly, users were reluctant to give out their e-mail addresses because they feared getting junk e-mail. In self-defense, many people have established secondary e-mail addresses so that they can give that address out to less trustworthy companies. In a few cases, our users entered a fake e-mail address.

Unfortunately, their fears about getting unsolicited commercial e-mail are justified, given the unethical practices of some websites. In fact, after this study, some of the facilitators have been getting more junk mail. We suspect one or more of our tested sites sold our e-mail addresses without asking us first.

- Iflorist: A user wondered aloud why they wanted her e-mail address: "Probably so they can send you stuff. So you can get junk mail on the Internet, just like in your mailbox. They may want to confirm the order. I don't know."

- Nordstrom: When asked for her e-mail address, one user said, "No. 'Cause there's cookies that can be hooked onto it." She confused cookies with viruses that arrive as e-mail attachments.

Someone Else's Personal Information

Seven users expressed reservations about entering a gift recipient's phone number, mostly because it was personal information. Four said they might have refused to give out the number, or put in a bogus number. One user didn't want the surprise spoiled for his gift recipient. When users said they would enter the recipient's number, the typical reason was that it might be needed for delivery purposes. None of the users, however, saw any such explanation on the sites we tested.

- Disney: A user didn't want to enter recipient's phone number: "If I was sending someone a gift, I wouldn't want them to get a phone call before they get it."

- eToys: "That's [the] personal information of my nephew, so I'd just leave it blank." Upon learning it was required, the user said she'd put in her own phone number.

- NorwaySweaters: "I have an unpublished phone number. I never give it out [online]. If I have to, I put my husband's business phone." She got error message because she didn't enter a shipping telephone number. "I don't like that at all. They don't need a phone number to ship something out. At that point, I would say forget it. I wouldn't give out anybody's phone number."

Tip: Ask for the purchaser's phone number in the case of gifts being shipped to others.

➡ *Provide a clear and easy-to-find privacy policy.*

Make it perfectly clear that you will not give or sell the customer's sensitive information, such as phone number and e-mail address, to anyone else. (For more on privacy issues, see the section "Trustworthy Security" later in this chapter.)

A user of Sears said, "I like that, that [the guarantee and privacy policy] is at the bottom of every page, not something I had to go search for." T17

➡ *Use opt-in for all marketing information sent to customers.*

Several of the websites we tested offered free e-mail newsletters. Most required users to delete a checkmark in a box on the registration page if they did not want the newsletter. All but one user carefully deleted the checkmark.

The following remark from a user of Reel.com illustrates the attitude of users toward this kind of marketing ploy: The user read out loud, "YES, I want to receive NewsReel, the twice-monthly e-mail update for Reel customers!" As he unchecked the checkbox, the user exclaimed: "This is dangerous! — Good that I noticed it!"

All but one user noticed the "subscribe me to the CustomDisc newsletter" checkbox. By default, this box was checked. Our users "opted out." That is, they unchecked it — and many of them made a point out of doing so. T18

Often, the terms "opt in" and "opt out" are used to describe this marketing tactic. We recommend opt-in — that is, customers must positively confirm that they wish to accept some kind of intrusive service like a regular e-mail subscription to a newsletter, or permanent storage of name, address, telephone number, credit card, and such.

Sometimes, to opt out, a customer must check a box instead of unchecking it. We know from other tests that some users find it hard to understand what it means to leave a checkbox unchecked for a negatively phrased statement. We consider it unethical to trick customers into getting unwanted e-mail. In any case, this ploy is counterproductive in the long run. Customers will come to distrust the site, because they will remember that they wanted to opt OUT.

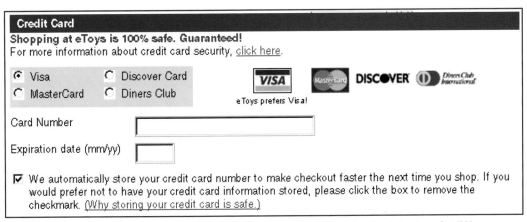

Join Cluboo

Please enter the following information about yourself. All required info is in bold.

Converse		Basketball		Acid Jazz	
Cosmic Girls		Bike		Blues	
Everlast		Climb		Classical	

☐ We'd like to email you from time to time when we have special promotions, limited editions or new brands and products. If you'd prefer we didn't, check here.

☐ Occasionally, we may share your personal information with selected partners or other third parties for reasons other than the execution of your order from boo.com. If you would prefer we didn't pass your personal info to anyone other than those required to process your order, check here.

On Boo, users had to check the box if they did NOT want the subscription. Note the deceptive wording. T19

Credit Card

Shopping at eToys is 100% safe. Guaranteed!
For more information about credit card security, click here.

◉ Visa ○ Discover Card
○ MasterCard ○ Diners Club

VISA MasterCard DISCOVER Diners Club International

eToys prefers Visa!

Card Number [＿＿＿＿＿＿]

Expiration date (mm/yy) [＿＿＿]

☑ We automatically store your credit card number to make checkout faster the next time you shop. If you would prefer not to have your credit card information stored, please click the box to remove the checkmark. (Why storing your credit card is safe.)

On the payment page of eToys, one user un-checked the box for "We automatically store your credit card number… ." The user un-checked it "just so it's not hanging around." T20

In other studies, we have found that people may be willing to subscribe to e-mail newsletters if the following information is provided:

Tip: Offer an example of the e-mail newsletter. Allow customers to view a sample to find out before they subscribe if they are really interested.

Tip: Say how often the newsletter will be sent. For promotional newsletters that are not time sensitive, one newsletter per month seemed acceptable to our users. Some were willing to accept a newsletter every two weeks. Few were willing to accept this kind of newsletter more frequently. But daily newsletters can be acceptable to some, especially when they are interesting, contain time-sensitive information, and can be read quickly.

Tip: Guarantee that the e-mail address will be used only for sending this one company's newsletters.

Tip: Emphasize how easy it is to unsubscribe. The simplest and most usable way of unsubscribing is to return the newsletter to the sender with the word "unsubscribe" in the subject line or body of the e-mail. Each and every newsletter should contain a brief description of how to unsubscribe or change the subscribed e-mail address.

➡ *Allow customers to purchase without registering.*

Forcing users to register creates a real barrier for first-time customers. Registration erodes trust, because people don't perceive benefit to themselves in registering.

- 1800flowers: "They want me to register so they can keep sending me junk?"
- SmarterKids: The user registered reluctantly: "I don't want to be a member."
- Gevalia: One of our users found himself on the Join Portal page. "I think they're building a mailing list. I don't want to join anything. I just want to buy coffee." Later, he rated the site negatively for how they might use his credit card and personal information, saying, "I think they'd harvest it. Marketing it out to e-mail lists."
- Gevalia: Another user found out that he had to register in order to get regular deliveries. As a result, the user dropped the idea of regular deliveries.
- Wal-Mart: A user considered "speedy checkout," but it required registration. "I would do that normally, if it was a site I was going to visit often ... . Something that only works for very well-established [stores]."
- Reel: A user entered a fake e-mail address on the registration page. He said he was very careful about giving his personal information.
- Iflorist: "I do like the thing about privacy policy [in About Us]. ... 'Will not be shared with others.' I like that. It talks about cookies — I like this, informative besides. I think every site should have something about personal information."

➡ *Do not require registration before or during a purchase — offer it as an option after the purchase.*

Many online consumers don't want to be "members" and have personal information permanently stored. Consider: What's more important to your business? Registration or a sale?

➡ *Explain the benefits of registration and consider offering an incentive.*

Make your customers want to join. Explain discreetly how much easier life would be if the customer were registered.

Tip: Make it easy for customers to cancel their registration. Tell how easy it is to cancel a registration and explain how to do it in an easy-to-find place.

Tip: Promise customers that if they cancel their registration, you will delete all information about them.

For more guidelines on registration, see the Checkout & Registration chapter.

Trustworthy Security

In this study, 10 out of 39 US users expressed interest in knowing whether the site was secure, and looked to the site or the browser for security information. Concerns over security may actually be under-represented in this study, because most users weren't even entering their own information, let alone a credit card number.

➡️ *Use secure connections.*

We were surprised at how many users looked for secure servers. We were even more surprised at how many users looked at the browser for indication that the site was secure.

- 1800flowers: "One of the things I like about this site is you see the security code up here" (referring to a small lock icon at the top of the page).

- CustomDisc Account page: "One of the first things I want to know is do they have a secure server, regarding credit card numbers and stuff. I want to make sure that once I send my [order] into cyberspace, it's secure. It's between them and me, and no one else."

- Unrelated to any of the sites he tested, one of our users commented that some sites have an option for secure or unsecure. He said he didn't understand what the difference was, or why anyone would choose unsecure. The facilitator explained that many older browsers do not support current security protocols.

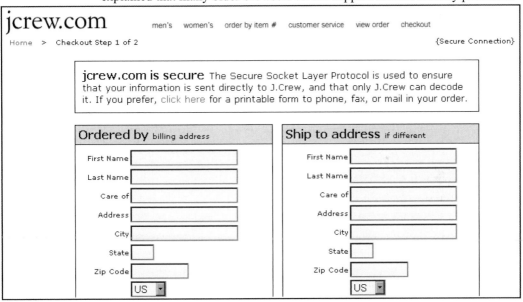

Jcrew did especially well at showing their server was secure, both in the shopping cart and on the checkout page. T21

> Iflorist allowed customers to choose between secure ordering, standard ordering, and telephone ordering. Some of our users weren't sure why they had a choice, though. T22

Iflorist explained the advantages and disadvantages of the security options, but the explanation only confused some of our users, who weren't sure why they had a choice. The choice raised more questions than it answered — no one understood why anyone would use the less secure standard order form.

One Iflorist user noted, "People who don't have this encryption are in some trouble if they start to order. ... Gotta encrypt this information so hackers can't get to it." Another Iflorist user decided she wanted to use the secure order form. "What I would do in real life is probably call, instead of putting in information. I'm not all that confident about the Internet yet."

Iflorist's approach, offering to educate customers first and then asking them to choose, is bad. Ideally, the browser and server should negotiate the highest level of security possible, and the site should explain the security status where interested customers can easily find it. Other approaches may introduce doubt about the whole process.

Tip: Don't scare people with security questions. Customers should never have to make a decision about the security of the technology they are using in the middle of trying to buy something.

Tip: Display information about your security precautions in a prominent place. Explain your security precautions in plain language. Avoid technical jargon.

Tip: When security is unavailable for any reason, tell the customer right away. Online shoppers don't like to waste their time entering an order that is unsafe or impossible to transmit.

➡ *Provide alternative methods of ordering.*

A person's comfort with buying online depends heavily on recommendations and warnings from others. Many people are more likely to fax or phone in their order when they order from an unknown company.

When one BasketHaus user saw a message that said the secure server was temporarily down, he refused to enter his credit card number. "Very reasonable that you can call when security is down," he said. "I would do that."

Tip: Make it simple for customers to order by fax, phone, or mail.

Tip: Provide a toll-free phone number.

Tip: Make alternative ordering methods easy to find. Give clear instructions for the ordering alternatives you offer.

Access to Helpful People

Access to real human beings can increase trust — providing, of course, your service people are helpful and trustworthy.

We have found that users expect that they can gain access to helpful people through:

- Fax
- Phone
- E-mail
- Traditional mail.

Furniture.com, 1800flowers, and Reel also offered a live chat feature with a customer service representative. Although only three users tried it (two on Furniture, one on 1800flowers), their responses were quite positive. The user who tried the chat on 1800flowers to obtain the answer to a delivery question was pleased that she got the correct answer right away.

Live chat on Furniture.com enabled two users to locate wine racks, which were difficult to find on the site. Both users raved about how great they thought the chat facility was. Despite connection problems and delays of up to a minute between responses, the users received the assistance they wanted. The delays didn't seem to bother the users at all, and they were impressed that the salesperson made a page containing wine racks appear. We have more to say on how live chat enhances sales in the Selling Strategies chapter.

> ### Show that people, not machines, are responding to customer requests.

Identify customer service representatives responding in e-mail by name, not just by weird signatures like, "The Disney Catalog International Department hd767/int."

> ### Back key statements with named persons.

For the sake of credibility and trust, back up key statements, company policies, and product reviews with the names of the people responsible.

> ### Present a consistent face to each customer.

One user complained that it was a bit disturbing that each message from customer service was written by yet another customer service representative. Whenever possible, assign one service person to handle a customer's question or problem from start to finish.

Fulfill Customer Expectations

The primary objective of this study was to test online shopping, not sales fulfillment. However, to get an idea of the problems that might appear in the fulfillment phase, we asked three of our Danish users to use their own credit cards to buy products from three different websites. We reimbursed them later for all costs, and they were free to keep the products they had ordered.

The three Danish users made a total of nine attempts to buy products from Disney, CustomDisc, and Iflorist. Only one of the nine attempts to order was completely successful, as shown in the table.

Seven of the nine orders ended in sales catastrophes during the ordering phase, only one of which was related to trust (User 2, CustomDisc). With help from the facilitator, four additional orders were completed, so a total of six orders went on to fulfillment.

Only two of the six fulfillments were completely without trust-related problems.

Fulfillment Results

	Disney.com	CustomDisc.com	Iflorist.com
User 1	Ordering Failure – User did not want to order, because she considered shipping costs outrageously high.	Ordering Failure – User was unable to find out how the music would be delivered. The user could not find suitable music.	Ordering Success, Fulfillment Failure – Order disappeared. *See **Note 1.***
User 2	Ordering Failure – User was unable to find a suitable product within a reasonable time (17 minutes).	Ordering Failure – The user would not have continued after the website deleted her billing information. Fulfillment Success – The facilitator asked the user to continue, and she completed the order. The CustomDisc was delivered without problems.	Ordering Failure – User thought the website did not ship to Denmark. Fulfillment Success – The facilitator asked the user to continue, and she completed the order. The flowers were delivered without problems.
User 3	Ordering Failure – The user gave up when he got a message about server connection problems. Fulfillment Failure – The facilitator asked the user to continue and he completed the order. The user later cancelled the order because of delivery delay. *See **Note 2.***	Ordering Failure – The user would not have continued after the website informed him that four of his selected songs could not be shipped outside the US. Fulfillment Partial Success – The facilitator asked the user to continue, and he completed the order. The CustomDisc was delivered, two weeks later than expected.	Ordering Success, Fulfillment Partial Success – The flowers were delivered, but they wilted quickly. Both the sender and recipient were unhappy with the quality of the flowers.

Note 1: (User 1, Iflorist) The flowers were never delivered. An inquiry to Iflorist resulted in the following explanation:

> Your credit card came up with an "Invalid Code or Account Number" message and we cancelled your order. We sent you an e-mail to this effect ... however, the e-mail bounced. The e-mail was sent to the same address as listed above. We had no other means to reach you.
>
> If you would care to have the order sent, we can replace it, but you will have to supply us with the correct credit card information.

After reading the message, the user gave up, noting that Iflorist had been able to send her a confirmation message using the e-mail address she provided. She suspected that they had not actually sent her any e-mail.

Note 2: (User 3, Disney) The user placed his order for an *Aristocats* DVD on Jan. 17. He did not receive a delivery date. He was unable to find out how to use the Disney order tracking system (because of confusion about his password). On Jan. 29, he inquired by e-mail about the status of the order. On Feb. 1, a Disney customer service representative told him that the DVD would not be shipped until April 4, which was the official re-release date of the cartoon. The user then decided to cancel the order.

➡ *Tell the customer when the products will be delivered.*

Provide a realistic delivery date. Give an absolute rather than a relative date, that is, "25 September 2000" rather than "within 10 working days." Show the estimated date when the products will arrive at the customer's door rather than the date when you will hand them over to the shipping company.

➡ *When there are delays, inform the customer promptly.*

Offer the customer the option of canceling the order, but don't make it sound as if that's the only option.

➡ *Make sure your order-tracking system is usable.*

One of our users spent 30 minutes after the test attempting to get useful information from Disney's order-tracking system. He finally sent an e-mail instead.

➡ *Conduct regular checks of delivered product quality.*

Quality assurance testing is particularly important when fulfillment is carried out by a third party. When the flowers one of our users ordered from Iflorist were delivered (by a local florist), they quickly wilted. Neither the sender nor the recipient were pleased, to say the least.

Category
Pages

" Good sites show clearly organized, representative merchandise starting right on the homepage."

Store Home Pages

The home page of an e-commerce site is like the first paragraph of a news story. Journalists are taught to convey the five "W"s (who, what, when, where, and why) early in the story, so the reader can decide whether to read the rest. Similarly, the home page of an e-commerce site should present the following essential elements and links, so a visitor can decide whether to go shopping on your website:

- **Show merchandise.** Display the products and / or services for sale.
- **Enable shopping.** Provide direct access to the catalog and / or online store.
- **Organize merchandise.** Classify goods and services in a user-oriented hierarchy.
- **Sell and deliver.** Provide links to purchasing options, return policy, shipping, and delivery information.
- **Build trust.** Link to customer service, privacy policy, and company background information.

In our study, we did not explain what each site was about. Instead, we let users click on whatever interested them for the first two or three minutes of the test. Then we asked three questions:

1. What does this site have?
2. Who is this site for?
3. At first glance, does it appear that this site would have things you might want or need?

Users' answers to the first two questions revealed whether they had the same overall understanding of the site as we did, based on the home page and any other pages they'd seen. The third question helped us understand the users' level of motivation in approaching the tasks.

➡ *Show what merchandise you sell and don't sell.*

The home page is a high-level category page. As such, it should show what merchandise the site does — and does not — offer. Compare the home pages of Wal-Mart and Sears. Both are large department stores that carry a variety of merchandise, but it was easier for users to get started on Wal-Mart than on Sears. It was also easier for users to form a correct impression of what Wal-Mart sold.

From the list of links down the left side of Wal-Mart's home page, users could readily see that the website offered a variety of merchandise, just like Wal-Mart's physical stores do. As one user who tested Boo and then Wal-Mart said, "Very typical kind of layout — which isn't a bad thing. Won't have that same fun factor as Boo does, but a feeling of home, that you can find your way around it." When looking for a specific item on Wal-Mart, most users chose a link quite quickly.

In contrast to Wal-Mart, the Sears site was misleading to our users. Although Sears is also a large department store, it doesn't offer all its merchandise online. The website sells primarily tools, appliances, and replacement parts. Users who were familiar with Sears immediately assumed that the website had all of Sears' products. This was not the case — the links to Around the House, Under the Hood, and Fashion File went to pages containing buying tips and ads promoting in-store (not online) specials. Users couldn't actually buy anything in those departments. The problem was even worse for the Danish users, who were not familiar with Sears. One Danish user who saw the image of the car and the words "car and garage" concluded that Sears sold cars.

The links on Wal-Mart's home page correspond to the departments in their physical stores. Users could easily tell what was for sale there. CP2

Sears' home page obscured the fact that they sell primarily tools, appliances, and replacement parts online, rather than all the merchandise offered in their brick-and-mortar stores. CP3

CustomDisc was another site where users had a tough time determining what the site actually sold. Despite the name "CustomDisc," users assumed that the site sold standard music CDs. It was not apparent from the home page that the site let customers make a custom CD by choosing songs. Three out of 10 users realized that the site offered custom CDs only when we gave them the task to create one.

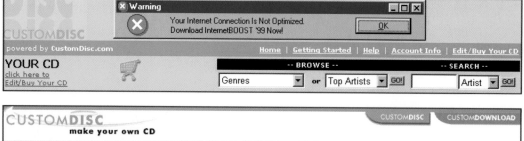

For a time, CustomDisc changed its home page to make it clearer what the site offered. CP4

➡ *Beware of over-emphasizing promotional items.*

Images of promotional items appearing on the home page shape peoples' perceptions of what the site offers. Promotional items can work against the site's interests if a potential customer mistakenly concludes that the site doesn't have merchandise of interest.

- Reel: One user didn't realize the site had VHS videos, because on the day he tested the site there was a prominent image that said "DVD Shopping Guide" on the home page.

- Nordstrom: One user said that the home page had given him a completely incorrect impression of the site. During the test he found out that Nordstrom primarily sells clothing, shoes, and high quality merchandise — not trinkets and other cheap stuff as he initially thought. The version of the home page this user saw featured a large image of inexpensive jewelry.

We only saw a few examples of wrong first impressions in our study, but it made us realize it's important to watch for unintended side effects of promoting certain items.

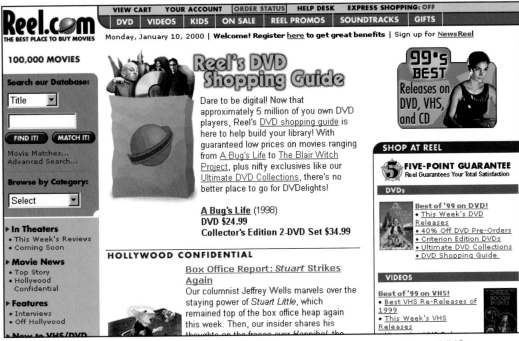

➡ *The home page should show the purpose of the site.*

Some websites have multiple purposes, with e-commerce being only one of them. For example, we can infer from HermanMiller's home page that the site sells consumer products, provides information to investors and business partners, and sells wholesale products to vertical markets such as health care and government.

After looking around the site for a couple of minutes, our users could tell us what HermanMiller did, so this home page did reasonably well at communicating the site's purpose — except, as explained below, it was hard for some users to find the retail store.

As e-commerce websites proliferate, it becomes increasingly important for sites to communicate their particular approach to doing business. Do they emphasize low cost? Variety of merchandise? Fast delivery? Free delivery? Specialty products? Customers' initial impressions of a site should match the messages the site is trying to communicate.

For instance, it was apparent to American users that SmarterKids specialized in educational toys for children. Interestingly, this purpose was not as clear to the Danish users. They could tell the site sold children's products, but they didn't immediately recognize the educational emphasis. By asking users to tell us what the site sold, we discovered these types of discrepancies.

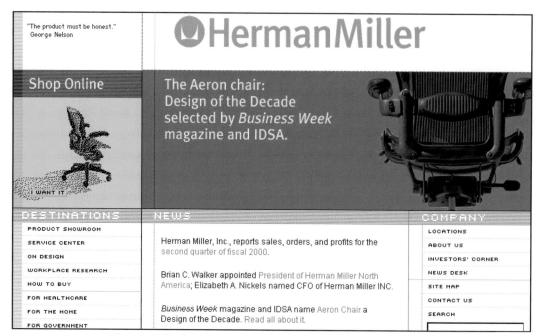

"The product must be honest." George Nelson

HermanMiller

Shop Online

I WANT IT

The Aeron chair:
Design of the Decade
selected by *Business Week*
magazine and IDSA.

DESTINATIONS

PRODUCT SHOWROOM
SERVICE CENTER
ON DESIGN
WORKPLACE RESEARCH
HOW TO BUY
FOR HEALTHCARE
FOR THE HOME
FOR GOVERNMENT

NEWS

Herman Miller, Inc., reports sales, orders, and profits for the second quarter of fiscal 2000.

Brian C. Walker appointed President of Herman Miller North America; Elizabeth A. Nickels named CFO of Herman Miller INC.

Business Week magazine and IDSA name Aeron Chair a Design of the Decade. Read all about it.

COMPANY

LOCATIONS
ABOUT US
INVESTORS' CORNER
NEWS DESK
SITE MAP
CONTACT US
SEARCH

HermanMiller's home page shows an emphasis on information for investors and business partners, not e-commerce. Depending on their goals for the site, this may be appropriate. CP6

➡️ *Don't hide the catalog — enable shopping from the home page.*

There are two approaches an e-commerce site can take regarding the display of its online catalog of merchandise:

- Provide a link to the catalog from the home page, or
- Use the home page as the front page of the catalog.

We believe the second approach is more effective, because it enables customers to start shopping right away. eToys, SmarterKids, Wal-Mart and 1800flowers are examples of sites whose home pages functioned as top-level category pages. These sites had a navigation panel that allowed users to access the main product categories (such as subject, brand name, or child's age on the toy sites). And they devoted space in the center of the home page to featured products. Even though there was a lot of information on these home pages, users didn't hesitate very long when we asked them to find something — they were off and clicking. Thus, these home pages were successful at getting potential customers started.

SmarterKids let visitors start shopping right from the home page. CP7

In contrast, it was harder for users to get started on sites where they had to navigate into the catalog (or store) to begin shopping. Compare SmarterKids' start-from-the-home-page approach to the Gevalia home page, where the user must explicitly enter the catalog. On Gevalia, users took significantly longer just to find the link to the catalog so they could start shopping.

It wasn't obvious how to start shopping on Gevalia — it took some users a few minutes to find the catalog. CP8

We saw even worse problems on HermanMiller, where the store entrance was effectively hidden. Some users went to the Showroom first, only to discover they couldn't buy anything there. Unlike their real-world equivalents, the Showroom and Store are totally separate parts of the HermanMiller site. One user got stuck in the Showroom and needed help from the test facilitator to continue. If HermanMiller wants to facilitate online buying, they should make the store a more central aspect of their home page.

▶ Reveal the product hierarchy.

It's difficult to explain what merchandise a site sells. It's much easier — and more effective — to show it. Sites that contained well-organized sets of links made it easier for users to identify what was on the site and to get started finding a particular item. Both eToys and SmarterKids clearly showed how the products were organized on the home page.

Nordstrom and Jcrew revealed their hierarchies one click down from the home page — as soon as the user chose the Men's or Women's link. This approach was also effective. On each of these sites, the high-level categories were visually scannable from a single page, without requiring the user to drill down.

This Gevalia catalog page concealed the product hierarchy by spreading the menus across several pages. It was hard for users to find coffee makers. CP9

In contrast, Gevalia's design had the most concealed product hierarchy. Many of Gevalia's catalog pages showed a large decorative image and a handful of links, requiring the user to drill down to pages containing submenus. Gevalia paid a usability price for this design. The issue isn't only that it required more clicks, but also that the contents of the subcategories were obscured from the user.

For example, it was not obvious that Coffee Makers would be found as a subcategory under Gevalia Coffee and Tea. When asked to find a coffee pot, users explored links like Gifts, instead. Also, because there were no links from one subcategory page to another, users had to back up to try a different path.

Gevalia's recent redesign revealed more of the product hierarchy at a higher level. Not only was the link to the catalog prominently featured on the much shorter home page, but the top catalog page also had more links. Unfortunately, much of the page is still filled with large decorative images. Although we didn't test this new design, it appears to be a step in the right direction — our task to find a coffee maker would likely be much easier with the new design.

Gevalia's redesigned catalog page (which we did not test) was somewhat better at revealing the product hierarchy. CP10

Similarly, even though Sears offered a narrower selection of merchandise than Wal-Mart, users still found it harder to get started when we asked them to find a specific item, such as a cordless drill, probably because Sears didn't have an organized hierarchy of links that users could quickly scan. One user never found the Tools tab, for example, even though he did explore the Parts tab right next to it.

Disney also obscured its product hierarchy, making it harder to find goods and services. Compare the links on the Disney Store main page to the links on eToys (below) and SmarterKids (Image CP7). On eToys, no one had trouble finding Hot Wheels products. However, on Disney, it wasn't obvious where to find a stuffed Pooh doll. Some users just gave up.

The product hierarchy was readily visible via links on eToys, but it wasn't on Disney. CP11

Reel's home page also tended to confuse users:

- "A little congested on the first part of it. Not self-explanatory enough. I'm scrolling through it for a minute or so before I realized what [kind of site it] was. A lot of words and not much for you to do."

- "It just looks like a search engine, not a store. … looks very technical." This user would prefer to see more pages like the *Toy Story* page "where they show pictures of the movies."

It was hard for users to tell what Reel had, and how to get started shopping for something specific. The home page had a lot of information, but it lacked a visible hierarchy of products. Revealing the full product hierarchy requires a major amount of screen real estate, and at some point, the page just becomes too long and unwieldy to be an effective sales tool.

According to users, Reel's home page had too much verbiage and not enough videos. CP12

In sharp contrast, Boo made it perfectly clear what its site was all about. Right on the home page it says, "sports and streetwear on the net." Our users didn't have any trouble recognizing that Boo sells clothing.

Boo had an interesting approach to the product hierarchy / screen display trade-off. Although Boo's high-level menus didn't reveal the subcategories, submenus popped up when the user moved the mouse over the main menu categories. This progressive disclosure didn't work perfectly, but users said they liked it.

One problem occurred because of the male and female symbols used on the submenus. Some users figured out that clicking on the symbols would provide only men's or women's clothing, but not everyone did, even those who said they wanted to look at only men's or women's clothing. Those who didn't discover how to use the symbols ended up looking at pages that contained both men's and women's clothing.

We have some strong reservations about Boo's approach to categories, which required technologies and features (such as Java or Flash) that some browsers don't, won't, or can't support. Boo also required excessive load time and it was less robust than standard HTML. Finally, Boo's menus might not always offer a usable compromise if too much information is hidden and the user must repeatedly sweep the mouse over the menus to make submenus pop up.

Even so, Boo tried to strike a balance between a minimalist high-level design and one that revealed all the merchandise for sale. From a usability perspective, it deserves an honorable mention, because the submenus worked fairly well (on a PC), aside from the confusion over male / female symbols, and users liked them.

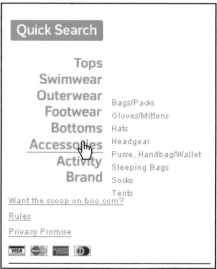

Users liked Boo's pop-up menu approach, although some never realized they could click the male and female symbols to see gender-specific clothing. CP13

> ### Provide links on the home page to purchasing options, return policy, shipping and delivery information.

Sometimes people need answers to important questions before they begin shopping, such as whether the site delivers to their country, whether they can have a product delivered by a certain date, or whether they can use a particular credit card.

For example, about 10% of our users spontaneously looked to see which credit cards the site accepted — even during tests when they knew they weren't being asked to buy anything.

Although delivery areas weren't an issue for the New Hampshire users, many Danish users had a hard time determining whether the site would deliver to Denmark or not. As e-commerce sites strive to reach a global audience, the issue of showing delivery areas will become more important. (See the International Users chapter for further discussion on this issue.)

◆ **Provide links on the home page to customer service, privacy, and company background information.**

In the US tests, we gave users the option of using a false identity — and in many cases the users chose not to enter their own personal information. Even so, the majority of users expressed concern about how their personal information would be used. Thus, having a link to the privacy policy on the home page (and on any other page that asks for personal information) helps to alleviate users' worries. Of course, there's no way to guarantee that users will actually read the privacy policy. Similarly, some users clicked About Us links before deciding to purchase the merchant's goods or services, even though nothing in our tasks asked them to research the company first.

Classification Schemes

The best way to classify merchandise depends on the subject matter of the site — shopping for tools by brand name makes sense, whereas shopping for flowers by brand name is less meaningful. Effective classification is difficult, so it's not surprising that we found problems related to classification on all of the sites we tested.

◆ **Choose classifications that are useful to your customers.**

In general, the flower sites (Iflorist and 1800flowers) and toy sites (eToys and SmarterKids) used classifications that were meaningful to our users. But on many of the other sites we tested, users had problems because the classifications were not clear to them. On Furniture, users had to start by picking a room, such as Dining Room. Then the subsequent page let users pick from a list of pieces for that room, for example.

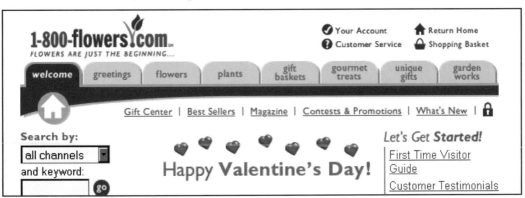

1800flowers showed classifications of their products on their home page. CP14

We asked users to shop for a wine rack on Furniture, but it wasn't obvious where to start. In reality, wine racks can go in the dining room, kitchen or cellar (or in any other room, for that matter), but on Furniture, wine racks were available only in Kitchen. Three out of 10 users were unable to find any wine racks on Furniture, though the site had several. Introducing room as a higher-level classification scheme made it harder to find a specific piece of furniture.

Living also classified furniture by rooms, but the "Browse for…" selection list on the home page allowed users to choose a specific piece of furniture.

Living's "Browse For …" list let the user navigate to a particular piece of furniture, regardless of what room it goes in. The Furniture site had no such option; users had to first pick the correct room. CP15

Other classification problems:

- Boo's subcategories of outerwear — Fleeces, Jackets, and Vests (body warmers) — didn't work very well for users who were trying to find a warm coat.

- CustomDisc's top-level classification of music by genre (Rock/Pop/Oldies, Alternative, Jazz/Blues, etc.) worked reasonably well, but once users clicked a genre, the subclassifications made no sense to them. Most users expected to see names of artists, but instead they had to peruse subcategories with titles like "Songs for the Car" or "Great Oldies."

- Jcrew classifies its men's shoes as Classic, Modern, and Rugged. We asked users to find brown boots. There were brown boots in both the Modern and Rugged categories. But users who opted to go directly to Rugged shoes instead of viewing all of the footwear missed seeing some of the brown boots.

- At the top levels of the site, SmarterKids showed both the age and school grade (called a "form" in some countries) together, but deeper in the site they dropped the age information and presented only grades. Someone who has no school-age children might not know a child's grade. Our tasks gave the age of the child, but not the grade, and we observed some age / grade confusion with two of our nine users. For example, one Danish user who was not familiar with the term "grades" mistakenly went to Grades 7–9 when looking for something for an 8-year-old.

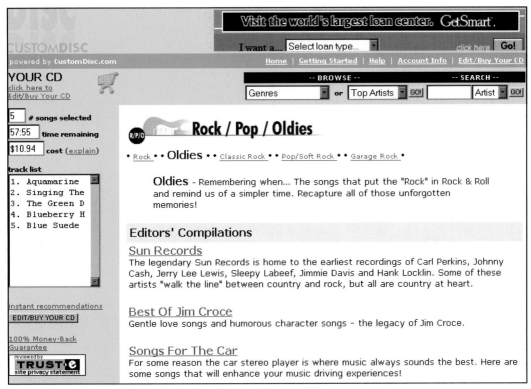

These collection titles made it difficult for users to find the exact songs they wanted. CP16

What constitutes good classification depends on the intended market and how familiar consumers are with the subject matter of the site. If SmarterKids views their primary market as Americans who have children in their lives (including teachers, who write many of the product reviews), the age / grade issue may not be important. However, if SmarterKids also wishes to sell merchandise to countries that don't use the term "grade" or to childless people who sometimes give gifts to children, they should modify their classification scheme to age-appropriate gifts.

This age / grade classification dilemma shows how site designers must take cultural assumptions into consideration when selling to an international market. It's important to know foreign holidays and gift-giving customs. (See the International Users chapter for more on this critical subject.)

▶ *Consider multiple classification schemes.*

SmarterKids and eToys effectively categorized their merchandise multiple ways. Whether a customer approaches the site by looking for the child's age, a specific brand, or the type of toy, there are links to support that method of shopping. The flower websites used multiple classification schemes also. In our study, users took different but equally successful paths to find items on these sites.

▶ *Provide cross-references.*

Not everyone classifies items the same way. If an item can be classified in more than one way, it's probably best to do so. Cross-referenced classification makes elegant sense online because it makes excellent use of the hypertext medium.

In contrast, Wal-Mart used a more limiting floor plan metaphor that closely matched the way the departments are organized in their physical stores. Although this classification scheme worked fairly well for US users, it wasn't completely unambiguous for the Danish users, who weren't familiar with Wal-Mart. All three Danish users looked for an infant car seat in the Automotive department — logical enough, but this didn't match the way the site was laid out.

On Wal-Mart, users found car seats under both Car Seats and Travel, but not under Automotive. CP17

Similarly, some users (including Americans) had difficulty with the difference between Wal-Mart's Housewares and Appliances categories. They mistakenly went to Housewares first when looking for a toaster. Housewares contained dishes and non-electric kitchen tools — but no cross links to appliances.

Wal-Mart does cross-reference. It just doesn't cross-reference enough. Users who looked in the Baby Shop were able to find car seats from either the Car Seats link or the Travel link. Most users chose Car Seats, but one user found an infant seat through Travel. Adding a link to Car Seats from the Automotive department and adding a link to Toasters from the Housewares department would have helped our users find these items.

▶ *Classify items consistently.*

Some sites didn't follow their own classification schemes:

- One user couldn't find *Doctor Zhivago* in Reel's list of Romantic Dramas, even though the site classified this movie as both a romance and a drama.

- Furniture returned up to seven wine racks (the exact number varied from day to day) when users searched for "wine rack." But other users only saw one wine rack when they selected the Wine Rack option on the Kitchen page. It is unclear how one would locate these other wine racks without using site's search engine. (See the Search chapter for information about improving search results.)

➡ *Don't over-classify.*

Cross-reference classification is mandatory for large websites, but we saw some smaller sites doing just fine with little or no classification. NorwaySweaters and BasketHaus — the sites in our study with the smallest selections — did not seem to suffer any ill effects from simply dumping all their products on one page.

NorwaySweaters offered six sweater designs; BasketHaus had 14 gift baskets. Users did not complain about a lack of organization on these sites. They simply clicked and scrolled until they'd seen all the products, and then chose the one they wanted.

We also saw some intriguing behavior on sites where the users were very interested in the merchandise. 1800flowers presented its 38 products containing roses on seven pages, in no particular order. Some users looked at all seven pages — which was noteworthy because we rarely saw a user go past the third page on any other site.

Possibly, looking at flower arrangements is inherently enjoyable for some people. Most of the US users commented during their initial site explorations that they enjoyed flowers or gardening. The selection available to the Danish users was much smaller, so we don't know if they would have looked at the same number of pages if given the opportunity.

Similarly, coffee lovers spent more time looking at coffees on Gevalia and Peet's than did users who don't drink coffee. These observations might suggest that it is less important to organize content on sites where the user enjoys just looking at the merchandise — but only when the number of products is small.

Methods for Classification

Classification is hard to do — and it's especially tricky when the people charged with creating the classification schema for the website are much more familiar with the product or service than are the sites' customers. Designers and database specialists simply don't think of the merchandise the same way the site's customers do. Customer behavior, therefore, must be observed.

We suggest two techniques for letting your customers define categorizations and classifications that will work for them — and you:

- Card-sorting exercises. In card-sorting, you give the user a pile of slips of paper, each with the name of one product written on it. The user sorts the items into groups and then names each group. After a number of users complete this exercise, you can find the common patterns and use them as guides for classification.

- Learning from mistakes. During usability tests, look for problems users have when navigating to products. If the user chooses a category that you didn't anticipate and fails to find the item, that item should probably be cross-referenced or recategorized.

Product Listing Pages

➡️ *Where feasible, limit product listings to two or three pages.*

One of the patterns we saw in our tests was that users didn't review very many pages of product listings. SmarterKids, Furniture, and Reel, for example, offered product listings that were hundreds of items long, spanning a dozen or more pages. Most users didn't look beyond the second or third page — either they simply chose something from these pages (a behavior that might not be so common in real life as it was in our artificial test environment) or they adopted a different strategy. What's especially interesting about this finding is that the websites we tested had varying approaches to product listings. For example:

- SmarterKids had eight products per page, each accompanied by a paragraph describing the item.
- Furniture showed thumbnail images with a price but no description, 20 per page.
- Boo showed about four products per page, without description but with relatively large images.

Despite the different display designs, on all three sites users rarely looked beyond the third page of product listings, and many didn't go beyond the second. And although slow-loading pages could have been an inhibiting factor on some sites, users still didn't go much farther on the sites that downloaded quickly. This user behavior pattern suggests that winnowing tools — described later in this chapter — are essential to ensure that users don't just abandon their searches on large sites.

When a website has a large number of products, it's impossible to put the best products on the first few pages without knowing more about what the user is looking for. The purpose of winnowing is to reduce the number of products to a set small enough to fit on a maximum of two or three Web pages.

The first page of Math products for 4th–6th graders on SmarterKids: Most users didn't look past the second or third page of product listings. CP18

➡ Scrolling is acceptable on product listing pages.

All users scrolled vertically on product listing pages (and horizontally on Boo) during our tests. We observed only a few scrolling-related problems, so we can't say that eliminating scrolling on product listing pages would make a site more usable.

We did observe a scrolling problem on HermanMiller's Chairs page, however. Some users didn't realize how many chairs there actually were, so they missed seeing some very nice office chairs located at the end of the list. The top of the page didn't indicate how many chairs were shown (37), and the white space between chairs in the list could have created an illusion that the user had reached the bottom of the page.

To solve this problem, we suggest:

- State the number of items listed.

- Make the images smaller so the products can be shown two or three to a row, putting more of them in front of the user at once, which would also shorten the page.

- Design the page so the last row of items is only partially visible and separate the rows with a minimal amount of white space. Of course, this tactic requires that you take into consideration the various combinations of browser window size and screen resolutions, so it's not easy or foolproof.

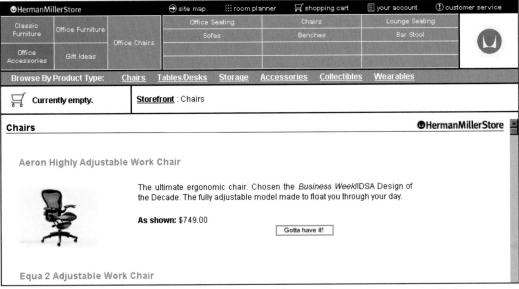

There are actually 37 chairs on this page, but some users scrolled only far enough to see the first few. CP19

➡ Use download time to determine the number of products per page.

There is no ideal number of products that should go on each page — it depends on the product and the amount of information you need to provide with each item. As described above, SmarterKids and Furniture used quite different approaches, but both page designs seemed useful, given the type of merchandise.

Instead, use download time to help determine the number of products to show per page. Put as many products on a page as you can — within a prescribed time limit. Jakob Nielsen recommends that 10 seconds is probably the maximum page load time, after which you risk losing the customer's attention. Of course, faster is better.

In our study, pages on Boo, Furniture, and HermanMiller took the longest to download, often a minute or more at 56k modem speed. Naturally, users complained that these sites were too slow. Although we did not time every page, most of our test sites had product listing pages that downloaded in an acceptable amount of time for our users.

Tip: Reduce the perceived download time. Some page layouts use big tables that enclose all the content on the page, which can cause apparent delay in page download times, because current browsers wait for all of the content inside a table to download before displaying any of it. Content-heavy pages should be laid out in a series of small tables instead of nesting smaller tables inside one big one. By using a series of tables, the designer can insure that the user gets something to look at as soon as possible, while the rest of the tables continue to load invisibly below the "fold" (the lower edge of the browser window).

Sorting Product Listings

▶ *Allow customers to sort products by the factors they care about most.*

The majority of the sites we tested didn't show product listings in any recognizable order. Although alphabetizing is a tempting way to organize a list, it is useful only if the list uses the words customers look for.

For example, we asked users to visit Boo to buy clothing to wear in freezing temperatures. Only one of the nine users noticed that Boo's jackets were displayed in alphabetical order by manufacturer — and that observation was largely irrelevant to the task at hand. For our purposes, it would have been ideal to see jackets organized by warmth.

Admittedly, categorization by warmth might not be so easy to do, and it might frustrate brand-name buyers. Multiple, cross-referenced classifications would be more appropriate. When we asked users to find warm gloves, they tended to assume that an $80 pair of gloves would be warmer than a $30 pair. Even if their assumption was mistaken, these users were mentally sorting items by price.

Interestingly, most sites we tested didn't sort product listings by price, although we observed our users frequently used price as a sorting factor. Nevertheless, we cannot assert that sorting by price is a must-have classification. Living did have a sort-by-price option, but none of our users clicked it.

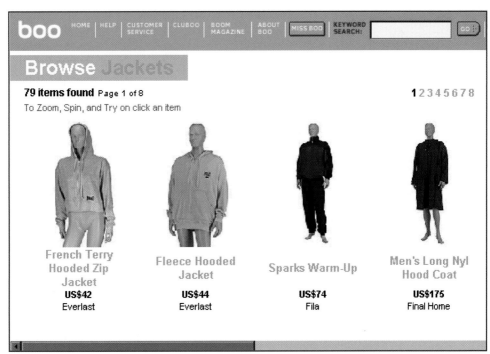

79 items found Page 1 of 8

1 2 3 4 5 6 7 8

To Zoom, Spin, and Try on click an item

French Terry Hooded Zip Jacket	Fleece Hooded Jacket	Sparks Warm-Up	Men's Long Nyl Hood Coat
US$42	**US$44**	**US$74**	**US$175**
Everlast	Everlast	Fila	Final Home

Boo's merchandise was presented in alphabetical order by manufacturer, which didn't help users find a warm jacket. CP20

Some products, like coffee, are harder to sort than others. One way that Peet's organized its coffees was by name, in alphabetical order. Is this useful? For returning customers who know what they want, perhaps it is, but it's definitely not helpful to new customers. Again, there was no option to sort by price.

Peet's did provide other organizing schemes, however, such as Type, Decaf, and Best Sellers. As described later in this chapter, Peet's also had a Taste Guide to assist users who weren't sure which coffees they might like. So, even though Peet's was not a model of best-practice site design, it still had several good ways to help users find what they wanted.

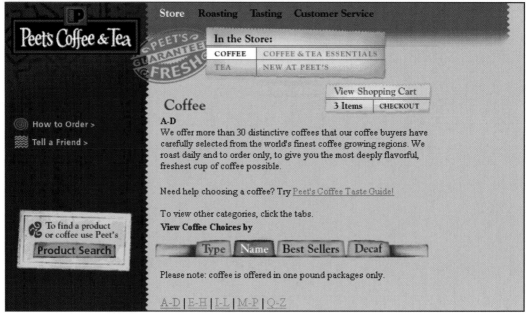

Coffee is hard to sort. Peet's organized its coffees by Type, Name, Best Sellers, and Decaf — but not by price. CP21

➡ *Show item availability at a high level.*

The more clicks users invest to learn they can't buy something, the worse their resentment is. Present availability information on a high-level category page to avoid annoying your customers.

Informing customers that the item they just put in their shopping cart is out of stock (as Jcrew does) is certainly too late. Sears, Disney, and Nordstrom were also guilty of showing merchandise on product listing pages that later turned out to be unavailable. In contrast, eToys showed which items were in stock right on the product listing page.

➡ *Show visually similar things together.*

Our theory (supported mostly by user behavior on the HermanMiller site) is that people may stop looking as soon as they start seeing items in a list that look less like what they want. This guideline depends, of course, on the nature of the merchandise. Grouping by visual similarity is more useful for items like clothing, furniture, and flowers (where seeing a picture helps the user identify key characteristics), but is less useful for videos and coffee. So when visual appearance counts as a sales factor, it's important to group products by visual similarity.

On HermanMiller, the products on the Chairs page got less office-like as users scrolled down the page. Gradually, the chairs were replaced by stools and benches. Unfortunately, there were some great office chairs at the bottom of the list, but some users gave up before they got that far. In one case, a user missed seeing a chair she would have preferred to the one she chose. She found this out only when we showed her the end of the list.

1800flowers shows visually similar things together. The Rose pages start with rose-only bouquets and then move on to other arrangements containing both roses and other flowers.

➡️ *Support navigation by letter for alphabetical lists.*

Alphabetical lists can be useful when users know what they're looking for. But on some sites, we watched frustrated users look for an item with a known name in a series of alphabetically ordered pages that were *numbered*.

- Reel: The Contemporary Classics listings were presented in an alphabetical list of 238 products that spanned eight pages. To find the movie *One Flew Over the Cuckoo's Nest*, the user had to guess which page it was on. He guessed right on the first try but said he was just lucky.

- Disney: A user tried to find a Winnie the Pooh doll in Collectibles and had to guess which of the 10 pages would contain items starting with "W."

Although both users eventually managed to navigate to the page containing the desired item, both of them grumbled about it.

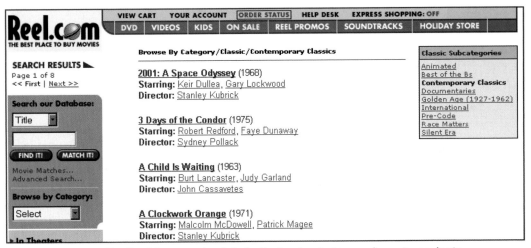

Reel's videos are in alphabetical order, but users have to navigate these pages by number. CP22

➡️ *Use both numbers (or letters) and Next / Previous for navigation among pages.*

Unless they were looking for a particular item in an ordered list, users generally went through the pages in linear order. In most cases, users clicked the Next option if there was one, but this does not mean numbered pages should be abandoned in favor of Next and Previous buttons.

Although random access to a numbered list vs. Next / Previous buttons did not prove to be a very important usability issue in our study, we believe it is best to allow users free access to all pages in a set of product listings, rather than forcing them to go through the pages in sequence. Our strongest recommendation, however, is that e-commerce sites use the alphabet — rather than numbers — when presenting alphabetized product lists.

Furniture and Boo let users go to the Next or Previous page, or jump to a specific page. On 1800flowers, users had to go back and forth in sequence. CP23

Images on Category Pages

Images of products are useful, and sometimes absolutely necessary, but a major trade-off exists between large, detailed images, or the faster download times afforded by "thumbnails" (small pictures that usually can be clicked to show a full-size image).

Fast-loading thumbnails are commonly used to speed up page download time. The real question is: How good do the thumbnails on category pages need to be?

Tip: Avoid using developer jargon like "thumbnail" in the interface. Users aren't generally familiar with design terms.

➡ *Image quality should be good enough to identify a known item.*

When a site carries merchandise that users could recognize from advertising or some other previous exposure, the thumbnails need to be good enough to support recognition of those items.

We saw this need on the video sites we tested. Users liked seeing covers of videos, but many of the pages that listed videos on Reel don't show the covers. One user complained about this lack, but then when he saw the On Sale page (which showed rows of video covers), he commented, "That's the way it should be. That's much better." We saw similar behavior on toy sites — one user scanned images of all 34 Barbie dolls looking for ones his wife wanted for her collection, and he quickly found Austrian Barbie by recognizing her picture.

➡ *Images should show the product characteristics*
that are most important to users.

The image producer must know which characteristics users need most to see. During testing, we looked for evidence that users were getting — or not getting — the information they wanted most from the thumbnail images on the product listing pages.

- Flower sites: The images on the category pages were good enough for users to identify one or two items they were interested in. They then used the product pages primarily to confirm the decision they'd made.

- BasketHaus: Users complained that the thumbnails were indistinct and didn't show the exact items in the basket. Users had to read the accompanying text to get an idea of what was in the basket (and there wasn't always enough detail there either).

- Living: When looking at bunk beds, one user rejected those that had a full-size bed on the bottom. She was looking for bunk beds that had built-in storage. From the thumbnails, she could spot which ones had full-size bottom bunks, but she had some trouble seeing whether the bottom bunk had a drawer beneath it.

It's hard to tell from these images which beds have drawers underneath. CP24

The product thumbnails on Boo (see Image CP20) were quite good, allowing users to see details of construction, like whether a jacket had a drawstring or how well it covered the wearer's neck. These large, detailed images unfortunately caused the product listing pages to download slowly, and users became impatient. Experiment with the size of thumbnails — find the smallest size that still conveys the information users want to see before clicking to view a larger, more detailed image.

It is difficult to see useful details on thumbnails of dark-colored products. Jcrew's Footwear page suffered from this problem, as did shoe images on Nordstrom. We wonder if it would have been better for them to use sketches instead of showing black blobs; however, we did not test any sites that used sketches.

➡ *Thumbnail images don't have to answer all the users' questions.*

If users are interested in a product, they'll click to learn more — and that's when they expect to see a larger and more detailed image that answers their questions.

Dark-colored images like these made it hard to see details. CP25

Winnowing

Many e-commerce sites have far too many products for the customer to consider all at once. Many users of these sites won't be successful unless the site helps them find the products they want — 27% of the sales catastrophes in our study were caused by failure to locate a suitable item. (We designed our tasks so that there was always at least one suitable item on the site.) People need to limit the number of visible offerings, or else they may miss the best product for their needs — and you lose a sale.

What is Winnowing?

We'd like to reintroduce an ancient word: *winnowing*. To winnow is to separate the useful from the non-useful, as in wheat from chaff. It also means to get rid of something undesirable or unwanted, to remove, separate, sift, and select. A broad selection of merchandise is good (as described in the Selling Strategies chapter), but a site with many choices must help users arrive at a manageable set to consider.

Winnowing capabilities separate great sites from good ones. The need for winnowing was most apparent on SmarterKids, where search or home page clicks often resulted in hundreds of products spread out over dozens of pages. SmarterKids is certainly not a bad site — users had many good things to say about it — but it was frustrating for users to find products that met the goals of our tasks, such as "software related to science for a 6-year-old" or "something to help a 10-year-old who's having trouble in math." Once users got to the right part of the site, there was no way to narrow the selection down further.

Winnowing is a subjective concept on e-commerce sites — no one offers a product unless they believe it's of interest to *someone*. And the definition of what's useful to a particular person varies as well, because people often refine their goals while shopping, or they may look for different items from one day to the next. So, we define winnowing as any method of interaction that lets the user refine a set of products, reducing the number of items in the set according to criteria chosen by the user.

Tip: The winnowing tool should also let users expand the set again.

Winnowing is more important for some sites than others. For small sites, it's probably overkill. But for sites that offer a wide selection of similar products, winnowing tools can decrease the chance that users will become overwhelmed and give up.

Examples of Winnowing Tools

Here is an overview of all the winnowing tools we saw in our test sites. Each tool is described in more detail below.

Site	Winnowing Tools	Optional / Required
Sears	Sears had two winnowing tools: • For tools, the user specified price range, brand name, or other factors, such as voltage. When the user clicked Search, the site returned the list of products that met the criteria.	Required — It's the only way to navigate to the product pages.
	• For microwaves, the user specified price range, color, brand, size, and several other factors. With each choice, the site dynamically updated the number of matching products. The user clicked View List to see the list.	Required — It's the only way to navigate to the product pages.
Furniture	Furniture had two winnowing tools: • The Furniture Finder	Optional
	• To find an item of furniture, users had to first specify the room, which then took them to a page asking them to pick the item, style, finish, and price range. The resulting page(s) displayed the set of products that match the criteria.	Required — It's the only way to navigate to the product pages.
Disney	The Gift Finder let the user specify the Disney character and type of product (clothing, toy, etc.).	Optional
Wal-Mart	The Gift Finder asked users to specify the occasion, recipient, and price range, then returned a page of suggestions. The user had no control over what type of items were shown, however.	Optional
Peet's	The Taste Guide asked five questions about the user's coffee-drinking behavior and preferences and then returned a list of suggested coffees.	Optional

Tools on Sears

We asked users to find a cordless drill with a power rating of about 10 volts. First, users clicked the Tools tab, then chose Portable Power Tools from the selection list, then Cordless Drills.

Because it had 33 cordless drills, Sears provided a winnowing page to narrow the selection further. This page allowed the user to identify a subset of drills based on features. Each time the user clicked the Search button, the list showed the number of products that matched the criteria.

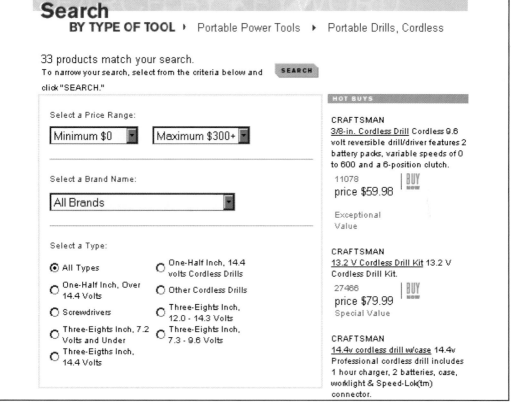

This winnowing page on Sears worked well except for the radio buttons, which were a little confusing. CP26

All the users who got to this point did succeed in finding a suitable drill. But the sizes and voltages were confusing — users had to study those carefully.

Microwaves on Sears

Sears had a different winnowing feature for microwaves. Unlike the method for finding tools, which required the user to click Search before the page reloaded, the microwave page updated dynamically as soon as the user specified each criterion, such as size or color.

In theory, this dynamic approach is more sophisticated and efficient (because it omits one click). In practice, it was quite confusing for about half of the users who tried it, because they didn't understand why the page kept changing.

Sometimes the page updated product aspects the user hadn't specified. For instance, if users picked an over-the-range microwave, the capacity and width were changed automatically. Compounding the problem, at 56k modem speed the site couldn't respond fast enough. If the user specified several products without pausing to let the site catch up, the site would respond only to the last criterion chosen. In these cases, users didn't get what they had asked for, and naturally, they became frustrated. Worth noting, Sears' microwave winnowing design is the only one we saw that offered an Undo option, which several people used.

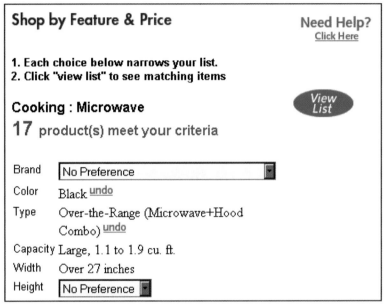

Users understood these winnowing criteria well enough, but the dynamic page updates confused them. CP27

It's possible that a dynamic winnowing tool could eventually prove superior to a click-to-update one, but only if it responds fast enough, and (even more important) if users expect the dynamic response.

Furniture.com

Like Sears, Furniture provided two different winnowing tools, but they did not work as well as Sears' tools. The most flawed tool was the Furniture Finder. Only three users tried it, and it wasn't clear to them how to fill out the form. When we reviewed the Furniture Finder after the tests, we couldn't quite figure it out either.

Our users couldn't figure out how to use the Furniture Finder ... and neither could we. CP28

It seemed to be buggy, sometimes simply reloading the same page. With only one exception, neither we nor our users were able to use it successfully.

The regular interface on Furniture was a winnowing tool in and of itself. But it also had some problems. The user had to select a furniture piece, style, finish, and price range before the website would deliver a search results page. Users had no way of knowing whether their criteria would yield 100 pieces or none. It was hard to adjust the criteria to get a reasonable set of furniture to look at. Worse, the style names, like Traditional and Country, weren't clear to the users.

Users weren't sure what the styles meant, and they had no way of knowing whether they'd get many hits or none. CP29

In contrast, Sears always showed how many things matched, for example: "17 product(s) meet your criteria."

Disney and Wal-Mart: Gift Finders

Gift finders are winnowing tools, also. Disney and Wal-Mart both had gift finders, but we obtained only a little data about them because most users didn't try them. Only two or three people tried Disney's gift finder. In one case, it failed to find any stuffed Winnie the Pooh dolls, even though the user seemed to have filled out the search form completely and correctly. One user tried to use Wal-Mart's gift finder to locate a car seat but gave up after the gift finder didn't find any seats.

➡ *Allow winnowing by the most useful differentiating factors for that type of product.*

From the patterns of user behavior we saw on different sites, we can identify ways in which the sites could have helped users winnow more than they did. Often there was a particular factor that people wanted to use:

- **Toys by age.** When buying for children, the age of the child is a key factor. All users demonstrated at least some concern about age appropriateness of toys. Both SmarterKids and eToys provided links based on the age of the child. (Disney's version, allowing the user to search for "Youth" or "Infant," wasn't specific enough.) The problem on SmarterKids was that other navigation tactics such as search yielded results for all ages, not the age range of the page the user had been on. Users found this discrepancy annoying. In contrast, when users searched from eToys' 3-year-old page, it returned only things that were appropriate for 3-year-olds. This approach worked better.

If users searched from eToys' 3-year-old page, all the results were items appropriate for a "3 yrs" page. CP30

- **Clothing by size.** On all the clothing sites, we watched most users exhibit the same pattern of behavior: They would find an item they wanted and then look to see if it was available in their size. When an item wasn't available, no one looked for it in a different size. We think it might be better if clothing sites first determined the user's size (from measurements, since sizes vary so much), and then showed only available items in that size range. Fit, however, is a subjective experience, so it might be necessary for the site to obtain more detail about the customer's measurements and preference for loose- or tight-fitting clothes.

- **Videos by media.** Reel and TowerRecords both showed all the variations of media and languages for each title. If a customer has only a VHS player, there's no need to see DVDs and laserdiscs. Offering every possible format increases the possibility that the customer will buy the wrong thing. We saw one user get a DVD instead of a VHS and another user mistakenly choose a video with Spanish subtitles. Finding a VHS or DVD format that would play on a Danish VHS or DVD player was even more difficult. (Read more about problems with abbreviations in the International Users chapter.)

- **Shopping on a budget.** Some customers have only a limited amount of money to spend and may wish to winnow out products that exceed their budgets. eToys let users specify a price range, and several used this feature successfully when we asked them to stay within a budget. 1800flowers had a similar feature, but none of our users tried it.

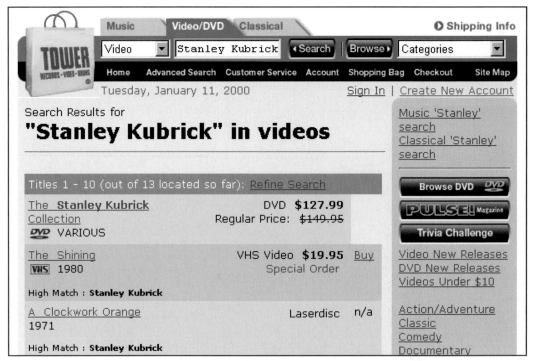

TowerRecords shows VHS, DVD, and laserdiscs all mixed together. Chances are good that the user is interested in only one of these formats. CP31

➡️ *Pick winnowing criteria your customers understand.*

The Taste Guide on Peet's offered an interesting way to make coffee choices. After asking five questions about taste preferences, the site presented the user with a list of suggested coffees. Several questions seemed odd, however, especially one that asked about "winey, fruity" flavors. Users weren't quite sure what this meant. So, although this winnowing tool showed promise (three users tried it, and one ended up choosing one of the recommended coffees), Peet's could explain the wording of some questions.

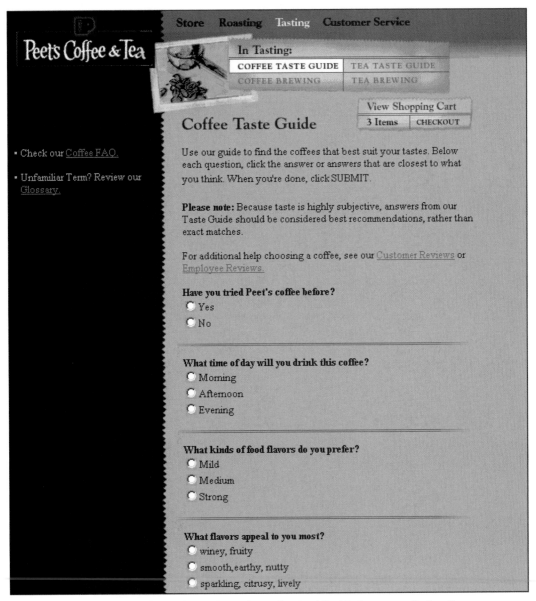

Store   Roasting   Tasting   Customer Service

Peet's Coffee & Tea

In Tasting:

| COFFEE TASTE GUIDE | TEA TASTE GUIDE |
| COFFEE BREWING | TEA BREWING |

View Shopping Cart

| 3 Items | CHECKOUT |

• Check our Coffee FAQ.

• Unfamiliar Term? Review our Glossary.

Coffee Taste Guide

Use our guide to find the coffees that best suit your tastes. Below each question, click the answer or answers that are closest to what you think. When you're done, click SUBMIT.

Please note: Because taste is highly subjective, answers from our Taste Guide should be considered best recommendations, rather than exact matches.

For additional help choosing a coffee, see our Customer Reviews or Employee Reviews.

Have you tried Peet's coffee before?
- Yes
- No

What time of day will you drink this coffee?
- Morning
- Afternoon
- Evening

What kinds of food flavors do you prefer?
- Mild
- Medium
- Strong

What flavors appeal to you most?
- winey, fruity
- smooth, earthy, nutty
- sparkling, citrusy, lively

Peet's Taste Guide is a winnowing tool that helps users find coffees they might like. This design worked reasonably well, but it might have worked better if users understood the question about flavors. CP32

It's not necessarily true that the product specifications make good winnowing criteria, as we saw during the Sears microwave task. For example, most consumers probably wouldn't know the exact cubic measurement (US or metric) they wanted when buying a microwave. Sears' Feature & Price page tried to address the measurement problem by classifying microwaves as compact, medium, large, or extra large, but this classification wasn't entirely satisfactory.

When users filled out the microwave specifications form, they tended to start at the top and work their way down, choosing criteria in the order presented. But as we discovered, this was not at all how users approached the process of choosing a microwave normally. They thought not in terms of watts and cubic feet, but rather in terms of what *foods* they wanted the microwave to cook.

- One user wanted to know, "What's the difference between medium, one cubic foot, and large size? I want to be able to put a small pizza in it, but not get lost inside the machine. A Hungry Man [frozen dinner brand] should be able to fit inside."

- Another user first talked about the types of food she planned to cook (mostly leftovers and popcorn). Then she stated how much she had to spend. She didn't have unlimited money but didn't want to get something too cheap. When we asked her if she could find a microwave based on what she'd just said, she pointed out that the site didn't seem to be set up to work that way.

These user comments call for a rather different set of winnowing criteria than the one the Sears site offered. So, although we applaud Sears for their efforts at helping customers narrow the selection, we'd like to see a winnowing process that more closely matches the way consumers approach their buying decisions.

Tip: Go to a store that sells products your site sells and watch the sales people assist customers for a day or two. Good sales clerks know which questions to ask, and these questions would probably make better winnowing criteria than the product specifications.

▶ *Support search as a winnowing tactic.*

We observed that users sometimes searched to narrow down a broad set of choices. Search is an important function to support, because it can work for you — or against you:

Fortunately, the search function on SmarterKids could get users out of a wrong category. Unfortunately, a search started on the Software tab for "space" returned results for all types of products, not just software. This failure to limit by chosen category was frustrating for users who were trying to find software related to space.

The dilemma is how to detect when the user needs a full search instead of a refinement search. Some sites use a "new search" button to return users to the top level and a "search again within these results" option for refinement searches. We didn't test any sites that used refinement, however, so we can't comment on how well those options actually work. (For more information about refinement searches, see the Search chapter.)

Product Comparisons

An essential element of the buying experience is comparison shopping. Many websites don't — but should — support product comparisons. Without a tool designed to help with comparison, a user must click the first potential item of interest, review its details, click back to the product listing, click the second potential item, and continue back and forth until the right item is found. User interface engineers call this behavior "pogo-sticking," which refers to a spring-loaded children's jumping toy. We saw many instances of pogo-sticking in our tests as users tried to determine how items differed.

➡️ *Provide a way to compare the details of similar items.*

Our users wanted a way to compare products when shopping for furniture, car seats, appliances, and in some cases, clothing.

One user wanted to compare Smart Fit and Room-to-Grow child car seats on Wal-Mart. "It would be nice if this had the comparison like Sears did. … Other than price, all I see are minor things. This more expensive one doesn't have a level indicator … but it's $10 more." Finally, he decided to buy the cheaper car seat, but he never determined why there was a $10 difference, which bothered him.

Another user wanted to compare bunk beds on Living. The online store had a mission loft bed on one page for $494 and on another page for $629. "I'm assuming it's better quality." Both show the same picture. She said the difference might be size. She printed out both pages to compare them, but can't find any real difference. "Dimensions are the same … this one's heavier."

The product-comparison features seemed to be more important on some sites than others. No one complained about the lack of a way to compare products on the flower, coffee, toy, music, or video sites. And we didn't observe much pogo-sticking on these sites either. So, in the absence of problems and user complaints, some sites might do just fine without comparison features.

➡️ *Design comparison tables to highlight differences.*

Sears and HermanMiller were the only two sites we tested that provided any explicit means to compare products. HermanMiller's site had a table showing the features of their chairs. Three out of nine users saw this table. They liked using it to compare all the chairs at once, but it bothered them to scroll horizontally, because then they could no longer see the row headings.

Some rows showed "Yes" for all chairs. Showing a common feature does not help the user detect the differences among models. It might be useful to know about that feature when comparing these chairs to those from another site, however.

We've got chairs for every size, every budget, all at extremely reasonable prices, and all ergonomically designed for healthful support.

And when you buy any chair between now and January 31, you're automatically entered in our **Office for the New Millennium Giveaway!**

Every chair in our "Office Chairs" section is eligible. Your chair order enters your name in our random drawing (one entry per person, please). You could win sleek, mobile, **high-tech office furniture** that's valued at $7,000! And since it's one of those no-purchase-necessary, void-where-prohibited deals, you can drop us a **note** with the subject "Enter The Office Of The New Millennium Giveaway" to enter, too.

Everybody deserves a good seat, and when you buy yours don't forget to choose either our UPS/RPS or standard freight carrier delivery option, and we'll ship your chair FREE OF CHARGE anywhere in the continental USA. Shop from anywhere on our site, or check out the convenient list below. And take comfort!

Work Chairs

	Aeron	Equa 2	Ergon 3	Equa 1	Ambi	Reaction	Avian
Base Price	$749.00	$479.00	$449.00	$364.00	$349.00	$363.30	$225.00
Adj. Arms	Yes	Available	Available	No	Available	Available	No
Adj. Back Height	No	No	Yes	No	Yes	Yes	No
Adj. Lumbar Support	Yes	Yes	No	No	No	No	No
Adj. Seat Depth	No	No	No	No	No	Yes	No
Adj. Tilt Tension	Yes	Yes	Yes	Yes	Yes	Yes	Yes
Forward Tilt Angle	Yes	No	No	No	No	Available	No
Tilt Lock	Yes	No	Yes	No	Yes	Yes	No
Pneumatic Lift	Yes	Yes	Yes	Yes	Yes	Yes	Yes
12 Year Warranty	Yes	Yes	Yes	Yes	Yes	Yes	Yes

Users who saw this table liked the concept of comparing all the chairs but disliked having to scroll horizontally. CP33

An inconsistent list of features draws attention to differences that might not exist. When users compared products on Sears and the side-by-side comparison showed a feature listed for product A but not for product B, they couldn't decide whether product B lacked the feature or the comparison just didn't mention it.

Even on sites without a comparison facility, it would help if product pages for similar products contained the same sets of information in a similar format. We saw users attempt to compare infant car seats on Wal-Mart. They pogo-sticked from page to page, trying to pick out relevant details from the text and keep them in mind when they looked at subsequent products.

The most important element of designing a product comparison facility is knowing which features your customers want to compare. The dilemma for content providers is that it might not be best — from a usability perspective — to rely on information that comes directly from the manufacturer. After all, how many manufacturers clearly list the features that their products *lack*? Some businesses might not have the legal right to rewrite information provided by the manufacturer, however.

➡ *Let customers choose the products to be compared.*

If you have a large number of products, let customers choose which products to compare. HermanMiller got away with putting all the chairs in one chart only because they carry a small number of models.

With 33 cordless drills and 114 microwaves, Sears needed to provide good comparison features. In our test, Sears was the cutting-edge site in the product-comparison arena. Their site had two different approaches to comparison, one in Tools and one in Appliances. For cordless drills, the user first picked two to four drills to compare. The selected drills were shown side by side after the user clicked the Compare button.

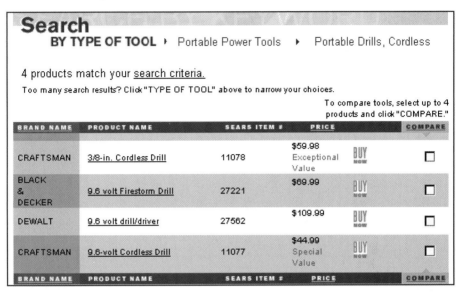

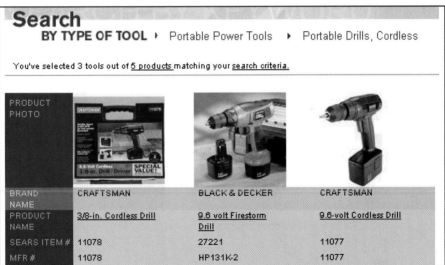

On Sears, the user could select as many as four drills by checking the Compare box. The resulting page showed the drills side by side. The type and format of the information for each drill varied, however, making direct comparisons more difficult than they should have been. CP34

This method of comparison worked reasonably well. Users understood the mechanics and liked seeing the comparison information. But it was still difficult to compare products directly, because each drill showed different information listed in a different format. Worse, users had to pogo-stick down a level each time they wanted to read details for a particular drill.

Comparing microwaves on Sears was more difficult than comparing drills. After the user finished picking the winnowing criteria, clicking the View List button displayed the list of microwaves. Users generally wanted to see pictures at this point, but the site displayed only a list of text links.

The "add to list" approach confused and frustrated our users. They wanted all the microwaves to fit on one screen without scrolling. And they strongly objected when the image of the microwave appeared in the wrong color. CP35

From the list, users could click "add to list" for microwaves they were interested in. Clicking the "compare" button brought up a side-by-side list. Although all users who tested this feature succeeded, it was more confusing and less easy to learn than the comparison feature for drills.

Once they were looking at the side-by-side comparison, users disliked having to scroll. One user commented that Sears should omit the right part of the page (where the list was) so he could see more of the microwaves. Worse, the color of the microwave in the image often didn't match the color the user had chosen. Users were quite disturbed by this discrepancy.

Conclusion

Users can't buy products that they can't find. Along with a good search facility, category pages are essential to helping users locate the products they want. Good sites show clearly organized, representative merchandise starting right on the home page. As e-commerce sites expand their offerings, they often expose weaknesses in their category pages. When the available selection within any category becomes too large for the customer to see all the items quickly, winnowing tools become important. Good tools help the customer to eliminate less interesting merchandise and to compare features among the few items most similar to their purchase criteria. Providing such tools is a key strategy for improving the customer experience and increasing sales.

Search

" *Site designers must create sophisticated — but simple —
search engines capable of delivering the goods on the
user's first search query.*"

A Model for Search

To build a website that enables your customers to search successfully, you must look at the process from the user's point of view. Our tests showed that the search process can be split into the following aspects:

- **The user notices the website supports search.** Users do not always know to look for search functionality when they enter a website. Our users told us they wanted a clearly visible search box on every page.

- **The user formulates a wish.** The search engines our users tested misinterpreted many perfectly reasonable wishes and questions that our users had. (For example, "I want to buy yellow roses for my mother.") Site designers and developers must learn what users actually search for and tune search engines accordingly.

- **The user expresses the wish as a search query string.** Many of our users' searches failed because the search engines were literal and unforgiving — spelling errors, synonyms, variant forms of keywords, and multiple-word input were small mistakes that caused big failures.

- **The user enters the search string and submits the query.** Our users wanted the simplest possible search: one search box, one search button.

- **The user receives and interprets the search results.** The user must then decide whether the results are satisfactory, or if a refinement or new search is necessary. Interpreting the results was often a challenge to our users. Too often, they were confused by results that were seemingly irrelevant, overwhelming in number, or written in technical jargon.

If the search fails, the website provides an error or "No Results" message.

- **The user notices the message.** Making sure the user notices the message is hard. Some No Results pages looked like search results pages.

- **The user interprets the message.** What you say, and how you say it, in a No Results page can make the difference between a sale and a sales catastrophe. Not all of our users understood the message. Some thought they understood the message when, in fact, they didn't understand it at all.

- **The user corrects the problem if possible.** If the user properly understands the message and acts upon it, the search continues. If the message is not understood, the user gives up on search or resorts to other means.

Any of these process components can fail for a multitude of reasons. Breaking the search process down into discrete aspects is useful, because each of the aspects is manageable. The process is easier to optimize piece-by-piece than as a whole. The rest of this chapter analyzes the search process in the light of this model. In the following sections we will show you what went wrong during our tests, and how you can prevent similar problems on your website.

Search Visibility

Some of our users complained about the lack of a search engine on some sites that actually did offer searching. At the end of many of our tests, the users were uncertain whether there was a search facility that they had overlooked. One user said, "They must smash it [the search facility] right in my face, or else I won't see it." Another user cited as one of his dislikes "the fact that there wasn't a search box or blank that hits you in the face when you first open [the website]."

➡️ *Use a text box instead of a link to a search page.*

Several users told us that when they looked for the search function, they looked for "one of the little boxes." Tabs and links to a separate search page just didn't work for them.

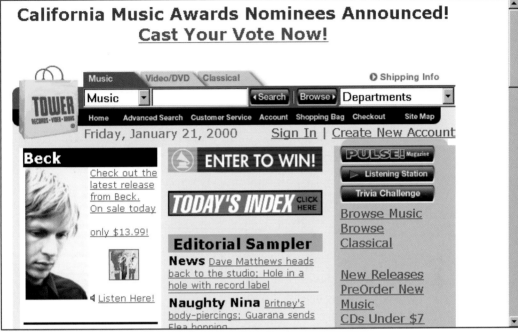

On the TowerRecords home page, our users had no problems locating the search text box. S1

The search link on this Nordstrom page was not easy to find. The search link is located in the middle of three tiny links (checkout | search | help) just to the right of center at the top of the page. S2

Compare the screenshots of TowerRecords and Nordstrom. Our users had no problems locating the search text box on TowerRecords. On Nordstrom, however, several users looked in vain for the search function. Expecting a text box, they did not notice the search link at the top of the page.

One user, who eventually did find the search link on Nordstrom, complained: "Why would you have to work so hard to get to where you'd want to buy something? I'm looking for a Lego watch, and it took me 10 minutes to find the search box. And it was in the smallest of print."

When a user on the HermanMiller Product Showroom page accidentally triggered the search function, the woman in a chair changed into a man's head (upper left corner of both screenshots) and a search dialog box opened. The problem was that the "Find" link itself was hard to find. S3

The HermanMiller Product Showroom page had a technologically interesting — but functionally ineffective — search feature. One of our users discovered it only by accident. When the mouse pointer hovered over the word "Find," a man's head appeared and a search dialog box opened.

We do not recommend this kind of feature, because most of our other users did not discover the search link at all. Even one of our experienced facilitators missed it. Many people do not know how to sweep a mouse over a page to discover hidden features.

A Case Study: www.useit.com

Jakob Nielsen redesigned his website's home page — www.useit.com (which we did not test in this study) — to replace a link to a search page with a search text box on the home page. As shown in the before and after screenshots, this was the only change Nielsen made.

Before the change, Search was just a link in the upper right corner of the page.

After the change from a link to a text box, use of the search function increased dramatically. s4

This minor change created a major result. Use of the search function on the site exploded:

- Searches per week before the change: 1,161
- Searches per week after the change: 2,223.

The number of searches increased 91%, while traffic on useit.com increased by only 2% during those two weeks.

We don't know, however, whether making search more available actually improved search results. We know only that nearly twice as many people tried the search function. Some people might equate an increase in the number of searches with an increase in the success rate of those searches. We don't want you to do this. We want you to back up the numbers with your own observations to see whether your customers' searches are indeed more successful.

➡ Put the search box on every page.

People want easy access to search. Start by assuming that there should be a search box on every page. Then, remove the box only from page sequences in which users would risk losing their work. For example, going off on a search might be hazardous when a user is in the middle of filling out a form or during the checkout process. In this study, however, we didn't see any users get into trouble because they started to search on a particular page.

On eToys, our users liked the clearly visible search box on the shopping cart page, "instead of having to go back to the previous page." S5

Search Formulation

Before your users can search, they must formulate a wish or a question, for example "I want to buy yellow roses for my mother," or "If I don't like the new cupboard I ordered, what can I do?" This chapter explains how to discover the high-level goals that users pursue when they search on your website and how you can tune your website in accordance with those goals.

➡ Learn what your customers actually search for.

To tune your search engine, you must know what typical customers search for on your website. You cannot learn this by guesswork or armchair analysis.

Tip: Perform usability tests. For a thorough discussion of usability testing, see the Methodology chapter.

Tip: Listen to technical support and customer service calls. Find out, in their own words, what customers ask for, and how they phrase their questions. Even more instructive is to hear how your best technical support and customer service representatives express themselves when they explain to customers how to solve the most common problems.

Analyze search logs.

Ask your webmaster to log each query string for several weeks or more. Rank the queries by frequency of occurrence. Some search engines have built-in facilities to provide such statistics. If your search engine doesn't, you can sort and count the queries using a spreadsheet program.

Because we conducted our study autonomously, we had no access to statistics from any of our test sites. We do, however, have a list of the top-100 search strings from approximately 20,000 queries of Jakob Nielsen's website useit.com. The numbers show how many times each query string was input by visitors.

Query String Frequency for Jakob Nielsen's Website useit.com					
frames	553	newsletter	66	bandwidth	45
intranet	333	scrolling	66	alertbox	45
navigation	274	back button	64	breadcrumb	45
search	221	focus groups	63	hci	44
usability	170	design	63	portals	42
css	147	javascript	63	accessibility	42
color	144	content	61	icons	40
wap	142	registration	59	focus group	40
heuristic	130	help	59	colors	39
subscribe	111	search engine	59	amazon	39
flash	107	yahoo	58	download time	39
heuristics	106	html	56	e-mail	39
xml	105	tabs	56	banner ads	38
portal	105	banner	55	hypertext	38
style sheets	98	micropayments	54	consistency	37
writing	97	response time	54	screen size	37
site map	94	graphics	54	pdf	37
e-commerce	92	microcontent	53	sun	37
personalization	90	frame	53	why frames suck	36
writing for the web	89	top ten	51	user testing	36
forms	86	affiliate	51	tables	36
font	85	survey	50	zipf	36
search engines	82	marketing	49	ecommerce	35
testing	81	web design	48	dhtml	35
asp	81	splash	48	font size	35
links	79	java	48	interface	35
advertising	76	animation	48	multimedia	35
test	75	resolution	47	url	35
fonts	73	google	47	community	34
webtv	72	screen resolution	46	gui	34
email	72	browser	45	user interface	34
heuristic evaluation	71	trust	45	international	34
information architecture	70	statistics	45	evaluation	34
usability testing	67				

Note that both "focus groups" and "focus group" appear in the list, as #38 and #75 respectively. Combined, they would have ranked #15. There are several other similar pairs, such as "heuristic" (#9) and "heuristics" (#12).

Also, note that of the top-100 queries, 76% are one word. Another 2% of the queries are one word with a hyphen. The remaining 22% of the queries are two words or more. In contrast to the predominance of one-word queries on useit.com, only 46% of the 151 queries in our e-commerce study consisted of just one word.

Real data about the length and nature of search queries are important to prevent development team holy wars over the need vs. difficulty of providing or teaching phrase searching to users.

If the search queries on your website are mostly common phrases or titles in the subject matter (as on useit.com), you can just enter a list of the most common phrases that your search engine can recognize in a simple character-by-character comparison. If, however, the multiple-word search queries on your site are unpredictable and complicated (as they were in our study), you may have to support full-fledged phrase-searching. (We discuss phrase searching later in this chapter in the "Search Expression" section.) Analyzing the query strings from your search engine log can help you to:

- Decide whether there are any frequent queries that need special treatment.
- Discover synonyms your customers use and configure your search engine to recognize them.
- Find out which goods or services your customers search for that are not available on your site.
- Learn which important words your customers sometimes misspell.
- Determine which keywords you might want to include in FAQs, Help, or other documentation.
- Decide whether to make often-used terms prominent on your home page.

In addition to the above, you can use the search log to test the quality of results your search engine delivers on frequent queries. Enter each query string in your top-100 list, or each query that accounts for more than 0.2% of the total number of queries submitted to your search engine. Subjectively evaluate the usefulness of the results the search engine delivers for each query. Are the best answers at the top of the list, "above the fold?"

When you analyze search logs, always remember that what the user entered and what the user was actually looking for might be very different things. To find out whether there are any important differences, you must conduct usability tests and continue to collect information on customer goals using all possible means. Customers' needs will change over time — and so will the top-100 query list. Search log analysis is not a one-time endeavor — it's an ongoing process.

➡️ *Adjust your search engine to respond to how your customers actually search.*

Once you have found out what your customers actually search for, you must configure your search engine so that it better answers their needs and queries. The following guidelines and tips present detailed advice on just how to fine-tune your search engine.

➡️ *Provide special treatment of frequent queries.*

Some queries occur so often that you might want to consider giving them special treatment by creating custom search result pages. In our test, eToys delivered custom results pages for its most popular toys, but SmarterKids returned only standard search results pages on all toy queries.

When our users typed the name of a well-liked toy (for example, Thomas the Tank, Barney, or Hot Wheels) into the eToys search text box, the search engine returned specially designed category pages instead of the usual set of links. This result worked quite well for most of our users, and they thought it was great. The custom pages confused some users, however, because the page layout was different from the standard search result page they expected.

The eToys strategy of delivering custom pages for its most popular toys did not work perfectly. Spelling can make a big difference in how a search engine responds. When our users typed in "Hot Wheels," they were treated to a custom page dedicated to Hot Wheels. When they typed "hotwheel," however, they got a standard search results page.

These screenshots clearly illustrate the difference between a custom search results page (left s6) and a standard search results page (right s7). Most, but not all, of our users preferred the custom page.

Consider making a customized results page if:

- The query occurs often enough to justify special treatment.

- The query is a general and vague term that indicates the user needs a general introduction to the website. Example: Searching for "toys" or "kids" on eToys, or searching for "usability" or "test" on useit.com.

- The query generates too many results. Most of our users looked at the results "above the fold" on the first results page. Fewer looked on the rest of page 1. Only a few determined users made it past page 3.

- There is no existing single page that provides a reasonable overview of the product or concept.

➡️ *Support search for nonproduct terms.*

Search engines aren't just for products and services. They are also for policies and customer support. We were surprised at how many of our users entered nonproduct terms into search engines — without success. Site developers might assume that search engines are only for products, but as our users demonstrated, customers expect much more. Note that if our users had called customer support, any service representative could have answered the nonproduct questions in the table below immediately.

Nonproduct Search Queries That Search Engines Did Not Support

Site	User searched for			Meaning
Boo	"returns"	"free returns"	"exchange"	product returns, exchange policy
eToys	"gift reg"	"gift records"		gift registry
Furniture	"catalog"			paper catalog (not available)
Wal-Mart	"price protection"			price guarantee
1800flowers	"payment"			how to buy an item

None of the websites we tested appeared to support nonproduct searches. Take, for instance, an episode we observed on 1800flowers. One of our users clicked "Buy now" on a category (product overview) page to purchase a box of cakes. The site took him to a product page instead of a checkout page where he could complete the purchase. Confused, he entered a search query for "payment" to find out how to buy the cakes. The search engine returned a "No products found" message. The user asked in exasperation, "Don't they want my money?"

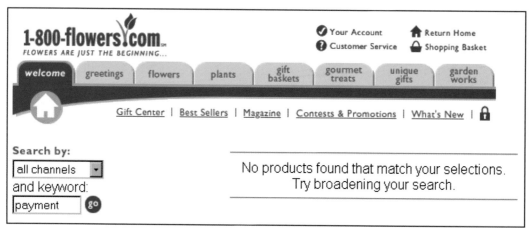

The search engine on 1800flowers interpreted a user's query about "payment" as a product it could not find. s8

➡ *Tell customers what you don't have.*

Just as their brick-and-mortar counterparts generally do, Web stores should promptly inform customers when they are looking for something the store doesn't have. A user on Peet's wanted flavored coffees but couldn't find any. A search for "flavored" returned information on flavored teas. A search for "flavored coffees" returned nothing. It would have been helpful to her if the search results had simply told her that the site doesn't sell flavored coffees. It would have been even more helpful if Peet's had promised to consider adding flavored coffees to its product line. It would have been most helpful if Peet's had told her where she could buy flavored coffees.

There is a difference between merchandise a site sells but doesn't have in stock, and merchandise the site doesn't sell at all. Reel and TowerRecords both sell videos and other products. Both websites had information on many videos and CDs that they did not have in stock, stating where appropriate that the product was hard to get. When our users searched for an unavailable title, the websites often returned useful information about the title — and added that the product was not available. Our users liked this, because the website acted just like a knowledgeable, service-minded sales clerk.

Both Reel and TowerRecords handled out-of-stock items with reasonable grace, but neither site came right out and said they didn't carry an item. If people assume you sell certain products that, in fact, you don't sell, it's good customer service to tell them so.

In another case, our users' searches were unsuccessful, because they quite reasonably assumed items would be in stock that actually were never in stock due to certain limitations on the website. CustomDisc sold music by the track, making custom CDs of songs chosen by the customer from CustomDisc's huge 200,000-song inventory. Unfortunately, CustomDisc's inventory was not limitless, and selections were restricted to only some popular artists and songs, mainly from the past.

One user typed "elvis" in the search box. CustomDisc returned "Melvis / The Megatones." The user searched again on "presley," and got one result for a band called Presley. The user then typed "elvis presley." CustomDisc returned a message that it could find no matches. "At this point, I'd say forget Elvis," said the disgruntled user. What the user didn't know — and the search engine did not explain — was that CustomDisc could not sell Elvis Presley songs due to copyright restrictions.

CustomDisc explained well why many searches for popular artists fail. This information, however, was located in Help, which only one of our users saw. This explanation should have been part of the error message for all failed searches for music.

Can't Find a Song?

Most songs are owned by an artist or record label. If they choose not to participate in our CustomDisc service, then we cannot legally sell their music. However, we're constantly expanding our roster of artists and record labels, so you may want to subscribe to **our newsletter** for updates on new music.

You may not find every song you want. But you'll probably find more than you planned. With over 200,000 songs available for your disc, browsing CustomDisc is your best bet.

CustomDisc showed the right information in the wrong place. This message (or something shorter) should have been shown whenever searches for songs and artists failed. S9

Search Expression

After your customers have formulated a wish or a question, they need to express it as a query (search string) that they can enter into the search box. For example, the wish: "I want to buy yellow roses for my mother" could be expressed as "yellow," "roses," or "roses, yellow." The question: "If I don't like the new cupboard I ordered, what can I do?" might be expressed as "return policy," or "take it back."

Most users know that you can't just enter a natural language question into the search box. This chapter tells you what you can do to prevent common problems that arise when users express a reasonable wish or question in a few search keywords.

➡ *Accept synonyms typically used by your customers.*

Customer queries may contain words that refer to products or concepts that do not appear on your website, because the designer just didn't anticipate them:

- On Wal-Mart, we asked our users to search for "a suitable car seat for a baby."
  - One of our users searched for "Child Seat" — no results.
  - The user then searched for "Children's Seat" — no results.
  - The user then searched for "Child Restraints" — no results.
  - The user finally complained, "These are commonly used terms!" — and gave up.
- On Living, we asked our users to search for a kids' bunk bed. We phrased the task so we did not disclose the term "bunk bed." Several users searched for "children's bed" but got no results. One user concluded, "They don't have any children's beds."
- On HermanMiller, we asked our users to find information about a "cleverly designed bag for a portable PC, which also functions as a desktop." HermanMiller calls this bag a "Lap Dog." Our users entered the following keywords in their unsuccessful searches to find the Lap Dog: "portable," "brief," "case," "laptop," and "bag."

Tip: Make sure the search engine recognizes synonyms customers use. This tip applies even if the synonyms don't appear anywhere on the website or in the product database. Add them to the search engine's dictionary.

Tip: Return the same results whether the user inputs the word that your website normally recognizes or a synonym that you've added.

Tip: Show the user, in an inoffensive way, the "correct" term your website uses for the product or concept. This feedback will help your customer understand why the results do not seem to correspond to the query, because the website has substituted the "correct" word for the synonym.

Tip: Elicit synonyms from your customers. During the usability testing and development process, show customers representative products from a product category. Ask them, "What do you call this?"

➡ *Consider offering limited vocabulary search.*

Instead of asking a website search engine to recognize users' sometimes unpredictable text input, it is often more efficient to present a number of options in a selection list. Limited Vocabulary Search (LVS) eliminates some of the main problems with text searches:

- The user does not know which choices are available.
- The user misspells a search term.
- The user enters an unrecognizable synonym into the website search engine.

LVS helps the user both in formulating and expressing a search query.

We are *not* recommending that LVS should replace text box searches. We *are* suggesting, however, that LVS can be a valuable supplement to search engine functionality.

Furniture, for example, used LVS lists but still offered the more versatile text box search. Furniture offered its customers LVS options on the category pages of each of the major subsections of the website, such as the Dining Room Furniture department.

Our users had some success with Furniture's LVS function for the Dining Room page, although one user complained that important search criteria were missing — for example, the number of people that a table could accommodate. Another user commented that wine racks were not available under the LVS dining room options. The search criteria seemed based on the standard parameters available in the search engine database — not on people's real-life needs. Usability tests would have revealed this oversight.

Each of the selection lists contained options that users could select. The default initial selection in each selection list was "All" — for example, "All Pieces" or "All Price Ranges." S10

Despite LVS shortcomings, our users generally appreciated this form of search. They used it frequently and successfully.

➡ *Make your search engine error-tolerant.*

Many of our users' searches failed because the search engines did not tolerate the slightest deviation from the "correct" input. The rest of this section describes ways in which you can make your search engine more accommodating to your customers.

➡ *Tolerate spelling errors.*

People don't always spell correctly. A website should be tolerant of spelling errors. Slight spelling errors should not prevent your customers from finding your products.

- On CustomDisc, a user went to search and typed "bee-gees." The user volunteered, "My spelling's lousy though, so I don't know." The "bee-gees" query produced no results. The user then tried "bee gees" (no hyphen). This query produced two song tracks. (Despite its huge inventory, CustomDisc can only offer some, but not all, of the most popular music.)

- On Reel, a user wanted a movie about "Babar," the elephant. The user searched for "Barbar" and got no relevant results. Another user unsuccessfully searched for *Dr. Zhivago* by spelling it "Dr. Zhivargo." Reel stocked both these videos. A more spelling-lenient search engine could have returned positive results.

- On Peet's, a user searched for "coffe maker." Again, an error-tolerant search engine could have turned a failed search into a success.

Many people are quite aware of their imperfect spelling abilities. One of our users said that search was fine, "if I spelled it right."

Here's how some of our users coped — or failed to cope — with spelling challenges:

- He knew that the main actor in *One Flew Over The Cuckoo's Nest* is Nicholson. He considered entering Nicholson in the search box, but he gave up because he was not sure how to spell Nicholson's name correctly.

- Another user copied "cuckoo" from the written task description the facilitator had given him.

- Yet another user, who wanted to find Arnold Schwarzenegger movies, said he wasn't sure how to spell Schwarzenegger, so he entered "Arnold," which worked.

Tip: Provide a search engine that includes a spell-check function. A word processor can do it — so why not a website? Spell check makes it more likely that customers will find what they look for even if their spelling is not perfect. Note, however, that most websites use special terms that you must add to the spell checker's dictionary.

Tip: Make frequent misspellings "aliases" of the correct words. In this context, an "alias" is any misspelled or misused word that you instruct the search engine to recognize as "correct" for a certain item.

In the example we saw previously in the "Search Formulation" section of this chapter, eToys tolerated two different spellings for the same thing: "hot wheels" and "hotwheel" (Images S6 and S7). The misspelling brought up a different page than the correctly spelled word, however. We recommend that even misspelled words bring up the same results as correctly spelled words.

TowerRecords compensated quite well for misspelled queries. S11

TowerRecords boasted about its smart search engine: "We are very proud of our new search engine. It will account for misspellings, use a thesaurus, and search every bit of our data to find exactly what you are looking for. Just give us a name, a hint or a clue, and we'll figure it out for you."

The TowerRecords search engine was indeed better than average, as these examples show:

- A search for "Fatasia" worked just as well as a search for "*Fantasia.*"
- A search for "parth of glory" worked just as well as a search for "Paths of Glory."
- A search for "Dr. Zarvago" located "Doctor Zhivago." (Reel failed on a similar search.)

As good as the TowerRecords smart search engine was, however, one of our users disagreed with the "Just give us … a hint" claim. He tried searching for a video with "James Bond" — and got no results.

➡ *Support variant forms of keywords.*

In some cases, searches were unsuccessful because our users entered a variant form of a keyword. Some search engines, for example, couldn't recognize the plural form of a keyword, because they were configured to accept only the singular form.

- On Living, several users typed "Bunk beds" into the search box and got nothing. "Bunk bed" would have done the job. The facilitator had to help one of these users. After the test, that user said: "I really disliked having to take away the 's' on bunk beds. I thought that was an almost insurmountable problem. I would have never guessed."
- On 1800flowers, we saw users search for "tulip" and "tulips," "rose" and "roses."
- On eToys, a user searched for "hotwheel," with and without an embedded space separator, with or without a hyphen, singular or plural. Examples: "hot wheel," "hotwheel," "hot wheels," and "hot-wheel." The user was confused because the search results were quite different. Our analysis reveals that the website itself spells Hot Wheels in at least two different ways.

➡ *Accommodate multiple-word input.*

Some of our users were confused by their search results when a site didn't respond as expected to their multiple-word queries. They didn't understand that the website looked for exact matches only.

Of the 151 queries in our tests, 54% consisted of more than one word. Many of these queries were either movie titles or names like "Winnie the Pooh."

No users enclosed multiple words in enclosing quotes, which are used in this chapter only to set off query strings from surrounding text.

We noticed two kinds of search strategies in our tests — inexperienced and experienced:

- The inexperienced users' search queries often approached natural language. The users entered as much information as possible, for instance: "*One Flew over the Cuckoo's Nest.*" We know from other studies that many novice users believe they're doing the computer a favor by entering as much information as possible. They don't realize that computers are literal. Unlike human sales clerks, most search engines are confused by extra details and typos.
- In contrast, our more experienced users chose the most unusual or unique word from their queries. In the *One Flew Over The Cuckoo's Nest* search task, one of our more experienced users entered just the word "cuckoo," and met with immediate success.

We believe the best solution is to present search results pages that offer constructive advice on search tactics. (For more on this topic, see "Search Error Recovery" in this chapter.) Natural-language search engines like Ask.com can be another way to assist inexperienced shoppers.

There are many ways searches can go wrong:

- On Sears, one of our users narrowed his search too much. He typed, "10v cordless power drill" — and got nothing. In actuality, Sears had 33 cordless drills. The problem was that there were no cordless drills on the site that were exactly 10 volts, so strictly speaking, the search results were correct.

- On 1800flowers, many of our users searched for "Yellow roses" and got no results. One user tried "Roses, yellow," but this didn't work either. This user then searched for "Yellow." He got 21 results, but none for yellow roses. Our users argued that "yellow" and "roses" were reasonable keywords. They were also convinced that yellow roses were available on the website: "Yellow roses — of course you can buy them" (and you could indeed).

On Living, a user searched for "rocking chair." The search was successful: The website showed a page with an overview of three rocking chairs. Another user searched for a "canadian rocking chair" (one that glides). The search engine found nothing, but on the search results page, the engine correctly suggested a less specific search. A third user searched for "rockingchair," which yielded no results. What we'd really like to see is a search result that says: "Nothing found for 'Canadian rocking chairs,' but we do have these rocking chairs."

Tip: When a user enters more than one word in the search box, do an exact search for the whole string. If your search engine cannot handle this, then it should issue a suitable error message.

Tip: When a user enters more than one word in a search box, and the search returns no results, issue a No Results page that explains — in plain language — how to conduct multiple-word searches on the site. For more information on how to write customer-friendly search instructions, see "Search Error Recovery" in this chapter.

➡ *Recognize all possible search operators.*

Some people will try to use techniques they learned from other search engines on your site. Although we didn't see many examples of this in our online shopping study, we do know from other research that some people attempt to apply Boolean, delimiting or wildcard search operators. Here are some examples of special characters your search engine should be able to respond to intelligently:

- software AND space
- (lincoln county)
- +mr. john smith
- *price*
- "winnie the pooh."

Tip: Check your search logs to see if your customers are submitting unexpected search characters or strings.

Tip: Ask a clarifying question when you detect potential search operators.
When a user enters characters in a query that might be search operators, such as
*, +, –, " ", or ( ), then politely ask a clarifying question — just as a human
being would. The same applies to potential Boolean operators like "AND," "OR,"
and "NOT."

Tip: Don't ignore search operators without a proper warning. A user searched
for "barney & thomas" on eToys and got a No Results page even though the website
sold these toys. The feedback on the No Results page indicated that the search
engine had interpreted the user's query as "barney thomas." The website should
have warned the user that it ignored the "&" character. The search engine also
ignored the word "and," and then performed a search for the remaining phrase.

Search Query Entry

➡ *Make default search simple to use.*

The best advice we can give you about the layout of the basic search function is:
Keep it simple. Most of our test sites adhered to this principle.

Limit yourself to:

- One search box (text entry field) for the search query.

- One button to start a search. The button label itself seems to be less important.
  "Search," "Search for," "Go," "Find," and "Find it" all worked well.

- A discreet link to advanced search. Make the advanced search link less
  prominent than the search button. If user testing shows that inexperienced users
  click the link out of curiosity or by mistake, then make it even less prominent.

Reel's search facility was clearly visible on the home page, but it was
also too complicated for our less experienced users. S12

The complex search facility on Reel's website demonstrated several reasons why
keep-it-simple is good advice when it comes to designing your search engine:

- Two of our inexperienced users ran into trouble when they selected the
  Advanced Search link. There are more details about the problems our users
  encountered in the guideline below, "Provide a clearly marked link to
  advanced search — and back."

- Many of our users didn't understand the difference between the "Find It!" and "Match It!" buttons.
- On Reel (and other websites we tested), some users didn't understand the selection list (which says "Title" in the image above) and simply ignored it, which caused otherwise reasonable searches to fail.

Generally, users need only one text box and one search button in a search tool.

Tip: Limit yourself to one search facility per page. Some websites — Wal-Mart, for example — had several search boxes in different areas on some pages. The boxes were labeled "Search our Site," "Find … in Baby Shop," and other site-specific names. Many of our users did not understand the differences among the boxes.

Tip: Make sure your search box accepts at least the number of characters in the longest likely query. Some people think they are doing your website a favor by entering long queries. What's more, some search strings can legitimately be quite long, as in the case of movie titles. On Reel, several users tried to enter "one flew over the cuckoo's nest," but the search box would not accept the final "t." Apparently, 30 characters was the maximum query length the search engine could handle.

Tip: Consider the function of the Enter key carefully. In several cases, our users typed a search query and hit the Enter key, which often just brought up the same page again, giving the impression that the search had returned nothing. Whenever the user hits the Enter key, the website should check for user input in the search box, if present.

Tip: Design the search facility so that the cursor is already in the text box if there are no more important form fields on the page. Several of our users typed a search query without clicking in the search box first.

Tip: Do not distinguish between upper- and lower-case characters in the search box.

➡ *Provide a clearly marked link to Advanced Search — and back.*

If your customers require advanced search functionality, offer it; but keep simple search as the default and allow an easy return.

Advanced search offers manual control over many parameters that refine the search process. The main problem with advanced search, however, is that people may interpret the additional parameters to mean that they can adjust the search differently than the designer intended. Here are some examples from Reel:

- A Danish user thought that if he selected "Country = Denmark," he could then search for the Danish title ("Gøgereden") of the movie "*One Flew over the Cuckoo's Nest.*"
- A user thought that if he wanted to search for an English actor, he had to set "Country = England."
- Yet another user did not understand why he could not select "Country = USA." We don't understand this either.

During our study, only two users looked at advanced search on Reel. It didn't give them any advantage. They had the same problems as in simple search. Additionally, they encountered unforeseen interpretations that were not possible in simple search.

Tip: State clearly that advanced search is only for experienced users with special needs.

Tip: When the user gets a "no results" message in advanced search, offer a highly visible link back to simple search.

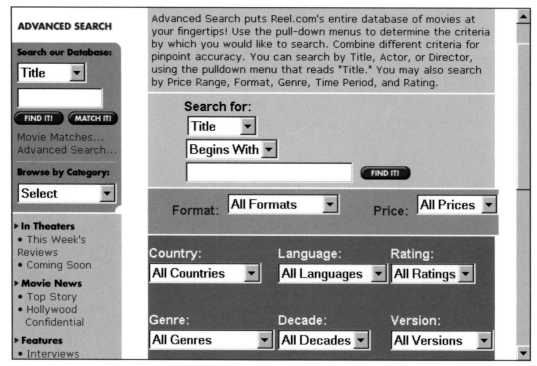

Two of our inexperienced users misinterpreted the extra controls on Reel's Advanced Search page. s13

▶ *The search default should be "contains" rather than "begins with."*

When people enter a search query, they usually don't care whether the search string is recognized at the start or somewhere inside the product title or product description. We observed that many of our users were time conscious. They selected what they considered the most unusual keyword from the title and used this word in their search, for efficiency. Unfortunately, some websites do not support this behavior, because, by default, they find only products whose name begins with the query string.

When one of our users searched on Reel for the film *One Flew over the Cuckoo's Nest*, the user typed in "cuckoo." The search engine returned no results, because the default search criterion was "Begins With" instead of "Contains," as the user had assumed. Like most users, this individual did not notice the default setting in the selection list, even though it appeared clearly on the page. Although the No Results page described some of the various selection lists, it did not mention the list that was the most likely cause of the problem. Without this knowledge, the user was stymied.

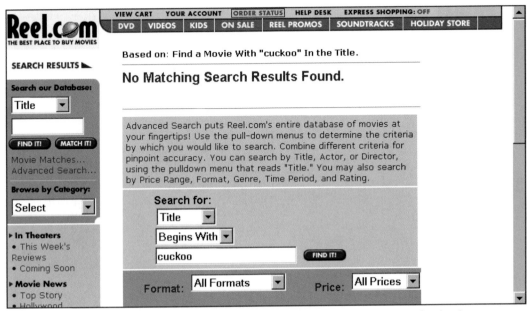

A user typed in "cuckoo" to search for *One Flew over the Cuckoo's Nest*. The search failed because the default search criterion in the selection list was "Begins With" instead of "Contains." S14

▶ *Explain the scope of the search.*

A search can cover:

- The entire site (full search).
- A part of the site previously selected by the user (limited search with implicit scope). For example, when a user searched on TowerRecords, the search results depended on whether the Music, Video / DVD, or Classical tab was previously selected.
- A part of the site explicitly selected by the user as part of the search (limited search with explicit scope). For example, when a user searched on CustomDisc, the search results depended on whether Artist or Title was chosen from a selection list in the search area.
- The results of a previous search (refinement search).

Our study showed that users most often expected search to cover the entire website or all products. We found, however, that when a search returned a long results list, users sometimes expected their subsequent search to search only within the current results.

Some of the websites tried to distinguish between these two possibilities — full search and refinement search. Our users did not always understand or agree with the choice that the website made. Problems arose because the search scope rules were not familiar to users and the website feedback was inadequate.

- **User misinterpreted the scope because of the number of results.** On SmarterKids, one user selected first "Ages 6–9" from a selection list in the search area (explicit scope) and then searched for the term "computer game." The website returned 650 results. The 650 results actually covered only ages 6–9, but the user first thought that the large number of results indicated that he had inadvertently searched the whole website.

- **User misinterpreted feedback and so expected one scope, but got another.** The same user then noticed feedback on the page: the age he had selected appeared in the upper left corner of the page. He searched again with the same keyword, hoping that this time he would get fewer results, assuming the search would be limited this time to the age group indicated by the header. This time, however, the website returned 1,026 results, because the search now covered the whole website — contrary to the user's expectations, the search was automatically broadened. Even though broadening the search might be a good strategy when a first search fails to find the wanted item, the problem here was that the user wasn't sure what was happening, in part because the website did not provide suitable feedback.

- **User expected a refinement search, but searched all instead.** On TowerRecords, two users searched for the Disney video "*Fantasia*." They searched for "*Fantasia*," and then "Disney." The users believed that they were doing a drill-down refinement search for *Disney's Fantasia*. They thought that each new search was carried out only from within the results of the previous search. In reality, the search engine started from scratch for each new search.

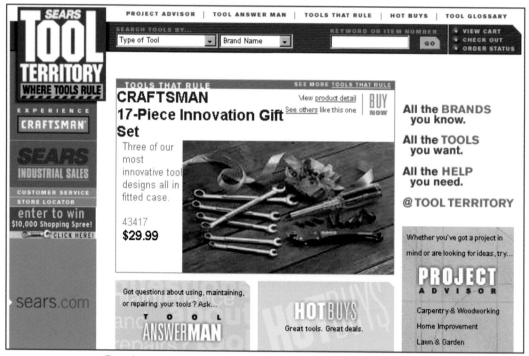

People sometimes expect search to cover the whole site, but on Sears Tool Territory, our users couldn't find microwave ovens from this page. s15

The following two complementary examples show how complicated it can be to determine the right scope automatically. Users' expectations may depend on whether they know that they are in the right department or not. The website can't possibly have this knowledge.

- **Users expected a search of the entire site, when they knew they were in the wrong department.** On Sears, we asked our users to find a microwave oven. Some users started from the Tool Territory category page, where the previous task ended, so the tools department was the implicit scope. Several users typed "microwave" into the search box. They got no results. One user said, "I know [a microwave] is not a tool, but I thought maybe it would bring me to the appliance section." Another user remarked, "This reminds me of looking under the Yellow Pages. You're looking under lawyers, and it's attorneys. I think I'm in the tool thing. I have to get out of the tool thing."

- **Users expected a search of only the department they were in, when they knew they were in the right department.** On SmarterKids, we told our users: "You want to get some software for your niece, who is 6. She is interested in science, especially space." In response, most users clicked the Software tab and then entered "space" in the search box. All users were surprised when the website returned space results from the other departments, too (Books, Toys/Games). "I didn't like when I thought I was under software, and it gave me books," one user said. "I thought it was going to be software and it wasn't."

It appeared that a search for "space" under the Software tab would be restricted to software — but to our users' annoyance, the search for "space" returned space-related products from every category on the website. s16

Tip: Provide a refinement search option when the search originates from a search results page and the search results list is long. Otherwise, start the search from scratch.

Tip: If multiple interpretations of the desired search scope are possible, offer the user options. For example, the options could be: "Search the whole website, just the music department, or only these search results?"

Tip: Make alternative scopes available and visible. Put the search scope right on the search button or on the search link. For example, "Search All Videos" or "Search Entire Catalog."

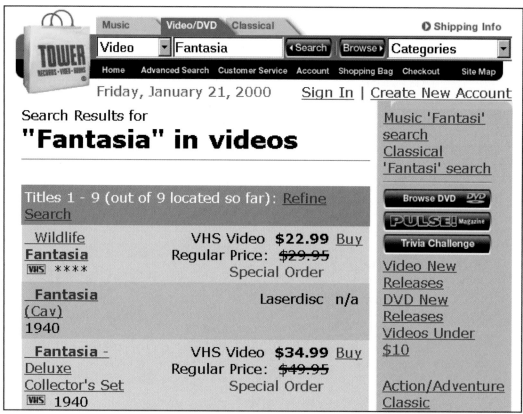

TowerRecords showed the scope for the search result list "Search Results for 'Fantasia' in videos" and provided links to new searches with different, explicit scopes "Music 'Fantasi' search" and "Classical 'Fantasi' search." This worked well. Note the unfortunate truncation in the word "Fantasi." S17

▶ *Add the selection "All" to all search selection lists —*
and make "All" the default.

Most users we've observed in this and other tests do not understand the purpose of selection lists that limit the scope of a search. They just ignore them. Still, scope-limiting lists are fine — as long as their default value is "All." This means that if the user does not take any special action, the whole database or the whole website will be searched.

• One of our users entered "Ipanema" in the search text box of CustomDisc and clicked Go. The search returned no results, because the user did not know or notice that the default scope on the selection list was set for "Artist," not "All." In fact, "All" wasn't even an option. The search engine interpreted the user's query as a request for an artist named Ipanema. Compare what would have happened if the user had asked a good sales clerk for an artist named Ipanema. Most likely, the answer would have been: "I've never heard of an artist with that name, but there's a famous old song called *The Girl from Ipanema*."

- Another user on CustomDisc thought it was not possible to search for a song title, because the selection list said "Artist." The user did not recognize the selection list for what it was, and thus, did not understand that "Artist" was just the default choice.
- On Furniture, "All" was the search default, which worked well for our users.

Our users had problems understanding the scope-of-search configuration on CustomDisc's search engine. They did not realize that the selection list displaying the default "Artist" limited the search scope. They also did not realize that they could change the default from "Artist" to "Song." S18

Tip: Ensure that the widest reasonable search scope is the default. Fewer users will search within a limited scope unintentionally when the default is set to search the broadest information space.

Tip: Give users suggestions for limiting the scope of the search when the default search yields too many results. If possible, make the suggestions clickable so that clicking initiates the search it suggests. (See Image S17.)

Tip: Provide a helpful message when the search gives no results. Explain carefully that the scope may not have been what the user intended.

Search Result Interpretation

After a user has entered one or more search keywords and activated the search, the website returns a list of search results that should correspond to the query. Some searches in our test failed at this point because the search results list:

- Contained insufficient information for the user to select the right product.
- Presented a list that appeared to be in random order to the user.
- Contained too many items or had too many results on the first page.
- Contained only one item.
- Had incomprehensible or inadequate page-to-page navigation within the results.
- Contained links with difficult-to-understand wording.
- Included items that appeared to be — or actually were — unrelated to the user's search criteria.

Tip: Always include the following in a search results page:

- Search criteria
- Website areas covered by search (scope)
- Total number of search results (items found).

For example: "You searched for 'microwave oven' in Appliances. 30 results were found."

➡ *Provide relevant information about search results.*

Our users expected the following information in a search result:

- **A short product description, including brand name.** The short description should link to a more detailed description, such as the product page.

- **The price of the product.**

- **A picture of the product.** Pictures should be so small and few in number that they do not delay download time considerably. Yet, pictures should be large enough to show the necessary details. Many users expected that a click on the picture would produce another, magnified version of the product that would show important details. The download time of the magnified version is less important, because users are willing to wait for pictures that they consider worthwhile. Provide an option to buy the item from the magnified picture, along with easy access to the product page.

- **Information on whether the product is in stock or not.** The Category Pages chapter describes how to present availability and shipping information effectively.

Writing a good, short product description requires knowledge of customer needs. Here are some examples of what our users looked for:

- On Reel, a user searched for "the jungle book," which resulted in multiple hits. She was able to identify the version she wanted easily — *The Jungle Book* (1967) — because the short product description contained the information she needed.

- On TowerRecords, a user searched for Disney's *Fantasia* video and got several hits. "It is *Fantasia* all right," the user said, "but is it *Disney's Fantasia*? How can I see who made it?" The short product description did not provide the brand name, so the user had to click to discover whether the right video had been found.

- On eToys, we asked a Danish user to look for a gift for a fictitious 3-year-old nephew who loves Hot Wheels cars and has several of them already, but needs tracks to run them on. The user selected "3 Years" in the "Shop by Age" selection list. He then searched for "Hot wheels" and got a search results list with 93 hits. He patiently clicked on some of the result links but eventually gave up. Among the reasons he abandoned the search were:

  - He did not know the English word for "tracks." He tried looking at the pictures, but the pictures did not provide the detail he needed to see in order to determine whether they had tracks.

  - The product listings appeared to be in random order, which gave him little hope of finding a grouping of Hot Wheels with tracks.

  - The search results page listed 93 Hot Wheels products. There was no way to further refine the search. The only way he could find tracks was to jump back and forth between the search result list and individual product pages. This user-unfriendly, time-consuming process is sometimes called "pogo-sticking."

eToys provided small pictures of products, but the pictures didn't provide enough detail for one of our Danish users to identify what he was looking for. The site did provide links to bigger pictures, but when faced with 93 results in apparently random order, our user was overwhelmed and gave up. S19

➡ *Offer appropriate sorting facilities.*

Many of our users wanted to sort products in the search results list by price. "Just like I sort my e-mail in-tray by date," said one user.

Tip: Allow users to sort by price. Consider showing the cheapest product first. Note, however, that there is a risk that users might mistakenly conclude the store doesn't carry the higher-end merchandise.

Tip: List products in an order that appears natural to customers. For example, list them by price, by product group, or alphabetically.

Tip: Indicate clearly how the results are sorted. Use a short text header to explain the current sorting order. If you use symbols, test carefully to make sure that users understand their meaning.

Tip: Explain how to apply other sorting criteria, if relevant. Although none of our users asked for any sorting criteria other than price, we can easily imagine cases in which alphabetical sorting by product name or product category would be useful.

➡ Speak the language of your customers.

Avoid using technical jargon on search results pages. The technical terms are so familiar to Web developers that sometimes only a usability test will show which words are opaque to your customers. Our users had trouble over unfamiliar terminology.

- On Furniture, a user searched for wine racks. The search returned four results with this message: "Pictures 1–4 of 4." It took her a while to figure out what that message meant. Text that said, "All results displayed," would have been clearer.

- On Wal-Mart, our users ignored the prominent link on the search results page to the "Toasters — Toaster Ovens" category page (Image S22), because they didn't understand the jargony heading above it, which said "Category Matches."

Tip: Avoid showing scores to indicate how relevant the search results may be. Relevancy scores are just noise for most users, who aren't aware of or interested in the factors that influence ranking. Use the scores only to order the list from highest to lowest.

➡ Beware of long lists.

Long search result lists can cause problems, like lost sales. During our study, we saw many searches return hundreds of items — without offering any way to narrow the search further. Only a few of our users looked past Page 3 of search results. Most didn't look past Page 2. Unless the desired item was on the first screen of the first page, most of our users' searches were unsuccessful.

Tip: Offer a usable navigation mechanism. For example, instead of listing "Results by Page 1 2 3 4 5 6 7 8 9 10," consider presenting lists arranged:

- **Alphabetically** — "Results by Title: A–Ang, Ann–Bri, Bro–Cr, Cy–Fo, Fr–I, I–Li, …"

- **By cost** — "Results by Price: $0.00–5.24, $5.25–9.99, $9.99–15.49, $15.50–39.99, $40–99.99, $100 or more."

Blue Velvet (1986)
Starring: Isabella Rossellini, Kyle MacLachlan
Director: David Lynch

Body Heat (1981)
Starring: William Hurt, Kathleen Turner
Director: Lawrence Kasdan

Bonnie and Clyde (1967)
Starring: Warren Beatty, Faye Dunaway
Director: Arthur Penn

Displaying Results 1 - 30 out of 236. For fewer Results, please refine your search

Results by Page : 1 2 3 4 5 6 7 8

© Copyright 1996-99
Reel.com, Inc.

On Reel, one user had to guess where *Doctor Zhivago* might be found in the numbered page scheme after he clicked the category "Romantic Dramas" and got 379 results split into eight pages. He tried Page 3, looking for titles starting with "D," but Page 3 only went up to "C." S20

◆ Avoid one-item lists.

One item does not look like a list. A search results page with only one item often caused problems for our users. They did not expect that they had to choose the item by clicking it. When a search returned only one matching result, users expected to be taken directly to the item.

One of our users searched on Reel for films directed by Stanley Kubrick. The user clicked on Reel's selection lists to set the search scope to "Directors" and "Contains." He then typed "kubrick" in the text box. When the search results page came up, the user hesitated. "And now it claims to have found … 'displaying results one out of one.' " He didn't immediately recognize that the search had in fact found something. The user finally clicked on the only link — "Stanley Kubrick" — and got the page with movies directed by Kubrick.

Another of our users encountered a similar one-item choice on CustomDisc. She typed "Platters" into the Artist search box. The website returned a search results page with one link to "The Platters." "Didn't do anything," she complained. "I expected to see a list of the songs in order of popularity." The user thought for a long while before she clicked the link that took her where she wanted to go.

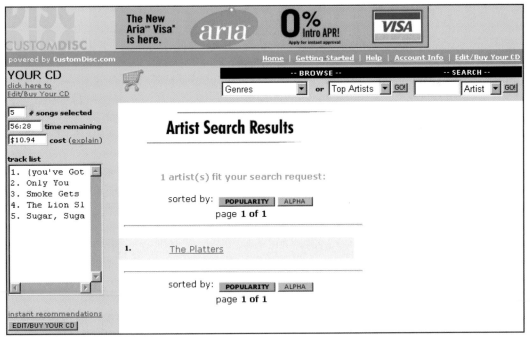

People are confused by one-item lists. Our user did not expect a page that looked like this. She expected CustomDisc to deliver a list of songs by The Platters. S21

◆ Show why results are included.

Several times our users got confused because the search results list contained seemingly irrelevant hits. For example, on TowerRecords, our users wondered why a search for *Fantasia* returned apparently irrelevant videos like *Dumbo* and *Pinocchio*.

A search for the cheapest toaster on Wal-Mart delivered a variety of items, not all of them toasters. One user clicked a link called "What were they thinking?" She said she hoped the link would lead to a toaster, but it didn't. "All I asked for was toasters, and then it gave me a book on how to cook." Other users wondered why the list contained products like "Ring! Tick Tock" and "The Complete Idiot's Guide to In-Laws."

- Home Improvement
- Household Goods
- Housewares
- Jewelry
- Movies
- Music
- Office
- Pets
- Photo Center
- Shoes
- Sporting Goods
- Toys
- Travel

Category Matches

1 matches found. Showing matches 1-1

- **Toasters-Toaster Ovens**

Product Matches

27 matches found. Showing matches 1-10   ▸ More Products

- **Black & Decker® VersaToast™ Wide Slot Toaster** $14.96
- **Sculpey III® Crafter's Clay Variety Pack** $9.97
- **Original Sculpey® Modeling Clay** $4.97
- **Camp Stove Toaster** $1.93
- **Proctor-Silex® SmartToast 2000™ Two Slice Toaster** $12.96
- **Proctor-Silex® SmartToast 2000™ Four Slice Toaster** $24.96
- **Toastmaster® Toaster Oven/Broiler** $26.86
- **Tubby Toast! Tubby Toast!** $3.49

A search for "toasters" on Wal-Mart produced this curious page, which included items like modeling clay. Note the "Toasters-Toaster Ovens" link to a category page above the "Product Matches" list. Our users ignored this link because they didn't understand the computer jargon "Category Matches." S22

Tip: For each search result, show where the search engine found the keyword. Highlight the keyword and show the sentences surrounding the keyword. Of course, surrounding sentences are not required when the keyword appears in the short product description.

▶ *Give customers only what they ask for.*

People expect a website to follow their instructions. They get confused and annoyed when they get results outside their search criteria and when the search engine overlooks items that should have matched.

- On SmarterKids, a user typed "software on space" in the search box. The website returned items that matched on space but not on software. (The second product on the search results list was frog pond puzzle.) The user scrolled down the list of the top eight products, looked at one of them, realized it wasn't software, went back to the software page, and searched for "software on science," thus broadening her search. This search gave better results for her than the first one had, and she decided on the "I Love Science CD." So she eventually found a product that she thought was suitable, but she never saw any software on space for this age group, even though it does exist on this site.

- On 1800flowers, a user searched for "yellow" in order to find yellow roses. The search found 21 yellow items — flowers, candles, and such — but no yellow roses, even though they were available on the website. Unable to find yellow roses, the user said, "If I were doing this at home, at this point, I'd say screw it. … I'd have gone to my florist."

- When Furniture was unable to find a dining room table that matched one user's criteria (Finish = Birch, Price Range = $0–500), the site returned a page that disregarded price and finish in order to at least present some tables. The user didn't notice the message that said there were no exact matches, and he got upset that Furniture had disregarded his search criteria.

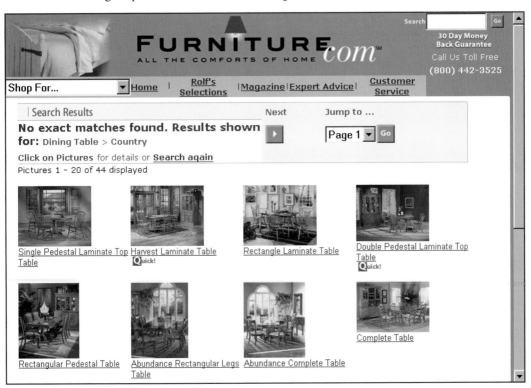

One of our users was very annoyed when Furniture apparently ignored his search criteria. He didn't notice the "No exact matches found" message. S23

- One of our users on Disney carefully narrowed the scope of her search. She chose "Department: Entertainment" and "Age group: Youth boy." When the Search Results page came back, she immediately noticed that the website had not adhered to her search criteria. "I searched for something for a boy. This shows a girl with a Dalmatians pajama set," she fumed.

A user was irritated when Disney presented a page showing a girl in pajamas while she was looking for something to give a boy. s24

Tip: Don't broaden the user's search automatically. People expect to get the search results they asked for. Our experience indicates that when no matches are found, it is safe to suggest that the user broaden the search. You are risking the user's ire, however, if you broaden the search without asking first. Also, it is not enough to say, "Broaden your search." This is geek-speak. We believe it's helpful to show users an example or two of how to broaden a search.

Search Error Recovery

Several of our users gave up searching for the rest of the test after getting a few error messages. We believe that they gave up because many of the error messages that our users encountered were not helpful. In a few cases, however, we saw error messages that were helpful because they helped our users recover from their errors without making them feel like they'd done something wrong.

After a search on Reel failed due to misspelling, a user said, "They say they haven't found any matches, and I'm wondering where else I can go." The search failure page on Reel, like many we saw in our test, didn't offer any suggestions. Some users felt that search was wasting their time.

▶ *Provide constructive advice.*

Whenever a user has problems, we recommend that you provide constructive, precise, and comprehensible messages, not just the inhuman, "No results found. Try again!"

Error messages should be:

- **Constructive** – Tell people how to proceed rather than telling them what they did wrong.
- **Polite** – Express yourself as you would if the customer were standing in front of you.
- **Apologetic** – Blame it on the website, not the customer ("We're sorry. This website is unable to …").
- **Comprehensible** – Shun technical slang and jargon. Speak the customers' language.

Tip: Ask yourself, "What would a competent sales clerk say to a customer if a similar situation occurred in a local store?"

Tip: Write error messages early. Bad error messages sometimes result from a flawed development process. Error messages are an important part of website design. They are at least as important as other text on the website. It is best to write the message when you create the page it belongs to.

Tip: Respect the rules for writing good error messages. Writing good error messages requires special skills. Not everyone can do it.

Tip: Review error messages. Show them to customers, your peers, developers, customer service, technical support, and technical writers.

Tip: Don't use default server messages for functionality errors. Customize the messages by wording them in user-level language. Suggest ways to recover from the error. Instead of "404 Not Found," a customized navigation page could suggest places to look for the wanted information, for example.

Creating a Good "No Results" Page

When a user enters a query for which the search engine can find no matches, display a No Results page. The No Results page should provide constructive and comprehensible advice about how the user can solve the problem.

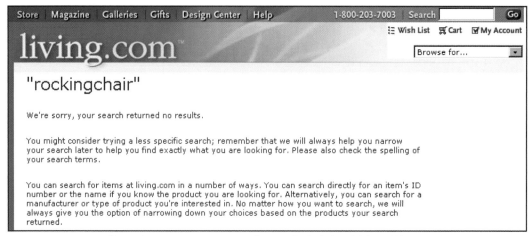

One of our users erroneously concluded that Living did not sell rocking chairs. We suspect the user did not know she was supposed to put a space between the words "rocking" and "chair." A more comprehensive error message explaining how to construct a search string (warning for example against spelling errors and missing spaces) could have helped here. S25

A user searched for "rockingchair" (note the missing space between words) on Living. She got "no results." The user mistook the feedback for a confirmation and concluded: "Well, the message shows that they understood my request. So it must mean that they don't sell rocking chairs." She gave up. We saw similar incidents on other websites. Incidents like these demonstrate why it is so important to show clearly on the No Results page why the search failed in terms the user can understand.

Although Living's error message did suggest the user check her spelling, it could have been more helpful to our user if the message had also shown how to use spaces in search strings. We suspect that some inexperienced searchers type search strings without spaces, because URLs can't have spaces.

➡ *Allow the user to begin a new search on the "No Results" page.*

Give the user another chance to succeed right away. Provide search functionality on every page, even on the search results and No Results pages. Don't make users navigate backward from the No Results page to try another query. Put new search features directly into the content area of the No Results page.

Almost invisible but present on the top right of the image above is the search box. It should have been in the content area. The Reel No Results page (Image S14) shows how to do this right.

On 1800flowers, many users searched in vain for "yellow roses." The No Results page suggested users "broaden" their search, but many users did not understand the suggestion. In response to the "broadening your search" message, we saw users searching for "roses, yellow" (no results), "yellow" (21 results, but no yellow roses), and "roses" (success).

A search for "yellow roses" yielded no matches even though 1800flowers actually did stock and sell yellow roses. An explanation, with examples, on "broadening your search" would have helped here. In contrast, the feedback on this page is reasonable. s26

CustomDisc's No Results page looked so much like a successful search results page that one of our users thought that the lists at the bottom of the page ("25 Top Songs" and "25 Top Artists") contained search results. The user started looking for matching songs in the lists and was surprised to find that none of the songs matched her search criteria.

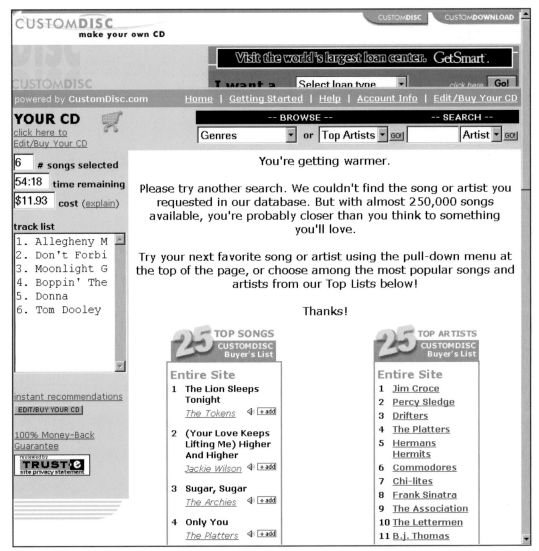

One of our users said she considered "You are getting warmer" to be an inappropriate response on CustomDisc's No Results page. Coincidentally, this remark was removed a few days after the test. s27

When there are no search results to chapter, it might be a good idea to make reasonable suggestions — although it can be hard to know what any one customer might think is "reasonable." Suggestions can be a little risky, so make sure you have a heading that clearly explains why you are making the suggestions. Such a heading is missing in the CustomDisc example, above.

Here are some tips for creating effective No Results pages:

Tip: Keep it short and simple. Even after an error, people won't read much text.

Tip: Provide feedback. Tell the user exactly what term(s) the website searched for and what was searched (scope). In the 1800flowers example (Image S26), the feedback is reasonable — it informs the user precisely what the search criteria were.

Tip: Phrase messages so the customer does not mistake the feedback for a confirmation of an erroneous assumption. Some websites expressed themselves in such a way that users misunderstood why the search failed. The No Results page (Image S25) on Living was misunderstood by some of our users. The 1800flowers No Results message (Image S26) worked better.

Tip: Make it clear why the search failed. Distinguish clearly among the following reasons:

- We did not understand your request.
- We understood your request, but we do not carry this product.
- We understood your request. We know the product, but it is temporarily unavailable.

Tip: Prevent the No Results problem by making sure that the search uses appropriate default values. On the Reel No Results page (Image S14), the website could safely change the default from "Begins With" to "Contains," because tests show that this behavior is what users expect. Users have a better chance of getting good results when their terms can be located anywhere in a title.

Tip: Ask users to check their spelling, or provide bad-spelling tolerance. TowerRecords had considerable success with the latter approach (Image S11).

Tip: Ask users to broaden their search. The website could suggest, "No products found that match your selections. Try broadening your search." We saw a few examples in which a user noticed this message and it actually helped. We're not sure, however, that everyone understands this meaning of the word "broaden." A more helpful suggestion might be, "Use fewer words." Offering an example or two might be even better.

Tip: Use appropriate language — don't try to be funny in an error message. A customer who is already annoyed might misunderstand your well-intended humor. Don't make CustomDisc's mistake and say, "You're getting warmer" (Image S27).

Tip: Consider providing just-in-time hints. Put these hints right on the No Results page. A rotating set of short tips displayed one at a time can teach without much interruption. Because the user must view this page anyway, it can be helpful to have some information on how to search more effectively. Because the user is motivated only for a very short time (perhaps 15 seconds), you might want to use examples instead of text. People view examples, but they have to read text. Viewing is fast, reading is slower.

Tip: Provide information about alternative ways of locating products. When a search fails, suggest other means of finding products or information right on the search error page. For example, you could include navigation, a table of contents, the site map, product and category pages, customer service options, or the site's FAQ (frequently asked questions) list.

Tip: Consider offering Help. None of our users looked at Help instructions for search. Having to pause in one's quest and learn a tool is a cognitive burden that most people aren't willing to shoulder. People are going to do whatever seems easiest to them. If you want to experiment with Help, however, here are a few suggestions:

- Base Help on observed problems.
- Provide a few carefully selected examples of realistic search strings.
- Avoid humorous examples.

Usable search functionality, usable error messages, and usable Help require a deep understanding of how customers actually interact with your search engine. Error messages and help instructions that result from armchair analysis or personal opinions may help an idealized rational shopper — but such customers are rare.

How Users Search

The key points from the following survey of user search behavior were:

- Users tried search about 28% of the time.
- Search was a successful strategy about 64% of the time users tried it.
- When users weren't successful with the first query in a search, their likelihood of success dropped off sharply with subsequent queries.
- Typically, users tried variations of the same search text, not something different.

Main Results

Our users employed text search in 95 (28%) out of 344 tasks in which search was possible. Of those 95 searches, 61 (64%) were successful, and 34 (36%) were not.

By our definition, during a search a user enters one or more queries (search strings). During their 95 searches, our users entered a total of 151 queries.

- 81 queries (54%) did not yield useful results. In many cases, however, users immediately entered another query in the same search, sometimes with more success.
- 70 queries (46%) yielded useful results.

The data reported in this section do not include limited vocabulary search, which was available only on a few websites, and which only a few of our users tried.

Multiple Searches

After each query, there were four possible next steps:

Useful results found — work with them	40%
Useful results found — but enter another query anyway (sometimes with less success)	7%
No good results — enter another query	30%
No good results — abandon search	23%

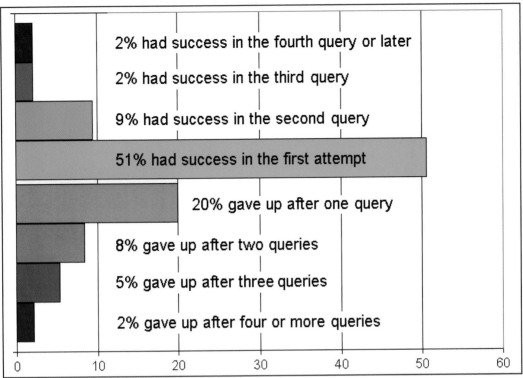

2% had success in the fourth query or later

2% had success in the third query

9% had success in the second query

51% had success in the first attempt

20% gave up after one query

8% gave up after two queries

5% gave up after three queries

2% gave up after four or more queries

Success and Failure Rates in Multiple Searches — The bar chart shows, by percentage of users, how many queries our users had to enter before they got a good search result. It also shows, by percentage of users, how many queries users entered before they gave up. S28

The probability for success declined sharply as one needed more and more queries.

First query	51% success rate
Second query	32% success rate
Third query	18% success rate

More detailed explanation: The 51% success rate for the first query is immediately noticeable from the chart. The 32% success rate for the second query is the success rate for the users who failed in the first query but continued to do a second query (and perhaps a third or fourth query). The 32% can be seen from the chart as 9% out of the 28% who continued after the first query. (28% = 13% who had success in the second, third, fourth query or later, plus 15% who gave up after two, three, four or more queries. 32% = 9% / 28%.) In this model, people only get to query N+1 if they have failed in all previous queries 1 … N. In our study, people continued to enter queries in 7% of the cases even after they got useful results, but the model gets too complex if we have to account for that.

The following list shows which query led to success when a user was successful:

First query	79%
Second query	15%
Third query	3%
Fourth or following query	3%

Our users slightly preferred multiple-word queries: 82 queries (54%) contained more than one word, compared to 69 queries (46%) that contained just one word. The average length of a query was 2.0 words.

When users entered multiple queries, they were usually a variation of the same word(s), for example, "coffee pot" and "coffee maker," or "returns" and "exchanges." We think this lack of variation partly explains the dramatic drop in success rate with subsequent queries.

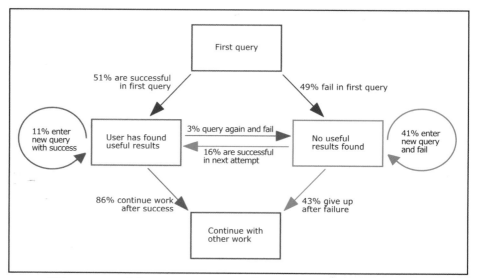

This success–failure state transition diagram shows what our users did when they were in the state in which they had found useful results — and when they were in a state in which they had found no useful results. s29

For example: When a user had just found a useful result, there was an 86% chance that the user would continue with other work. There was an 11% chance that the user would enter another query and be successful again, and there was a minuscule 3% chance that the user would enter another query and fail.

Thus, search will rarely be more than a two-step process. If a user succeeds with the first query, then searching is complete. If the first query does not succeed, the user might try one more time.

Unsuccessful searches on one site did not seem to scare users away from trying search on subsequent sites. We had 15 users who abandoned search on one website but used it again on another website. Of these, 2 failed with search on two websites but bravely fought a new battle with search on a third website that they tested. (Both of them were somewhat successful on the third website.)

Product
Pages

" *The true tests of a product page are whether it provides shoppers with enough information to make their buying decisions and whether it presents an effective mechanism for purchasing.*"

Three Examples of Product Pages

Here are three examples of product pages that have both good and bad aspects. Later in this chapter, we'll go into more detail about each example and explain what we saw in our testing that led to our guidelines and recommendations.

1) The Ergon 3 Chair: HermanMiller.com

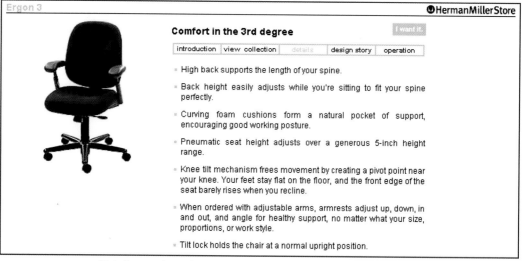

This layered product page shows the features of an office chair from HermanMiller.com. P1

PROS (what this page did well)	CONS (what was missing or not done well)
• The Introduction tab (not shown) contained only one paragraph, instead of overwhelming users by showing everything at once.	• Price ($449) was not shown.
	• Price of the option was not shown. (Adjustable arms were $55.71.)
• Additional information was available by clicking the tabs at the top of the page. The Details tab (shown here) had good information on the features of the chair.	• The chair came in a choice of four colors, but the page didn't say that.
	• There was no information on availability. (Most configurations shipped in four days.)
• Image of chair could be enlarged, and other views were shown when the Operation tab was selected.	• There were no links to the guarantee and return policy. (The chair could be returned within 60 days for any reason.)
• The I Want It button was an unusual way of putting an item in the shopping cart, but it didn't confuse any of our users.	• Cost of shipping was missing. (The standard shipping rate is free.)

2) The North Face Ak-Su Jacket: Boo.com

A jacket on Boo.com. The Spin button — sometimes — opened a second window that let you rotate the jacket. P2

PROS (what this page did well)	CONS (what was missing or not done well)
• Price was prominently shown.	• The Spin and Zoom buttons didn't always work, or were very slow over a 56k modem connection.
• Image was good enough to see details of construction, such as the neck protector.	• If a user selected a different color, it didn't match the swatches. (For instance, blue looked black.)
• Users liked the Spin function because they could see the back of the jacket.	• When a size or color was unavailable, users weren't told that until they tried to put the item in the "boobag" (shopping cart).
• "Free shipping, free returns" appeared on every page.	
• Swatches of other colors were shown (left side of page), and the jacket changed when a user clicked on another color.	• A couple of users tried "Buy Now" instead of "Add to boobag." (Buy Now took the user into the checkout process with an empty boobag.)
• All sizes were shown.	• There was no mention of a product guarantee.
• A detailed description was available, but was not visible all at once. (Users liked this.)	

3) The Attic Loft Bed: Living.com

The Attic Loft bed on Living.com. Users didn't realize that the chest shown in the picture was not included with the beds. P3

PROS (what this page did well)	CONS (what was missing or not done well)
• Description discussed usage and durability — things users cared about. • Dimensions and weight were shown. • Image was good enough for users. • Prices were clearly shown. • Available finishes were shown. • The Add Selected Items to Cart button was an unusual way of putting an item in the shopping cart, but it didn't confuse anyone.	• Image didn't change when the user selected a different finish. • There was no information on shipping costs (free). • It was hard to tell what was included. (The chest was sold separately and some users were misled.) • There was no mention of time to process the order. (Many items took six weeks or longer to ship.) • There was no link to the product guarantee. (The Certified Merchant Guarantee at the bottom pertained to privacy and credit card fraud, not the merchandise. Living had a 100% satisfaction guarantee, but it was not mentioned here.)

Product Description

➡ *Provide the product details customers want and need.*

This advice sounds obvious, but it wasn't always done well. Although no two users had exactly the same criteria, there were some patterns in the type of information they wanted to know about products. Here are some examples:

Product Details Users Wanted

Type of Product	Factors Users Typically Considered	Sample User Quote
Toys	Age appropriateness, size, durability, accessories	Toy: (Princess Dress-Up Trunk) "I couldn't stand ordering it and then find out that it is too small."
Clothing	Color, material, details of construction, lining, pockets, sizing	Jacket: "Color really matters. … White always gets dirty. … If it has a hood or not. If it's thick. I don't like the ones that have elastic bands around the bottom. If it's a zipper, or a button, or just a pullover. If it's got a fleece liner. I snowboard, so the fleece keeps you really warm."
Furniture	Finish, type of wood or fabric, comfort, dimensions, adjustability, construction	Bunk bed: The user was concerned with the ease of getting into the top bunk and whether it had drawers underneath. "I'd like to see how these drawers are made, if they're dovetailed or what." She wondered about the "steadiness of the drawer, how it will hold up" and whether it was made of "wood or that pressed crap."
Videos, Music	Actors / artist, year released, description of plot or tracks, image of the cover	CD: "Actually, I am only interested in one particular [sound] track. If that track is not on the CD, then I don't want the CD."

Sometimes, the users' questions were answered by looking at the picture. Other times they got the answers by reading the accompanying text. But many times product pages left key questions unanswered:

- Boo: It was hard to determine the relative warmth of gloves. One young skier suggested they could show temperature ratings, a feature he'd seen elsewhere.
- TowerRecords: The site sometimes omitted pictures of the video cover. One user gave up on finding Disney's *Fantasia* even though he'd been on the right page, because he was looking for the picture.
- Disney: Users looked for but didn't find information about age-appropriateness for many toys.

The less familiar users were with an item, the more detailed information they wanted before deciding whether to buy it. When buying known videos or toys, some users needed only to recognize the item, such as the man who quickly picked Austrian Barbie (one his wife wanted for her collection) out of a list of 34 Barbie dolls.

If customers have already done their research elsewhere, they may need little more than the product name, an image, the price, and a Buy button. Some customers may want to buy directly from a higher-level category page (as our Barbie buyer did) because they do not need to see the product page to make their decision.

On Boo, one user readily put a vest in his Boobag without much investigation, but he spent more time scrutinizing his second item, a jacket. He explained: "This vest is an item I've seen in stores and I know I like it. This [jacket] I haven't, so I'm relying more heavily on the site to communicate the value of it."

Tip: Talk to the experts. Researchers have been watching people shop in physical stores for decades. Paco Underhill's Book *Why We Buy* gives a fascinating look at how real-world shopping behavior is affected by the layout of the store. To obtain the same level of sophisticated knowledge about online shopping, website owners and designers must tap into existing marketing wisdom — but not assume that all of it transfers directly to the online customer experience. Whenever possible, you should talk to store owners, salespeople, and manufacturing reps to find out what they've learned about selling their goods and services in stores and through paper catalogs. Even so, you must conduct usability tests to be sure what actually works online.

▶ *Speak the customer's language; avoid jargon and clever names.*

Unfamiliar words sometimes confused our users. Although we might have expected the Danish users to have trouble if they didn't speak English fluently, in fact, many of the Americans stumbled over the terms as well. Here are some examples of words users said they didn't understand:

Site	Troublesome Terms
Nordstrom	Sanyo Microfiber (Terms like Polartech on Boo, however, didn't seem to be a problem.)
BasketHaus	Chocolate spoons, truffles
HermanMiller	Lumbar
Wal-Mart	Rear-facing (for a child seat)
Jcrew	Shetland, boucle
TowerRecords	"n/a," "pre-order" (Some users figured out the meanings of these terms when they tried — and failed — to purchase a video.)
Disney	Pooh Gram, Disney Gram
1800flowers	Rugelach

It's not necessarily bad to use such terms — as long as there is enough context for customers to learn how the term relates to what they want to know.

For example, one user on Furniture had trouble deciding whether he needed a table with two leaves or four leaves to seat six people: "They're speaking their language, not mine. I don't know how many leaves I need."

Furniture listed the dimensions of the table and leaves, but the user didn't want to know that. He wanted to know how many people could sit at the table. Ultimately he couldn't decide and said he would use the site's chat facility to ask an expert.

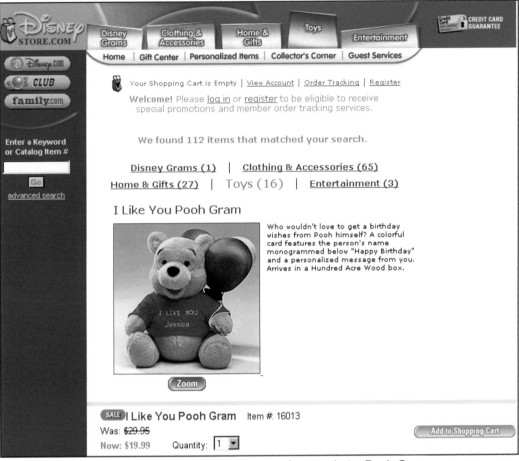

On Disney.com, a few users weren't sure what a Pooh Gram was even after seeing this page. (We had asked them to get a stuffed Winnie the Pooh bear.) P4

Some users were baffled by the term "Pooh Gram" on Disney's website. A Pooh Gram is a customized stuffed Winnie the Pooh bear (from A.A. Milne's classic children's stories) that wears a shirt with the gift-giver's personalized greeting, such as, "I like you, Jessica." When given the task to find a stuffed Pooh, several users complained about not knowing what a Pooh Gram was. As far as we could tell, nowhere on Disney did it explicitly state that a Pooh Gram was a stuffed doll with personalized words printed on its shirt.

Tip: In usability testing, listen to the vocabulary people use as they are looking at products. If they use different words than those the site uses — or if they appear confused — either change the terms to match whatever users said, or provide definitions.

➡ *Be specific.*

Users appreciate information that is specific rather than general. As we have also seen in other studies, users tend to take things literally when reading online. Thus, it is important to describe products accurately. In this study, we found that when a product page used vague terms, it raised more questions than it answered:

- BasketHaus: The contents of the gift baskets were not shown or described in enough detail for users to know what they'd be buying. Users wanted a better list of the exact items, including amounts and brands. When BasketHaus said "cheese," users wanted to know what kind and how many ounces.
- Wal-Mart: It wasn't clear to some users what the upper age limit was on car seats for "infants."
- Sears: One user was confused by a cordless drill "kit." He interpreted the word kit to mean the drill would come with something besides the battery and charger (which are integral parts of a cordless drill). The product page made no mention of other components.
- eToys: The description of the Super Highway Playtrack stated, "Not for use with some Hot Wheels vehicles." One user complained that the site didn't say which vehicles wouldn't work.

➡ *Don't present too much detail at once. Layer the information.*

Sears actually showed too much detail about its microwaves. As one annoyed user quipped, "You have to be a microwave oven engineer to understand this!" This user just wanted basic information about power consumption and cleaning.

Another user was amused to discover that the description was so detailed that it even mentioned having a steamed fruit pudding sensor (which she was not interested in).

Feature	Description
Microwave Capacity	Mid-Size (.9 - 1.2 cubic feet)
Product Type	Microwave
Microwave Type	Countertop
Manufacturer Brand	Kenmore
Color Oven Door	Black Glass
Color Overall	Grey Stone w/Black
Type	Countertop
Type Size	Medium, 0.8 to 1.09 cu. ft.
Configuration Heating Type	Microwave
Configuration Watts	1000 Watts
Configuration Power Levels	10
Configuration Capacity	1.0 cu. ft.
Configuration Interior Dimensions	13 13/16 in. W x 8 3/4 in. H x 14 5/8 in. D
Configuration Turntable	Removable Recessed Turntable
Settings One-Touch, Foods	Quick Touch POPCORN
Settings Defrost/Preheat	AUTO DEFROST, 1-Course, Enter Weight
Settings Cook	Quick Touch AUTO COOK
Settings Multi-Setting Cook	Super EVENWAVE(r) Cooking System
Settings Extend Cook	MORE/LESS
Settings Warm/Reheat	Quick Touch AUTO REHEAT
Settings Custom	Super EVENWAVE(tm) Cooking
Controls Type	Electronic Touch & Quick Touch Keys w/Digital Display
Controls Maximum Setting Time	99 Minutes/99 Seconds
Controls Ease of Use	DEMO MODE Touchpad Sequence
Quality Installation Flexibility	Countertop
Styling Door Swing	Left
Styling Door Open/Handle	Push Release Door Open
Materials & Finishes Turntable	Glass
Power Source Power Ratings	Electric
Power Source Requirements	12.9 Amps
Dimensions* Width	20 11/16 in.
Dimensions* Height	11 3/8 in.
Dimensions* Depth, to Edge of Door	16 1/2 in.
Dimensions* Weight, Shipping	39 lbs.

Sears had too much detail about its microwaves. P5

Here are some ways that our test sites avoided overwhelming users with details:

- Boo displayed text in a scrolling box. The detail text didn't take up the whole page, but it was available when users wanted to see it. Users had no trouble with the scroll control, and they seemed to like this approach. As one user said, "That's nice. The way it scrolls through, it doesn't inundate you with text, which normally would turn you away from reading it."

- HermanMiller used a tab approach for layering the information about chairs. The product page initially displayed a one-paragraph introduction. Details about the features and operation of the chair could be seen by clicking the tabs.

➡ *Consider providing reviews and / or ratings.*

This is not a hard and fast rule — the need for information provided by experts and other customers depends on the product, how familiar customers are with the merchandise, and the degree to which one person's opinion will be relevant to others.

In our study, SmarterKids provided expert ratings for all their products. eToys had ratings from parents and kids for some of their products. And Peet's had customer and employee reviews of their coffees. Although many users ignored this information, a few appreciated the reviews and found them helpful. Sample comments:

- Peet's: One user looked at Employee Reviews, saying they were "for people like me who don't know much about coffee, which I think is very user-friendly."

- eToys: Another user commented on a toy car: "That's cool — kids rate it four out of five. Kids like it better than adults, which is actually good."

Other users expressed skepticism, however, that such reviews could be unbiased. For more information about how second opinions can affect the credibility of an e-commerce site, see the Trust chapter.

➡ *Explain details that can't be seen in the product image.*

Sometimes words can explain things the picture doesn't show. A user who was looking for a jacket on Nordstrom had trouble getting his questions answered. Did it have pockets? What kind of lining did it have? The text on the product page didn't reveal the answers.

The text for the weatherproof microfiber jacket was much better: "This gives you more information about what the jacket is than the leather one did," he said. "It tells you it has pockets, zipper, liner, machine washable. The leather jacket said nothing about the jacket." Note that the features the user mentioned — lining, pockets, zipper — are not readily apparent from the microfiber image.

NORDSTROM.com

gifts

Browse Leather. ◀ ▶

▶ GIFTS FOR
  WOMEN

▼ GIFTS FOR MEN
  • Basics
  • Executive Gifts
  • Golf Gifts.
  • Great Coats.
  • Great Sweaters.
  • Leather.
  • Men's
    Accessories
  • Performance
    Wear
  • Robes &
    Sleepwear.

▶ GIFTS FOR
  TEENS

▶ GIFTS FOR
  KIDS

▶ GIFTS FOR
  PET LOVERS

LARGER VIEW

EXPERT Leather Bomber
Rich lambskin with straight, open-bottom styling updates the timeless bomber jacket. Its sleek cut makes it an option for dress-up as well as a casual wear-with-everything jacket. Italian lambskin. Professional leather care only. By EXPERT by Evergreen; imported. For color and size selection, click on the pull-down menu below.
#15454 $295.00

▶ SELECT

men

Browse Casual ◀ ▶

▶ TROUSERS &
  JEANS

▶ SHIRTS

▶ SWEATERS

▼ OUTERWEAR
  • Casual
  • Leather.
  • All-weather
  • Hats, Gloves &
    Scarves

▶ SPORTCOATS
  & SUITS

▶ NECKWEAR

▶ UNDERWEAR &
  FURNISHINGS

▶ EXTENDED
  SIZES

LARGER VIEW

Weatherproof Microfiber Jacket
Designed of a polyester/nylon blend that is sandwashed five times for a feel as soft as suede. Wind and water repellent; two front pockets with zip closure; cotton poplin lining. Machine wash. By Impermeable by Weatherproof; imported. For color and size selection, click on the pull-down menu below.
#17820 $79.50

▶ SELECT

These two Nordstrom pages had the same layout, but the description of the microfiber jacket did a better job of answering the user's questions than the description of the bomber jacket did, because it explained details the photo didn't show. P6

Our recommendation to explain details isn't foolproof. Often, text is only an imperfect substitute for better images. Many users do not read very much on websites, so they miss details that are provided only in the text. We saw this behavior on Furniture, where one user wanted a picture of the inside of a Hardware Dry Bar to see whether it had any shelves. The text on the same page clearly stated that it had one adjustable shelf, but the user never saw that. He was sufficiently bothered by what he perceived as a lack of visual information that he gave up on the item.

Ideally, product text and images should work together. The images should show as much detail as possible. The accompanying text can reinforce key features and explain intangibles.

Technical Issues

▶ *If you must use downloads and plug-ins,*
make the installation process as transparent as possible.

On CustomDisc, users could listen to audio clips of songs with RealPlayer, a third-party plug-in program. During our research, we found it made a huge difference to users whether or not RealPlayer was installed on the test computer.

For the US tests, the computer had RealPlayer already set up. All six users chose to listen to one or more audio clips. After a user clicked CustomDisc's Listen button, RealPlayer automatically launched itself, downloaded the audio file, and played the music — all with no user intervention required. Even users who had no prior experience with RealPlayer were able to stop the clip when they wanted to and close RealPlayer when it was done. Playing audio samples was an important aspect of the user experience on CustomDisc, and the US users appreciated being able to hear the songs.

But in Denmark, it was a different story. The Danish test computer did not have RealPlayer installed. We watched all four users attempt to listen to the music by clicking the Listen button. A standard file transfer dialog box appeared indicating that the website wanted to transfer an audio file. The browser asked the users to indicate where they wanted to place the file. The users downloaded the file to a default location without really understanding what they were doing. The result was that even though the computer could run audio files, none of the users knew how to make the computer play the music. None of the users made the slightest attempt to find out what the problem was.

The issue here is that CustomDisc made no apparent effort to help customers with the technical aspects of downloading and playing music samples. It's not necessary to have RealPlayer to download a music file, but our test proved that potential customers who don't have RealPlayer, and who don't have the technical know-how to download and play an audio file, will miss out on one of this website's major sales attractions.

Ideally, playing a music sample should be transparent to the user. If that's not possible, CustomDisc — and other sites that depend upon third-party technologies — should make overt efforts to provide as much help and troubleshooting information as possible.

▶ *If the technology isn't reliable, leave it out.*

On Boo, half the users couldn't get the Spin and Zoom features (described later) to work. This was a technical problem, not a usability problem, because when users clicked the buttons labeled Spin and Zoom, nothing happened. Usually they tried a couple of times and gave up. Other users, who appeared to be doing exactly the same thing, got a response from the buttons. This technical problem was unfortunate, because users who were able to make Spin and Zoom work liked this functionality and found it helpful. Those who couldn't make it work, however, expressed their frustration out loud. Their shopping experience was worse because of the technical glitch than it would have been if this functionality had been absent.

Interestingly, after our study, Boo introduced "modes" as a method of dealing with some of the site's technical constraints. Users could choose between Simple and Full Modes. The main difference was that Full Mode supported Spin and Zoom, and the Simple Mode didn't.

Shoppers who weren't sure which mode they should use could click a link to test their connection speed, and the site would recommend whether to use the Full or Simple Mode. We didn't test this approach, so we don't know if users would have grasped the concept of modes and what this rather technical page was telling them.

Boo was checking connection speed only through this link — not other factors such as the browser version. We ran our tests using 56k modems and the latest versions of Netscape Navigator and Internet Explorer, so theoretically our test setup should have met their criteria.

Although we credit Boo for these innovative approaches to displaying merchandise, we can hardly call Boo's implementation a success. The site's behavior was too unpredictable, and it frustrated users who couldn't get the highly attractive Spin and Zoom features to work. Boo might have been better off removing the troublesome features rather than running the risk of irritating and confusing potential customers.

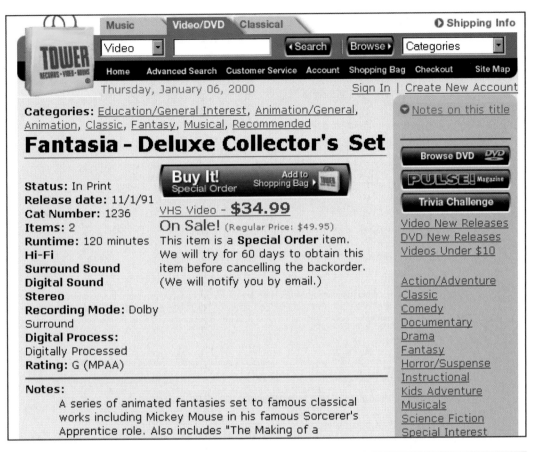

Users who knew that the cover of Disney's *Fantasia* featured Mickey Mouse in a sorcerer's hat had trouble identifying the video on TowerRecords — they had to read the notes carefully. The *Fantasia* video would have been easier to identify on Reel.com. P7

Product Images

Some users made a point of mentioning that they were visually oriented and wanted to see pictures of products. Whether they mentioned it or not, all of our users relied upon images to some degree when shopping for products. (On CustomDisc, the downloadable music samples were the audio equivalent of images.)

▶ *Provide a recognizable image for familiar items.*

This guideline is especially important when the customer might recognize the item from advertising or previous experience. Recognizing a familiar item visually is easier for some people than recalling its name.

For Disney's *Fantasia*, users wanted to see the image of the video cover. One user was completely unable to identify this video because he was looking for the picture of Mickey Mouse with the sorcerer's hat, but the product page didn't show it. We also know from other tests that it can be impossible for users to identify even simple products if no picture is available.

To accommodate users who have difficulty seeing, or who turn off images on their browsers, it remains important to provide meaningful ALT text. ALT text is what appears when the user has turned off images, and it's also what screen readers, or voice browsers, speak.

▶ *Provide images that are big, detailed, and free of visual distractions.*

As one user said, "The biggest problem with any kind of shopping I've done online is that it's not a big enough picture for me to assess whether or not I like it." Of course, the need to provide an enlarged image depends partly on the merchandise. Potential buyers should be able to see the product details that are important in making their purchase decisions.

Sites had different approaches to displaying images and enlarged images. Here is a breakdown, listed from worst to best:

Image Display Approaches

Functionality for Displaying Images	Site and Comments
Needs Improvement: Images were missing or not large enough to show the details users cared about.	• BasketHaus: There were no separate product pages. Instructions said: "Please click on the thumbnailed pictures, to enlarge the image!" Clicking an image showed a slightly larger image (the size varied) on a separate page with nothing but a Back button. Users complained they still couldn't see what was in the basket. • NorwaySweaters: A decent-sized image could be enlarged by clicking on it (no instructions). About half of the images did not display any larger than the image on the product page, though, and the page had nothing but the image — not even a Back link. • TowerRecords: Product pages did not have images of the video covers, which users wanted. • Wal-Mart: Images of products were fairly small, with no way to enlarge them. • Sears: Images of microwaves were relatively small, and there was no way to enlarge them. Users wanted to see the control panel.
Acceptable: Images on product pages were usually large and detailed enough to satisfy users, but users occasionally tried to click to see a larger image.	• 1800flowers • eToys • Gevalia • HermanMiller • Reel • SmarterKids • Iflorist
Acceptable: Sites offered larger images, which either opened in the same window or in a second browser window.	• Living: Images on product pages were fairly large and detailed. Some images could be enlarged further, others couldn't. • Sears: Images of tools could be enlarged by clicking the words "Larger photo," but not by clicking the image itself. • Furniture: Instructions below the image said, "Click image for a larger photo," but you couldn't click the instructions too. • Peet's: No separate product pages were provided. Clicking an image from the category page opened a second window containing a larger image. The site provided no instructions except for a small symbol of a magnifying glass. • Disney: Clicking the Zoom button or the image opened a second window that showed the image about four times larger.
Good: Enlarged images sometimes showed a different angle. Clickable thumbnails offered views of the item in different colors.	• Nordstrom: Images could be enlarged by clicking the magnifying glass or the words "Larger view" (but not by clicking the image itself). Some enlarged images were very clear; others less so. Sometimes the enlarged image was the same as the thumbnail, other times it was a different view of the product (which users liked). • Jcrew: Instructions said "click for larger view," but you had to click the image, not the instructions. The enlarged image appeared along with clickable thumbnails of other colors. Most enlarged images were very crisp and detailed.
Honorable Mention: Sophisticated options for viewing images were used, such as rotation and multilevel zoom. Unfortunately, they worked only about half the time — otherwise Boo might have deserved an Excellent rating.	• Boo: Images on product pages could be rotated and zoomed. Zoom and Spin buttons each opened new windows. For footwear, there was a "Heel + Toe" feature. When the user moved the mouse over the Heel + Toe button, the image changed from a side view to front and back view (one shoe facing front and the other facing back).

The critical factor in determining how large images should be, and whether enlarged images are necessary, is whether or not shoppers can see the product details they need in order to make a purchase decision. For some products, such as videos and coffee, the visual details aren't very important, so it was acceptable for some sites to use relatively small images that could not be enlarged. The need for an enlarged view was strongest on the clothing and furniture sites, because users were most concerned about details for these products.

The toy and flower sites we tested showed thumbnails on the category pages and larger images on product pages that were large enough to satisfy users. BasketHaus needed real product pages with images as large and detailed as those on Iflorist in order to meet user needs.

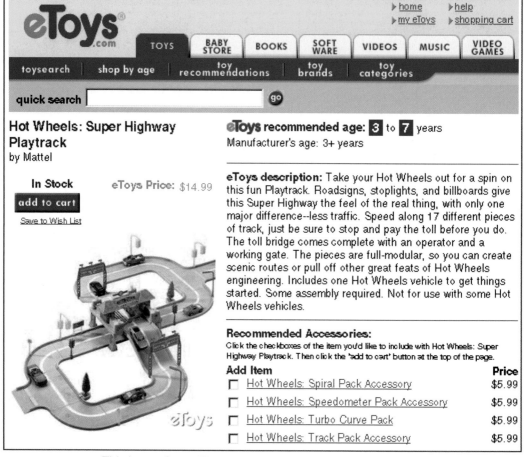

This image from eToys could not be enlarged, but it was enough to give users a good idea of the toy. P8

The Jcrew site provided especially large, clear images. Its enlarged images were shown as big as possible against a white background. With the exception of some dark-colored items, the details were clearly visible. Nordstrom deserves an honorable mention for the clarity and detail of some of its images, although not all of them were useful enough. Users of these sites responded positively to the enlarged images, as these example remarks show:

- Jcrew: One user clicked Upland Boot. "Got a good [image] of the boot, telling me whether it's low-cut, high-cut, how it's laced. Gives you a good illustration, and it's clear and distinct." User clicked for larger view. "It will blow it up even further, which is an excellent thing. Almost life-size of the boot." The image of the boot was so sharp and detailed that you could see the grain of the leather.

- Nordstrom: A user looking for pants explained there were some pleats she liked and others she didn't. She clicked a pair of pants for a larger view. "That gives me a better idea." She was satisfied that those pants had the type of pleats she wanted.

In some cases, users decided after looking at an enlarged image that they didn't want the item, which is good because one important purpose of images is to help users eliminate products they would not be happy with. For example, the enlarged image of a bunk bed on Living showed one user that the bed had no storage underneath, when she was looking for beds that had drawers. Another user decided he didn't like the weathered-looking leather of the Upland Boot because "it looks like an old brown shoe."

Contrast Jcrew's clear sweater image (Image P10) with the enlarged image from NorwaySweaters. It's hard to see the sweater colors and pattern, let alone the type of fasteners it has. The leaves in the background, the dappled lighting, and the model's patterned pants all create visual distractions — as does a red version of the same sweater, which appears in the lower left corner.

On NorwaySweaters, it was hard to see the color and pattern of the sweater even in this enlarged image. P9

Cashmere ribbed crew

blue
heather

charcoal
hea

black

grey
heather

J.CREW

This is the kind of enlarged view on Jcrew that users found very helpful. You can clearly see the collars, cuffs, and texture of this sweater. P10

We don't know whether it's really necessary to have a Zoom button or explicit instructions to click the image for a larger view (although instructions probably don't hurt). Users consistently clicked images when they wanted to see a larger view, even in the absence of instructions.

On Sears and Nordstrom, users had to click the instructions and not the image, which caused some momentary confusion. On Furniture and Jcrew, it was just the opposite — you had to click the image and not the instructions.

Tip: When you offer enlarged images, the thumbnail should always be clickable.

Tip: When you provide instructions, make them clickable too.

➡ *Beware of losing details in dark-colored images.*

Dark colors make it especially hard to see product details, or even the shade of the color itself. Users sometimes rejected dark-colored items (typically, clothing and footwear) because they couldn't see them clearly. Dark-colored images were a problem even in enlarged views. As one user said of an enlarged Black Watch Blazer on Jcrew. "It looks like a big black mountain." Unable to see any details of the blazer, the user went on to a different item. Similarly, photos of black microwave ovens on Sears made it hard for users to see the control panel.

Tip: When showing dark-colored items, be innovative. It might help to show a sketch or wire-frame drawing of the item (in addition to its picture), or to default to showing the color that allows the details to be seen most clearly. Another option would be to show a grayscale image that has been brightened, traced, or otherwise digitally enhanced to improve clarity. We did not test a site that had a good solution for the inherent problems in seeing dark-colored items.

➡ *Consider showing alternative views of a product.*

As with image size, the importance of showing multiple views depends on the product. In our study, users sometimes wanted to see other views of items (especially clothing and furniture). Seeing the side or back of an item was important to their purchasing decision.

Boo was the only site we tested that provided several ways to view each item. Unfortunately, the multiple-view features frequently didn't work or were annoyingly slow. When the Spin function worked, it allowed the user to rotate the item on its vertical axis. Users liked Spin because they could see the sides and back of the item.

Only three users saw the Heel + Toe feature on Boo. (We had asked users to shop for warm clothing, and most spent their time looking at jackets.) Users liked this feature, which was activated when the mouse cursor was positioned over the Heel + Toe button. There was no way, however, to view the sole of the shoe, which can be an important factor in determining the quality and suitability of a shoe for various activities.

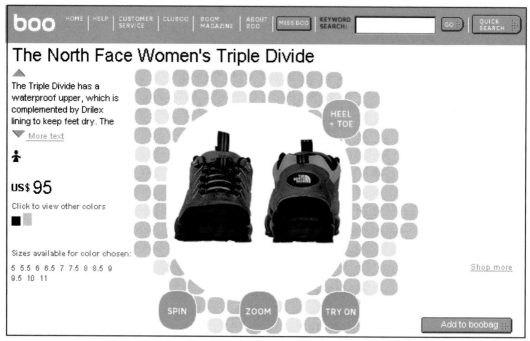

Boo showed footwear from the back and front when the cursor was placed over Boo's Heel + Toe button.

Jcrew showed some of its shoes from two angles — a simple way to implement multiple views. P11

Showing alternative views doesn't necessarily involve the use of advanced technology. When we looked at Jcrew after we completed our study, we noticed that some of their photographs of footwear showed both shoes — one from the side and one from the top. We didn't test this method, but it seems to be a simple and useful way to show the user more information about the product without demanding additional technology be installed.

➡ *Show only what's included for sale.*

When several items appeared in on a product page, it was sometimes hard for users to determine exactly what was included — and what was not. Furniture and Living had the most problems with multiple-item confusion. These sites showed photos of furniture sets and even entire furnished rooms.

Multiple items were also a problem on Gevalia, where the photo of the French Coffee Press showed a matching decanter that was not included in the $24.98 price. In other cases the accompanying text didn't always help to clarify what was actually being sold.

Users tended to assume they were getting what was shown in the picture. One user was so confused by this issue on Living that he abandoned the bunk beds he originally wanted. After discovering that the matching chest was not included, he started questioning whether he was getting both the top and bottom bunk. Unable to tell, he gave up.

French Coffee Press

Prepare coffee right at your table in a bold French press. Delicious gourmet coffee is as easy as 1-2-3. Add your favorite Gevalia® roast, pour boiling water and let it steep, then press the plunger down. Made of glass with a beautiful jeweltone top and handle and matching coffee scoop. Makes 6 cups. Specify sapphire blue or ruby red.

Users weren't quite sure how many of the pictured items on Gevalia they were getting for their $24.98. (Answer: only the red-handled French press (left) and matching coffee scoop were included.) P12

We're not implying that it's bad to show several matching items together in one picture — as long as it's crystal clear that the items are sold separately and there is a way to see more detail about each item. For example, one rocking chair on Living appeared in a whole room full of matching furniture. There was no way to see just the chair, and users complained about that. For other rocking chairs that were not part of a set, however, the site did show an image of just the chair.

Tip: Don't reinvent the catalog. Paper catalogs have also faced this context problem, so we can look to them for ideas about how to solve this problem on the Web. For example, Staples' paper catalog sells sets of office furniture. They show the entire set in the photograph, but they put letters on top of each item. A nearby list shows the price of each item next to the corresponding letter.

Users complained that there was no way on Living to see the rocking chair in the middle picture separately, the way the other two chairs were shown. P13

Price, Other Costs, and Availability

➧ *Put price (and currency) on both*
the category page and the product page.

Our users said they wanted to see prices at the category page level, not just when they got down to the individual product page.

Most sites showed prices well, with the exception of Living, where prices for some items were available only by e-mail. (As documented in both the Selling Strategies and Trust chapters, users had strong negative reactions to this approach.)

When a site sells goods in multiple countries, it is helpful to indicate the price in the user's local currency. Boo put "US$" before its prices to indicate US dollars. When a user chose Denmark from the home page, the prices were shown in Danish kroner.

▶ *Show all costs — or lack thereof.*

Users appreciated seeing information about additional costs right on the product page, rather than waiting until the checkout process. Iflorist showed the $6.95 service fee right on the product page; 1800flowers didn't. But 1800flowers had delivery information on the product page, which was good, because users wanted to know this information also.

Some — but not all — users recognized that the total cost would depend on where the item was shipped. The Danish users were especially concerned, because many of them had encountered high shipping costs in the past.

One user on 1800flowers suggested it would be nice if you could enter the destination (probably a postal code) right on the product page and have the site calculate what the total cost would be, including delivery charges and tax. She emphasized that she wanted to see the total cost on the product page rather than in the shopping cart, because total cost was part of her purchase decision.

Showing total cost on a per-item basis is more complicated for sites that have a per-order charge as well as shipping costs for each item. One solution would be to show the total cost of the order in a corner of the page, and then show the incremental cost of adding this item to the shopping cart on the product page. An even better solution would be to simplify the shipping and handling charges so that this problem just goes away.

Some sites such as Furniture, Living, and HermanMiller offered free shipping, but this benefit wasn't clear to most users when they were looking at products. Instead, they discovered shipping was free only when they were completing the order form. Sites like these that carry high-priced, high-quality items could lower the risk of shocking potential customers with their high prices by advertising free shipping earlier in the shopping process.

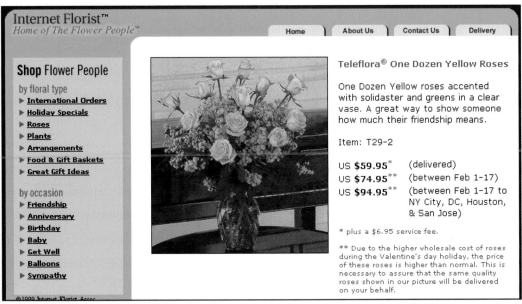

Iflorist showed the service charge on the product page. 1800flowers showed delivery information. Users wanted to know both the service charge and the delivery information. P14

➡️ *Link to guarantees and policies.*

It is a good idea to provide links to guarantees and return policies on the product page. Although not every customer will use these links, a few of our users commented on them:

- Disney: The user readily found and clicked the link to the return policy at the bottom of the product page.

- Sears: "I like it that the guarantee and privacy policy is at the bottom of every page — not something I have to go search for."

- Living: "Free delivery, 30-day money back guarantee kind of hit me before I even got into it." (At the time of our test, some product pages had links to free shipping and the money-back guarantee down the right side of the page.)

- Wal-Mart: The user appreciated the link to the manufacturer's warranty for a car seat.

Prices and promotions are for the continental U.S. only.
© 1999 Sears, Roebuck and Co. Satisfaction guaranteed or your money back.
Please view our privacy policy and terms and conditions. * Credit Details
Questions? Call 1-800-349-4358

Contact Us | Return/Exchange Policy | Shipping Information

Please click here for legal restrictions and terms of use applicable to this site.
Use of this site signifies your agreement to the terms of use.

Please click here for Disney Online's Internet Privacy Policy.

© Disney. All rights reserved.

Sears and Disney had links to guarantees and return policies at the bottom of their product pages. A few users followed these links when they wanted to know about returning an item. P15

Not all sites had convenient links. It was hard for users to find the low-price guarantee on SmarterKids — it was available only from the About Us page. Some users couldn't find the guarantee at all.

It is also good to provide information on manufacturers' warranties. Wal-Mart did this for a couple of its car seats, and one user reviewed this information thoroughly. He was more inclined to purchase a particular car seat after learning it had a manufacturer's seven-year warranty.

Finally, when any page makes a reference to a guarantee or return policy, make sure these references are links, because people might try to click on them:

- Boo: A user tried to find the return policy. "They had all the things about free delivery, free returns. ... I don't know where to find out information about it." The user tried to click on "free returns" at the bottom of the home page, but it wasn't a link.

- Reel: A user wanted to read about the five-point guarantee indicated by an icon in the upper left corner of the registration page, but the icon was not clickable.

➡ *Clearly indicate when the customer will get the order.*

There are two main factors that influence how long it will take for a customer to receive an item ordered online, as explained by this page excerpt from HermanMiller:

Shipping Lead Time
_____

How long will it take to get your order? The answer is the sum of two parts.

1. The first part deals with how long it takes us to make the stuff on your order. That's the "manufacturing time" listed above for each product you've put in your shopping cart. Since we ship all of the items on your order at the same time, we use the longest "manufacturing time" shown above. So, this order will be ready for shipment in 4 calendar days.
2. The second part depends on the delivery option you'll choose in a moment. Once you do, we'll add the "manufacturing time" to the delivery time and give you a date on or before which you can expect your order to arrive.

You won't know your final cost until you choose your delivery option in a few moments. This subtotal doesn't include taxes or shipping charges. We can't compute them until you decide how you want your order delivered. You'll get a complete picture of your total price to review before you commit to this order.

Please note that right now we're licensed and equipped to sell only within the continental USA. If you live elsewhere, check out www.hermanmiller.com for a list of Herman Miller showrooms and representatives worldwide.

Secure Server On
_____

Please note: We work hard to protect our customers by using the latest and greatest encryption software to make our ordering process secure. Unfortunately, not all browsers are designed to process secure server orders. If your browser delivers an error message, or if you are connecting to the Internet through AOL, you may need to switch to our non-secure server. Read more about security, or switch to non-secure server.

HermanMiller's shopping cart explained the factors that affected time to delivery. P16

Users generally expected to find information about shipping options in the shopping cart rather than on the product page, so delivery time was not a key issue for most product pages.

The exception was the two florist sites, where delivery time could be a crucial issue in whether a user decided to buy the item. (For more information about delivery time issues, see the Selling Strategies and Checkout & Registration chapters.)

Most of the test sites didn't do very well with what HermanMiller called "how long it takes us to make the stuff on your order." We call this "availability." In most cases, it was not apparent from the product page whether an item was out of stock or if it would take a long time to be delivered. Availability information was important to users, even in our test setting, even though most of them weren't actually completing purchases. eToys did well at reporting availability. "In Stock" was displayed prominently above the "add to cart" button.

Items may be unavailable for immediate purchase or simply unavailable for other reasons:

- **Out of stock or back-ordered** –The online merchant is waiting to receive the next shipment of the item from the manufacturer. For example, inventories of popular toys run low during the Christmas holiday season. Sometimes the online merchant knows when the next shipment is scheduled to arrive, but other times the merchant may be at the mercy of unpredictable delays from the manufacturer.

- **Discontinued or clearance** – The item is no longer being manufactured, or the store has no plans to replenish the inventory. We saw several examples of older movies that were no longer offered for sale. Many clothing retailers hold "clearance" sales to get rid of leftover merchandise. Usually, not all sizes, colors and styles are available.

- **Custom-made** – The item is built to the customer's specifications. This feature is more likely to be offered for large items such as furniture, because it is expensive to keep finished goods in a warehouse. For custom-made products, the site should tell the customer the length of time needed to manufacture the item, which can range from a day or two (CustomDisc) to 10–12 weeks (HermanMiller).

Regardless of the reason for delay, customers just want to know how long it will take to receive their purchase — they don't really care about the distinction between the online merchant and the manufacturer. The length of time that the user is willing to wait can depend on several factors, including how badly the user wants the item and whether the user can obtain a suitable alternative more quickly.

If a product is not available right away, the user may opt to:

- Wait for the site to ship the item.
- Shop elsewhere.
- Give up on that item, perhaps choosing something else.
- Buy nothing.

The bottom line is that product page should clearly indicate whether an item is in stock, and if it is not, the page should explain the situation, telling when the item will be available or showing the color and size combinations that are available. And of course, successful online retailers must deliver what they promise.

The best way to show availability depends the merchandise. Here are some examples:

Methods of Showing Availability

Type of Merchandise	Availability Issues	What Sites Did
Clothing and toys	Shoppers may not be willing to wait for an item, especially when they believe they can find it elsewhere. Beyond having a store locator on the site, none of the test sites attempted to steer customers to their physical stores or offered any way to check those stores for hard-to-find items.	• Jcrew indicated when the item would be available and informed the customer if other color options were available sooner. The problem was that this information appeared only after the user had added the item to the shopping cart. This approach wasn't very satisfactory. After choosing a couple of items that turned out to be unavailable, two users said they would have given up and gone to the mall. • Nordstrom's approach was to show availability on the product page by graying out unavailable size / color combinations in the menu. Users understood that gray meant not available, but unfortunately, these menus had other significant usability problems, so they were not an effective solution. Also, no information was provided about when the item would be available again — if ever.
Videos	Some videos had not yet been released, but their release date was known. These videos were likely not available at other stores either. Some videos were no longer being produced, so another store might still have had a few in stock.	• Reel offered not-yet-released videos by using a Pre-Order button and announcing the availability date. This feature was good as far as it goes, but they did not define what "pre-order" meant. • TowerRecords showed "n/a" when a video was not available, but the meaning of "n/a" was not explained, and the term was not clickable. Reel simply said the video was not available.
Furniture	Some users balked at the idea of waiting several weeks for furniture to be custom-made. We don't know how long they would wait if they ordered a comparable item from their local store. Eventually, retailers who sell products with long delivery delays may lose business to those who can deliver more quickly, because on the Web it's very easy to go to another store to see if a comparable product can be obtained sooner.	• HermanMiller said "some configurations of this product ship in two calendar days" for its office chairs. The site gave a more definite estimate in the shopping cart, once the configuration was known. Some items took several weeks for delivery, causing one user to exclaim, "When I make up my mind to buy something, I want it then, not six weeks from now! When I do online shopping, it's because I know I can get it right away." • Living made no mention on its product pages of how long it would take to process the order. • Furniture explicitly mentioned the number of weeks until delivery on the product page. The delay was as long as 10–12 weeks for some items, which the page mentioned were custom-made.

In the future, sites might have to do better than just showing when the product will become available. Consider what happens when you walk into a store and ask for a product that is sold out. The mediocre sales clerk will say, "Sorry, we don't have that." The good sales clerk will tell you, "Yes, we normally carry that, but we don't have any right now. We are expecting a shipment on Thursday." The excellent sales clerk will say, "We should have some on Thursday, but Smith's shop down the road might have it in stock now. Would you like me to call and check?" Although a few of the test sites behaved like the good sales clerk, we've never tested one that acts like the excellent clerk.

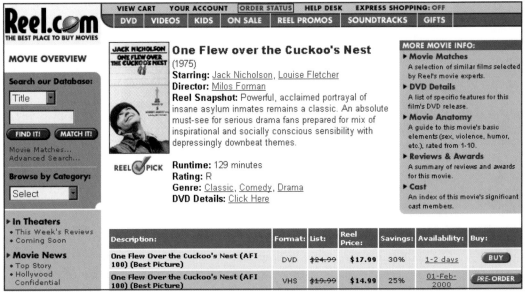

Reel showed the exact date when a movie would be available, so the user could decide whether it was worth the wait. (This image was captured on January 6, 2000.) P17

Specifying Product Options

For many products, customers must specify options. For videos, there are different media (for example, VHS or DVD). For clothing, choices of size and color are usually required. For coffee, regular or decaffeinated must be selected. For furniture, there are often fabric and finish alternatives.

▶ *Show all options on the same page.*

Most of the test sites showed all the options on the product page, except for Furniture. Some wooden items there were offered in as many as 30 different finishes, but only four finishes were displayed at a time, making it impossible to review all the choices at once.

One user never realized how many choices he had, making his selection from the first four shown. He was puzzled that there were so many in the selection list, but he never explored the More button. Although we saw this particular problem with only one user, we've seen many other users wish for side-by-side views when they needed to make a choice. Showing all options is especially important when choosing colors, which are difficult to compare from memory.

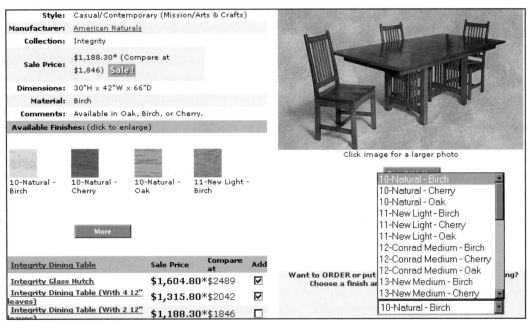

Style:	Casual/Contemporary (Mission/Arts & Crafts)
Manufacturer:	American Naturals
Collection:	Integrity
Sale Price:	$1,188.30* (Compare at $1,846) Sale!
Dimensions:	30"H x 42"W x 66"D
Material:	Birch
Comments:	Available in Oak, Birch, or Cherry.

Available Finishes: (click to enlarge)

10-Natural - Birch
10-Natural - Cherry
10-Natural - Oak
11-New Light - Birch

More

Click image for a larger photo

Integrity Dining Table	Sale Price	Compare at	Add
Integrity Glass Hutch	$1,604.80*	$2489	☑
Integrity Dining Table (With 4 12" leaves)	$1,315.80*	$2042	☑
Integrity Dining Table (With 2 12" leaves)	$1,188.30*	$1846	☐

Want to ORDER or put
Choose a finish and ng?

10-Natural - Birch
10-Natural - Cherry
10-Natural - Oak
11-New Light - Birch
11-New Light - Cherry
11-New Light - Oak
12-Conrad Medium - Birch
12-Conrad Medium - Cherry
12-Conrad Medium - Oak
13-New Medium - Birch
13-New Medium - Cherry

10-Natural - Birch

Furniture made it hard to compare finishes, because it showed only four examples at a time. P18

➡ *Use conventional names for colors.*

Some users were confused by the names of colors, especially on Jcrew, which had fanciful color names, like prussian, lake, iris, and surplus. The problem was worse in the order form, where users were given a choice of remaining colors — by name only — when their initial choice was out of stock. Here are two examples that show the severity of the color-naming problem on Jcrew:

- Tipped terry polo shirt. A user clicked "navy" from selection list and added the shirt to his order. He didn't notice the "sold out" message for the navy shirt. He thought the word "surplus" meant they had "a surplus of color." (Surplus is Jcrew's name for "army surplus" green.) He was certain he was getting a navy-blue shirt until we explained otherwise. He said he would have been very upset if he had received a green shirt.

- Lambswool scarf. "I couldn't tell you what the prussian is, whether it's black or brown or blue," complained one user. "It's called prussian, but that doesn't mean a thing to me. And flannel, I can't tell you what color that is either. I wouldn't order either of them for that reason, because I don't know what color I'm getting." She eventually hit the Back button and went to a different product. The facilitator couldn't determine what color prussian was either.

A few users even had trouble with less exotic color names such as navy and taupe. (Navy is dark blue, and taupe can range from brownish gray to yellowish brown.) On NorwaySweaters, one user mused, "Navy … is 'navy,' navy blue? I'm not sure if that means blue … but I'm pretty sure it is." A minute later he commented, "That's a lot of money to spend if I'm not sure." (Coincidentally, the site changed right after that user test and described the color as navy blue.)

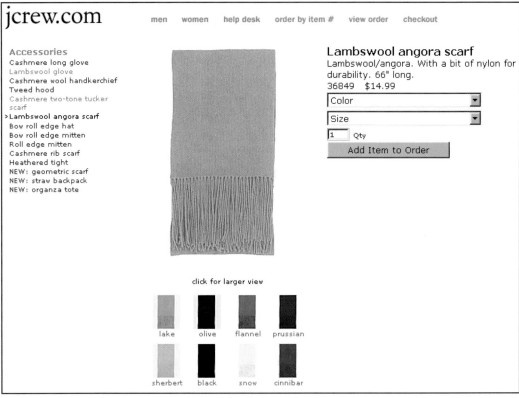

jcrew.com   men   women   help desk   order by item #   view order   checkout

Accessories
Cashmere long glove
Lambswool glove
Cashmere wool handkerchief
Tweed hood
Cashmere two-tone tucker
scarf
> Lambswool angora scarf
Bow roll edge hat
Bow roll edge mitten
Roll edge mitten
Cashmere rib scarf
Heathered tight
NEW: geometric scarf
NEW: straw backpack
NEW: organza tote

Lambswool angora scarf
Lambswool/angora. With a bit of nylon for durability. 66" long.
36849 $14.99

Color ▼

Size ▼

1   Qty

Add Item to Order

click for larger view

lake   olive   flannel   prussian

sherbert   black   snow   cinnibar

One user could not determine what color prussian was, even after viewing the full-size image of the scarf in that color. She gave up on this item. P19

Tip: Use conventional color names. Because choosing the right color is so important to customers, we recommend using color names that are as recognizable as possible or at least translating them into conventional terms. For example, "surplus" might be called "olive green," and "lake" could be "light blue."

Tip: Use text descriptions. For people who have difficulty seeing colors or who turn off images in their browser, having a descriptive color name (in both text and ALT tag) is even more important.

Tip: Test color names for recognition. The recognition of colors can also depend on cultural factors. People who recall the popularity of green kitchen appliances in the US during the 1970s will know exactly what color "avocado" is, but customers from other times and places may never have heard this term. Usability testing will help identify troublesome color terminology.

➡ Show the product image in each available color.

Users expected to see the image of the product in each of the different colors available. When users chose a color, they wanted to see the photo change to display the product in that color. Jcrew included thumbnails for each of the color options. Clicking the thumbnail displayed a large image of the item in that color, which worked well except for the confusing color names. Sears irritated users by showing black microwaves when they had specified a white one:

- "I asked for white. Looks like black. Very poor. I would never buy it. I can't see it at all. It's terrible," one user fumed. A few minutes later, he found another "white" microwave depicted as black. "Terrible. I'd leave this site. I'd probably go to Best Buy" (a discount appliance chain).

- "It says 'white on white,' don't you think the picture would be white?" asked another user. "It didn't display the product that it said it was."

Disclaimers didn't help. Even though Sears clearly stated that the color of the image might not be representative of the unit selected, users still found this practice unacceptable. They doubted that Sears could deliver the microwave they wanted, because Sears couldn't even show the right product to them. Living also used a disclaimer that the image might not change to show the color selection. Once again, we saw the same reaction — users didn't want to buy the item without seeing it in their chosen finish.

Although some swatches on Furniture and Living were quite good at showing details of color and finish, they were not sufficient to help users make a choice. Anyone who has ever bought wallpaper or paint knows that what looks bright and cheerful in a small swatch at the store can be overwhelming on an entire wall at home. Depicting an item with the chosen options reassures customers that they're going to be happy with their purchase.

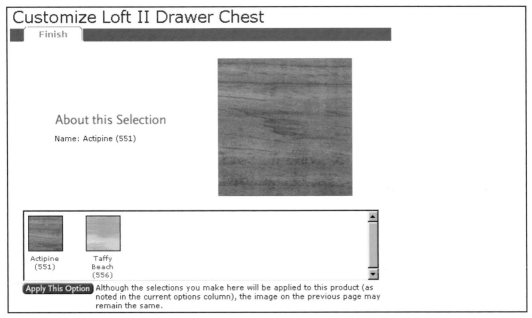

Living's disclaimer that the image might not change was not good enough for users. They didn't want to buy a piece of furniture without seeing it in their chosen finish. P20

➡ *Make sure images match color swatches.*

Furniture, HermanMiller, Boo, and Living used swatches (small rectangles in each available color or pattern) to display the options for a product. Users expected the color of the image to match the color of the swatch they had chosen. When the colors didn't appear to match, users were deterred from buying the item.

- Boo: A user clicked a blue swatch. "I thought I'd like the medium blue they have, but it came out looking like that." (The color was a very dark blue that appeared black in the image.) The user chose green instead.

- Living: "This makes me curious, because I think this blue is supposed to be the same. ...This [swatch] doesn't look the same as that [rocking chair]. That would make me nervous. ... I would assume this is the brilliant blue, which doesn't match this, which makes me wonder what the red and yellow and cream are going to look like."

- HermanMiller: "This is not good — I can't see the color of that green, or that blue. ... I'm not happy that I can't see it too good." The user said the colors looked black to her. "Colors were so poor, if I had to order something and I'm not sure ... . To be honest I wouldn't do it, especially if I'm ordering a $500 chair. If they're going to offer the colors, they should handle it better."

- Furniture: One user rejected a set of items he'd chosen because the finish didn't appear to be the same color on the selections page, although all items indicated an "Actipine" finish.

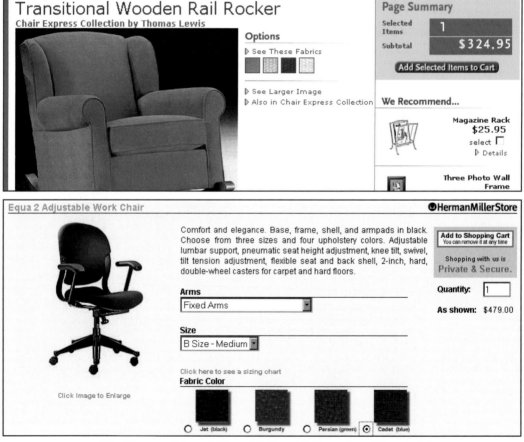

The blue swatch on Living didn't match the color of the chair in the photo. On HermanMiller, the swatches were so dark the user had no idea what the actual color would look like. P21

Jcrew avoided the whole swatch vs. item-color problem by offering enlargeable thumbnail images of the actual item in all its various colors. In general, accurate representation of color online is much more difficult than in a paper catalog, because too much translation happens on the way to the viewer's eye:

- The color in the original photograph depends on several factors, including the lighting, film, and processing techniques (or the resolution and lighting if the photo is digital).

- When a photograph is scanned, the color is changed by the scanner and its software.

- Image editing is a crucial step in the process, because sometimes problems present in the original or scanned image can be corrected. Ideally, the person editing the images would have the original item to look at, otherwise he or she would be able to match the color only to the photograph.

- Even when the graphic editor has done a good job, color fidelity can be compromised by the user's monitor, browser, and operating system, which introduce variables in how colors are displayed.

- User-adjustable controls such as monitor brightness and contrast can also degrade the quality of the picture.

Tip: Use tools and testing to prevent image problems. Although there is nothing as good (or as humbling) as testing a site on many platforms, some image programs can simulate other computer environments. Also, some monitors have changeable settings for number of colors, gamma, and resolution, so the careful developer can often take a good guess at the best possible image. Usability testing will also help show whether the image is good enough.

➡ *Have the customer select options before the product goes in the shopping cart.*

There are two main reasons for having customers select all options before the product goes in the shopping cart:

1. Once customers believe they have selected the item they want, they may not read carefully enough to discover that they aren't quite finished specifying it, or — even worse — that they aren't actually going to get what they requested:

   - Peet's asked customers to choose the grind of the coffee after they put it in the shopping cart. Even though the selection list was visible and it clearly stated, "Select a Grind," four users out of nine skipped right over it. Although three of these users eventually figured out that they needed to select a grind, the fourth didn't notice the red error message at the top of the page (Image P22) and needed help from the facilitator to complete his order. Gevalia's shopping cart also asked customers to select between ground and whole bean, but the default is ground, which at least allowed our users to proceed with the order.

   - When an item wasn't available in the chosen color, Jcrew used a selection list in the shopping cart to let customers pick from the remaining colors that were available. One user never noticed this list and would have ended up with a green shirt instead of the blue one he wanted.

2. Users often pressed the Back button to get out of the shopping cart when they wished to shop for additional items, thus losing any customization they'd made within the shopping cart:

   - On Peet's, one user chose four different coffees. After each of the first two, she used the Back button to get out of the cart after choosing the grind, so her choice of grind wasn't retained. Each time she re-entered the cart, she patiently respecified the grinds. After adding her third coffee, she finally used the Continue Shopping button. This action retained her choices, but it also took her to the top catalog page, causing her extra navigation steps to get back to the page she wanted.

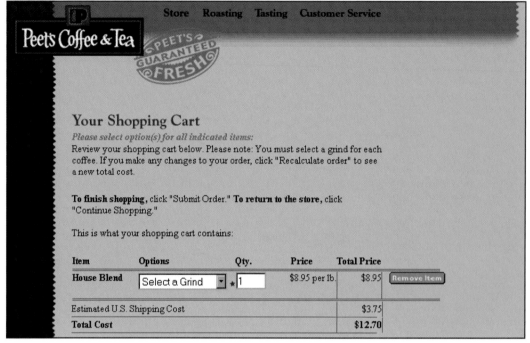

Specifying the grind within the shopping cart was confusing on Peet's. Some users didn't respond to the selection list. One user needed help even after reading the red error message that said "Please select option(s) for all indicated items." P22

This backing-out behavior was common even on sites that provided a Continue Shopping button. There appear to be several reasons why users chose the Back button instead of the Continue Shopping button:

- Clicking the Continue Shopping button preserves choices made in the cart, but many people didn't realize this, so the benefits of using this button were not clear to them.

- The Continue Shopping button often forced extra navigation steps.

- Users couldn't tell where the Continue Shopping button would take them.

- People simply didn't notice the Continue Shopping button.

Overall, the Back button is the most familiar and predictable choice for users. Because there is no simple solution to the "continue shopping" ambiguity, we expect that many users will continue to use Back. For more information about the Continue Shopping issue, see the Checkout & Registration chapter.

➡ *Avoid using multilevel lists or menus to select options.*

This guideline is based on data from only one site (Nordstrom) but the problems we saw were so severe that we caution designers to avoid using multilevel selection lists or menus on product pages.

Of nine users, seven had some kind of difficulty on Nordstrom specifying options or getting products into the shopping cart. Users had difficulty traversing the menus, which displayed sizes and colors in a branching tree structure. Users tended to let their mouse stray too far from the perpendicular when moving to submenus, causing all the menus to disappear. Adding to the confusion, making the selection didn't take the user into the shopping cart — and there was no feedback that anything had happened.

Traversing these menus was prohibitively difficult for some users. One user spent seven minutes trying to figure out how these menus worked, and eventually gave up. P23

➧ *Don't make the buyer specify a "choice" when there is only one option.*

Sometimes there really weren't choices for an item, because it came in only one size or color. The way the Nordstrom and Jcrew product pages were implemented, users were forced to pick size and color from selection lists, which caused confusion when there was no choice to be made. For example, the Black Watch Blazer came in black only, but the user still had to specify the color.

One Nordstrom user was completely baffled by the selection lists for a Lego watch, and she gave up after a painful seven minutes of wrestling with them. It wasn't clear to her that she had to click the rightmost option (which said "One Size") to actually add the watch to her shopping cart.

Tip: Use smart defaults. One user suggested that Jcrew's selection list should default to whatever color item he was currently looking at, and the default should change when he clicked a different colored thumbnail. In other words, he wanted the site to assume that he was most likely to choose the color that he had looked at most recently. Although this may be difficult technically, from a usability perspective it is an intriguing idea.

As one might infer from the name, Jcrew's Black Watch blazer came in black only. It didn't make sense to one user that he still had to choose a color. P24

➤ *Show chosen options in the cart.*

Users wanted to see their specifications appear in the shopping cart as well as on the product page. NorwaySweaters didn't show the color in the shopping cart. This omission perplexed some users who weren't sure they were actually getting the blue sweater that we had asked them to find. In the rest of NorwaySweaters' checkout process, the color was indicated, however.

Users wanted the shopping cart on NorwaySweaters to show the color, as later pages of the checkout process did. P25

Adding Products to the Shopping Cart

Inability to get an item into the shopping cart accounted for 6% of the sales catastrophes we saw in this study. Although this might not seem like a large percentage, these problems were especially painful to watch, because the user had invested time and effort in choosing a product and was ready to complete the purchase.

Before we discuss the problems users had in getting items into the cart, we should first mention that users had no problems with Disney, NorwaySweaters, or Reel's shopping carts. Additionally, users had only minor difficulties on eToys and Gevalia. When we found a site where users did have trouble, it was instructive to compare it to the sites where users had few or no problems.

No users had trouble getting a sweater into the shopping cart on NorwaySweaters, even though they had to scroll down to see the "Add to shopping cart" button. P26

➡️ *Beware of using clever names for the shopping cart and Buy button.*

When we use the terms "shopping cart" and "buy button," we don't mean to imply that these exact terms are the only ones that should be used. Calling the shopping cart something other than "shopping cart" does not automatically mean there will be usability problems. Boo's "boobag" didn't confuse anyone, for instance. Because of the potential for confusion, however, any unusual name like "wheelbarrow" or "sledge" should pass usability testing before being implemented on a live site.

Similarly, the exact wording on the Buy button varied among successful websites. "Add to cart," "Add to shopping cart," and "Buy" all worked just fine, leading us to conclude that there are probably quite a few valid wordings for this button.

Conversely, using "shopping cart" doesn't guarantee an absence of problems. The meaning of the term "cart" wasn't always clear, especially to our non-American users. One Danish user on Peet's wasn't sure what a cart was and tried to look it up in the site's glossary but did not find it. Another Danish user decided that "empty cart" would be the way to pay for her items, because she thought in terms of literally emptying the cart onto the counter as one would do in a real store. These kinds of problems are difficult to predict, so we watch for them carefully in usability tests.

Even a normally unambiguous word like "basket" can confound shoppers, as we saw on 1800flowers. The word "basket" was too similar to the terminology used to describe the merchandise. 1800flowers sells gift baskets, leading at least one user to infer that "add to basket" was a means of customizing what she was trying to purchase — by letting her choose a different basket for the arrangement — rather than the way to buy it. With that impression firmly in mind, she became completely stuck and couldn't complete her purchase. Two other users had similar problems but eventually figured it out for themselves. Three of nine users had significant difficulty with the "add to basket" button.

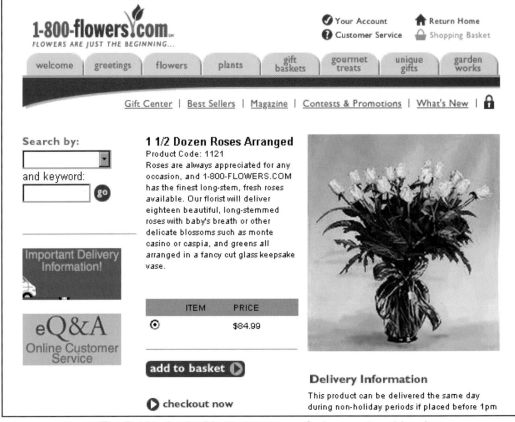

The "add to basket" button was a confusing way to add an item to the shopping cart on 1800flowers. Users tended to click "checkout now" instead. P27

➡️ *Use a simple button for the buy mechanism.*

On two of the test sites, users had a surprising amount of difficulty identifying the mechanism that would let them buy a product:

- HermanMiller: Three users out of nine had some trouble figuring how to buy a chair. One user was temporarily confused, because she scrolled the Add to Shopping Cart button off the page while she was selecting the fabric color. Another user clicked Private & Secure and got completely distracted. A third user hesitated before she figured out how to continue.

- TowerRecords: One user spent more than eight minutes trying to find the Buy It! button (Image P7). He didn't notice it, even when he was actively looking for it. He even looked in Help to find an answer. We finally had to show it to him. Another user had similar difficulty but did manage to find the button after a couple of minutes.

Three users had trouble identifying the "Add to Shopping Cart" button on this page. P28

The interesting similarity about the Buy buttons on these two sites is that they both contained extra words and visual elements. It's possible that the users skipped over the buttons after subconsciously identifying them as ads. (This study and others have noted "ad blindness" behavior.) Although it's never a good idea to over-design something, it seems to be particularly risky with Buy buttons. In this study, Buy buttons worked best when they looked like simple push-buttons.

Tip: Test to make sure page elements are noticeable. Once you know where something is, it becomes very obvious to you, and it's difficult to imagine that someone else doesn't notice it. Thus, testing with customers is the only way to know whether a buy button (or anything else, for that matter) is noticeable.

➡ *Put a Buy button on enlarged views.*

Jcrew, NorwaySweaters, and BasketHaus did not provide any way to add an item to the shopping cart from the enlarged image page. Instead, the user had to click the Back button to return to the product page in order to add the item to the shopping cart.

For example, three users wanted to order from an enlarged view page on Jcrew, because that was the page that helped them decide they wanted the item. We saw users try the "order by item #" option (which would work only if you knew the item's catalog number) and "checkout." All three users eventually got past this problem, but they spent up to several minutes figuring it out (Image P10).

Include a Buy button on any page containing product information, even on pages that contain only enlarged pictures. Never force customers to back up to make a purchase. Instead, give them a way to proceed with their purchase from right where they are.

➡ *Provide shopping instructions in the empty cart.*

When they wanted to buy something, users sometimes clicked the shopping cart icon or checkout button without adding the item to the cart first. Typically, the result was an empty cart with no explanation. We saw this happen on many sites: Boo, Sears, SmarterKids, HermanMiller, Jcrew, Living, CustomDisc, and 1800flowers.

Danish users were somewhat more likely to be confused about the difference between "shopping cart" and "check out" than their American counterparts were, but we saw this behavior on both sides of the Atlantic. Sites that also had gift registries or wish lists added more confusion about what was actually going to be purchased.

We saw several users click View Cart or Add to Gift Registry when they were trying to purchase an item on SmarterKids. P29

- Boo: Two users initially clicked the Buy Now button instead of the Add to Boobag button. Two more debated which to click before deciding on Add to Boobag. They all figured it out on their own eventually. All users seemed to understand what the Boobag was.

- SmarterKids: One user clicked the shopping cart icon, instead of Add to Cart, when he was on a page with an item he wanted. He interpreted the empty shopping cart to mean he needed to register first.

- SmarterKids: A Danish user clicked Add to Gift Registry instead of Add to Cart, which is quite understandable, because the concept of a gift registry is totally unfamiliar to Danes, and our task involved buying a gift.

All the sites that had the empty cart problem could have done more to solve it. 1800flowers actually had a help topic called, "Why is my basket empty?" But no one noticed it. Users did notice the empty basket, though, which said simply, "Your basket is empty." This text was followed by a fine-print explanation that the problem might be caused by the user's browser not accepting cookies, which was not the issue in any of our tests.

1800flowers seemed aware of the empty cart problem and provided some information intended to help, but this information wasn't where shoppers were most likely to need it. The empty shopping cart is the best place to explain how to purchase items.

Why is my basket empty?

If the products you select are not showing up in your basket, one of two things is probably happening. You may not be fully adding the product to your basket or your browser may not be set up to work properly with the basket.

First, when you select a product, make sure you completely fill in the shipping information and click on either the "Shop More" button or the "Check Out Now" button on the bottom of the page. This should add that product to your basket. (You can confirm this by clicking on the "Shopping Basket" button which is in the top navigation bar on every page.)

If your product is still not showing in your basket, your browser could be set up to not accept "cookies". This site uses cookies to keep the items you've added to your order associated with you. We do not put any personal or billing information in these cookies, so there is no security

---

1800flowers had a FAQ called "Why is my basket empty?" but no one saw it. At least two users saw the empty basket, where this explanation does not appear but easily could. P30

Tip: Separate buttons that users can easily confuse. In comparing the sites where users had trouble with empty carts to the trouble-free sites, we noticed that the trouble-free designs had the checkout or shopping cart link located on a different part of the page than the Buy button. We believe that it might help to keep these buttons separated (such as by having the shopping cart link in the top navigation bar and the Buy button in the middle of the page). Separating the buttons can reduce the chance of a customer clicking the wrong button.

➡️ *Provide strong feedback when an item has been put into the cart.*

When customers put an item in their shopping carts, they need to see that something has happened. Most sites provided feedback by taking the user to the shopping cart page where they could see the item they had just added.

Peet's, Nordstrom, and Boo didn't take the user to the shopping cart page automatically. Instead, when the user added an item to the shopping cart, the product page persisted, but the shopping cart area changed to show that something had happened. This approach is not a bad idea if the change in the cart area is easily noticed and if the customer usually buys several items from the same page in one shopping session, which isn't always the case.

Compare the "before" screenshot of the Lego watch page on Nordstrom to the "after." This change was a bit too subtle for a few users, who wondered aloud whether the site had done anything. Sometimes they tried adding the item again.

Nordstrom added a My Order and Checkout area to a bar near the top of the page after the user put the first product in the cart. This form of feedback was too subtle for some users, who weren't sure the item had really gone into the cart. P31

Boo maintained an omnipresent shopping cart area (the Boobag) at the bottom of the page, which changed when an item was added. Unlike Peet's and Nordstrom, however, Boo's page design worked.

In Boo's design, when a user added an item to the Boobag, a thumbnail of the chosen item appeared in the Boobag section of the page. None of the nine users had trouble determining that they'd succeeded in placing an item in the shopping cart. So, even though the user remained on the product page, we count Boo's design as successful at providing easily noticed feedback.

Boo's very effective boobag showed pictures of the items inside. P32

One factor that seems to affect whether a change is noticeable or not is how close it is to the area of the page where the user's eyes are focused. To get an item into the cart on Nordstrom required navigating a tricky series of multilevel menus at the bottom of the page. Thus, it's a fair bet that the user was looking at the bottom of the page, making it easier to miss the feedback that happened near the top of the page. Peet's had a similar design flaw. On Boo, however, the "Add to Boobag" button was positioned just above the Boobag. This made it easier to see the thumbnail when it popped onto the page, which probably helped.

Tip: Use rapid prototyping and discount usability testing, because it is often much faster to experiment with improved designs rather than to over-analyze a flawed one. In order to be sure exactly where a user is looking on the page, you have to use an eye tracker, which we did not do in this study. It takes specially trained people to operate eye trackers and interpret their data. For most usability tests, however, eye trackers are unnecessary, because you can determine what you need to know by simple observation. We had to test only a handful of users to discover that Nordstrom had a feedback problem. If we'd been designing Nordstrom's site, we might have tried simply moving the Buy button to the top of the page. Then we would have tested another handful of users to see whether this change was enough to solve the feedback problem.

Conclusion

The true tests of a product page are whether it provides shoppers with enough information to make their buying decisions and whether it presents an effective mechanism for purchasing. Problems with product pages — when users couldn't get their questions answered or couldn't get a product into the shopping cart — accounted for 17% of the sales catastrophes in this study.

To create a successful product page, you must first know which factors your customers consider when they shop for the merchandise you sell. Some information is conveyed best by words, and other information by pictures, so good product pages employ an effective combination of words and images. As you conduct your own usability tests, you will discover which information sells products — and which doesn't.

In usability testing, listen for unanswered questions shoppers have about the merchandise, because these will point to areas where the product pages can be

Checkout & Registration

" When your customer is unable or unwilling to complete an online order after finding a desired product, it is a disaster for your site. Not only do you lose that sale, but often you lose the customer as well."

The terms "shopping cart" and "cart" in this chapter refer to the single page on an e-commerce site that shows items the customer has chosen to purchase. The subsequent pages needed to complete the order are called the "checkout process," or simply "checkout."

What to Include in the Shopping Cart

The purposes of the shopping cart are to:

- Show a summary of the items the user has selected.
- Provide links to information the user may wish to review before purchasing, such as the return policy and product page for each item.
- Provide a means to modify quantities and remove items.
- Provide navigation mechanisms so the customer can begin the checkout process or return to the store for more items.

Once users got an item into their carts, the shopping cart page itself caused few problems in most cases. Problems users had in putting items into the cart are discussed in the Product Pages chapter.

➡️ *Show items, all costs, and the subtotal.*

Users expected the shopping cart to show all the items they'd chosen and the subtotal. Our test sites generally met these expectations.

Tip: Show estimated shipping charges in the shopping cart. See "Shipping Methods and Delivery Options" in this chapter for more information.

TowerRecords properly showed the availability of each item in the shopping cart; but as discussed later, it wasn't clear to users how to remove items or proceed with the checkout process. C1

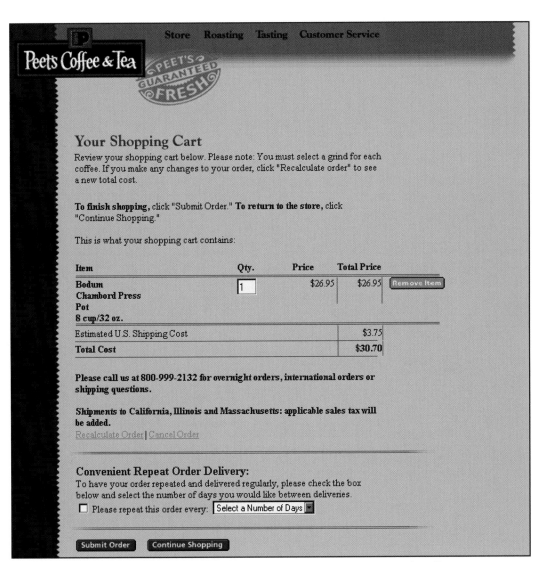

Your Shopping Cart

Review your shopping cart below. Please note: You must select a grind for each coffee. If you make any changes to your order, click "Recalculate order" to see a new total cost.

To finish shopping, click "Submit Order." **To return to the store**, click "Continue Shopping."

This is what your shopping cart contains:

Item	Qty.	Price	Total Price	
Bodum Chambord Press Pot 8 cup/32 oz.	1	$26.95	$26.95	Remove Item
Estimated U.S. Shipping Cost			$3.75	
Total Cost			**$30.70**	

Please call us at 800-999-2132 for overnight orders, international orders or shipping questions.

Shipments to California, Illinois and Massachusetts: applicable sales tax will be added.

Recalculate Order | Cancel Order

Convenient Repeat Order Delivery:

To have your order repeated and delivered regularly, please check the box below and select the number of days you would like between deliveries.

☐ Please repeat this order every: [Select a Number of Days ▾]

[Submit Order]   [Continue Shopping]

Peet's showed estimated US shipping cost and had a clear Remove Item button. C2

▶ *Provide information about return policies and guarantees.*

Before purchasing, some users wanted to read the return policy. They were interested in the deadline for returning goods and whether there were any costs associated with returns (such as not having shipping charges refunded or having to pay return postage).

Nordstrom had a prominent link to its return policy on the first page of the checkout process. One user said, "I would want to know what their return and exchange policy was, before I went any further. It's good they've got that right there. That's a definite plus."

On Reel, another user wanted to read about the five-point guarantee indicated by an icon in the upper left corner, but the icon was not clickable.

Nordstrom provided a link to the return policy from the "shopping bag." C3

Navigation in the Shopping Cart

▶ *Provide a "return to shopping" link.*

There are several possible things a customer would like to do after verifying that an item is in the cart and noting the total purchase price including shipping:

Go someplace else:

- **Complete the purchase.** The customer needs to find the button to pay and exit.

- **Buy more items from the same department.** The customer needs to go back to the previous category page.

- **Begin shopping for an entirely different item in the store.** The customer needs to go to the list of departments or begin a search.

Do something further about the products in the cart:

- **Accessorize the chosen items.** The customer needs some suggestions about what other items might be needed, with a link to the product pages where the features of the additional items are shown. As discussed in more detail in the Selling Strategies chapter, we don't recommend adding accessories to the order automatically, but offering suggested items in the cart seems to be acceptable.

- **Change the number of items or delete an item.** The customer needs a button that removes items and the option to change any item's quantities. These features of the cart are discussed later in this chapter.

In many instances during our test, the Continue Shopping button didn't go where users expected. Here are some examples from Jcrew:

- The user put a jacket in the shopping cart and then clicked the Continue Shopping button. The website displayed the product page for the jacket he had just bought. The user said he had expected to return to the Men's directory and not to the jacket he had just ordered. It seemed unlikely that he would buy more jackets.

- The user had selected a pair of shoes and was on the View Order page. "Okay, where is the I-don't-want-anything-else button?" He clicked the Continue Shopping button and the website returned him to the Rugged Shoes page.

Tip: Name navigation buttons so that they clearly indicate where they will take you. It's hard for customers to be sure where a Continue Shopping link goes. Some sites use it for "back to where you were" and others create a "top of catalog" link. The name on the button could clear this confusion up right away, for example by calling the button "back to previous page" or "return to product search results," and so forth. In any case, test your designs with users and ask what they expect to happen when they click on each button in the shopping cart and observe which buttons they choose when shopping. In other tests we've seen longer button names work better than short labels.

One common behavior pattern we saw was users clicking the Back button from the shopping cart when they wished to continue shopping, despite the presence of a Continue Shopping button. Because the Back button is such a frequently used method of website navigation, it is not realistic to expect users to stop using it in this special case.

For example, both Gevalia and Peet's requested that the user specify a grind for the coffee on the shopping cart page. However, the user's choice of grind was lost if the user used the Back button to continue shopping. One user patiently re-specified the grinds for all her chosen coffees each time she returned to the shopping cart, without ever realizing that use of the Back button would cause her choices to be lost.

Tip: Consider an integrated shopping cart. Like Boo did, some sites integrate the shopping cart with each product page so that both cart items and items for sale are always visible. This approach requires a highly noticeable shopping cart in order to be successful, but it seems promising because it avoids the need for a Continue Shopping button and perhaps unnecessary or premature trips to the shopping cart during a shopping session. Boo used a prominent "Buy Now" button in the "boobag" to begin the checkout process.

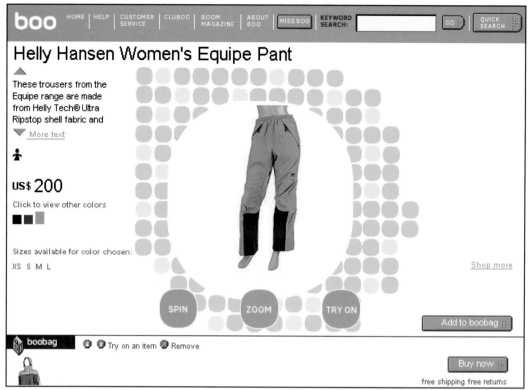

Helly Hansen Women's Equipe Pant

These trousers from the Equipe range are made from Helly Tech® Ultra Ripstop shell fabric and ▼ More text

us$ 200

Click to view other colors
■ ■ ■

Sizes available for color chosen:
XS S M L

SPIN   ZOOM   TRY ON

Shop more

Add to boobag

boobag   ⊕ ⊕ Try on an item ⊗ Remove

Buy now

free shipping free returns

Boo avoided the need for a Continue Shopping button by making the contents of the shopping cart ("boobag") visible. C4

Removing Items from the Shopping Cart

➡ *Provide a Remove button for each item in the cart.*

In our test, individual Remove buttons for each item in the shopping cart — even the fancy remove icons like the US-style trash can on Reel — were readily understood. Changing the quantity to zero and clicking "Update" didn't work as well, though, because some users didn't realize they had to click Update.

SmarterKids separated the change-quantity function from the remove-item function, an approach we recommend, but the Update Quantities button could have been closer to the fields it referred to. C5

One Gevalia user got completely stuck while trying to delete items, because he couldn't understand that he had to both change the quantity and press the I Changed It button. There were instructions but he didn't read them. The buttons were near the bottom of the screen and he said they were hard to read.

Tip: In general, buttons should state what they do from the user's point of view, not what the user did or what the system did. "I Changed It" is not as good a label as "Change It" would be. "Show my new quantities" would seem to be a better label than "I Changed It," but it doesn't address the real problem, which is that because the user has changed the quantities, he or she is now looking at the new numbers and so appears to be done. It isn't apparent to the user that the change must be sent to the server and back to the browser before it is really changed.

Quantity	Description	Unit Price	Total Price
☐ 1	Proctor-Silex® SmartToast 2000™ Two Slice Toaster	$12.96	**$12.96**

☑ Remove checked items

(UPDATE TOTALS)

SUBTOTAL $12.96

Tax, shipping and handling will be calculated during checkout.
(sales tax added for AR, UT & CA only)

Wal-Mart gave one user trouble because the "Remove checked items" label was placed too far away from the checkbox. Also, because checkboxes are often used to denote positive choices, it might be that the checkbox itself was a confusing mechanism for item removal. c6

On Wal-Mart, a user checked the small checkbox to the left of the Quantity field to indicate that he wanted to buy the product. After clicking Checkout, he found that his shopping cart was empty. When the user repeated this action in the following task, the facilitator asked him what the checkbox meant and why he checked it. The user said he didn't know what it meant but it seemed necessary to check it. He didn't relate the checkbox to the text underneath, which explained that checking the box meant the item should be removed.

Tip: If users might have to scroll to see the action buttons or navigation in the shopping cart, repeat those items where they will be visible. Buttons that didn't appear on the screen were a problem for one HermanMiller user. It took her about three minutes of clicking on various things before she scrolled down and saw the delete and modify buttons.

Tip: Every time the user clicks any button or link in the shopping cart — even if it's the Help button — the cart should update any changed quantities automatically.

Shopping Instructions

➡ *Provide shopping instructions in the empty shopping cart.*

Some users wanted to read details about the ordering process before beginning to shop. The users who needed this information the most were those who had tried to put an item in the cart and failed and those who explored the shopping cart because they didn't know exactly where to begin.

Put shopping instructions in the empty shopping cart that explain how to place an item in the cart. Also provide navigation back to the page the user entered the cart from, so users won't rely on the Back button. The Product Pages chapter discusses in detail the problems users had putting items into the cart and their resulting confusion caused by seeing an empty cart.

Many users don't read instructions, at least until they have a problem. In this study, when users looked in Help, they did so because they were unable to get *started* in the checkout process. Once they had products in the cart, they didn't want to read about how to check out; they simply wanted to do it.

If the steps in the shopping process are made explicit and they match what the user expects, the need for additional help in the checkout pages can be alleviated.

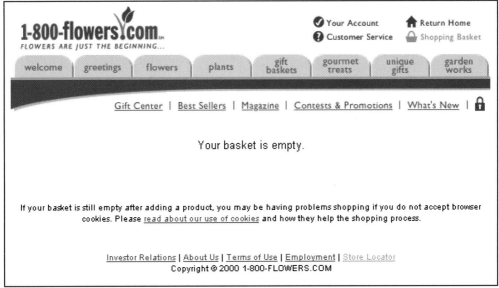

1800flowers, like most of the sites we tested, didn't provide any shopping instructions in the empty shopping cart. The message referred only to information about the site's reliance on cookies. Cookie preferences are not the only likely cause of having an empty cart, and this kind of message is of no help to users who don't understand how to put items into the cart. c7

The Checkout Process

Steps, Procedures, Diagrams

Navigation during the checkout process usually consists of a way to move through a linear procedure. One step must be completed before the next one can be started, and no skipping around is allowed. This process generally starts in the shopping cart or order form and ends with the confirmation page. The problems we saw were mainly the site's checkout process not matching the user's mental model of the process, and the location, appearance, and labels on the navigation buttons themselves.

➡️ *Order the steps in the checkout process according to users' expectations.*

Typically, after reviewing their items and other charges, users wanted to complete the steps in the following order:

1. Specify any gift options such as wrapping and a card message. (See the chapter on Selling Strategies for more information about gift options.)

2. Choose shipping method. (Sometimes this step may be more important than the gift options, so the order of these two steps should be determined by the patterns of behavior you notice on your own site.)

3. Enter shipping address information.

4. Enter billing information (the address is often the same as the shipping address).

5. Give a credit card number.

Note that users did not expect registration as a natural part of the above process. As discussed later in this chapter, placing registration before or in the middle of the checkout process can confuse and alienate users — sometimes enough so that they stop shopping at the site.

▶ *Show the steps of the process.*

Users liked illustrations that showed the steps in the checkout process. The only problem with these graphics was that users sometimes tried to click the graphic to skip to a later step — typically shipping — because they had questions about that step of the process.

Ordering the steps of the checkout process to match what the majority of users expect and providing enough information at the right steps might have prevented this mistake. Alternatively, the graphics could be clickable or have rollover tips. That said, much of the need for steps or clickable graphics would probably go away if sites moved the shipping information and specification step to the beginning of the checkout process, before asking for personal information.

HermanMiller had a step diagram (below), but users clicked on it to try to navigate around the Customer Login. These attempts failed, because the graphic wasn't clickable and registration wasn't optional.

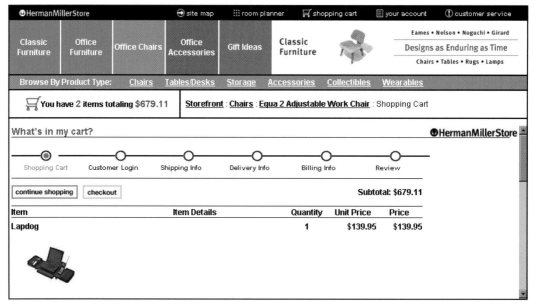

HermanMiller's checkout process had an unnumbered graphic step diagram. Some users wanted to skip the Customer Login step, however, so they tried clicking on Shipping Info or Delivery Info, which didn't work, because the process is linear, not random access and registration / login was required. C8

▶ Make the next-step button prominent and visually distinct from the site navigation and other page elements.

When the action buttons were more graphical and less button-like, our users had trouble finding them, particularly in the shopping cart. Because the entire checkout process often cannot be completed if only part of the information is submitted, making sure customers notice the process buttons and know when to click on them is extremely important.

Accidental early exit from registration or checkout can occur when site navigation is present and more attractive than form buttons. If they do not look like push buttons, submit buttons can be confused with other graphical elements. In general, the more distracting and complex the page or button looks, the more confusing it can be to use.

Tip: Don't over-design buttons. In particular, buttons that have images, animations, or slogans on them can be confused with advertising and thus ignored. Several studies of "ad blindness" show that many people report not even noticing items on pages that look like ads. In this study we saw evidence of ad blindness several times.

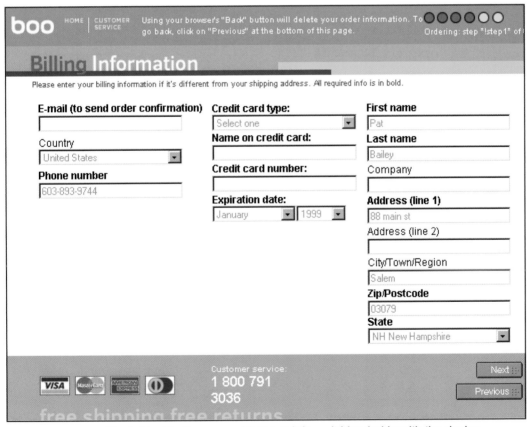

Boo's Next button was a bit too subtle — it blended in with the design of the page. Some users tried to click the circles at the top to proceed to the next step. Also see the TowerRecords example (Image C1), where the over-designed buttons made it hard to identify the Continue Checkout button. C9

| Step 2 (of 3): Enter Your Billing & Delivery Information   Order Number: 2160195135

Billing Information

Full Name	Pat Bailey
Address Line 1	
Address Line 2	
City	
State	
Zip Code	
Country	**United States of America**
Daytime Telephone	
Evening Telephone	

Delivery Information
☐ **Same As Billing Information**

Full Name	
Address Line 1	
Address Line 2	
City	
Telephone	
State	
Zip Code	
Country	**United States of America**
Special Instructions	

Click Continue to provide your credit card information SSL-encrypted for your protection!   Continue ▶

Furniture's prominent Continue button provided a good cue for going on to the next step. C10

When and How to Show Shipping Charges

▶ *Reveal shipping charges before asking for personal information.*

Users wanted to know the total, including shipping and tax, before they entered any of their own personal information. This user desire creates a site design challenge, because the delivery address sometimes determines the costs for tax and shipping.

Most of our test sites required the user to enter at least a shipping address before revealing the shipping charges, and some sites required much more information.

Users grumbled about having to give out personal information before they were ready to commit to the total amount of the purchase:

- Wal-Mart: "This says that shipping, tax, and handling will be added during checkout. My time is valuable. ... I want to see from the [beginning of checkout]. I don't mind paying shipping and handling, because it's a convenience, but I want to know when I might be getting ripped off or not. If I had to put in my credit card without knowing [the total cost], I wouldn't."

- BasketHaus: "I don't like the idea you don't know what your shipping cost is. They're asking you to give your credit card. ... Somewhere I read that shipping could be as high as $60. That seems like a ridiculous amount — that would make me nervous. You can call, but you've gone through this whole thing. You should have a standard rate you pay."

The following table shows how much information the user had to enter before a site revealed the shipping charge. The table is ordered from best to worst, depending on the amount of personal information users had to enter. Note that sites that offer free shipping avoid the issue of when to present shipping charges.

When Shipping Charges Were Revealed

Rating	Site
Excellent – User was required to enter no personal information and / or shipping was shown as free.	• Iflorist – Delivery fee appeared on the product page. • Furniture – Shipping was free. A link to information about free delivery was shown in the shopping cart. The order preview page, which was shown before users entered shipping and billing information, said: "Delivery: FREE." • Peet's – Estimated shipping charge appeared in the shopping cart, before shipping or billing address was entered.
Good – User was required to enter little or no personal information.	• Boo, Living – "Free shipping" appeared on the home page. • Boo – Some users tried to click on the words "free shipping" to learn more. Shipping charges were shown during checkout as $0 rather than "free," which concerned some users.
Fair – User was required to enter shipping and / or billing address but not credit card number.	• eToys, NorwaySweaters, SmarterKids, 1800flowers, CustomDisc, Disney, Jcrew, Nordstrom, Sears, Wal-Mart – Shipping charges were presented after the user entered a shipping address (and sometimes billing address), but before credit card entry. • HermanMiller, TowerRecords – Same as those above, except the user also had to register or log in before site revealed shipping charges.
Poor – Shipping charges were not provided at all, or they were shown after the user entered credit card information.	• Gevalia – Shipping charges were shown on the order summary page, after users entered all information including credit card number, but one step before confirming the order. • Reel – The choice of shipping methods, with prices, appeared on the payment page below the credit card number. • BasketHaus – Final amounts were not shown on site at all; the user had to call or e-mail the store to discover the total charge.

Tip: Ask for a ZIP or postal code and country for the purpose of calculating shipping charges. With two pieces of information, the ZIP / postal code and the country name for the delivery address, a site could potentially calculate shipping charges and taxes and present the grand total in the shopping cart. Although none of our test sites used this method, we believe that users would be willing to enter this information on the first page of the shopping cart in return for the exact charges and a total. A simpler alternative that would please customers even more would be to make all extra costs "free" and clearly show the word "free" in the shopping cart. This approach may not be possible if the site has a legal obligation to collect tax or duty, however.

Enter U.S. ZIP Code

To view real-time inventory availability, please enter the ZIP code where products will be shipped.

U.S. ZIP Code:

[   ]

[Continue]

Canadian Shoppers: Click Here
Other International Visitors: Click Here
Go to Staples.com

Staples (which is not a site we tested) asked users for a ZIP Code early in the shopping process. A previous version of this page failed to explain why the site was asking for what seemed like personal information. After Staples added an explanation (to view real-time inventory availability), the number of users who abandoned the site at that point was dramatically reduced. c11

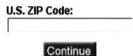 *Provide exact shipping charges and tax, not formulas.*

Shipping charges and tax were responsible for 7% of the sales catastrophes in our study. Users preferred free shipping, but in any case they wanted to know the cost of shipping as early as possible — before committing themselves to a purchase. Sites that had formulas for shipping charges and tax made determining total cost more difficult.

1800flowers had the most confusing shipping charges. One user said: "How do I know what they're charging me? I've found with all of them [websites] their shipping information is not clear. I don't like shopping to be this difficult. If I'm on the phone, they say 'your total will be ...'. Shipping needs to be clearer." C12

Shipping Methods and Delivery Options

▶ *Give the user a choice of shipping methods and carriers, if possible.*

Users recognized that there are tradeoffs in cost, speed, and service depending on the shipping method and carrier. Examples:

- "If it was being shipped someplace when someone might not be home, then I'd rather have it kept at the post office than UPS leaving it under the porch. On the other hand, during regular business hours, UPS works fine."

- "Depends on how fast I want it. I didn't see any options for UPS or overnight."

Although the Wal-Mart example was confusing because it required the user to calculate the total shipping charge, at least it showed the cost / speed tradeoff for the various shipping methods. (See Image C13.)

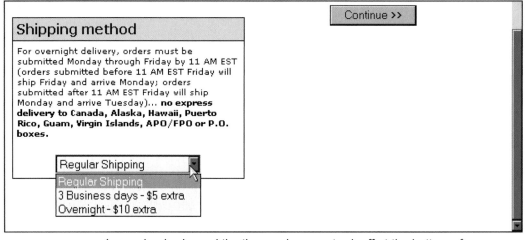

Shipping Options

How would you like to ship your order? Choose one of the following:

⊙ **Standard** (5-8 business days) $4.00 + $0.97 per item

○ **Premium** (3-5 business days) $6.00 + $2.47 per item

○ **Express** (2-3 business days) $12.00 + $5.97 per item

*Shipping information applies to merchandise shipping within the Continental U.S.

Wal-Mart offered customers a choice of shipping methods and their associated prices (good) but forced them to perform calculations when they wanted to know the total (bad). C13

Tip: When a customer provides a post office box for the shipping address, show the postal service as the default shipper and allow the customer to change shipping address and shippers easily. If an incompatible address and shipper are chosen, provide a helpful error message that tells the customer exactly what is wrong and what to change.

Tip: Ask customers whether any items are gifts before asking about delivery options. If gifts are flagged early in the process, the site can show gift options only when appropriate, such as wrapping, cards, or additional delivery addresses.

Continue >>

Shipping method

For overnight delivery, orders must be submitted Monday through Friday by 11 AM EST (orders submitted before 11 AM EST Friday will ship Friday and arrive Monday; orders submitted after 11 AM EST Friday will ship Monday and arrive Tuesday)... **no express delivery to Canada, Alaska, Hawaii, Puerto Rico, Guam, Virgin Islands, APO/FPO or P.O. boxes.**

Regular Shipping

Regular Shipping
3 Business days - $5 extra
Overnight - $10 extra

Jcrew clearly showed the time and money tradeoff at the bottom of their shipping options form. C14

Tip: Consider providing a shipping instruction field. If possible, offer a shipping instruction field, because some customers have requirements such as "deliver to back of house," "deliver to manager's office," "deliver before 6 pm," "accept my signature only," and so forth. These instructions are even more important when customers are ordering large and expensive items (such as furniture and jewelry) and emergency or surprise items (such as mission-critical equipment and gifts). Delivery instructions can also be useful when a person needs to sign for a package or bring it indoors. Many of our users expressed the desire to include such instructions.

Tip: Provide detailed information on delivery for large or perishable items.
Some items are harder to deliver than others, so the customer may want more information about what to expect. One user who read Living's delivery information was glad that items weighing over 150 pounds would be delivered for free by people who would make sure the furniture was brought inside: "It's nice to know if they're going to show up at my door with a 150-pound box. What if the box doesn't fit in my aunt's front door?"

Free Premium Delivery Service

For certain products, we also offer a FREE Premium Delivery Service as part of our limited-time FREE shipping policy. Available in the 48 contiguous United States, the Premium Delivery Service is offered on all items that weigh 150 lbs. or more, and for any piece - whatever it weighs - that is considered fragile. All other items weighing less than 150 lbs. are shipped via Airborne@home.

At no extra charge, two delivery specialists will unpack your order (and assemble it if necessary) and move the piece(s) to its final location. Premium Delivery Service, however does not include final installation, such as hanging a mirror on the wall.

Premium Delivery Service can take place only if there is full and complete access to the area in which the order is to be setup. If there is limited access to its final destination, delivery will be made to the nearest accessible area to avoid any risk to your home or the product(s) you ordered. Please read **Preparing for Premium Delivery Service** for full details.

Preparing for Premium Delivery Service
(Fragile items, and all individual items over 150 lbs.)

If you cannot be present at the time of delivery, please arrange to have a responsible person present so that the carrier may rely upon his or her signature as authorized to inspect and accept delivery. After ascertaining that the items will fit in your home, please be certain to clear a path for the items to pass through, and make sure the final locations for all items are free of any obstructions.

If your home is not accessible to the carrier's trucks, your merchandise will be transported to the nearest accessible point and it will be your responsibility to provide a means of transportation from the truck to your home.

△ back to top

Scheduling Premium Delivery Service
(Fragile items, and all individual items over 150 lbs.)

If you are unable to schedule a date that falls within 30 days of the completion of your order, your credit card will be charged any remaining balances. If you elect not to schedule delivery within 30 days of the completion of your order, storage fees may apply.

Although not all users bothered to read Living's additional information about delivery, those users who did read it appreciated this level of detail. C15

Shipping and Billing Address Forms

Asking for Personal Information

If you ask customers for more than is required to complete the purchase, you risk losing their trust and the sale. Even when entering demographic information is optional, it takes longer to fill out the additional information and increases the likelihood of errors.

➡ *Ask for only the information needed to complete the transaction and clearly state how it can be used.*

Refusal to enter personal information caused 4% of the sales catastrophes in our study. A larger proportion of users entered something, but they weren't happy about it. Some users simply made up false information when they didn't want to enter it. The issues related to gaining and losing customer trust are discussed primarily in the Trust chapter, but some specific observations are mentioned here when they relate to the checkout and registration process.

Many users expressed concern about why a site wanted certain information. They particularly balked at entering phone numbers because they didn't want their numbers used for telemarketing. Users were also worried that their e-mail addresses would be misused to send unsolicited commercial e-mail. Revealing street addresses was not generally a concern, probably because users recognized that this information is required in order to deliver the items purchased. Even so, users were not as concerned about receiving unwanted postal mail as they were about being contacted by phone or e-mail.

Not only were users concerned about revealing their own personal information, but they also resisted entering the information of others. One user said she would never give out the telephone number for her young nephew if she was sending him a gift, out of concerns for his safety and privacy. Another user explained that if he were sending a gift, he would not want to include the recipient's phone number, because if the recipient got a phone call about the delivery it would spoil the surprise.

Sometimes the issue with providing phone numbers and e-mail addresses was that the user just didn't have that information. Not all Web shoppers possess an e-mail address — as was the case for several users in our study. Some people shop from someone else's computer, so just because they have access to he Internet does not guarantee that they have an e-mail address. Also, not everyone knows the phone number of a gift recipient.

Tip: If marketing resists removing registration because of the desire to collect customer data, make a separate questionnaire and offer customers an incentive to complete it after their purchase. Information collected is likely to be invalid either way, but customers who choose to answer questions might give more accurate information, and the site will lose fewer sales due to registration resistance.

Tip: Explain the benefit to the user of entering phone numbers and e-mail addresses, and make entering them optional. If customers don't understand or agree with your reason for needing their e-mail addresses, they will be more likely to enter false information. A false email address can cause more trouble for them (for example because they can't receive important information about their order) than would entering no information.

Privacy Policy

The vast majority of users who expressed a concern about the use of their personal information did *not* attempt to look up the site's privacy policy to find out how their information would be used. In some cases, the users expressed their distrust that a site's policy would be followed, which is not unreasonable.

Tip: Place explanatory links next to information customers are likely to have questions about. Proximity and the name of the link can both help indicate that the link contains brief contextual help. We don't know if it would help to place links to the privacy policy next to the fields users are concerned about, though. Most of our users didn't go out of their way to look for privacy policies, but they did click on informational links that seemed to promise a specific answer to the question they had at the time. For example, on CustomDisc, when they wondered why the disc cost so much, they clicked a link called "(explain)" that was right next to the field called "cost."

Address Forms

➡ *Use clear labels and show examples of valid entries.*

Users sometimes didn't understand the purpose of a field or the format of the information they were supposed to enter.

Shorter isn't always better. International users may need more examples, instructions, or longer labels for form fields. In our study, none of the American users had trouble with the MI (middle initial) field, but several Danish users weren't sure what "MI" stood for. (See the International Users chapter for more information about international form issues.)

Not every field needs an example. Labels such as "Name" and "City" were self-explanatory. An "Address 2" field confused some users, because they didn't understand its purpose. Phone number and e-mail address fields should definitely show examples. Examples do not remove the need for validation and descriptive error messages, however.

➡ *Make the size of the field indicate the length of the expected input.*

Make sure type-in fields are the right size for the data. One user truncated her e-mail address in the mistaken belief that it had to fit into the visible part of the field, for example.

Tip: Provide tools for forms. Where appropriate, offer tools such as address books, currency converters, ZIP / postal code lookups, area code lookups, and so forth, if the tools could be useful in order to complete the form.

When a user selects a state, then the country could be assumed to be the USA, unless the state menu includes military addresses, Canadian provinces, or Australian states.

- Iflorist: The user could not remember the postal code of the recipient. She had to guess since there was no support from the website.
- Sears: "I think if you type in your ZIP Code, they should pull up your state. They know where you are."

➡ *Differentiate shipping address from billing address.*

Address forms look alike. The difference between "shipping" and "billing" is subtle and the user must translate this difference into people. We noticed that a few users reversed the shipping and billing address information on

NorwaySweaters — the pages looked very similar, with only the words "billing" and "shipping" to indicate which address went where. In contrast, Iflorist asked, "Who will be receiving your Internet Florist gift?" which was much less ambiguous.

2. Choose the shipping address

First Name: [ ]   Last Name: [ ]

Address: [ ]
[ ]

City: [ ]   State: [AL Alabama ▾]

Zip: [ ]   Phone: [ ]

○ **Same**: (Use shipping address)

◉ **Enter**: First Name: [ ]   Last Name: [ ]

Address: [ ]
[ ]

City: [ ]   State: [AL Alabama ▾]

Zip: [ ]   Phone: [ ]

The shipping and billing forms on NorwaySweaters appeared on two separate pages. They looked so similar that a few users reversed their addresses. C16

Who will be receiving your Internet Florist gift?

Recipient's Name: [   ]

Business Name or C/O: [   ]

Street Address: [   ]

Continued Address: [   ]

Town: [   ]

Postal Code: [   ]

Country: Denmark

Telephone Number: [   ]

Additional Delivery Info:
(no delivery times please) [   ]

Your message for the card enclosure

Card Message:
(3 sentences or 30 words or less.)

Please remember to include the sender's name.
(e.g. Love, Jane)

[   ]

Desired date of delivery

Next business day delivery is available to most areas for orders received by 11 AM CST. We can guarantee delivery dates for orders received three business days in advance.

[Friday ▼] [January ▼] [21 ▼] [2000 ▼]

Payment Information

Cardholder Name: [Rolf Molich]

Card Type: [Visa ▼]

Card Number: [4571155000406341]

Expiration Date: [8 ▼] / [00 ▼]

Sender Information

Please use your credit card billing address.
This information is needed to contact you if we have a question regarding your order and to authorize your credit card. This information will not be given to others.

Sender Name: [Rolf Molich]

Unlike NorwaySweaters, Iflorist avoided the shipping / billing confusion by asking "Who will be receiving your Internet Florist gift?" C17

In general, sites that used "Billing address same as Shipping address" checkboxes worked well for our users.

▶ *Use a type-in field, not a selection list, for the state.*

One of the more surprising results of this study was how much selection lists (the HTML form elements sometimes called drop-down lists or pop-up menus) for selecting the state annoyed users. (See Image C9, C10, or C16) Although none of the problems prevented users from buying, state selection lists irritated 16 of 39 of the US users (and these were just the people who expressed their feelings).

Some users were confused when typing "N" showed the states whose name begins with N and then typing "H" (which users expected would show NH for New Hampshire) showed Hawaii instead. Most users did not understand why they got this result.

One theoretical argument in favor of selection lists is that they reduce errors by providing predefined valid choices, but we saw many users select the wrong state the first time, by accident. Although all the users in this study noticed and fixed the problems themselves, selection lists could be a source of error as well as irritation for customers.

International Form Issues

Phone Numbers: Require an area or city code for phone numbers and allow a country code to be entered. Most people are not used to providing this information routinely because they communicate within their country or region primarily. Also accommodate + ( ) - and other commonly used characters in phone number fields, such as x for extension.

Phone area codes and country codes are not necessarily tied tightly to geography any more (particularly in the case of cell phones). So a person's phone number could be in a different region than his or her shipping or billing address. For these reasons, it is better to require the user to enter complete phone information rather than to assume the phone number prefix matches the shipping address or the ZIP Code.

See the International Users chapter for more information about these and other considerations for international sites.

Multiple Recipients

Tip: Consider whether it is necessary to support multiple shipping addresses. The need for accommodating multiple recipients depends on how common it is for a site's customers to need to ship to more than one recipient. For some sites, allowing customers to ship various items to different recipients could be a better choice than asking customers to repeat the checkout process for each gift recipient.

Some sites allow customers to save an "address book," or collection of past recipients. Amazon.com, for example, stores address information its customers entered in prior transactions. Previous recipients can be chosen from a list with a radio button, so customers don't need to retype the shipping address. Providing such an address book is probably a reasonable approach, but we have not tested it.

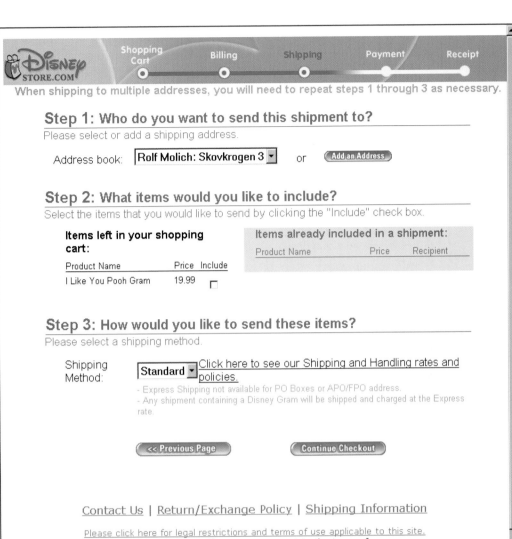

Disney's shipping form allowed multiple recipients, but the process was difficult to understand. Disney also provided an address book feature, but we didn't test it in our study. C18

Tip: If multiple recipients are allowed, don't make customers who want to ship to only one recipient fill out the more complex form.

Form Entry Problems

▶ *Save and autofill all previously supplied information.*

In our study, 11 of 39 US users experienced some kind of situation where they had to fill out the same form or fields more than once, because the site hadn't stored their information. Users expected that any information they entered into a form would be preserved. We saw these expectations in the following cases:

- **Partial information entered** – Users filled out and submitted some forms during the checkout process but stopped short of completing the purchase at the facilitator's request. During the next task, they expected that the site would still have all the information they'd entered from the previous task, even though they acknowledged that they hadn't actually completed a purchase.

- **Information entered during registration** – Users registered during the checkout process, then they expected all their registration information to be retained and automatically filled into subsequent forms during checkout.

- **Information entry interrupted** – Users clicked a link from a checkout page in order to read about something, such as the return policy. When they clicked the Back button afterward, users expected the form to be the same as when they left it.

- **Information entry errors** – Users completed a form but made errors. They expected all the correctly completed fields would remain filled in when they returned to fix the form.

Some users refused to click on links to helpful information during the checkout process, because they were afraid their data would disappear. Provide links to helpful information from the checkout forms, but don't erase the information the user has already entered.

▶ *Validate information submitted.*

Don't assume that customers will enter information in the expected format, even if you provide instructions and examples. Make flexible forms and perform reasonable error checking. Allow users to enter addresses and phone numbers in the formats they are used to, but trap common mistakes.

In our study, 16 of the 39 US users made at least one typographical error while filling out order forms. The majority of these users didn't notice their errors unless the site pointed them out.

Errors Users Made During Form Entry

Field	Problems We Observed
Name	• Both first and last name were typed into the First Name field by 11 of 39 US users, but all of them noticed and corrected the problem themselves.
Second line of address	• Users didn't understand what to enter in the second address line "I only have one address," was a typical remark.
	• Three typed a city name in this field. (Two of the three noticed and corrected this error on their own.)
City, State, ZIP	• Seven users mistyped city names or ZIP Codes, but only two of the mismatches were caught by error checking.
	• Two users typed both city and state in the city field. (One noticed and fixed it.)
E-mail address	• One user omitted the domain name "@aol.com," likely because AOL lets its users send e-mail to other AOL users with only a user name.
	• Two users omitted ".com."
	• Some users hesitated before typing the @ symbol, which is hard to type on some keyboards; we saw more Danish than US users hesitate. A few users entered no @ or typed @@.
	• Three users omitted one or more characters, typing: "aol.cm," "ao.com," and "name@.com."
	• One user entered a URL instead of an e-mail address.
Phone number	• Four users omitted an area code. One of these users filled in the area code field with the first three digits of the local phone number.
	• One user typed "same" for an evening phone number after entering the daytime phone correctly.
	• One user typed "1" before the area code.

Tip: Consider breaking the e-mail address into pieces. Reel had two separate input fields for the user and domain name, with the @ supplied in between. Some users were annoyed by this solution, but further testing should show whether it helps more users than not. This approach may not be well received, even if it works better. One user complained that "it's easier to type it all in one shot."

Enter your email address:

[   ]@[   ]

If you don't have an email address, click here.

Reel broke the e-mail address into two pieces. This tactic removed the need for users to type the @ symbol and also indicated clearly that the portion after the @ could not be omitted, as some AOL users did on other sites. C19

▶ *Expect users to hit the Enter or Return key while filling out forms; handle it gracefully.*

Keyboard shortcuts are necessary for good accessibility and rapid form completion, but they can cause errors too. Test carefully before implementing shortcuts.

On many sites, the Enter / Return key on the keyboard submits a form to the server. Although most users in our test pressed Tab to move between fields, 9 of the 39 US users experienced difficulty — ranging from being confused by a beep sound to losing the whole form contents — because they pressed Enter instead of Tab after they finished typing in a field. Other people used the mouse to navigate from field to field — apparently unaware that the Tab key would do this for them.

On one site we tested, which shall not be named, the form coding that allows the Tab key to move the cursor between fields was incomplete, so only a few of the first fields on the page plus the Location (URL type-in) field were accessible using Tab. The user typed quickly, pressing Tab to change fields. When the Tab key didn't correctly go to the address field but went to the Location field instead, the user typed a few characters before noticing that her keystrokes weren't filling in the address field. After filling out the rest of the fields, she pressed Enter to submit the form. Instead, the Location field (which had the mistyped characters in it) was activated and a pornography site appeared.

Sites that beeped when people hit the Enter key prevented accidental form submission, which is a great error-prevention feature. Some users were annoyed by the beep, but they succeeded in filling out the form.

Tip: Make smarter forms for pages with multiple submit buttons. On a page with both a search box and another form, either submit button could be activated by the Enter key. A good form would check and choose: If the search box contains data, do a search; if the form contains data, submit the form; or if both contain data, ask the user what to do. We haven't tested any sites that perform this kind of data detection.

Tip: Test and implement accessible solutions. People with text browsers, screen readers, or various other Web-access devices might not be able to use your site if the Enter key does not activate the Submit button on a form.

Our study did not seek to discover anything about keyboard shortcuts or accessibility, but there are some good resources online. See the References section for more information about forms and Web accessibility.

▶ *When errors occur, clearly tell how to fix which fields.*

Error recovery is extremely important to user success. If users don't understand or don't notice an error message, sometimes they can't proceed.

Every computer user has experienced bad error messages, because good error messages are difficult to write. Many are written from the system or developer's point of view and tell users nothing about how to fix the problem.

Good error messages:

- **Tell the user politely that a problem exists.**

- **Explain clearly which field(s) had the problem.** The error message appears both prominently at the top of the page and right next to the field where new information is required.

- **Explain what information was expected or how to fix the error.**

In our study we found messages that users didn't understand, messages that users didn't notice, and messages that users had to scroll down to see:

- Boo: The user typed his full name for his user name in the registration form. His name was longer than the website permitted, so he got an error message, as a comment from Miss Boo. (Miss Boo was an animated character that popped up in a separate window and responded to the users' actions.) The user did not understand Miss Boo's comment, so he ignored the message. After completing the registration form, he clicked "Join Now." The website refused the form by simply repeating Miss Boo's message: "Hey you! Take a break. We're not asking you to write a book. Try a name of 4 to 10 characters." The message said "Name," not "Username" as in the field label. The user said he thought that the error occurred because he had not specified his favorite brands on the registration form, so he went back and entered his favorite brands.

- Peet's: In the shopping cart, users had to select how the coffee should be ground for brewing or choose whole beans. Users who didn't select one of the options received an error message and couldn't proceed with their purchase unless they figured out what was required and selected a grind. The badly worded error message caused sales catastrophes because some users didn't notice the red text and others didn't know what it meant. It said, "Please select option(s) for all indicated items:" and there was a tiny star between the grind selection list and the quantity type-in field three paragraphs below the message. (See Image P22 in the Product Pages chapter.)

- Nordstrom: The user submitted the form without entering his phone number. "It just came back to the same address," he said. At first he didn't notice what was wrong because he had to scroll down to see the error message, which appeared next to the address field. (See Image C20.)

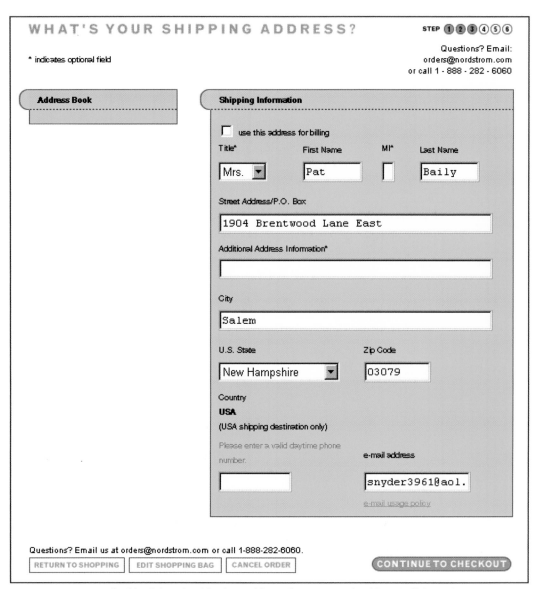

WHAT'S YOUR SHIPPING ADDRESS?   STEP ① ② ③ ④ ⑤ ⑥

Questions? Email:
orders@nordstrom.com
or call 1 - 888 - 282 - 6060

* indicates optional field

Address Book

Shipping Information

☐ use this address for billing

Title^   First Name   MI^   Last Name

[Mrs. ▼]   [Pat]   [ ]   [Baily]

Street Address/P.O. Box

[1904 Brentwood Lane East]

Additional Address Information^

[ ]

City

[Salem]

U.S. State   Zip Code

[New Hampshire ▼]   [03079]

Country
USA
(USA shipping destination only)

Please enter a valid daytime phone
number.   e-mail address

[ ]   [snyder3961@aol.]

e-mail usage policy

Questions? Email us at orders@nordstrom.com or call 1-888-282-6060.

[RETURN TO SHOPPING]   [EDIT SHOPPING BAG]   [CANCEL ORDER]   [CONTINUE TO CHECKOUT]

On Nordstrom's shipping address form, users had to scroll down to see
the error about the phone number. Nothing on the immediately visible
part of the page informed the user that there was a problem. C20

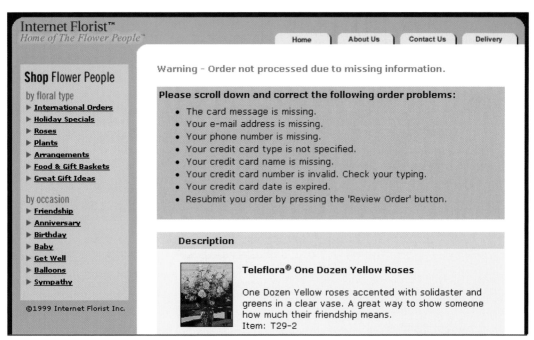

Internet Florist™
Home of The Flower People™

Home | About Us | Contact Us | Delivery

Shop Flower People

by floral type
► **International Orders**
► **Holiday Specials**
► **Roses**
► **Plants**
► **Arrangements**
► **Food & Gift Baskets**
► **Great Gift Ideas**

by occasion
► **Friendship**
► **Anniversary**
► **Birthday**
► **Baby**
► **Get Well**
► **Balloons**
► **Sympathy**

©1999 Internet Florist Inc.

Warning - Order not processed due to missing information.

Please scroll down and correct the following order problems:

- The card message is missing.
- Your e-mail address is missing.
- Your phone number is missing.
- Your credit card type is not specified.
- Your credit card name is missing.
- Your credit card number is invalid. Check your typing.
- Your credit card date is expired.
- Resubmit you order by pressing the 'Review Order' button.

Description

Teleflora® One Dozen Yellow Roses

One Dozen Yellow roses accented with solidaster and greens in a clear vase. A great way to show someone how much their friendship means.
Item: T29-2

Iflorist summarized all the form errors at the top of the page and also put a red asterisk next to each field that had a problem (not shown). Error messages for invalid entries did not clearly indicate the expected format of the information, however. C21

Required Fields

At the time of this study, it was common for Web application developers to indicate required fields in a form by putting red asterisks (*) next to them. In another user test, all users did not understand this use of asterisks. As mentioned previously, it is better to ask for only required information on forms, to cut down on possible errors and to avoid losing customer trust. (See the Trust chapter for more information about trust and personal information.)

Tip: If you use a symbol to denote something as important as a required field, explain what the symbol means right there on the page. Asterisks have often been used to indicate a footnote reference, so users who understand that meaning of asterisk may look at the bottom of the page for it. We have not tested this theory, however. If you use the asterisk for required fields, you should not also use it to designate an error.

Order Summary, Payment, and Confirmation

Order Summary

➡️ *Provide an order summary with all information about the transaction.*

A good order summary shows all the who, what, how much, and when information. It sets expectations correctly, before a customer commits to the purchase, and it allows the customer to make corrections easily. The summary should not be confused with the order confirmation page, which is shown after the purchase so that it can be printed. Most of the sites we tested showed good summaries, although some could have shown the summary earlier in the process.

CustomDisc's Order Review had the right information on it. C22

Wal-Mart provided a succinct summary of items and prices along with security information, but it did not show billing or delivery address, even though the users had entered that information already. C23

The main purpose of the summary is to allow the customer to verify that all information is correct before the order is submitted. The page should allow the customer to make changes easily and address any remaining concerns about the transaction that might prevent the customer from being comfortable enough to continue.

A good order summary shows the:

- Items to be shipped, including gift messages and wrapping options.
- Total charge including price for each item, shipping, tax, and other additional costs.
- Shipping and billing addresses.
- Shipping method.
- Estimated delivery date.
- Payment options.
- State of the transaction. (For example: "The order is not placed until after you provide payment information on the next screen and press the Confirm Order button.")
- Links to information the customer might want, such as privacy, security, customer service, returns, guarantees, and customer profile.
- Method for making changes to the order.

Payment Forms

Although most of our users did not actually complete purchases in our study (because we asked them not to), we learned a few things from those who did. Our users had little trouble filling out payment information on most of the test sites.

BasketHaus had the most difficult form because of its free-entry text fields. (See Image C24.) The fields' lack of structure and disappearing instructions made it hard to use. Each instruction had been placed inside the field it applied to, so users generally typed over the instructions when filling out the form. After typing over the instructions, many users had questions that they couldn't answer because that information was now gone.

The other notable problem occurred when, on another site, one user typed "Visa" in response to a field labeled: "Name on card."

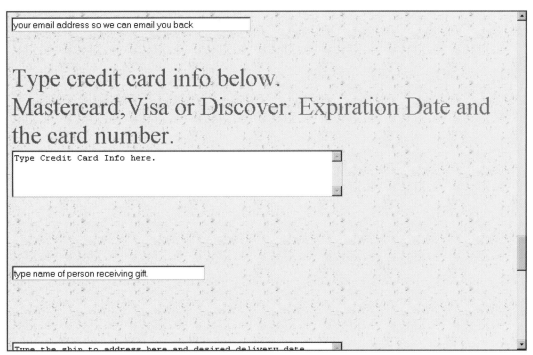

your email address so we can email you back

Type credit card info below.
Mastercard, Visa or Discover. Expiration Date and
the card number.

Type Credit Card Info here.

type name of person receiving gift.

Type the ship to address here and desired delivery date

After the user typed some information over the instructions, he wondered what else he had been asked to enter because the prompt was gone. C24

➧ *Offer a toll-free number for placing orders over the telephone.*

In our tests, users said many positive things about being able to place telephone orders instead of using their credit cards on the Web. Some people are afraid to leave credit card information stored on a website because of the potential for theft later, especially if the store is not familiar to them or well established. Also, many users in our study who got stuck — when they couldn't figure out how to check out, register, or log in — said they would normally give up on the website and try calling the company to complete their purchase.

➧ *Include a prominent link to privacy and security policies.*

Although we allowed them to enter fake personal information, almost 25% of our US users expressed interest in a site's security. We believe even more people would have been interested in security if they had been asked to enter their own information. (See the Trust chapter for more information about where and how to present effective security information.)

Order Confirmation

➧ *Provide an order confirmation page after the purchase.*

The order *summary* is the last page that is shown before the user authorizes the purchase. The order *confirmation* is the first page that appears after the user has confirmed the sale and completed the payment transaction. In our tests, only three users (all Danish) saw the confirmation pages.

Tip: Make the confirmation page as helpful as possible.

Although we tested only a few order confirmation pages, no discussion of the checkout process would be complete without covering this important topic. These then are our best suggestions based on our experiences as both test facilitators and customers.

A good confirmation page has the same information as a good summary page (see "Order Summary" earlier in this chapter), but it also shows:

- A thank-you message that clearly states that the order has been successfully *received* (not just sent) and payment status (for example: "your credit card has been charged $25.95").
- Which credit card or other payment method has been used and the last few digits from the card number (for example: "Visa XXXX XXXX XXXX 9876").
- The order confirmation or reference number.
- The shipping method and estimated delivery date.
- Customer service contact information.
- A reminder to print or save the page for future reference.
- Which e-mail address the confirmation e-mail has been sent to.
- The URL for the site.

A terrific confirmation page would also include:

- The tracking number with a URL for the shipper's tracking system.
- How to get back to the store now and order more items without having to log in again.
- How to manage any stored personal information.
- How to rate the site or comment on the shopping experience.
- Coupons or special offers for the next purchase.
- Site navigation links.

Tip: Provide information that's easy to skim. Use bullets or other scannable short texts on order confirmation pages instead of paragraphs, and make links from any of the text that could usefully guide the customer to more information about that topic.

Tip: Design for printability and offer email options. Make sure the page prints out acceptably on several kinds of computers, printers, and browsers. If necessary, provide a separate printable version. Offer to e-mail the page contents to any address the user specifies. Even though a confirmation mail might have been sent, some customers will not be able to receive, print, or access it for any number of reasons. Others will want to send the information to another account or another person, or print it at work, and so forth.

Tip: Make sure the confirmation page can act as both a receipt and a tracking aid. Some people will need to submit this page for expense reimbursement or keep it for their tax records. Others will have it in hand when they contact customer service. Make sure the information on the page serves both purposes well.

➧ *Send a confirmation e-mail as soon as possible after the transaction.*

Although we didn't ask users in our test to comment on e-mail confirmation messages, we believe it signals good customer service when sites send e-mail confirmations as soon as possible after a purchase.

At a minimum, the confirmation should include:

- The ordered items and total price
- Date and time of purchase
- Order number
- Customer service contact information, including telephone number, business hours, and time zone of call center
- Delivery status
- Delivery method and tracking information.

The e-mail should not include sensitive information such as the password or credit card number, of course. It could include the last four digits of the card, however, and all the other information shown on the confirmation page of the website. Many customers would find this information very useful to have in e-mail, even if they already have a printout of the page (and particularly if they don't).

Registration

Why Registration Fails

Registration accounted for 8% of the sales catastrophes in our study. At the time of this study (January 2000), it was quite common for sites to require users to register during the process of making their first purchase. Many users:

- **Misunderstood an important aspect of registration.** One user thought the process would open a charge account. Another user thought there might be a fee for membership. Other users weren't quite sure what registration was for and were unsure how to proceed.
- **Were reluctant to "join" anything or unwilling to complete a registration form.** Many users said, "I don't want to be a member," when they were asked to register while trying to buy something.
- **Typed into the form fields for returning users, even though they were new users.** (See Image C26.) Those who did not understand the subsequent error page became stuck.
- **Didn't realize they were supposed to invent a password.** Some users expected the site to issue them a password, perhaps because they'd never had to invent one before. Others thought the site was asking for the password to their e-mail account.

If a user fails or refuses to register — and registration is required — the failure results in a sales catastrophe for the site, which is not what either the prospective buyer or seller intended. People who give up on a website may not be back again.

➧ *Allow customers to purchase without registering.*

We saw so many problems with registration in our test that we must recommend against requiring it at all. Of the eight sites that required registration, four sites experienced complete purchase failures with one or more users because of problems during login and registration. Allowing customers to register optionally after a purchase is much better, because then it doesn't interrupt or prevent the sale, and it is less offensive to customers because they have a choice.

In some countries, even the term "registration" can be problematic because of its negative connotations. For example, in Denmark there have been many news stories about registration of HIV-infected persons and registration of those who are slow at paying their bills.

Various Approaches to Registration

At the time of this writing, many sites required registration or login at different points, usually as an interruption to the user's task, such as:

- Before the user can look at the catalog of products.
- Before the user can read customer service information.
- Before the user can put a product in the cart.
- Before the user can access online help.

Almost no sites require users to register or log in before allowing them into the website anymore, because that practice failed miserably when it was first tried. (Could you imagine being forced to register before you entered a supermarket?) Users in our tests perceived these barriers to access quite negatively.

The table below shows the three approaches to registration we saw in our tests — none, optional, and required — and which sites fell into each category, in alphabetical order. Sites that appear in bold had one or more users who became stuck on a registration-related issue and were unable or unwilling to continue.

Three Approaches to Registration (Bold sites had one or more complete failures)

None	Optional	Required
• BasketHaus	• **1800flowers** – during checkout	• eToys – New customers entered their e-mail address before their shipping information but didn't choose a password until later.
• Iflorist	• Boo – you could become a "VIP customer," which promised special offers.	
• Jcrew		
• Nordstrom	• CustomDisc	• Furniture
• NorwaySweaters	• Disney – at any time	• HermanMiller
	• **Gevalia** – required only if ordering regular deliveries	• **Living**
		• **Reel**
	• Peet's – during checkout	• Sears
	• Wal-Mart – after completing purchase	• **SmarterKids**
		• **TowerRecords**

During our tests, users expressed their irritation again and again at being forced to register, even when they perceived some value to themselves in doing so. Resistance to registration was greater when the procedure was required early in the process.

Forcing users to register creates an unnecessary barrier for first-time and one-time customers, and it annoys even those who manage to comply. Many users didn't trust sites to use their information appropriately. Some complaints we heard:

- **Fear of unsolicited e-mail or privacy concerns** – "I think they're building a mailing list. I don't want to join anything; I just want to buy coffee."

- **Fear of being charged something** – "This is what I was trying to avoid. … I'm guessing this would be like a charge card. … It kind of looks like you might have to be a registered user. This would piss me off at this point. I would probably call their 800 number. I might even call their competitor and then call them and let them know about it."

- **Annoyance at the additional steps and inconvenience** – Inventing a password is "too complicated. They assume that I will patronize this website in the future. They don't care about one-time shoppers."

On the bright side, one user said he would register with companies he knew and used often.

Optional Registration

Some sites' approaches to registration were less interruptive, for example:

- Wal-Mart offered optional registration after a successful purchase.

- Boo and 1800flowers offered optional registration as part of the order form.

We didn't gather much data about the effectiveness of optional registration, except on 1800flowers. There we saw users opt to skip registration, although they didn't seem to mind seeing the offer. A few user comments about Wal-Mart indicated that its optional registration was well received. Boo tried to convince customers to register as a VIP customer. It was completely voluntary, but they promised special deals. We believe that optional registration has less risk of confusing or alienating the user, unlike the more aggressive attempts to get users' information.

The failures of optional registration in our test, one each on 1800flowers and Gevalia, occurred because users believed they were required to register, when they weren't. Because they were unable to figure out how to register successfully, they got stuck and couldn't continue.

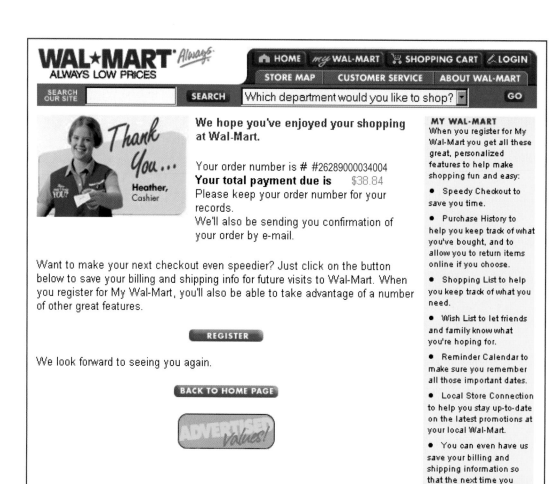

WAL★MART Always·
ALWAYS LOW PRICES

🏠 HOME | my WAL-MART | 🛒 SHOPPING CART | ✎ LOGIN

STORE MAP | CUSTOMER SERVICE | ABOUT WAL-MART

SEARCH OUR SITE | SEARCH | Which department would you like to shop? ▾ | GO

Thank You...

Heather, Cashier

We hope you've enjoyed your shopping at Wal-Mart.

Your order number is # #26289000034004
Your total payment due is $38.84
Please keep your order number for your records.
We'll also be sending you confirmation of your order by e-mail.

Want to make your next checkout even speedier? Just click on the button below to save your billing and shipping info for future visits to Wal-Mart. When you register for My Wal-Mart, you'll also be able to take advantage of a number of other great features.

REGISTER

We look forward to seeing you again.

BACK TO HOME PAGE

ADVERTISE Values!

MY WAL-MART
When you register for My Wal-Mart you get all these great, personalized features to help make shopping fun and easy:

• Speedy Checkout to save you time.

• Purchase History to help you keep track of what you've bought, and to allow you to return items online if you choose.

• Shopping List to help you keep track of what you need.

• Wish List to let friends and family know what you're hoping for.

• Reminder Calendar to make sure you remember all those important dates.

• Local Store Connection to help you stay up-to-date on the latest promotions at your local Wal-Mart.

• You can even have us save your billing and shipping information so that the next time you shop at Wal-Mart it's even quicker and easier!

Wal-Mart offered optional registration after the customer completed a purchase. Although we didn't test optional registration after the purchase, we believe it's the right approach. C25

Users perceived a site more positively when registration was optional:

- Reel: "I've shopped on sites that say 'would you like to save this' — that was great, I did that." The user made this remark (about sites we didn't test) after objecting to having to register during the checkout process.

- Disney: Comparing Disney to an earlier site she tested that required her to register, the user said: "I'm just entering [required information], for my credit card. That makes sense. … This looks like a billing form. It doesn't look like I'm doing a password thing. I feel much better about that. I can just pay and get out of there."

⮞ *Explain the benefits of registration and consider offering an incentive.*

Although it can be to the customer's advantage to register, the value of doing so may not be fully realized until the second visit. A big advantage to offering registration at the end of a purchase is that one of its key benefits — not having to fill out so many forms next time — is then more apparent to the user. If customers don't understand the benefit to themselves of registering, they simply go somewhere else to shop.

Tip: Make sure to explain the convenience benefit explicitly. On 1800flowers, one user read in the FAQ that registering was supposed to result in "faster, easier shopping." But she commented, "I'm not sure how it's faster or easier."

Tip: Say that membership is free of charge. Membership can cost something in other contexts. We suggest including the word "free" in the list of benefits to avoid the kind of concern we saw:

- Tower: "There might even be a fee for membership, I'm suspecting."

- 1800flowers: "I could order things as I need them and not have to be locked in with a potential membership fee. That's what I believe — they would charge me fees."

Users were more willing to register when there was a clear incentive or value to them in doing so. They wanted to feel like they were getting something back in return for giving up the requested information. Customers are already trading money for goods, so it's only fair to offer something further in exchange for their registration information. On every site that offered an incentive, at least one user volunteered a positive reaction to it.

▶ *Clearly explain the privacy policy and make it easy to find.*

We believe we saw an unusually low incidence of users looking at the privacy policy, probably because in the US tests most users were not entering their own information. In other studies, however, users expressed concerns about both privacy and security, which users may not distinguish between to the degree that developers do. Privacy and security are really the same problem from the users' point of view (their information might be used without their consent), with various likely causes (the site released the information on purpose or allowed it to get away through accident or negligence).

Tip: Make it easy for customers to cancel their registration. Tell customers how easy it is to cancel a registration, before and after you ask them to register. Promise that if they cancel their registration, you will delete all information about them. For example: "Any personal information you enter will be deleted as soon as any current order has been completed." Of the 15 sites we tested that required registration, none offered a way to delete a user account.

Creating a User Name and Password

Creating a password and user name for future login was part of the registration process on many sites, and the forms for creating a new login (which look similar to the forms used to log in on most sites) created some difficulties for users. This form confusion is discussed in detail in the section, "Login Problems: Using the Wrong Form," later in this chapter.

➡ *Allow (but don't require) an e-mail address for the user name.*

Using a person's e-mail address as a user name has two advantages: it is easier to remember and it is already unique. Picking a unique user name can be one of the big hurdles in registering, as we have seen in this study and others. We saw two problems with using an e-mail address in our tests:

1. **Lack of e-mail address**. Not all Web shoppers have an e-mail address, or they share one with others. (Consider the complications of sharing an e-mail address with the person you are ordering a gift for!) Out of 64 users in our study, about 5% told us they didn't have their own e-mail address. It's possible that the percentage of customers without an e-mail address may be smaller — perhaps even small enough to ignore — for sites that target business customers instead of the middle-class consumers we tested, however.

2. **Password confusion.** Four users mistakenly thought a site was asking for the password to their e-mail account, which they were understandably reluctant to provide.

   • Living: "It asks for my name and e-mail address, but what password? My e-mail password? Not clear on what they're asking for. … I'm not going to go any further. I don't want to give out my password for my e-mail account."

   • Wal-Mart: The user typed her e-mail address in the field for User Name and her AOL password in the Password field.

Although we didn't see it in our study, there is a third problem worth mentioning:

3. **Customer e-mail addresses can change quite often**. Allow users to change their e-mail address after proper login, and transfer their properties seamlessly.

Living's Sign In page is an example of the kind of forms that caused users to mistakenly believe the site was asking for the password to their e-mail accounts. These dual-purpose forms confused users, many of whom used the wrong half of the form to try to create a new account (See "Login Problems: Using the Wrong Form," later in this chapter, for a detailed discussion of this problem.) C26

○————————————◉————————————○————————————○————————————○————————————○

Shopping Cart   Customer Login   Shipping Info   Delivery Info   Billing Info   Review

New Customers: Give Yourself a Username & Password

Welcome! Give yourself a User Name and Password for shopping now and later. In addition to speeding up future shopping sprees, your User Name and Password entered on the "your account" page will give you info on the status of your order and let you review past orders.

User Name: [   ]

Password: [   ]

Confirm Password: [   ]

[sign in]

Returning Customers: Sign In Now

If you've shopped with us before, enter your User Name and Password.

User Name: [   ]

Password: [   ]

[sign in]

Forgot Your Username or Password?

Call Customer Service at 1-888-520-7646 Monday through Friday, 7 a.m. to 11 p.m. EST

HermanMiller's login page attempted to explain the purpose of creating a user name and password. This page was better than Living's Sign In page, but HermanMiller also didn't clearly explain what to enter. C27

➡ *Explain how to select a user name and password and why.*

Some users in our tests needed assistance from the facilitator to fill in these fields, because they didn't understand the purpose of the user name and password. Instructions and explanations on the sites were often inadequate.

Explain what the user should enter — full name, e-mail address, a nickname, and so forth. If the user name will be used by the site to greet the user, mention that fact — it might deter the user from entering a foolish or derogatory name. If the user name first chosen is already in use, the error message should suggest how to create a unique user name and provide available variations on the name the user asked for.

Several users got quite upset when their password was turned down because of some reasonable but unexplained rule, such as the minimum length of five characters on Reel. The rule was revealed only on the registration error page, shown here. C28

Problems creating a user name paled in comparison to problems we saw with creating a password. The main issues were how to get one and how to remember it.

The user must *invent* a password. Tell users to invent their own passwords and not to wait for one to be given to them. Make sure this explanation is provided again in the error message if the user skips the password field, because this misconception can cause some users to leave the password field blank.

Five users were unsure what to enter for a password. Two became stuck and needed help from the facilitator in order to proceed. These users believed the site would email them a password.

- Living: One user explained, "You're not supposed to make passwords up. You're supposed to get passwords."

- Living: Another user said, "The password thing gets me. I didn't have a password to begin with. So I never know what to do there. It's not going to let me skip them." She tried to sign in without entering a password." She tried the "Forgot my password" link, then "Request a password," then "Create a new password." She ended up on the login page she'd just filled out, but her information was gone. "I'm in a loop." She spent several minutes struggling until the facilitator explained she had to make up a password.

- HermanMiller: "So that means I have to get a password in order to order? So do I make one up, or do I gotta go to Your Account first?"

The user must create a secure but memorable password. Some users make bad passwords or use the same ones every time. Explain any limits on number and type of characters. Show an example or two, but don't allow the examples to be used as passwords.

Once users entered a password, the Confirm Password field didn't cause any problems. No one seemed confused by it or questioned why it was there.

Tip: Let the user choose who should make up the password. Add explanatory text: "Make up your own password, or let us make up a good one for you." Make sure the generated password is pronounceable nonsense, for example quotanbil.

Tip: Check for weak passwords. Passwords such as aaaaa, 123456, or the user name should be trapped by error checking. Many passwords selected by our users were easy to guess or defeat by trial and error, but we didn't notice any sites in our study that checked for weak passwords.

Tip: Motivate users to create secure passwords. Explain what a good password looks like and why it's to the user's advantage to make one. An excellent reference about motivating users to create secure passwords is: *Users Are Not The Enemy*, by Anne Adams and Martina Angela Sasse, in Communications of the ACM December 1999, pages 41–46.

➡ *Avoid using secret questions and hints for password recovery.*

Many e-commerce websites have a feature that is designed to allow the customer to recover a forgotten password. Although password recovery seems like a good thing to offer, hints and questions create more problems.

One method, sometimes called a "secret question," requires the customer to choose a question and a corresponding answer (unrelated to the password) that can later be used to verify his or her identity. The site poses the question and the user must respond with the pre-defined answer.

The other method in common use requires the customer to save a "hint" about the nature of the password, and if the password is forgotten, the site can prompt the customer with the hint.

Both methods have two significant downsides:

- **They can alienate customers**. Several users in our test liked the concept of a password hint, but others hated using them. One user was so annoyed by the password question and answer on SmarterKids that he refused to continue. Even if customers don't mind having to create hints or questions, it does take them extra time and effort to understand and complete the additional fields, especially for secret questions.

- **They can weaken security**. One user summed up the issue: "I don't like when they do these questions and answers for passwords. If I put in a question that's obvious enough to have an answer come up, then it's obvious enough for someone else; and if I enter something foolish, I'll never remember." A few users entered the same thing into both the question and the answer. Some users chose questions other people could answer, such as "daughter." Others used their password as the hint, which destroyed their security completely. During multiple tests of a popular free e-mail site, users defeated password security in this way so consistently that the hint process was identified as the site's most severe security and usability problem. (See Molich, et al in the References section.)

Tip: Instead of using hints or questions, send the customer an e-mail containing the forgotten password at the registered e-mail address (if there is one), or simply require the user to make a new account. Suggest the customer log in immediately and create a new password, because e-mailing passwords is insecure. Even so, this method poses less risk than allowing an insecure hint to reveal the password when someone is trying to break into a user's account.

☑ **SmarterKids.com™** | **Registration**

Home | MySmarterKids | Parents Center | Gift Center | Help | 🛒

SEARCH [_____] (Go) | Toddler | Preschool-K | Grades 1-3 | Grades 4-6 | Grades 7-9

Please enter some information about yourself. The information you provide will be secure and not shared with others. Click here to read our Privacy Policy.

Already registered with SmarterKids? Click Here to Log-in.

Personal Information

First Name: [_____] — We will use this information to greet you when you return to SmarterKids.

Last Name: [_____]

E-mail: [_____] — We use your e-mail address to identify you and communicate with you. Please ensure that your e-mail address is correct.

Password: [_____] — Your password will be used to protect your personal information from others. The password must be at least 5 characters.

Verify Password: [_____]

Please Type a question that only you would know the answer to. This question should have a one-word answer. If you should forget your password, we will ask this question to verify your identity. (**example:**"What is the name of my child's favorite toy?")

Question: [_____]
Answer: [_____]
(one word)

On the SmarterKids Registration page some users typed the same word in both the Question and Answer fields or simply typed their password into one or both fields. C29

Login Problems: Using the Wrong Form

➡️ *Allow new users to register even if they use the returning customer login form.*

On most sites that had separate fields for new and returning customers, we saw users try to invent a new user name and password by typing into the fields for returning customers. (See Images C26 and C27.) It may seem at first like a case of "clueless user" when new customers complete user name and password fields intended only for returning customers, but we saw this problem happen often enough that we believe websites should actually support or work around this behavior. Even when the fields for new customers looked distinct from those for returning customers, our users picked the wrong set again and again. They didn't always read the instructions, but instead simply began entering data into the first field they saw on the page.

Login fails for one of two reasons on the system side: either the user name is not recognized, or the password doesn't match the user name. The system detects which type of problem occurred, but the user has a more complex situation. The user might have used the wrong form when trying to create a login, typed the right password incorrectly, entered some other account's password or user name, typed the password with the right characters but capitalized the wrong letter, and so forth.

None of the websites we tested explained which of the two kinds of system login failure occurred (it might compromise security to do so). But in our test, no error messages hinted at the real problem, which was that the users had mistakenly typed into the returning customer form instead of the new customer form in an effort to create a new login and password.

Users typically assumed the error message meant that they had simply invented an unacceptable name or password. So they made up a new name or password. A few users could not proceed beyond that point because nothing they typed (into the wrong form) worked and they never realized their mistake.

SHOPPING CART

FIVE-POINT
GUARANTEE

- The account name/password combination provided is not valid. Please note that your password is case sensitive.

I HAVE NOT YET REGISTERED OR PURCHASED FROM REEL'S NEW WEBSITE:

When you come back to Reel.com in the future, you can use your account name and the password you choose to access your account.

CONTINUE ▶

I AM A REGISTERED CUSTOMER ON REEL'S NEW WEBSITE:

My E-Mail Address is:

snyder3961@aol.com

If you have no email address, please enter the account name under which you registered.

and my password is:

CONTINUE ▶

Forgot your password? We're here to help!

If you haven't set up an account at Reel.com within the last few weeks (i.e. since August 3, 1999), you aren't yet a registered customer and you don't have a password. So why don't you register without further delay?

Reel's message said, "The account name / password combination is not valid. Please note that your password is case sensitive." Unfortunately the user believed this meant her password was already in use. She got stuck and couldn't continue with her purchase. The real problem was that she was a new user who typed her information into the form instead of clicking the top button. Although well-constructed, case-sensitive passwords can provide better security from password cracking programs, they are a much less usable choice for most websites and most users. C30

- Reel had a new customer button (called "Continue") and a returning customer form with type-in fields. The user typed her e-mail address and a password and clicked Continue. When the site gave her an error, she said, "Someone already got my stupid password." She never realized that the user name and password fields are for previously registered users only, not for those who are creating a new account. She never read the instructions on the bottom of the page. She didn't get past that point.

- On Living, one user started out typing into the correct set of fields (for new users) but switched to the simpler set of fields (for returning users) after getting her first error message. She didn't read the labels. (See Image C26.)

Another kind of form confusion occurred in our study. When sites showed a prominent login form for returning customers, our users assumed they had to register. We saw this mistake on Wal-Mart, which does not require registration:

- "I don't like this. … I don't know when I'll ever get back to this website, so why should they have the information?"
- The user typed a user name and a password even though he hadn't registered yet. A minute later he said, "I'm not a registered user" and deleted the information he had typed. "I assumed I needed to register."

Some new users tried to type a user name and password despite the big "or" that tried to divide new customers from returning ones. Two users mistakenly concluded that Wal-Mart required registration when they saw this page. C31

Worse, Gevalia's design led users to believe that they had to register in order to see the catalog. The option to enter as a guest was not immediately noticeable, and some users needed help from the facilitator to get into the catalog.

GEVALIA®
ONLINE CATALOG
Sign In

Account Maintenence
Log In
Search
Shopping Cart
Help

PREFERRED SHOPPERS SIGN IN HERE
Username:
Password: Go

Want to change your password?
Fill in the Username and current password
above and enter your new password below
New password:
Confirm new
password: Go

NOT A PREFERRED SHOPPING MEMBER?

You can still enter as our guest: Go

Gevalia created a perceived barrier on the front page of their catalog by providing a prominent registration and login form. Some users didn't notice the barely visible "guest" option (which was partly cut off by the bottom of the monitor, as shown) and concluded they had to register before being able to view the catalog, which they refused to do. C32

Tip: To alleviate confusion between new and returning user forms, we have three recommendations:

- **Buttons** – Try the Sears approach (Image C33), which seemed to work well for our users. Use two separate buttons for new and returning customers instead of type-in fields.

- **Error recovery** – Assume that, despite your best efforts, new customers will sometimes try to enter information into the fields for returning users. The resulting error page should clearly explain what might be the problem and offer new users a means of proceeding from there with new account creation if they wish.

- **Unified form** – Amazon.com, for example, designed one login form for all users (Image C34) that looks quite different from the typical login / password form. By providing one form for everyone, mistakes can likely be minimized. We have not tested this or similar designs, however.

SEARS   Appliance Advisor   Contact Us   Home

Shopping Cart

Here are the items currently in your shopping cart. After reviewing your order, you can continue shopping or move on to check out. For an error-free delivery, look through our pre-delivery checklist.

Currently, we can only accept orders in the Continental United States. For more information read our Terms and Conditions, or find out more about the shopping process in About Ordering.

View Item	Item Number	Description	Qty	Price	Total	Remove
View Item	02069299	Kenmore 69299 Grey Stone w/Black 1.0 cu. ft. Flex Style Middle Size Countertop Microwave	1	$99.88	$99.88	☐

Subtotal does not include delivery and tax.   subtotal: $99.88

You can set the quantity to zero or check "remove" to delete an item from your shopping cart.

Save Changes Now

check out

continue to shop online

First-time User   Registered User

Sears sorted the "First-time User" from the "Registered User" with buttons rather than instructions. This approach worked for our users, who had to read the buttons in order to choose one. No attractive login form was present to distract them. C33

amazon.com.   🛒 | YOUR ACCOUNT | HELP

WELCOME | DIRECTORY   — TODAY'S FEATURED STORES —   ELECTRONICS   MUSIC   AUCTIONS   BOOKS   CAMERA & PHOTO

What is your e-mail address?

My e-mail address is [   ]

Do you have an Amazon.com password?

○ **No, I am a new customer.**

◉ **Yes, I have a password:** [   ]
Forgot your password? Click here.

Sign in using our secure server

If you received an error message when you tried to use our secure server, sign in using our standard server. If you select the secure server, the information you enter will be encrypted.

Where's My Stuff?	**Shipping & Returns**	**Need Help?**
• Track your recent orders.	• See our Shipping Rates & Policies.	• Forgot your password? Click here.
• Use Your Account to view or change your orders.	• Read our Returns Policy.	• Redeem or buy a gift certificate.
		• Visit the Help Desk.

Top of Page

Amazon.com Home | Books | Music | DVD | Video | Toys & Games | Electronics | Camera & Photo | Software | Computer & Video Games | New Cars | Kitchen | Tools & Hardware | Lawn & Patio | Health & Beauty | Auctions | zShops | sothebys.amazon.com | e-Cards | 1-Click Settings | Shopping Cart | Your Account | Help | Sell Items

We didn't test Amazon.com, but we suspect this kind of unified form might work better than the now-typical dual login forms that use two similar entry areas for both new and returning customers. C34

Creating a Good Checkout Process

Although checkout — filling out a series of forms — seems simple, our study shows that its usability can't be taken for granted. Users expect to see all relevant details of their purchase before committing to it. Missing information or unpleasant surprises can drive them away from a site.

Even though form designers may have a clear picture of the database fields the information will go into, users don't care about database schema. Data entry errors can be prevented by allowing users to enter their information in a familiar order into appropriate-length fields. No matter how good the explanations and examples, forms should validate important data.

This study clearly showed that forcing users to register while purchasing is counter-productive. We believe that mandatory registration will soon disappear as consumers experience more e-commerce sites that don't require registration and as more companies begin to understand the cost in terms of lost sales. Instead, customers should be invited to register with the site after their initial purchase.

International Users

" Ultimately, the best way to improve your site's international usability is to make it more usable in its native country."

International vs. Localized Websites

Ten of the 20 websites we tested sold products to customers outside the US. The rest catered only to US customers. Nine websites were international and one (boo.com) was localized.

A *localized* website appears as though it were originally developed in the target language. The language, the culture, and general business issues of the original website are adapted to the local (national) market. Simply translating the text on a website is superficial localization. Perfect localization of a website requires not only translation but also replacement of original US product selections, names, specifications, prices, and business practices with those of the target country's market.

An *international* website is adapted to the global market. It appears as a US website but has been changed and extended in subtle ways that ideally make it usable in other parts of the world. For example, the website shows where it ships its merchandise; checkout and registration procedures cater to international users; and the language is a simplified form of English, suitable for people who know English but do not use it as their primary language.

One language does not necessarily correspond to one national market. The German language is used on German, Austrian, and some Swiss websites, for example. A careful analysis may be required to determine whether one, two, or even three different localized websites will be required to serve these three countries.

The table below shows how easy or difficult it was for users to find out where each website would ship goods and where that information was found. Even when a site did ship to Denmark, it was not necessarily easy for Danish users to realize it.

Ease of Finding International Shipping Information

Website	Type	Easy to find?	Where the site revealed which countries it serves
BasketHaus.com	International	Yes	Home page
Iflorist.com	International	Yes	International Orders
SmarterKids.com	International	Yes	Help – Do you ship internationally? – FAQ #16
TowerRecords.com	International	Yes	Customer Service – International
1800flowers.com	International	No	Contradictory *
CustomDisc.com	International	No	Help – Shipping and Handling
Disney.com	International	No	Disney Store – Guest Services – Shipping Information
Peets.com	International	No	Order form (not in Customer Service or Search)
Reel.com	International	No	Billing information page lets you select country
Boo.com	Localized	Yes	Localized version. Users were never in doubt
Jcrew.com	US National	Yes	Customer service – International orders
NorwaySweaters.com	US National	Yes	Shipping page during checkout
eToys.com	US National	No	Shipping options – Shipping Charges, Learn More
Gevalia.com	US National	No	Shipping form: Shipping country is USA (unchangeable)
Nordstrom.com	US National	No	Help – Shipping, International orders
Sears.com	US National	No	Shipping form: Shipping country is United States (unchangeable)
Wal-Mart.com	US National	No	Customer Service – FAQ #12
Furniture.com	US National	No	Shipping form: Shipping country is United States (unchangeable)
HermanMiller.com	US National	No	Shop Online – Customer Service – FAQ #1
Living.com	US National	No	Shipping form: Impossible to specify country in shipping address

*The 1800flowers case is discussed under the guideline: "Explicitly list all countries to which you ship," later in this chapter.

Superficial Localization

Skillful localization depends on a keen understanding of your intended audience. Boo was a superficially localized website. Localization there consisted mostly of simple translation. Boo's shipping information page was more difficult for our users than were similar pages on some of the websites that were not localized. For example, the State field confused users. In the US, the State and ZIP Code fields belong together (State – ZIP Code). In most European countries, the Postal Code and the City fields belong together (Postal Code – City).

On Boo's Danish shipping information page, the separation of the city and postal code fields confused our Danish users. Boo used the US layout for Danish customers. In Column 1, from top to bottom, the fields were: First Name, Last Name, Company, Address, Address, City. In Column 2, the fields were: Country, State (only USA / Canada), Postal Code, Telephone Number. IU1

Show Where You Ship

Our Danish users fell into two groups:

- **Inexperienced users** – They had never shopped on a non-Danish site. At first, these users did not suspect possible delivery problems. These problems appeared only when the users had collected the products they wanted to buy and attempted to specify their shipping address during checkout.

- **Experienced users** – They had previously shopped on non-Danish sites and knew that many US websites don't ship outside the continental US. These veteran users started by looking for information about shipment even before they looked at the merchandise.

➡️ *Place international shipping information*
where inexperienced users will notice it.

Danish inexperienced users invariably followed the same procedure when shopping on a website, regardless of whether the website shipped outside the US or not:

1. They located the desired products and put them in the shopping cart. None of them looked for or noticed shipping restrictions.

2. They attempted to check out. When they tried to specify a shipping address, they ran into problems if the website did not ship to countries outside the US.

These inexperienced users got irritated when they encountered the shipping information pages:

- On eToys: "It would have been nice if they had told me this a bit earlier!"

- On Jcrew: "They could have said this right from the start."

- On 1800flowers: "It's a bit late to find out that they don't ship to Denmark." (Actually, 1800flowers does ship to Denmark, but it isn't easy to figure out how. See the discussion under the guideline "Explicitly list all countries to which you ship" in this chapter.)

- On Jcrew: A user wanted to send an e-mail asking whether they would ship to Denmark anyway.

In many cases, users found out a website did not ship to Denmark when they realized the only choices for Country on the shipping address form were USA and possibly Canada. Some users were so convinced the website would ship to Denmark, however, that they attempted to overwrite even this non-editable information.

- On Jcrew, a user attempted to write "Denmark" in the State form field. He also typed in his Danish postal code (2100) in the ZIP Code field.

- The Nordstrom Shipping page does not contain a Country field. Danish users attempted to locate "Denmark" in the state selection list. When they were unsuccessful, they tried to type "Denmark" in the State selection list.

- On HermanMiller, users attempted to make their European address fit into the data entry fields provided. One user selected State=DE, which she thought represented Denmark. The website did not explain the code "DE." (DE is an abbreviation for the US state Delaware.) She was a bit worried, because the code DE differed from the ordinary country code for Denmark, which is DK. The idea that HermanMiller would not ship to Denmark occurred to her only after much searching. She eventually found the information that HermanMiller does not ship outside the US in the fine print at the bottom of the shopping cart page.

Tip: Show the shipping restrictions on the home page. If your site serves only a national market, state that clearly from the beginning.

Tip: Ask for the user's ZIP Code or country as soon as the user has selected a product. Explain you need this information to compute shipping cost. If you don't ship to the specified country, provide a helpful message — see the examples in Images IU3 and IU4.

Tip: Repeat any shipping restrictions on the shipping information page.
Don't just write "Country: United States" as Sears did on its Secure Check Out page, below. Instead, write: "Country: United States (Other Countries)" and provide a link to a helpful message when a user clicks Other Countries. Otherwise, users will try to change the fixed text. Some of our users highlighted the unwanted text and pressed the Delete key, or they attempted to type text in a selection list box. When these attempts failed, some of our users slowly started to realize they had a problem: "It seems that I can't buy anything if I'm from Europe." Others concluded you had to use a special procedure for delivery outside the US and started looking in vain for that procedure.

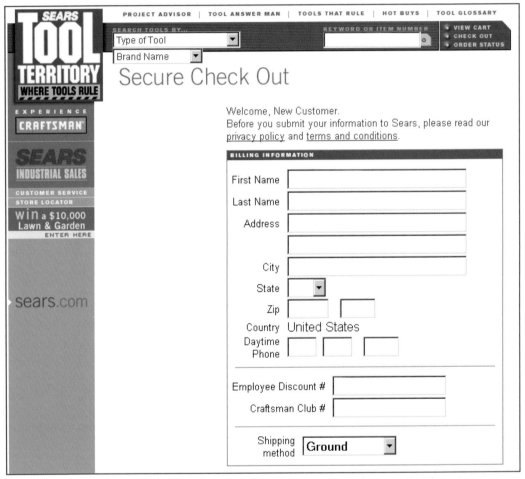

In several cases, our Danish users tried to modify non-editable text, like "Country: United States," on Sears. IU2

eToys.com

shipping address

Select Shipping Address

Please note: eToys currently only ships to the United States, most U.S. Territories, APO/FPO addresses, and Canada. For U.K. shipments, please visit www.eToys.co.uk.

ship all items to one address - [ship to more than one address]
OR-
Enter an address in the fields below.

Name: [   ]
Address: [   ]
[   ]
City: [   ]
State/Province: [Not Selected ▾]   Zip: [   ]
Phone: [   ]

☐ Save yourself some time later! Click this box if your Billing Address is the same as this shipping address.

On eToys' shipping address page, the first information on the page told users that products could be shipped only to US and Canadian addresses. IU3

➡ *Place international shipping information where experienced users look for it.*

Experienced Danish users knew many US websites don't ship outside the continental US. These users started site exploration by looking for information about shipment restrictions. Some users even put a dummy product in the shopping cart so they could access the shipping information page as early as possible. Experienced users looked in the following places (most frequently searched pages listed first):

1. **Customer Service**

2. **Home page**

3. **Shipping Information (during checkout)**

4. **FAQ**

5. **About Us.**

Experienced users looked to see if "Denmark" was available in the country selection list on the shipping information page. If there was no country selection list, they looked in the state selection list.

None of our Danish users looked in Help for shipping information. As one user said, "Help is technical stuff." Five of our 25 Danish users did consult Help at some point during their tests, Surprisingly, 23 of our 39 US users went to Help one or more times during their tests. In roughly half the cases, Help provided an appropriate answer to users' questions. Only a few users looked at the About Us pages for international shipping information.

An example: Experienced users started their work on Reel by checking to see if Denmark was on the list of countries Reel ships to. As one user explained, "I want to check this right away, because I have wasted some time on other websites, where late in the process I found out that they do not ship outside the US." After a while, experienced users found the information on the Billing page, where the country selection list included Denmark. "This information should have been on the home page," complained one user.

Tip: Put the shipping information, or a very noticeable link to the information, on the customer service page, the home page, and the shipping information page. Don't expect users to notice shipping information in unexpected places like the shopping cart (but it wouldn't hurt to put a link there).

Tip: Include information about countries you ship to, even if there are no restrictions. If you ship all over the world, state that clearly.

Tip: Place shipping restrictions no farther than two very noticeable links from the home page. The following link sequence works well:
Home > Customer Service > International Shipping. This sequence works even better: Home > Where do we deliver?

On NorwaySweaters, international shipping information was easy to find. Users simply clicked the Shipping link on the home page. The shipping page clearly stated, "We are unable to export our sweaters outside the US." A typical reaction was "Well, then I better get out of here." This is a good thing for users to say — they understood they shouldn't spend any more time on this site.

Danish users wasted little time on NorwaySweaters after they read this easy-to-find Shipping & Handling page. IU4

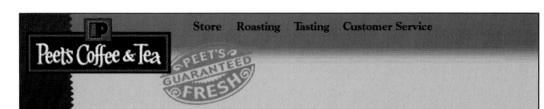

Your Shopping Cart

Review your shopping cart below. Please note: You must select a grind for each coffee. If you make any changes to your order, click "Recalculate order" to see a new total cost.

To finish shopping, click "Submit Order." **To return to the store,** click "Continue Shopping."

This is what your shopping cart contains:

Item	Options	Qty.	Price	Total Price	
French Roast	Select a Grind ▾	2	$10.95 per lb.	$21.90	Remove Item

Choose Multiple Grinds

Adjust the quantity of coffee in the Qty boxes, and the type of
grind in the pull-down menus.

Estimated U.S. Shipping Cost	$4.25
Total Cost	**$26.15**

Please call us at 800-999-2132 for overnight orders, international orders or shipping questions.

Shipments to California, Illinois and Massachusetts: applicable sales tax will be added.

Recalculate Order | Cancel Order

Peet's unsuccessfully tried to inform its users about shipping restrictions, but our users did not notice the shipping information near the bottom of the shopping cart. IU5

Tip: Make sure the words "international" and "shipping" stand out. Most of our users looked for these two keywords.

At Peet's, the shipping restrictions were shown in the shopping cart, where users did not expect to find them. In addition, the word "international" did not stand out. The result: Our users did not notice the restrictions.

The first clause of a sentence should let people know whether the rest of the sentence pertains to them. We'd revise the Peet's text to make the international information stand out: "International orders, overnight delivery, and … please call us at … ."

➡️ *Offer alternatives if you don't ship abroad.*

Presenting a clear, very noticeable message about shipping restrictions is good. Telling users where and how they can buy your merchandise through other channels is even better:

- HermanMiller provided links to international partners that carried their products.
- eToys offered its international customers a link to its subsidiary in the United Kingdom.

Tip: Provide links to international partners who carry similar products.

Tip: Provide links to subsidiaries that serve the user's country.

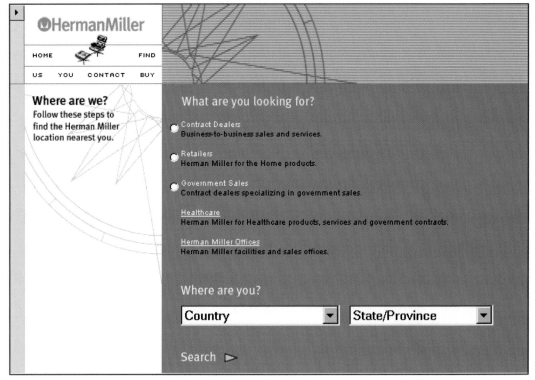

HermanMiller provided links to international partners that carry their products. IU6

Tip: Make sure the website you link to will actually meet your user's needs. If you refer the user to another website, clearly indicate any unusual restrictions that might apply to that site.

One of our users on eToys had already put products in his shopping cart when he found out eToys ships products only to US and Canadian addresses. He noticed the link, www.eToys.co.uk, for shipments to the United Kingdom. His reaction: "Oh, no, I have to start all over again!" (See Image IU3.)

Sometimes, a link is not enough. The user suggested he should be able to transfer his shopping cart to the UK website. Although this is an excellent suggestion, neither eToys nor any other website we know will let you perform this kind of shopping cart transfer yet.

All Danish users assumed the eToys.co.uk website would ship to other European countries, including Denmark. This assumption was incorrect, but the users never found out, because they did not try to place the order on the UK website.

➡ *Show both where you ship and where you bill.*

Although many of the websites we tested offered appropriate information about countries they ship to, few offered information about countries they bill to. Several of our users wanted to know, "Well, even if they don't ship to Denmark, will they accept orders from Denmark to a US shipping address?"

Product Information

Many companies offer significantly different products to each country they serve. The Mercedes-Benz main website (www.mercedes-benz.com) shows cars not for sale outside of Germany, for example.

➡ *If different models, prices, or procedures apply in different countries, make that clear.*

We didn't notice many violations of this guideline and have included it here mainly for completeness. In most cases, the product selection turned out to be adequate for the Danish users in our tests.

We did record one comment, however, about missing products. A CustomDisc user noted, "These are all Billboard songs. There are no Danish songs."

One of our users remarked that many of the movies displayed on Reel's home page were unknown in Denmark. US movies on videotape are released in Denmark several months after they are released in the US. Most of the brand new video titles on the Reel's home page might not yet be known to the international audience.

➡ *Warn about potential technical and legal problems with products.*

Some US products may not work outside the US. A website must warn its international customers as early as possible about possible compatibility problems. Reel's Format Notice (below) is a good example of fair warning.

Our users encountered several technical compatibility problems:

- US DVDs and videos may not play on European players because of protection codes and incompatible formats.
- US appliances that require 110V, 60 Hz may not work in Europe where the current is most often 220V, 50Hz.
- Few cellular phones will work in both Europe and the US.

Other US products might work outside the US, but owning or using them might be illegal. We didn't notice any problems in this study, but from personal experience, we know it can be illegal to ship plant or animal products to other countries due to agricultural import restrictions.

Tip: Set up important warnings as interactive barriers so users cannot overlook them. Reel wanted to warn and educate their international customers about potential videotape format incompatibilities. Users were required to confirm having read the warning message by checking the checkbox near the bottom of the page. They were not allowed to proceed with their orders until they had checked the box. This warning method worked well, although our users said this important information should have been shown earlier in the process.

Don't hide important warnings. On TowerRecords, two Danish users managed to complete their orders. Neither of them noticed the cryptic warning that appeared in a small grayish font near the end of each video description: "Non U.S. residents: please note that our videos are in NTSC format. We do not offer PAL or SECAM."

Tip: Make sure warnings are correct. You might need advice from local experts to provide correct warnings. If parts of a warning are incorrect, users may distrust the entire warning, even if the main part is accurate (Image IU7).

- As well designed as it was, Reel's International Format Notice contained incorrect information. Many newer European players actually can play US NTSC videos without problems, but the picture quality is lower than for European PAL videos.

- The information, "Movies on Reel's site have a PAL button option," in the International Format Notice appeared to be wrong. We were unable to locate a "PAL button option" on any movie titles, and a Reel customer service representative could not point one out either.

Our users appreciated this incompatibility warning from Reel, but they wished Reel had shown this message much earlier in the shopping process. IU7

Tip: Make sure warnings are easy to understand. All our Danish users of CustomDisc (and a couple of Americans as well) wondered why US and Canadian flags sometimes appeared with the song tracks in the shopping cart. Several users tried to click the flags but nothing happened. The flags appeared only in the shopping cart — not in the search results.

Several steps (and several minutes) later, all users encountered the error message: "Your custom disc contains songs that cannot be shipped outside the US. Click here to update the contents of your custom disc." The users understood the meaning of the message, but they were irritated that the website had not told them about this restriction earlier. "In real life I would have stopped at this point," said one user. "It's my fault. I should have clicked those flags," said another. Clicking the flags, however, would not have worked. Only by chance, one user discovered that when the mouse rested (hovered) for about two seconds over a flag, a message appeared: "cannot be shipped outside U.S. or Canada." By not making the flags clickable, CustomDisc failed to present important information to users in a way they expected.

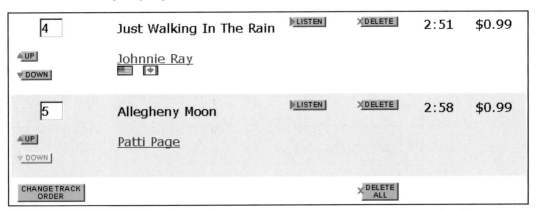

Users on CustomDisc did not understand the warning symbolized by the US and Canadian flags. They tried to click the flags to get an explanation but nothing happened. IU8

Tip: Address technical incompatibilities in your FAQ.

Tip: Get the legal department involved early. Site design changes may be required to accommodate legal issues. Consult a professional early in the design process.

➡ *Show all additional costs, especially shipping costs, as soon as possible.*

If you are unable to compute the exact total, tell users about potential extra costs and where they can get precise information. Danish users worried about additional costs, which they perceived as hidden costs:

- Jcrew: "The price applies within the US. They will add all sorts of different things."

- NorwaySweaters: "Tax should have been included in the price. That's what we are used to. Everything else is cheating." (This user referred to Danish law that requires Danish stores to display product prices, including sales tax. If a store displays a price without sales tax, the store must sell the product to the customer at the price shown, and the store must pay the sales tax.)

- SmarterKids: A user feared the products would be even more expensive if he had to pay tax and duty. He said it was impossible to figure out how much the actual cost for him would be.

Tip: Show non-US costs. Specifically, our Danish users were concerned about these costs:

- US sales tax (state sales tax)
- Local sales tax (Danish sales tax)
- Duty
- International shipping charges.

None of the sites we tested (and no other sites we know) warned users they might have to pay duty and local sales tax. One of our users, who was an experienced Web shopper, told us he would never order a gift shipped directly to the recipient. He had previously bought toys for himself and had received a call from the customs authorities demanding duty. He did not want to expose a gift recipient to demands for money from the government.

Tip: State clearly that international customers do not have to pay US sales tax. Danish users didn't understand the rules for US sales tax, which isn't surprising, because some of our US users had problems understanding sales tax rules, too. In addition to US sales tax, Danish users did not know whether Danish sales tax would be added to orders shipped to a Danish address. (For more on sales tax, see the chapter on Selling Strategies.)

- NorwaySweaters: "I think the tax varies from state to state. I don't know what this will cost me."
- Furniture: "[The website says] 'Massachusetts residents pay 5% sales tax,' but what if I live outside Massachusetts?"
- Iflorist: A user wondered about this tax notice: "State tax: Added to Minnesota orders only." She was bewildered by this irrelevant information, because she had already specified the order was for delivery in Denmark.

Tip: Explain that international customers might have to pay local sales tax in their own country. Consider showing how much the customer's local sales tax would be.

Tip: Support one-click or two-click access to information about additional costs. In our tests, experienced Web shoppers from both countries always checked a new site for shipping costs and any other unpleasant surprises. They searched in this sequence: Home > Customer Service > Shipping Costs.

Tip: Support this link trail: Home > Customer Service > Shipping Costs. Consult the Selling Strategies and Checkout & Registration chapters for more shipping cost strategies.

➡ *Consider offering a built-in currency converter.*

Some internationalized websites feature a built-in currency converter. The user can specify a currency, and all prices are then shown in that currency. If you choose to offer access to currency conversion, make it perfectly clear whether the converted price is legally binding, or if it is provided for information / estimation purposes only.

Most of our users knew one US dollar corresponded approximately to seven Danish kroner at the time of testing. Only one of our Danish users had problems converting US dollars into Danish kroner.

- Iflorist: Upon seeing the total amount of $44.95, the user wondered, "How much is a dollar? About seven [Danish kroner]?" The user was right, but a currency converter would have been useful.

Moisturising Body Gel

A cooling gel which is ideal for use after showing or exposure to the sun. The gel contains beads of vitamin E which disperse on contact with the skin.

Key ingredients : Pure New Zealand Spring Water, Carrageenans, Vitamin E, Horsetail Extract, Hyaluronic acid, Gingko Biloba Extract, Lanolin.

100ml tube costs $NZ 9.00

Beauty Spa Homepage / Secure order form / Currency Converter

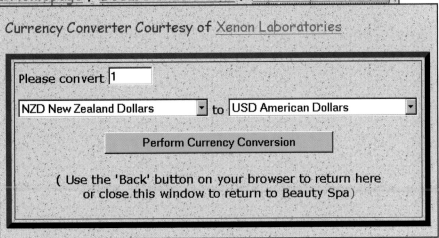

Currency Converter Courtesy of Xenon Laboratories

Please convert 1

NZD New Zealand Dollars ▼ to USD American Dollars ▼

Perform Currency Conversion

(Use the 'Back' button on your browser to return here or close this window to return to Beauty Spa)

Beauty Spa (www.beautyspa.co.nz) provided an external link to a currency conversion site (www.xe.net/cgi-bin/ucc/convert), but users were required to type in the price themselves. IU9

The majority of internationalized e-commerce sites outsource their currency conversion. For instance, Beauty Spa (not a site we tested in this study) linked to the Xenon Laboratories Currency Converter. Note that the price on the Beauty Spa product page did not transfer to the currency converter, although such a transfer is technically possible.

Tip: Use the keywords "currency converter" on any major search engine to find companies that offer currency conversion services.

Measures

Measures caused problems. Most Danish users were unable to convert US measures to the metric system. The problems mainly fell in three areas:

- Weight
- Capacity
- Size.

We did not test a site that dealt in temperatures. We would expect confusion, however, between the US Fahrenheit scale and the Celsius scale used in many other countries, including Denmark.

Weight

None of our users knew a US pound is 0.454 kilograms. More than half of the Danish users didn't recognize the abbreviation "lb." for pound.

➡️ *Provide translation of measures to and from metric units.*

A Danish user tried to buy coffee from Peet's. She was uncertain about the meaning of lb., so she typed in "2 kg" (two kilograms) in the Qty (quantity) box. Then she clicked the Buy Now button. The website did not react. She thought the website had understood her request, but she was unable to complete the purchase.

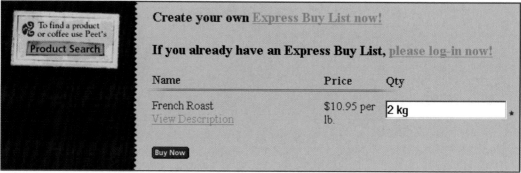

A user could not complete a purchase from Peet's because the site did not respond when she typed a metric unit in the Qty form field. IU10

Tip: Set up measure form fields to respond with a helpful error message when a user inputs unexpected values.

Capacity

Capacity measures, such as cubic feet, were difficult even for US users. All our users had trouble figuring out how much food would fit inside a microwave. The Product Comparison page on Sears (below) prompted these comments from the Danish users:

- "I don't understand the abbreviations and measures."
- "Inches? I don't recall how much it is."
- "These are difficult concepts for a European."

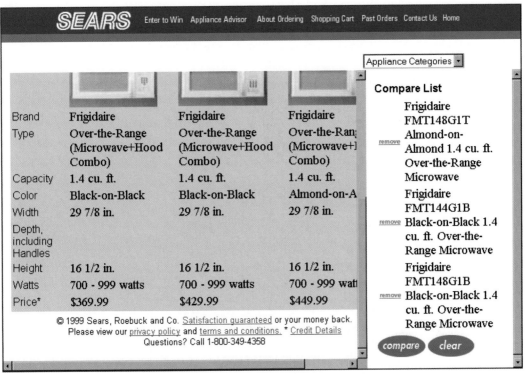

Enter to Win   Appliance Advisor   About Ordering   Shopping Cart   Past Orders   Contact Us   Home

Appliance Categories ▾

				Compare List
Brand	Frigidaire	Frigidaire	Frigidaire	Frigidaire FMT148G1T
Type	Over-the-Range (Microwave+Hood Combo)	Over-the-Range (Microwave+Hood Combo)	Over-the-Rang (Microwave+] Combo)	Almond-on- Almond 1.4 cu. ft. Over-the-Range Microwave
Capacity	1.4 cu. ft.	1.4 cu. ft.	1.4 cu. ft.	
Color	Black-on-Black	Black-on-Black	Almond-on-A	Frigidaire FMT144G1B
Width	29 7/8 in.	29 7/8 in.	29 7/8 in.	Black-on-Black 1.4
Depth, including Handles				cu. ft. Over-the- Range Microwave
Height	16 1/2 in.	16 1/2 in.	16 1/2 in.	Frigidaire FMT148G1B
Watts	700 - 999 watts	700 - 999 watts	700 - 999 watt	Black-on-Black 1.4
Price*	$369.99	$429.99	$449.99	cu. ft. Over-the- Range Microwave

remove (for FMT148G1T)
remove (for FMT144G1B)
remove (for FMT148G1B)

© 1999 Sears, Roebuck and Co. Satisfaction guaranteed or your money back. Please view our privacy policy and terms and conditions. * Credit Details Questions? Call 1-800-349-4358

compare   clear

This Product Comparison page on Sears was of no help to any of our users in figuring out how much food would fit inside these microwaves. IU11

Size

Although most Danish users knew an inch is a US length measure, just a few knew an inch corresponds to 2.54 centimeters in the metric system. Even those who knew the conversion formula found it hard to multiply by 2.54 to get an idea of a size in a familiar unit of measure.

A Danish user was unable to choose the correct size of a ring on Nordstrom. "These sizes don't mean anything to me," complained the user. "Are sizes shown in inches?"

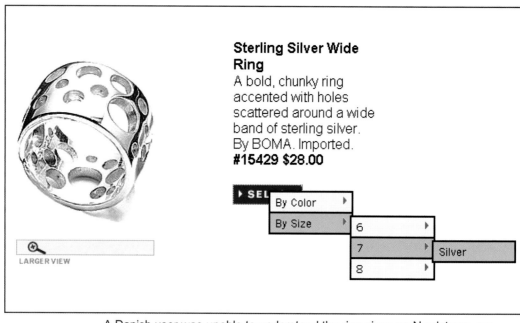

Sterling Silver Wide Ring
A bold, chunky ring accented with holes scattered around a wide band of sterling silver. By BOMA. Imported.
#15429 $28.00

A Danish user was unable to understand the ring sizes on Nordstrom. IU12

Size codes for clothing vary from country to country. Even within Europe, the size codes vary. US size codes are largely unknown in Europe, and information on how to convert size codes is not readily available. As one Danish user put it: "Even if I could choose a size it would be of little use since the Americans have their own size codes. This makes it difficult to order."

Only Jcrew gave our Danish users a size range (for a jacket) they could understand immediately (M, L, and XL): "Oh, good! The sizes are comprehensible!" None of the Danish users understood the size codes M and H–M for shoes on Jcrew, however.

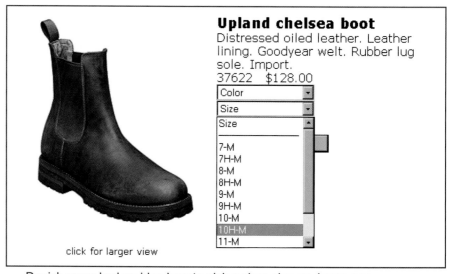

Upland chelsea boot
Distressed oiled leather. Leather lining. Goodyear welt. Rubber lug sole. Import.
37622 $128.00

Danish users had no idea how to pick a shoe size on Jcrew. IU13

Use of Language

Some users of any website speak a primary language other than the one the website is presented in. Many people get by with a working vocabulary of 200–1,500 words in their secondary language(s). Site designers and developers must make an active effort to accommodate users with limited vocabularies. Designers of English-language websites can make sites easier for international users by carefully choosing the words they use.

➡ *Write all text in EASL (English As a Second Language).*

Avoid the following language elements on international websites:

- **Words with multiple meanings** – "Basket" (Iflorist)
- **Abbreviations** – "MI" for middle initial (HermanMiller) and US state abbreviations
- **Colloquial expressions** – "DVDs that deliver the most Bang for your Buck!" (Reel); "Wrap up your search for the perfect gift with GiftFinder!" (Wal-Mart)
- **Acronyms** – FAQ, Q&A (1800flowers)
- **Jargon** – "French press" (Gevalia)
- **Humor** – "Luv songs" (CustomDisc). Not all humor translates from culture to culture. Avoid puns.
- **Slang, or language that is too informal** – "Hey you! Take a break. We're not asking you to write a book. Try a name of 4 to 10 characters." (Boo)
- **New words** – "Greeter" (Wal-Mart), "Tool Answer Man" (Sears), "Pooh Gram" (Disney)
- **Culturally dependent phrases**, for instance, phrases from popular commercials, TV series, cartoons, or songs – "Tools that rule" (Sears).

Some companies use Simplified English to communicate with EASL users (see world-ready.com/r_intl.htm#esl).

Product Descriptions

Users are hesitant to buy products when they don't understand the product description. In some cases, single words or phrases caused difficulties. Many of our Danish users had a limited knowledge of English. They looked for pictures and simple terms they could recognize and use as input to the search engine. For example, one user tried "track" when searching for "something that Hot Wheels cars would run on."

- A user on the HermanMiller furniture site didn't understand the word "lumbar," as in "lumbar support" (in a description of a chair).
- On Sears, a user did not understand several of the category names on the home page: " 'Around the house' — that sounds like an overview of the site," and " 'Under the hood' — I don't understand that." EASL users would find "Home and lifestyle" and "Car and garage" simpler to understand.
- On Wal-Mart, we asked users to search for "a suitable car seat for a baby." One of our users searched for: "Child Seat," "Childrens Seat," "Child Restraints," and "Child restraints." The user finally complained, "These are commonly used terms!" and gave up. The Wal-Mart website recognized only the word "kid," not "child."

- Two other users on Wal-Mart were also unable to find a car seat for a baby, because they did not know the US term for it. They said they would be able to recognize the right word if they saw it.
- On Reel, two users were not sure what a DVD was. One of them ordered a DVD anyway, thinking it was some sort of videotape.
- One of our Danish users on Peet's knew what a coffee press pot is called in Danish. He was unsure, however, what to call it in English ("French press"). The test facilitator provided a translation so he could continue. We would classify "French press" as jargon.
- On SmarterKids, one of our users was shopping for a gift for a 10-year-old child. The website expected the user to select the appropriate school grade-level. "Ten years old, what grade are you in?" the user wondered. After a while, the user chose "Grades 4–6."

Several users of Reel were severely limited in their selection of a suitable video. They did not know the US title of a video, although they knew the Danish title. One user shopped for the video "Seven," because it was one of the few English-title videos she knew.

Tip: Consider a translation facility for song, film, and video titles. The translation facility could be built into the search engine, so the user could choose a search language.

Shopping Terms

Even more problems surfaced with terms related to shopping. Some of our US users also had problems understanding specialized terms used in e-commerce.

➡ *Provide a glossary for both product and shopping terms.*

In particular, the phrase "check out" caused problems.

- On HermanMiller, two users didn't understand the words "check out." One of them asked, "Does it mean the same as 'drop out'? … That is, delete item or delete shopping cart?"
- On 1800flowers, a user declared: " 'Checkout' is a silly name. You might get the impression that you leave the shop without buying anything. 'Order' would be better."
- On Reel, users also misunderstood the term "check out." Some users simply didn't understand the phrase. Others thought it meant to search, as in "Check it out." Still others thought it meant "leave," assuming it was the opposite of "check in." One user clicked "Continue Shopping" when he wanted to check out.

Most of our users eventually managed to solve the "check out" problem by themselves. They employed the time-consuming process of elimination: "There must be a way to buy the items I have in the shopping cart. I have tried all buttons and links, except Check Out, so I will have to try that one."

Tip: Provide a "How to Buy" topic in customer service. About one third of the Danish users had trouble with the words "check out." "Pay Now" might work better, but we haven't tested it.

Tip: Use synonyms in definitions and explanations. On Reel, the explanation of the word "checkout" referred to itself: "To begin the checkout process, click on the Checkout Now button." It would have been better to say something like, "To pay, click the Checkout Now button."

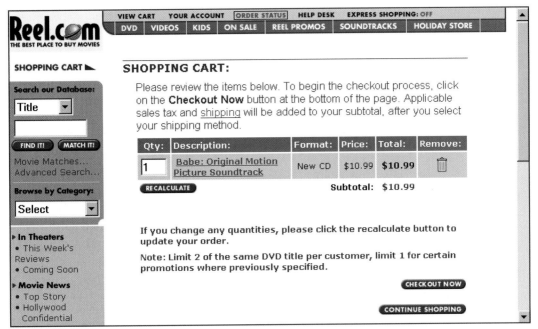

Danish users of Reel's Shopping Cart did not understand the term "checkout" — and they could not figure out what it meant from the context, because the term referred to itself. IU14

Other EASL examples:

- On Living, a user did not understand the terms "white sale" and "clearance" on the home page.

- On Reel, a user did not understand what a "clam shell package" is, so he did not order this product (even though it was the product he was looking for). The same user thought "pre-order" meant "currently not in stock." The site lacked an explanation of pre-order, which confused users in the US as well.

- Several users on several websites said they did not know what "UPS" meant. (United Parcel Service is a delivery service based in the US. It is not affiliated with the United States Postal Service.)

- On Peet's, a user asked, "What does 'Add to cart' mean?" The user was unsure about the meaning of the word "cart." The user tried to look up "cart" in the website's glossary but did not find it (it isn't there).

A final anecdote: During registration, a user of Reel said he assumed the password had to make sense in English. He first tried the password "Babe," which the site did not accept because it was too short. The user then chose "Movie." An example might have helped.

Character Set

The English character set (alphabet) contains 26 letters. The Danish character set contains the same 26 letters plus three more letters (æ, ø and å). Most European languages have their own character sets, which all have more letters than the English alphabet.

These additional characters sometimes cause problems when users type them on e-commerce sites. A user of Disney typed his first name as "Jørgen," which includes the special Danish letter ø. In the shipping summary, his first name displayed as "Jxrgen."

Most of our Danish users were aware of the character problem some sites have, so they typed the unofficial English equivalents of the Danish characters (ae for æ, oe for ø, and aa for å) without voicing any complaints. In most European countries, such equivalents are available and known to many people.

Other users, however, considered it demeaning to distort their names or addresses to fit the requirements of a limited-character website. They tried to input the correct, national spelling of their names and addresses, but some websites mangled their entries. These users accepted the distortions with resignation and no inflammatory comments.

Some of the websites we tested accepted Danish characters without problems.

Tip: Handle international character sets correctly. Character set and national conventions also affect alphabetical sorting.

Tip: If you decide not to support international character sets, inform the user as soon as possible when characters the user enters are not supported by your website. We've seen users in other tests become upset when they registered their personal information using national characters early in the shopping process, only to find out during checkout that the website refused to accept the "errors" in their entries.

Numbers

In Europe, decimal points are often shown as decimal commas. For example, 4,500 (or 4,5) means four and a half. Thousand separators are points instead of commas, for example 2.500 means two thousand five hundred (and not two and a half). As you might imagine, this ambiguity could cause rather serious misunderstandings. We didn't find any number interpretation problems in the current study. We know from other studies, however, that decimal conventions can cause serious confusion, even on European websites used by Europeans.

So, if a user inputs 200,00, the user is probably European and means two hundred (the comma is a decimal comma). If a user inputs 200,000, this user is probably from the US and means two hundred thousand (the comma is a thousand separator). Both 4,500,000 and 4.500.000 are probably unambiguous, as are 4.750,25 and 4,750.25. In many cases, however, you just can't be sure — it could be a typo.

Tip: Ask the user if there is doubt about the interpretation of a number containing dots or commas. Please avoid unhelpful, inhuman error messages like "illegal number."

Dates

The US way of showing dates (month-day-year) is not widely used in Europe, where dates are normally shown as day-month-year (and sometimes year-month-day). Although many Europeans are aware of the US date convention, some of our Danish users misinterpreted dates during our tests.

- On TowerRecords, two users entered their birthdays in the Danish format, dd/mm/yy, instead of mm/dd/yy, as requested by the website. The website accepted one of the dates, 17/05/67, even though it was clearly "wrong."

- Jcrew informed one of our users that a jacket could be shipped 02/11/2000. The user read the date as 2 November 2000, not as February 11, 2000.

- On Nordstrom, when several users tried to order "temporarily unavailable" products, they encountered this message: "The item you have selected is available to ship on 2/15/00." The users were puzzled at first by the date format, but they figured out it had to mean February 15, 2000.

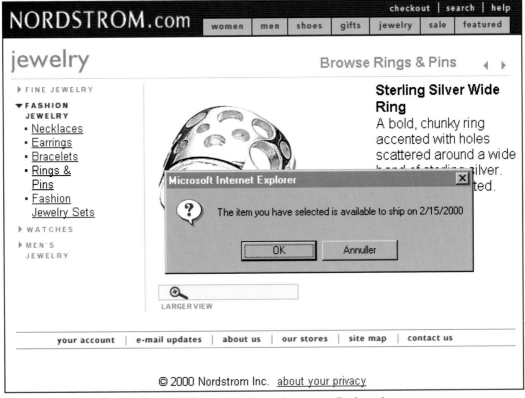

International differences in how dates are displayed can cause confusion. If this product from Nordstrom had been available just four days earlier, the date would have been shown as 2/11/2000, which most Danish users would have interpreted as 2 November 2000. IU15

Tip: Provide separate input fields for day, month, and year — label each field explicitly. Use the labels "Month," "Day," and "Year." Avoid abbreviations like mm/dd/yyyy. Many people do not understand that "mm" means month written as two digits.

Tip: Consider showing the month in text form. The only widely used, clear way to differentiate between day and month is to spell out the month name. For example, neither 2 Nov 2000 nor 11 Feb 2000 can be misinterpreted. As a bonus, this date format doesn't need punctuation.

Time

In Europe, the 24-hour clock is customary. European users might not understand, or might be confused by, the abbreviations "am" and "pm." We do not have any simple solution for this time problem, because writing "15.13" instead of "3:13 pm" could confuse US users. We did not encounter any problems in time translation during our study, possibly because the time of day was not relevant for most of our tasks.

On Iflorist, a user did not understand the abbreviation "CST" in: "Next business day delivery is available to most areas for orders received by 11 AM CST." The most common time zone abbreviations referred to in the US are EST (Eastern Standard Time) and PST (Pacific Standard Time). CST (Central Standard Time) and MST (Mountain Standard Time) are mentioned less often outside their regions.

One Danish user noticed the difference between the time on the receipt (10:23:49) and the actual, local time (19:23:49). A possible solution to the time zone issue could be to use GMT (Greenwich Mean Time), but few US and European users understand GMT. Another potential solution would be to translate the time into local times in a few major locations. For example, "the press conference starts at 1:00 pm in New York (GMT –5), corresponding to 19:00 in Paris (GMT +1), and 3:00 (GMT + 9) the next day in Tokyo." The best solution might be to have the site determine the user's local time zone from the user's browser, postal code, or country, but we don't know of any sites that provide local time information to users yet.

Checkout

Many problems with international shipping and billing information emerged during our study. As we mentioned at the beginning of this chapter, European and US addressing conventions are different. For example, CustomDisc presented a Billing and Shipping page with a State / Province field. Danish (and many other European) addresses do not contain state or province information. On CustomDisc, none of our users initially typed any information in the State / Province field, which generated an error message. After reading the error message, the users typed DE or DK in the text box. Ironically, the website accepted anything at all entered in the State / Province text box.

CUSTOMDISC
make your own CD

CUSTOMDISC

Our 100% Guarantee
Your online transaction is guaranteed.
Your CustomDisc is guaranteed. . . . . . **or you get your money back!**

powered by **CustomDisc.com**   Home | Help | Your Shopping Cart

Billing and Shipping Information
Please take two minutes and enter your Shipping and Billing information.
Fields which are required are marked in this color!!

Email Address
Enter the email address where you would like to receive notifications about your CustomDisc order.

your e-mail [   ]

Billing Information

first name [   ]
(as it appears on your credit card)

last name [   ]
(as it appears on your credit card)

address 1 [   ]

address 2 [   ]

city [   ]

state/province [   ]
(for U.S. addresses, please enter 2 letter state code)

zip/postal code [   ]

country [United States ▼]

telephone [   ]

Shipping Information

Please select a shipping address below or create a new address.

⦿ USE BILLING ADDRESS

○ NEW SHIPPING ADDRESS

first name [   ]

last name [   ]

address 1 [   ]

address 2 [   ]

city [   ]

state/province [   ]
(for U.S. addresses, please enter 2 letter state code)

zip/postal code [   ]

country [United States ▼]

click here to... [CONTINUE ▶]
click here to... [◀ ADD MORE MUSIC]

It was difficult, if not impossible, for Danish users to fill out the CustomDisc order form properly because state / province was erroneously required for non-US countries. IU16

Name and Address

> *Show examples of acceptable and typical information users should enter.*

Most of the problems caused by the form fields users encountered in our tests could have been avoided if a simple example had been included (for instance) to the right of each field:

- **MI**: Only one Danish user understood the abbreviation "MI" (middle initial), even though it appeared between the First Name and the Last Name fields. This abbreviation caused no real problems, because users just ignored the field. A middle initial example works best within an example of a whole name:

    First name: MI: Last name:

    John   F.   Kennedy

- **Apt. / Suite**: One of our users was uncertain about what to type in the Apt. / Suite field. In many European countries, it is not customary to specify apartment or suite number. Instead, you sometimes specify the floor number. Examples like "401" or "2nd floor" would be helpful.

- **Address 2:** After correctly filling in their street address in the first line, some users got very creative with the second address line provided. Several Danish users typed their postal code there, and others typed both postal code and city name. Even US users were confused by this often-unneeded second line. Examples like "Hempstead House" or "Apt 2A" would help clarify why the line was provided.

Several of our users were in doubt about which language they should use in the address. The city name was the one that caused the most concern. Our users wondered whether they should use the English spelling or the national spelling, for example "Copenhagen" or "København." After some hesitation, most of our users chose the English spelling.

> *Use the prompt "ZIP / postal code" rather than "ZIP" or "ZIP Code."*

About half of the Danish users weren't sure what ZIP means (Zone Improvement Plan — a mail routing system used by the United States Postal Service). Everyone understood "postal code." Simply replacing "ZIP" with "postal code," however, might cause trouble for some US users. We recommend "ZIP / postal code."

Tip: Place the postal code field right in front of the city name field on international forms. In most European countries, the postal code is closely associated with the city. Separating the postal code from the city with the State / Region field is unfamiliar to Europeans. From a Danish (European) point of view, the ideal arrangement would be these fields in the following order:

1. Postal code – City (on one line)
2. State / Province (if required, see the discussion in the following section, State / Province)
3. Country.

When one of our users came to the City text box on Disney, she was uncertain whether she should enter both her postal code and the city name, as is customary in Denmark (for instance, "2200 Copenhagen N"). She could not see the ZIP Code field, which was still hidden off-screen. The distance between the ZIP field and the City field had become so great that it caused a usability problem. In the

Checkout & Registration chapter, we discuss asking for the ZIP Code first, then auto-filling the state and city.

Tip: Accept non-US postal codes. The full format for a European postal code is:

- An optional country code followed by a dash. The country code is 1–3 letters.
- The national postal code. The national postal code is 4–7 characters, which can be digits, letters or spaces.

Examples: 3660, DK-3660, GB-W2 5RH, NL-2517 JR.

Tip: Provide good error messages for postal codes. "Invalid ZIP Code," which we saw from several websites, is not a helpful message. When a postal code appears to be wrong, make sure the error messages provide constructive advice in each of the following cases:

- The user mistyped the code.
- The user forgot the code. (Provide a link to help the user find the correct postal code.)
- The website does not ship to the user's country.
- The code does not match the chosen state, province, or country.

State / Province

Like many Europeans, Danes live in a region or province, but the region name is not a part of the address. As mentioned previously, users looked for the country name (Denmark) in the State selection list on many sites. Some of our users came to the State field with the firm but incorrect belief that the website shipped to addresses outside the US. Several of the websites we tested communicated that they don't ship abroad only by making it impossible to specify shipping addresses outside the US.

Tip: Write US state names in full in the State selection list. Several Danish users selected DE (Delaware) because they thought it meant Denmark. Some were slightly worried that DE could be misinterpreted as Deutschland (Germany). This abbreviation uncertainty happened on Living, CustomDisc, and HermanMiller.

Tip: Include "Other Countries" in the State selection list if you do not have a separate selection list for countries. The State selection list was the most common place users looked to find Denmark. When the user selects Other Countries, provide more detailed information.

Tip: Avoid the abbreviation "n/a" (not applicable). Many of our users did not understand it.

Tip: Don't expect international users to use the State field. Iflorist expected their international users to change the State / Province field from "Select State" to "Not Applicable" using a selection list, then enter the appropriate country name in a separate field. Our users didn't understand this procedure, which wasn't explained on the form.

None of our Danish users understood abbreviations such as AA, AE, AP, APO, or FPO in the State selection list. Many of our US users didn't understand these abbreviations either. Users made only brief negative comments about the abbreviations, because they had more important problems to worry about at the time.

➡️ *Explicitly list all countries to which you ship.*

We asked three Danish users to order flowers on 1800flowers. The users clicked "Deliveries Outside US" on the home page. The Deliveries Outside US page contained a selection list with the names of about 10 countries. Denmark was not among those countries. Users concluded the website did not ship to Denmark.

After the test, our facilitator contacted the website's Help Desk through the interactive chat facility on the website. She found out that 1800flowers actually can deliver to Denmark. Neither the users nor the facilitator was able to discover this shipping capability from the Web pages. The only hint was the text on the Deliveries Outside US page that said, "1-800-FLOWERS.COM can deliver floral items anywhere in the world through a number of international affiliations." All users and the facilitator dismissed this claim as a slightly exaggerated statement.

The 1800flowers Help Desk representative said you must type in the name of your country in the second address line. The Help Desk person also said this information is stated on the "Deliveries Outside US" page.

On 1800flowers, Denmark was neither on the State nor the Country selection list, so Danish users had to put "Denmark" in the second address line. IU17

Tip: Avoid seemingly irrelevant information in State and Country boxes. To get flowers delivered to a Danish address from 1800flowers, users had to ignore "Other Countries" in the State selection list. Instead, users had to type the name of the country in the second address field, because Denmark was not on the Country selection list. Danish users were also instructed to ignore whichever country appeared in the Country list. If you had to order that way, would you trust that your order would arrive in the right place? Asking international users to enter seemingly incorrect information might affect trust.

▶ *Let the user specify the shipping region first.*

After struggling with the shipment address for some time, one of our users concluded, "It would be practical if they asked for the country name first." If the website had detected from the beginning that the billing address was in Denmark, then the confusing questions about state and province could have been omitted.

Letting the user specify the shipping ZIP Code or destination country early in the shopping process is a good idea. Although none of the sites we tested asked for ZIP Code or country, this approach would provide two advantages:

- The website could compute the exact shipping cost.
- The website could display the address forms in a suitable format.

▶ *Provide different pages for US and European address formats.*

Many of our Danish users had problems with billing and shipping information forms. Usable formats for US and European addresses are incompatible with each other.

US and European addressing conventions are incompatible.

US Addresses	European Addresses
First name – Middle initial – Last name	First name – Last name
Company	Company
Address 1	Address 1
Address 2	Address 2
City	Postal code – City
State – ZIP	Country

Some websites adapted the address format automatically, for example Peet's. When a user changed the Country field from the default value (most often United States) to Denmark, the website replaced the page with the proper non-US address forms. This auto-replacement surprised our users completely — as predicted by the usability principle that computer systems should not initiate any actions when users believe they are in control.

Instead, the user should first select US or non-US address format. Separate Checkout buttons in the shopping cart — one for "US Checkout" and one for "Non-US Checkout" — would be a good way to accommodate non-US users. After the user has submitted this information, the website should present the appropriately formatted set of address fields.

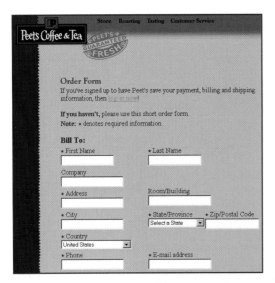

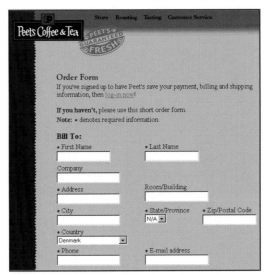

United States was the default value of Peet's Country field. Shortly after a user changed the Country field from United States to Denmark, the page became blank. A few seconds later, a slightly changed page appeared. The State / Province field was shown as N/A. After an exclamation of surprise, the user realized what had happened: "That's because I changed the country to Denmark." Not all users realized why the page suddenly went blank. A polite message would have been a good use of the otherwise blank page, which users on slow connections might get to look at for more than several seconds. IU18

The non-US address format on Peet's didn't correspond to international users' needs. For example, the City and the ZIP / Postal Code fields were still in an order that confused Danish users.

Telephone Numbers

➧ *Support international phone number formats.*

Telephone numbers often caused problems for our users. Many users were reluctant to give out their telephone number, as discussed in the chapter on Trust. Other users found it difficult to type in their correct international telephone numbers without getting an error message from the website.

Iflorist, which caters to international customers, scored pretty low for phone number usability. Our users didn't know how they should type in their telephone numbers on the order form. They had to consider all these possibilities:

- The correct international number, for example: +45 47 17 17 17. (The "+" is a common placeholder for whichever number sequence is required to get an international line and "45" is Denmark's country code.)

- The international number without the "+," for example: 45 47 17 17 17.

- The international number to call from most European countries to Denmark, for example: 0045 47 17 17 17.

- The 8-digit national number, for calls within Denmark, for example: 47 17 17 17.

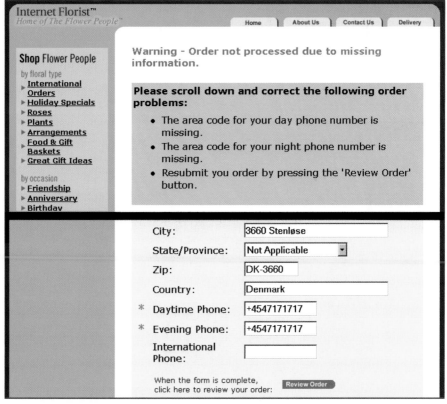

None of our users typed in a phone number in the "International Phone" textbox. Neither they nor we understood which phone number should go into this text box. The users typed phone numbers into the Daytime Phone and Evening Phone fields instead, which did not accept correctly formatted international phone numbers. IU19

The Iflorist website rejected the format +4547171717 in the Daytime Phone and Evening Phone fields. The user then changed the telephone number to 47171717, which the website accepted. It appeared that the website would not accept complete international telephone numbers, which include a leading +.

Tip: Explain that international prefixes and country codes are not required (but make room for them anyway). Your website should look up codes automatically. Some of our users could not remember the international telephone country code for Denmark (45). The true solution to this problem is to politely inform users that the website will supply the right code.

Tip: Make the input field sufficiently long to accept any international telephone number. We suggest making room for at least 20 characters.

Tip: Accept a leading plus (+), parentheses, dashes, digits, and spaces in any international telephone number input field. Because the sequence you must dial to get an international line varies from country to country, the variable numbers are generally shown as a +. Example: The international access sequence is 011 for some telephone companies in the US. To call +4547171717 from the US, you would have to dial 0114547171717. From Germany, however, you would dial 004547171717.

Tip: Provide a customer service telephone number for international customers. The number should be an ordinary phone number — not a special toll-free number. Toll-free numbers may be difficult to access from outside the US. In some countries, like Denmark, people can call US toll-free phone numbers, but a recording warns them that the call will be charged at normal international rates.

Tip: Avoid letter-only telephone numbers. US telephone numbers like 1-800-ASK-TOWER are unusable from Europe, because most European telephones don't have letters on their phone buttons.

Order by Phone: 1-800-ASK-TOWER   **Order by Fax:** 1-800-538-6938
Shop AOL: Keyword: Tower

Phone Outside US: 916-373-3050   **Fax Outside US:** 916-373-2930

TowerRecords provided ordinary telephone numbers without letters for international use at the bottom of their home page. The "Phone Outside US" number is not completely correctly specified, though. The country prefix should have been included, +1-916-373-3050. IU20

Cultural Differences

We saw just a few instances in which metaphors, mental model, navigation, or interaction confused or alienated our Danish users.

▶ *Don't use metaphors that are intimately connected with a specific country.*

A Reel user understood the US trash can icon for "remove product" in the shopping cart, but he smiled at it. "I guess it is an American trash can, but I'm not sure, because I've never seen one of those. To me it looks more like a Roman column." (Image IU14).

> **Test your site in each target country to find cultural problems.**

Some of the products, concepts, and phrases that appeared on some of the websites we tested amused, confused, or surprised our Danish users. The designers of these websites, apparently, had not taken into account that customs vary from country to country.

- BasketHaus: A user associated the basket offerings with Christmas Baskets. In Denmark, needy people can apply for a Christmas Basket in December with food and goodies.

- Iflorist: A user was amused by the idea of adding teddy bears and balloons to floral gifts. In Denmark, it is unusual to attach teddy bears and balloons to a bouquet of flowers. A bouquet of flowers is considered a formal present. Teddy bears and balloons are inappropriate.

- Furniture: A user didn't understand what a coupon is. Coupons are not allowed in Denmark.

- Jcrew: We asked a user whether there was a J. Crew shop in Washington, DC. The user went to the Customer Service page and selected the question, "Where are J. Crew retail stores?" A clickable map appeared. The user commented such maps work mainly for US users who know where Washington, DC, is. Foreign users often don't know another country's geography. The user scrolled through a list of shops and found a Washington, DC shop at the bottom of the list.

- eToys: None of our Danish users on eToys appreciated the wish list and gift registry features. (A registry serves to prevent duplicate gifts. Each wish is marked "available" or "already bought" in a password-protected registry.) "We talk, and it is most unlikely that everyone would use the same website for shopping," observed one user. Another user said that a wish list is irrelevant nonsense on a website. Two of our four users refused to perform the task related to the wish list or registry, because they considered the very idea ridiculous.

The eToys Wish List and Registry raised both conceptual and cultural issues. The concepts baffled all the Danish users and some US users, too. On a cultural level, the online wish list and registry were not acceptable in Danish society. Usability testing with US users could have uncovered the first issue, but only testing in Denmark could have revealed that the features were culturally unacceptable there.

Danish users thought wish lists were inappropriate on a website. IU21

Telephone Charges

Fast downloads and easy navigation are important to user satisfaction the world around. In the US, most users pay a flat rate for Internet service, but in many European countries, users pay per minute even for local telephone calls. Users worry about this cost of shopping time. A Sears user said: "I hate to get lost on a website, because it's me who has to pay the bill."

Designers of international e-commerce websites must keep in mind that anyone who pays by the minute for Internet access must balance the cost of shopping online against the discount and convenience of buying online. Graphics, animations, hidden information, and blind navigation alleys cost users money.

Special Days

Sites that support gift-giving, such as bookstores and flower sites, often celebrate "special days," such as Mother's Day, Father's Day, Valentine's Day, Thanksgiving, and so forth. Some of these holidays are not known all over the world, and some of them are celebrated on different days in different countries. Foreign users could be confused if a website features some great Mother's Day gifts when Mother's Day in the user's country was a long time ago.

Tip: Learn the holidays and other "special days" in your target countries. Two online sources are www.earthcalendar.net and www.holidayfestival.com. Check such sites carefully, however, before you rely on their data. We looked up holiday information about Denmark on both sites, and found both slightly inaccurate. Earth Calendar was the most complete, but included a number of outdated church holidays that are not commonly known. Holiday Festival had not been updated for more than a year but was honest enough to show the last revision date.

International Usability Tests

No guidelines yet published are sufficiently complete to guarantee perfect international usability. An empirical test is always a good idea. The best way to detect international usability problems in general — and cultural differences in particular — is to conduct in-country usability tests. We advise hiring competent local people who are familiar with the national culture and who speak the language of the site you'll be testing fluently.

If your website has already been carefully usability tested in your home country, chances are good that a small number of additional tests in different parts of the world will uncover issues specific to those cultures. Ideally, we recommend you conduct tests with three to six users in *each* target country. For example, testing in South Africa doesn't necessarily ensure a culturally appropriate site in Kenya.

Tip: If your budget doesn't allow for testing in each country, at least have a local usability person review the site for potential cultural issues. Testing is better, but it's not always possible.

Tip: Run the test with local users who match your user profile. Even if you have a local subsidiary or affiliate, don't use your local staff as test participants.

Tip: Run the test in the native language of the user. Just because it may be possible to run usability tests in English doesn't mean it's a good idea. Although many local users may speak English deceptively well, almost all of them will be more at ease in their native language. Local users who are fluent in English may be atypical users, also. When you run tests in English, native users are likely to suppress comments you would consider important, because they can't easily express themselves in a foreign language. People are more at ease when offering tactful criticism in their own language.

Tip: Hire a local usability specialist to run the tests. In true usability testing, facilitators must beware of providing inadvertent, unconscious help to users. At the same time, facilitators must make sure users don't blame themselves when they can't complete even the most basic tasks for which the site was built. Do not let your local marketing or sales staff run your tests, because they have an agenda and they seek opinions. Users must be observed without bias in order to discover how well a website performs for them.

Tip: Check the usability firm's quality. Often, it may be prohibitively expensive to visit the usability company that will do the testing for you. You can get an impression of the company's quality without visiting them, however:

- Ask for references and follow up on one or two of them.

- Request a sample usability report. If client usability reports are confidential, ask to read the usability report on the test of the company's own website.

- Look to see if their reports deal mostly with "micro-usability" issues (for example, graphics and use of color), or if they also address usability-in-the-large, such as suitability for common user tasks.

- Check their findings to see whether they are based on user observations. User opinions or expert opinions are less valuable.

- Inquire about the experience and qualifications of the employees who will handle your tests. Ask whether these facilitators are native speakers of the language.

- Visit the usability company's website to get an idea of whether their understanding of usability matches yours.

Tip: Check the quality of the test task translations. You probably will supply the test tasks in English to be translated into the local language. Ask for a copy of the translated tasks. If you don't understand the local language, have the tasks translated back into your language by a third party, possibly a colleague. Then check the translated test tasks for the usual task problems (hidden clues, unclear instructions, and similar errors).

Four Mistakes to Avoid

You can't expect to attract international customers unless you show you have made a true effort to accommodate them. Roughly speaking, we can divide the incidents described in this chapter into four groups:

- **Site showed no apparent interest in foreign customers.** Our Danish users sometimes sensed a lack of respect for foreign customers or felt they were being treated as second-class customers. Special offers were almost always restricted to the Continental US, sometimes without even saying so. We did not find one example of an offer that applied exclusively to foreign customers. In some cases, shipping was prohibitively expensive. In other cases, strange and hidden restrictions applied to what foreign customers could buy.

- **Pages used mainly by foreigners had elementary quality problems.** In general, text quality (complete sentences and correct spelling) was good, but in some cases it seemed that pages intended for foreign users had not been quality checked. For example, Reel's International Format Notice (Image IU7) contained an incomprehensible sentence: "I understand that U.S.-formatted tapes and disks do not play in most players manufactured below ... " (There was nothing "below" this statement.) Also, a vital link to the Internet Music Shop was not provided. In all, the quality of this page was considerably lower than most other pages on Reel.

- **Site designs showed unfamiliarity with foreign people, customs, and norms.** Our Danish users were confused by strange and unfamiliar procedures that worked well for US users, such as address specification, date format, and measures.

- **Usability problems that affected all users were even more severe for foreign users.** Examples: Both US and Danish users were perplexed by how much they would have to pay in state sales taxes. Likewise, US and Danish users wanted understandable size and measurement charts for everything from microwaves to clothes. This information was absent on many websites, although sizing guides are the norm in most mail-order catalogs. Like international mail-order catalogs, websites should provide US / metric sizing and conversion guides.

Almost all the international errors we found were well-known universal usability or quality-assurance problems. In relatively few cases were cultural differences the major usability obstacle.

We believe the differences we found in website usability between our US and Danish user groups would disappear if the sites we tested:

- Cleared up existing site faults, which confused even domestic users.

- Familiarized themselves with their international users.

- Conducted simple usability testing with non-US users.

Methodology

" Ultimately, the recommendations arising from any usability study can only be as good as the information on which they're based."

Type of Study

This study was exploratory in that we had no specific hypotheses we were trying to prove. We chose a broad focus (20 sites and dozens of users) because we wanted to identify patterns among a variety of e-commerce sites and to gain as many new insights as possible into what makes e-commerce sites successful.

We wanted to better understand what happens when a person goes to a website to buy merchandise or services. We were more interested in qualitative data — what users said and did — and what results they got. We were less interested in quantitative performance measurements, such as task completion time or error rates. We took copious notes but made few measurements beyond whether the task was successful or not. During the data analysis phase, we categorized our findings and calculated statistics as necessary, but this book is based primarily on the behavior patterns we observed during the tests.

Our Team

Our international team of five experienced usability professionals from the United States and Denmark conducted this study in Salem, New Hampshire, and Copenhagen, Denmark. We tested in two countries to cross-check our findings with two independent testing agencies and to uncover international usability issues with English-language e-commerce sites. We worked together over the Internet from locations in California, New Hampshire, and Denmark.

Team Assignments

What	Who
Propose, guide, and fund the study. Recruit the other usability professionals.	Jakob Nielsen
Survey the target audience.	Rolf Molich and Sofie Scheutz
Select the sites, create the tasks, and plan the tests.	Jakob Nielsen, Rolf Molich, Sofie Scheutz, Carolyn Snyder, and Susan Farrell
Facilitate the tests and observe the users.	Rolf Molich, Sofie Scheutz (Denmark), and Carolyn Snyder (US)
Write and review the chapters.	Jakob Nielsen, Rolf Molich, Carolyn Snyder, and Susan Farrell. (Sofie Scheutz was primarily a reviewer.)
Supervise editing, layout, and production.	Susan Farrell. (Tom Durkin provided editorial assistance and Steven Thomas designed and produced the reports and book.)

Study Overview

In this section, we describe the main parameters of this study, including the techniques of usability testing, number of users, test length, order in which the sites were tested, and other factors.

What Is Usability Testing?

Usability testing a website involves watching a person use the site in order to discover the ways the site aids or hinders people from reaching their goals. Traditional usability tests are conducted in a controlled setting, and the user is asked to attempt a set of predefined tasks. A trained facilitator manages the session. One or more trained observers take notes.

You can collect data about the usability of websites in many ways, such as expert reviews, surveys, online tools, and focus groups. We chose usability testing because we think it provides superior insights as compared to other techniques.

Common Misconceptions about Usability Testing

Usability testing is not universally understood. Usability testing differs from other techniques in these ways:

- **We don't try to determine whether the site functions — that's quality assurance (QA) testing.** In a QA test, a member of the development team follows a test script to make sure the site does what it's supposed to do. In a usability test, a person who is not part of the development team tries to use the site. The usability team notes how the site helps, confuses, or defeats the user.

- **We don't test the site ourselves.** A true usability test involves users who are not usability experts. Only users from the site's intended audience can provide a true picture of how well the site works. A review, sometimes called a heuristic evaluation, by a usability expert is often valuable, but a professional usability evaluation is not a substitute for a usability test. Sometimes even experts cannot predict a site's major usability problems, or they may find problems that don't bother actual users. Also, no two experts will find exactly the same set of potential problems or agree on their severity. Only usability testing can provide definitive answers about site effectiveness.

- **We watch user behavior rather than ask for opinions.** We don't just sit the users down in front of a site and ask them what they think. We give them something to *do*, then we take note of the obstacles they encounter. Sometimes people say they like how a site looks even thought they can't accomplish the tasks we give them. Of course, we don't ignore the opinions users express as they're working. We note them along with our other observations.

- **We test with only one or two users at a time.** Rather than showing site mockups to several people at once and asking for their reactions as focus groups do, we observe users working alone or in pairs so we can learn how well the site actually works for them.

- **We don't train users or explain how to use the site.** People often encounter a site for the first time having little knowledge of what the site does or how it is intended to work. Thus, for website usability testing it's generally not appropriate to give the users much information about a site before they test it. Once you start explaining the interface, it's no longer a usability test but rather a very expensive training session. Of course, we do sometimes help users when they become stuck or frustrated.

Number of Users

Research has shown that you don't need a large number of users to get meaningful results from a usability study. Jakob Nielsen's *Alertbox* column, *Why You Only Need to Test with Five Users* (www.useit.com/alertbox/20000319.html), explains why a handful of users is often enough to spot major problems, but be aware that:

- **They must belong to the same user group.** (Some websites have diverse populations, such as pediatricians and parents.)

- **They must test key areas only.** Unless the site has a very limited number of pages, a small number of users cannot cover the entire site.

- **Different facilitators tend to find different problems.** Other research has shown that facilitators' results vary, for example, the Comparative Usability Evaluation (CUE) Tests. (See Molich, et al in the References section.) In the CUE study, nine professional usability teams tested Hotmail.com — and arrived at somewhat different results.

Although these factors can be significant in some studies, we don't believe they affected the validity of our results. We tested each site with at least five US users. Five users alone were enough to show us the biggest usability issues for the commonly visited portions of each site, such as the shopping cart. Because we were trying to identify common patterns across a variety of e-commerce sites, it wasn't as important to go into depth as it can be when testing a single site.

We didn't stop with five users, however. We also conducted tests of each site with Danish facilitators and at least three Danish users. These tests, conducted in two countries with different facilitators, found essentially the same problems. Danish users found an interesting subset of problems when they tried to buy from American websites, which are described primarily in the International Users chapter.

We are confident that the problems we found in this study are indicative of the problems that exist on e-commerce websites.

Number of Sites

We focused on mainstream e-commerce retail sites that sold tangible products (toys, clothing, videos) so that our findings would have the widest possible practical worth to e-commerce merchants. We wanted to study at least two sites within each industry so we could closely compare sites with similar goals and different approaches. We decided to study three sites in each of seven different industries. (In one industry, we tested only two sites, for a total of 20 sites.) Site Selection Criteria, below, describes how we chose our test sites.

Test Length and Sites per Test

We decided to have each user come in for two hours and test three sites. Due to scheduling factors, a few tests covered two or four sites. We knew from experience that users (and facilitators) become fatigued during long tests, so two hours is a realistic maximum length.

Theoretically, we had 40 minutes to test each site, but in practice, the actual time spent per site was usually around 35 minutes, because of the test introduction and breaks. Thirty-five minutes is not a long time to watch a user on a site. We often wished for another 10 minutes. Even so, 35 minutes was enough time for most users to attempt most of the tasks we'd planned. Each site was tested by nine or 10 users, so we collected roughly six hours of observations for each site.

We had a self-imposed time constraint. We wanted to complete the tests within one month to minimize the chance that the sites would change drastically in the middle of our study. Spending more test time on each site would have meant cutting back on the number of users per site or the number of sites tested.

Which Users Tested Which Sites

As described in the Users section below, our users were almost equally divided between men and women. They ranged in age from 20–60. We made a reasonable, but not rigorous, effort to test each site with both men and women of various ages.

Strictly controlling for demographic factors was not important in our study. None of us has noticed any behavior patterns linked to age or gender in previous studies, and we didn't see any such patterns in this study either. We believe that usability problems on most websites are still severe enough to affect almost all users. Any age- or gender-specific user issues are masked by the broader problems.

Site Order

We varied the order in which we tested the sites because sequence can introduce bias. The effects of sequence bias are hard to predict. Sometimes users learn procedures on the first site that help (or hinder) them on the second. Users also become more tired as the testing progresses. It is also common for people to prefer the first procedures they learn over subsequent variations encountered, perhaps because of familiarity.

As with our effort to test with a variety of users, our method of varying site order was reasonable but not rigorous. We planned which users would test which sites and in what order. Unforeseen events occasionally disrupted this plan, though, for example when a site was temporarily unavailable so we had to substitute a different one. We are certain, however, that none of our test sites was always tested first, second, or last.

Timing Concerns

We conducted our tests in January 2000. We expected many sites to relaunch shortly after the first of the year, but none of the sites we tested changed substantially until after the test period.

To minimize the chance of a site changing substantially during our study, we broke the 20 test sites into three batches. We attempted to finish testing one batch before moving on to the next. Thus, most tests for a particular site were completed within a week or so.

We also coordinated the American and Danish tests so they were conducted within a few days of each other. We had to reschedule several of our tests, however, because of snowstorms, no-show users, site availability problems, or computer malfunctions.

We learned to capture screenshots *immediately* after the test whenever possible, because we could not rely on the pages to persist unchanged for any length of time. We expected the sites to change, but it was impossible to predict when the updated versions would be launched. For example, when we tested TowerRecords on January 10, our users complained because the site still had Christmas decorations. When we visited the website a few days later to capture the screenshots, the Christmas decorations were gone.

Site Selection Criteria

Choosing our 20 e-commerce sites wasn't easy. We had selection criteria to satisfy:

- **Include both small and large sites.** We sought to bypass large, overly visible sites (in terms of press coverage, other published usability studies, and reputation). For instance, we passed over Amazon.com because of its high profile. We also wanted to include a few relatively unknown sites like BasketHaus and NorwaySweaters.

- **Select sites that did not require special skills or interests.** We wanted to test with typical middle-class consumers from young to old. We avoided sites that focused too much on a particular skill, hobby, or need (such as software development, golf, or life insurance). Some of sites we tested targeted specific markets. Boo was aimed at the under-30 set. Peet's and Gevalia both catered to coffee drinkers. Although Boo, Peet's, and Gevalia were niche sites, their offerings were realistic for our users to consider.

- **Avoid sites that might present a conflict of interest.** This study was funded entirely by the Nielsen Norman Group, so we were not influenced in our choice of sites or our findings by any outside factors. We are all Web designers and / or testers, however, and over the years we have been professionally involved in the development of many commercial sites. We excluded all those sites from our study.

Because we were testing US websites in Denmark, we had some additional considerations:

- **Choose reasonable websites for participants outside the US.** We couldn't test sites that offered auto insurance or wireless phones, for instance. The American and Danish markets for these services are different, as are the regulations governing them. This criterion also eliminated drugstores, because US drugstores have no direct counterpart in Denmark.

- **Find location-independent websites.** This criterion eliminated websites like supermarkets or ticket-sellers, which require the customer to live in realistic proximity to a certain business or venue. The BasketHaus store was physically local to our New Hampshire participants (although none of them had heard of it), but the site itself had no apparent geographic restrictions.

Users

User Profiles

User profiles are determined by the goals of the study and the sites being tested. Our goal was to study broad patterns in e-commerce, so our site selection was diverse and our user profile was rather loose. We created a screening questionnaire for the characteristics we wanted, which included the following:

- Required: people who know how to use browsers. We did not want to recruit people who would be using the Web for the first time.

- Required: people who had already shopped online. We did not require users to have purchased online before; we just wanted to know that they'd used the Web to shop for products or services.

- Desired: people who were strangers to the facilitators. We made exceptions to this rule for some pilot tests and the tests in which we asked users to complete purchases.
- Desired: people who were employed full time. We wanted people who had disposable income, so this characteristic was intended to screen out those of very limited means. A few participants worked only part time or were retired, but they constituted less than 10% of our study population.
- Desired: A roughly equal mix of men and women.
- Desired: A wide range of ages for both men and women. We decided to limit our testing to adults, so the minimum age was 18. We did not have an upper age limit, although in practice it was difficult to find users over 50, especially in Denmark. Our users ranged in age from about 20 to 60, but we recruited fewer older users than we had hoped for.
- Excluded: Web developers and usability professionals. We did not want people who had an insider's view of e-commerce, because they would not reflect the typical customer.

The complete screening questionnaire and other testing materials are shown at the end of this chapter.

Demographics of the Study Participants

Of the 64 participants, 57% were female and 43% male. About three-fifths (62%) lived in the United States (specifically, New Hampshire) and the rest were residents of Denmark.

New Hampshire Users

	20s	30s	40s	50s	Total
Female	2	7	7	4	20
Male	8	4	6	1	19
Total	10	11	13	5	39

Danish Users

	20s	30s	40s	50s	Total
Female	5	7	4	1	16
Male	1	6	1	0	8
Total	6	13	5	1	25

Composition of Participants by Age
US and Danish Combined

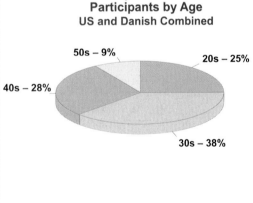

50s – 9%
20s – 25%
40s – 28%
30s – 38%

User Recruitment

For the US tests, a market research firm recruited the users. We described the profile and gave them our screening questionnaire (reproduced at the end of this chapter). For the Danish tests, we started out using a recruitment firm, but after some misunderstandings, we recruited the participants ourselves.

What Users Were Told

We prepared a short introduction to the study that gave participants some idea of what to expect. We didn't go into details about our purpose or methods. The US recruiting firm gave the following explanation in the confirmation letter to scheduled participants:

> This is a research study about online shopping. We want to understand what makes some websites easier to use than others. This study takes about two hours. We'll ask you to visit some websites and shop for various things. You will not be required to actually buy anything. One or two researchers will be in the room with you, observing and taking notes. We will not videotape or audiotape the session, and the office is very casual, so feel free to dress comfortably. We will safeguard the privacy of all participants — you will not have to enter any personal or credit card information online. Any personal information collected during this study will not be sold or otherwise released to any other company. Participants will be paid $80 cash at the end of the two-hour session.

DialogDesign used similar wording when describing the test to Danish prospects. We specifically avoided using words like "lab," "experiment," and "subject" when describing the sessions. Strictly speaking, the "subject" of a website study is the site, not the user. We did not want to give people the impression they would be guinea pigs in an unpleasant experiment. We wanted our wording to convey that users would be safe and that our procedures are well known.

User Payment

We handled payment differently in the US and Denmark. Compensation reflected both cultural issues and the local economies. The US users were paid $40 per hour for their participation. The US market research firm told us they usually paid their participants (residents of southern New Hampshire) $30–$35 per hour. The going rate for participants in the Boston area ranges from $50–$200 per hour, depending on profession.

DialogDesign's usual practice in Denmark was to offer a gift worth about $20. For this study, our incentive was six bottles of French red wine or a gift certificate worth about US$40. Users who completed purchases were allowed to keep the merchandise they ordered. The Danish marketing company that recruited about six of our users offered a gift of approximately $20–$25 for their focus groups. When we suggested a more expensive gift, they said the value of the gift was not important. We later learned they had never actually tried to offer a higher-priced gift.

Pre-Test Documents

Each user was mailed a consent form and a pre-test questionnaire. A consent form is a legal document that explains to the participant the parameters, data use, and conditions of the test environment. These conditions include their right to privacy and to end the test at any time. The US consent form and pre-test questionnaire are reproduced at the end of this chapter.

The pre-test questionnaire captures user demographics. We used a questionnaire in both countries. Although we asked the US users to fill out a pre-test questionnaire, it had so much overlap with the market research firm's screening questionnaire that it ended up being superfluous.

All the sites we tested were publicly available. We had no access to proprietary information about them, so we did not ask users to sign a non-disclosure agreement.

Scheduling Tips

We used several tactics to complete a large number of tests on a tight schedule:

Tip: Offer a higher incentive to reduce no-shows. The cost of a user includes the payment made to the user, the time or money spent on recruiting, and the lost productivity when a user doesn't show up. In both countries, we offered a higher incentive than local market research firms. We believe this incentive helped cut down the no-show rate, which was lower than in some of our other studies, thus reducing the total cost per user.

Tip: Send confirmation letters. We sent a letter with the test date, time, and directions to the test facility.

Tip: Call participants the day before the test. Showing enthusiasm about the test increases the likelihood that participants will show up. Our confirmation calls reminded participants of the session and gave the recruitment effort a personal touch. ("We are looking forward to seeing you. You make a difference.") Most of the Danish no-shows were recruited by a marketing agency rather than by DialogDesign.

Tip: Plan for cancellations. In order to stay on our tight test schedule, we planned extra sessions to cover no-shows and unforeseen circumstances. Carolyn Snyder scheduled 16 test sessions on Monday through Thursday of each week. She instructed the market research firm to fill 11 of those sessions. In retrospect four test sessions per day is too many. Three would have been better. We designated four additional test sessions on Friday and Saturday in case the original 11 sessions didn't happen as planned. This tactic proved valuable for the New Hampshire tests when snowstorms forced us to reschedule several sessions for one of the Friday or Saturday slots.

DialogDesign scheduled one extra test session but did not need to use it, because all scheduled participants showed up. The extra participant was so eager to participate, however, that DialogDesign decided to hold the extra test anyway.

Creating Good Tasks

Task design is one of the most important and difficult aspects of usability testing. All tasks created by someone other than the user, no matter how carefully done, constitute a form of bias. Probably more than any other factor, the task instructions influence where users go on the site and how they behave.

This section describes how we created our tasks. The actual task instructions appear at the end of this chapter.

Realistic Scenarios

Good tasks accurately represent actual use. Creating realistic scenarios is hard to do. You must have detailed information about real users and why they are visiting the site. In a different type of study, we might have:

- **Collaborated with the site designers to find out what they knew about their market.** If an e-commerce company had hired us to improve their site usability, we would have worked with the site designers.

- **Interviewed users first about their interests and then matched them to test sites relevant to their needs.** This technique is probably the best way to construct real tasks, but that would have taken more time than our schedule allowed. Because we wanted to watch several users attempt the same tasks, we did not attempt to match users with sites according to their needs and interests.

We created the tasks by reviewing the sites and coming up with scenarios we thought were practical. In some cases, we based the tasks on goals we had actually pursued on these or similar sites. So, although we can't claim that all our tasks were "real," we can say they were "realistic."

Motivation

When users are pursuing their own goals, they are self-motivated. The trick for task designers is to create scenarios compelling enough to motivate users to behave as if they were working on a task of their own. Creating tasks to motivate all users is difficult, unless you know something about the users ahead of time. Although we were testing with strangers, some users did find the tasks quite motivating, such as the loving grandmother who tested toy sites or the coffee lover who asked us to write down the URLs of the coffee sites so she could revisit them from home. Conversely, users who did not have children or who did not like coffee were not as motivated on the toy and coffee sites.

If a task is not motivating to a particular user, he or she might pick an item just to satisfy the requirements of the task. We observed this behavior in our study. We could still determine whether the unmotivated users could complete a purchase, but we couldn't learn from them which factors motivated shoppers might care about when buying products.

In a few cases, users made up their own realistic tasks after realizing what they could do on the website. A TowerRecords user immediately started looking for a CD containing a particular long-sought soundtrack from the movie "Babe." Realizing that the users' own tasks were probably a lot more motivating for them than our tasks, we let these users pursue their own goals. We found the same usability problems with both impromptu variations and preplanned tasks.

Task Independence

Good tasks should not depend on the successful completion of an earlier task. Unfortunately, we inadvertently violated this rule. Task 3 on Gevalia asked users to order coffee for delivery on a regular basis. This task proved unexpectedly difficult, because the form to join Gevalia's subscription service was on a separate part of the site from the product catalog. As a result, few users figured out how to set up regular deliveries. So, when we asked users in Task 4 to change the frequency of their deliveries, this assignment was impossible for those users who hadn't figured out how to join Gevalia. In retrospect, we wished that we had created a Task 4 that was unrelated to Task 3.

Cultural Issues

If the goal of a study is to test in multiple countries, the tasks must be suitable for users in all the test countries. Most of our tasks met this criterion. We did, however, find one issue that was probably a cultural problem with the task, rather than a usability problem with the site.

On eToys, Task 4 said, "Your child's birthday is coming up, and she has a long list of toys she wants. Several relatives will be getting something for her, and you want to avoid duplicates. Can this site help you manage this problem?" We planned that the eToys Wish List and / or Gift Registry would be the solution to this problem. But two Danish users found the idea of the Wish List so ridiculous that they refused to continue with the task. The third Danish user completed the task without really ever understanding how the Gift Registry worked. None of the six US users had any objection to the concept of a gift registry, but gift registries are not widely known in Denmark, so this task turned out to be culturally inappropriate.

Task Descriptions

We had four tasks for each site:

Task 1 – First Impressions

Allowing users to simply explore a site on their own and voice their impressions is not an effective testing method, because you can't be sure the user is having a realistic experience with a website that relates to his or her own interests.

Our Task 1 was a *limited* free exploration. We told users they could look at whatever they wanted to on the site. After two or three minutes, we stopped them and asked three questions:

1. What does this site have?
2. Who is this site for?
3. At first glance, does it appear that this site would have things you might want or need?

We used the free-form exploration for the initial task, because we didn't want to tell users what the site was about. We wanted the site to explain itself. We kept this initial exploration task very brief so we could devote most of the testing time to tasks 2 and 3.

Task 2 – Specific Item

In Task 2, we asked users to look for a specific item. In some cases, we asked for an item that matched rather precise criteria. In any case, there was a limited set of possible correct answers. For example, on Wal-Mart we asked users to find the cheapest toaster.

A straightforward task can act as a "warm-up" for more difficult tasks to follow. Thus, we hoped Task 2 would not require a great deal of effort, judgement, or time. Ideally, specifying an item to find should cause several users to visit roughly the same set of pages. But as so often happens in usability testing, users sometimes took different paths to the same answer.

Task 3 – Open-Ended

In Task 3, we gave users a more vaguely worded problem. We allowed them to use their own preferences and judgement to determine the answer. Unlike Task 2, in which we had a good idea which products the user would see, in Task 3 we allowed the users to visit a wider variety of pages on each site. For example, on the clothing sites, one of our tasks was, "Pretend that you have just moved from Florida to a cold climate and that you don't own any winter clothes. Please buy what you will need to be able to go for a walk in freezing temperatures." To satisfy this task, users were free to look at gloves, jackets, boots, or whatever they wanted.

Open-ended tasks make it harder to define success and failure. With specific tasks, the facilitator knows the right answer and needs to record only whether the user got it or not. When assessing the success of open-ended tasks, the user's feelings about the experience become more relevant. For example, one user on Nordstrom wanted to know about the lining of a pair of boots. The user explained that the lining affected both the comfort and the fit. A site that didn't supply this information would have failed for this particular user but might have succeeded for users who didn't care about the boot lining.

If we just wanted to prove a set of hypotheses, we probably would have used a greater percentage of specific tasks, as in Task 2, which allow facilitators more control (at least theoretically) over which parts of the site users visit. Our study was exploratory, so we included more open-ended tasks to see what unexpected insights our users might reveal to us.

Task 4 – Customer Service

In Task 4, we asked our users questions regarding the site's customer service policies, such as:

- Can you return the item if you're not satisfied?
- What happens if you find the same item elsewhere at a lower price after purchasing it here?
- Can you cancel an order after placing it?

Tips for Writing Task Instructions

Keep the following tips in mind when writing task instructions:

Tip: Describe the goal but not the steps. For example, we wouldn't say, "Go to the Men's section of the site and search for brown boots." This wording explains too much about how the site is organized and how the user is expected to behave. We avoid telling the user where to look or how the site works. Instead, we word the task more generally: "For his birthday, you want to give your brother a pair of brown leather boots in size 10 (medium width). Please buy the boots and have them delivered to your brother."

Tip: Avoid technical terms and product names that appear on the website. For example, on Gevalia and Peet's, we wanted users to find a french press (a type of coffee maker, also called a press pot or plunger pot). We didn't tell them what the coffee maker was actually called on these sites, because we didn't want to make the task artificially easy. Instead, we used a photo of a press pot so users could see what one looked like. (The photo came from a site we weren't testing.) We worded the task, "Your friend has one of these and it makes great coffee, so you want one."

Users were shown this picture of a specialty coffee maker, but they were not told the exact name of the item. M1

Tip: Put each task on a separate page. We printed each task on a separate page so we could give them to users in any order, and so users would not be intimidated by seeing how many tasks we had. If the user experienced significant difficulty or was extremely thorough, we didn't present all the tasks. We didn't want the user to feel bad about being "slow" or not getting through everything.

Task Refinement

We tested the tasks thoroughly before the study. We made sure the tasks could be understood by someone other than their author and that they could be accomplished using the site. Collecting success metrics was a goal for our study. So we didn't change tasks during testing, because that might have skewed the data. In contrast, when we work directly with a development team to improve a website design, we do sometimes change the tasks during a study, according to what the development team wants to learn from the next test.

Because we all helped create tasks, the first "test" of our tasks was when we tried them out ourselves. Although this couldn't be considered an actual test (because none of us fit our user profile), this exercise helped identify any apparent problems with the task: If we couldn't complete a task, that indicated the task was too hard. If usability professionals can complete a task, however, that still is no guarantee the task is appropriate for the target users. The best way to refine tasks is to conduct pilot tests with users, as we did in this study. As a result of our pilot sessions, we changed several of our tasks, as described in the Pilot Testing section of this chapter.

Testing of Complete Purchases

Potential ethical issues arise whenever you ask strangers to use their own credit cards to complete purchases in a study. Our motives were pure, but they might not have looked that way. Our US test facility was a nearly vacant office suite with a couple of folding tables and computers — a makeshift and clearly temporary facility. Probably no one would feel comfortable revealing their credit card numbers in such a setting. We didn't want users to be reluctant to buy products for reasons having to do with the test setting rather than the sites themselves.

For most of the tests, we stopped the user short of completing a purchase. Practically, this meant proceeding as far as possible before the site required a credit card. Once the user got to this point, we considered it a "successful purchase" for our study, even though there was no actual purchase.

We wanted to watch at least a few users complete their purchases, however, because the final pages of the e-commerce process can be seen only after the user actually types in a credit card number. For this reason, we conducted some of the Danish tests with people known to the facilitators. These people felt comfortable enough to buy merchandise on the test sites with their own credit cards.

We conducted these tests somewhat differently:

- The test participants were three good friends of the facilitators' families who agreed beforehand to use their own credit cards for the test.

- We ran the tests as usual, except we asked the test participants to order real products in Task 3.

- We told the test participants we would refund up to $50 of their purchases. If they bought for less, or if they were unable to buy anything, they did not receive the difference in cash. If they spent more than $50, they were responsible for paying the remaining balance. The $50 included shipping charges. For testing purposes, we did not tell them in advance that shipping charges to Denmark could consume a substantial amount of their allowance.
- Each participant also received the standard compensation given to other participants who were not asked to complete purchases.
- We followed up with the test participants after they had received the merchandise to hear about the post-purchase experience.

The most valuable findings from the tests of completed purchases were related to issues of trust. See the Trust chapter for more details.

Usability Test Facilities

We conducted the New Hampshire tests in office space rented on a short-term lease. We brought in a couple of folding tables, office chairs, and computers. With the addition of a phone line and Internet account, we had a discount usability lab.

We held the Copenhagen tests in a meeting room we rented by the day. The room was about 200 square feet with large windows. We used the meeting tables and chairs that came with the room. We brought in a portable computer, printer, and modem. We used the telephone line in the room to connect to one of DialogDesign's Internet accounts.

In all of our test sessions, the facilitator sat in the same room with the user and also took notes. (In some usability labs, two people perform these functions, but an experienced facilitator can do both jobs.) We did not have a separate observation room. On the rare occasions when someone wanted to observe the test, we let them sit quietly in the same room with us.

Some usability professionals think it is important to record usability test sessions. Because of the large number of tests we had scheduled in a relatively short time frame, we did not have time to review test tapes. Even if we'd had more time, we probably still wouldn't have videotaped. To review a videotape of a usability test takes more than two hours. In the same amount of time, you could run another test and learn more. So instead of recording the tests, we focused on taking clear and detailed notes.

Test System Configuration

Hardware

Both test machines were Pentium-class PCs running Windows 98 with monitor resolution set to 800 x 600 and a 56k dial-up modem.

- The US test machine had 96 MB of memory and a 15-inch monitor.
- The Danish test machine was a portable with 64 MB of memory and a 14-inch monitor.

We made a printer available during the tests, because in other studies some users printed Web pages. In the US tests, the printer was on the floor, so we pointed it out during the initial briefing. In the Danish tests the printer wasn't mentioned. It just sat on the table next to the computer.

Only one user printed anything during our study. There are several possible reasons why the presence of a printer wasn't as important as we'd thought it might be:

- **Some of the products and scenarios we tested didn't lend themselves to printing.** It is hard to imagine printing product pages for coffee or caring enough to print out the specs for Wal-Mart's cheapest toaster.

- **For the most part, we were not testing complete transactions.** The Danish users who completed transactions wanted printed or written copies of the order confirmation numbers. Having a printer was more important during those tests.

- **Users were probably not shopping as carefully during our tests as they would when they shop for themselves.** For example, no other decision-makers were involved who might have needed to see a printout.

Based on these results, we might forego a printer during future tests, unless we were testing complete purchases. It does no harm to provide access to a printer if one is available, however.

Software

Browsers

We allowed the users to choose either Microsoft Internet Explorer or Netscape Navigator. The US test machine had version 5.0 of Internet Explorer and version 4.08 of Navigator. The Danish machine had version 4.0 of Internet Explorer and version 4.08 of Navigator. About half the US users chose Netscape Navigator, but none of the Danish users did. We did not observe any issues that were attributable to the browser brand.

On the US machine, we configured the browsers with a default page we had created. The page provided links to all the sites in our study. Thus, we avoided the need to type in the URLs. This page was easy to create and worked well in practice. We deliberately made the links cryptic so users wouldn't see the whole list of test sites. The Danish machine was not set up this way, but it didn't seem to be a great inconvenience to have users type in the short site URLs.

Online Shopping Study Web Sites

A1 (re)	B1 (ns)	C1 (sm)	E1 (if)
A2 (to)	B2 (jc)	C2 (di)	E2 (18)
A3 (cu)	B3 (bo)	C3 (et)	
F1 (ge)	G1 (fu)	H1 (no)	
F2 (pe)	G2 (li)	H2 (se)	
F3 (ba)	G3 (he)	H3 (wa)	

For the US tests, this HTML page hid the identity of the test sites with cryptic hyperlinks. M2

E-mail Accounts

On Living, not all prices were shown. Users had to request prices be sent to them in e-mail. So, we needed to have e-mail accounts set up on the test machines. Only two users made use of the e-mail account.

Many sites require users to provide an e-mail address during registration. The Danish users didn't mind using their own e-mail addresses in the test. We anticipated many US participants would prefer not to use their own e-mail addresses due to concerns about privacy or unsolicited commercial e-mail. So we thought it was important to provide an alternative e-mail address they could use. We started the study with a few spare e-mail addresses. By the end of the study, we had used most of them, because many sites wouldn't allow two users with the same e-mail address to register as unique users. Next time we would prepare one fake e-mail address per user, unless we were sure users would supply their own e-mail addresses.

We didn't allow users to invent e-mail addresses. In a couple of cases, we stopped users from typing in fake addresses (such as bob@aol.com) to eliminate the possibility of other people receiving unwanted e-mail because of our study.

Tip: Print samples of confirmation e-mail messages in advance. In case a user wants to see an example of the e-mail order confirmation a site sends, it's handy to keep around a few printed copies of legitimate order confirmations from previous online purchases.

Between-Test Cleanup

After each test, we cleared the visited links and erased the browser history because they might provide artificial clues for the next user. We also deleted any cookies left by the tested websites, which was a bit difficult. Cookies were troublesome, because they could cause the computer to retain information from one test to the next. For instance, a user might encounter the contents of the shopping cart or the personal information left by a previous user, such as user ID and password.

To get rid of cookies, we deleted files from all the usual places on Windows-based systems: Windows\Cookies, Windows\Temp, Windows\Temporary Internet Files, and the subdirectories within Netscape. Some tracking mechanism survived this deletion effort, however. We suspect that CustomDisc tracked the IP address of one of our test computers, because the site continued to call users "Lisa" after one user registered on the site using that name. Starting a new dialup session fixed this problem. In the future, we will use a software utility to clean cookies from the hard disk between tests.

Pilot Testing

In addition to trying the tasks ourselves, we held several pilot tests before we began the main study. The objectives of pilot testing are to verify that the:

- Tasks are understandable and doable.
- Forms and questionnaires make sense to the users.
- Testing environment is functional: equipment and software operate properly, and the test websites are up and running.
- Users understand the pre-test introduction and instructions.
- Time allotted for each test is adequate.

In the US pilot test, we tested each task once with users. The Danish pilot tests covered a representative subset of the tasks. The results of the pilot tests from both countries inspired us to revise some aspects of the real study before we commenced testing.

What We Changed

Task Refinements

Before the beginning the study, we took what we learned from the pilot tests and made changes to the test tasks. Some of the changes were:

Tasks Changed Because of Problems in the Pilot Tests

Original Task	Problem	Revised Task
Iflorist: "Your significant other has recently been mad at you. However, s/he has just sent a bouquet of yellow carnations to you at work. Is this a good sign or a bad one?"	We decided that a task to decipher the meaning of particular flowers (in this case, that yellow carnations symbolize rejection) was too obscure, even though the information was available on the site.	"You're thinking of getting your significant other some flowers for Valentine's Day, but you tend to put things off until the last minute. How far ahead of time do you have to order the flowers to make sure they arrive in time?"
Disney: "Your friends had a 10-pound baby boy two months ago. You want to get him a sleeper with Disney characters, but you're not sure what size to get."	This task turned out to be too unrealistic. The pilot user commented that he would never have thought to look for clothing size information on the Disney site (the information is there).	"You bought your nephew a Baseball Pooh Mini Bean Bag, not realizing he already has one. You no longer have the original packaging — can you return it?"
HermanMiller: "At lunch you overheard a conversation between two colleagues. They were talking about a product called the Lapdog. Find out what it is and order it."	We realized that using the product name Lapdog would make the task artificially easy, because the user could simply type it into the search engine.	"You overheard a conversation between two co-workers about a product on this website. It seems to be a cleverly designed bag for a portable PC, which also functions as a desktop. Find out precisely what it is."

Site Replacement

Most of the changes we made because of the pilot study results were to the tasks. We did change one of the sites we tested, however. We originally included CDuctive.com, which offered custom CDs of underground music. The first pilot user found some of the song titles offensive, so we replaced CDuctive with CustomDisc, which also allowed users to make custom CDs. CustomDisc specialized in "oldies" (older music from the times when songs titles were just silly, not offensive).

Task Duration

Overall, we found the task timing was tight but workable. We planned to cut Task 2 (the specific task) short once the user had found a suitable item, then let the user complete the order process in Task 3. During the actual tests, however, we realized we needed to see the user complete the order form only once per site and it didn't really matter whether it happened in Task 2 or Task 3. Thus, we didn't cut Task 2 short if the user found the item faster than we expected, but instead we allowed the user to proceed with the order form. In these cases, we did not ask the user to complete the order form again in Task 3.

Test Facilitation

At the start of each usability test, we gave users an introduction similar to the one presented in the previous section "What Users Were Told" in this chapter. The introduction explained the purpose of the session and what we'd be asking users to do.

Description of Think-Aloud Protocol

We encouraged our users to explain what they're looking for, ask questions, and tell us what they were thinking. The typical statement we used to describe the think-aloud process to the users was:

> As you're working, I'll ask you to think out loud and describe what you're looking for, what questions you have, anything that surprises you, etc. I may not be able to answer your questions, but they will help us understand how to make these sites more user friendly.

We did not remain silent while the users were working. Instead, we used an interactive style of facilitation, encouraging users to expand upon interesting remarks. Whenever possible, we asked neutral, open-ended questions such as, "What do you mean by that?" We were careful not to help users inadvertently, reveal our own opinions about the site, or redirect users' attention (unless we'd made a deliberate decision to help them).

Sometimes, after the test was over, we asked users specific questions about the site, such as:

- See this logo here? Did you know that's actually a link to the home page?

- Did you notice this animated truck that says "Important Delivery Information?"

We always waited until the end of the test to ask such questions. Waiting allowed us to gather clean data about specific aspects of the site's design, without influencing the users' behavior while they were working on the tasks.

Personal Data or Fake Identity

One decision we had to make was whether to require users to enter their personal information or to allow them to use fake data. Ultimately, we chose to do things differently in the US and Danish tests. Some of the considerations were:

- Would users make more mistakes typing fake information than they would with their own?

- Would users be more willing to provide false personal information than they would their own information?

US Tests

At the time of this study, many US residents were quite concerned about privacy and fraud online. We opted to give the New Hampshire users a choice of using their own personal information or a fake name and address we supplied. In the pre-test introduction, we explained:

> The websites we're testing are real. It is up to you whether you enter any personal information on these sites such as your name or e-mail address. If you want to enter your own information, you may do so. If not, you can use this made-up identity instead. Or, you can use a mixture of your real information and the made-up identity.

Although most US users opted to assume a fake identity, they were quite vocal in situations in which they would not have wanted to give out their own information. We were relieved to get this feedback. One of our concerns in providing fake information was that it would mask user reluctance to release personal information, but that reluctance came through loud and clear anyway. When a user was adamant that he or she would not have given out personal information, we counted the task as a failure even when the user went on to successfully complete the task using the false information.

We also learned fake identities can introduce artificial confusion between shipping and billing addresses. Normally, people know which information belongs to them and which belongs to their intended recipient. Even so, they might type this information in the wrong places on the form. When we saw a shipping / billing reversal during a test, we checked for this confusion by asking the user, "Whose information is that?" If the user confusion was because both the sender and recipient information were unfamiliar to the user, we didn't count this as a problem with the site.

Danish Tests

We asked the Danish participants to use their own personal information, and none of them objected. Using real information provided diversity in names and addresses, which was especially important in identifying international issues during the checkout process.

Assisting with Technical Problems

A usability lab is an artificial environment. Results can be affected if the user is accustomed to a machine or environment that is different from the lab's. For example, one of our nontechnical users said that she asked her husband (a systems analyst) to help her when she had trouble using her computer at home. We could argue that she was less likely to be successful in our test setting than she would be at home. We could counter-argue that the goal of usability testing is to improve sites so users don't have to ask for help.

We did attempt to counter the "unfamiliar environment" bias when we could, by assisting users with any aspect of our computer setup that was unfamiliar to them. For example, some users used a different version of the browser or had theirs configured a different way. America Online users sometimes needed assistance to recognize common browser controls, because AOL had its own browser. Similarly, when users had questions that pertained to aspects of the machine configuration, such as modem speed, we answered those questions freely. We did not count these questions as usability issues.

Helping Users

One of the goals of test facilitation is to affect the user's behavior as little as possible. The facilitator has an ethical duty (and depending on the wording of the informed consent, a legal responsibility) to avoid causing the user psychological discomfort. Some people can be uncomfortable in a test setting, especially those who perceive that the problems they're having with the site are due to their own lack of skills. We told users during the pre-test briefing that we were testing websites, not testing them. When a user experienced difficulty during the test, we provided reassurance that the problems were not the user's fault.

Sometimes, the user became stuck and was unable to proceed. In these cases, we provided assistance to help the user overcome the problem, assuming we had additional time to spend on the site. For example, we helped one user on 1800flowers who had come to the conclusion that "Add to Basket" was not the way to put items into the shopping cart, when in fact it was. We helped her because we had gathered plenty of data about this particular problem. We wanted the user to move on so we could gather data about filling out the order form.

A Discussion of Bias

By "bias," we mean the potential for the test protocol to affect the results obtained from the study. In this section, we'll provide some insights about bias so you can better interpret the results of this and other studies.

This study — like every study of user behavior — contains bias. But bias is not necessarily bad, as long as we make an effort to identify its sources and to consider the effects.

We cannot observe and measure user behavior without affecting that behavior. The only way to have a completely unbiased usability study would be to watch users doing their real tasks in their real environments, unaware they're being observed. Another name for this method is spying, which is unethical, if not downright illegal.

Even a totally unbiased study wouldn't be ideal, because to get zero bias, we'd have to give up all experimental controls and all our interactions with users. As a result, we'd lose most of the benefits of usability testing.

We identified several sources of bias in our tests, including:

- **Order in which the sites were tested** – A good or bad experience with one site can shape users' expectations or behavior when they visit subsequent sites. In essence, users are biased by the sum total of all their online experiences. Even though we varied the site order, we noticed users' behavior or perceptions were still affected by an experience with a prior site. For example, one user who discovered he had accidentally ordered a shirt of the wrong color on Jcrew paid special attention to product color on the next site, NorwaySweaters.

- **Difficulty of the tasks** – Controlling for task difficulty is almost impossible when designing a usability study. In this study, our goal was not to compare the relative usability of the sites, so we did not control for task difficulty. For this reason, the usability results for one site in our study should not be compared with those of another.

- **Helping a user who has become stuck and frustrated** – The facilitator has an ethical obligation to assist a user who's having a sufficiently tough time completing a task. Clearly, such help affects the meaning of "success" for the task. We kept careful notes of situations in which we helped users, so we could evaluate whether we could count these tasks as successes or not.

- **Asking a user to clarify a remark** – When we interrupted people working on a task, we could never be sure they would continue on exactly the same path afterward. We always weighed the value of the insights we'd gain from the user's response against the possibility we were interfering with his or her behavior.

Taking into account the sources of bias in our study, we believe the data we obtained is a realistic proxy for the data we would have collected watching actual customers use these sites. As with any source of bias, we had to ask ourselves these questions:

- How might this bias have affected the results?

- Do we believe we would have gotten the same result in the absence of this bias?

We recognize intelligent disagreement on specific issues is inevitable, such as whether to count a task a success when the user received a hint from the facilitator. Although the results of specific tasks might be disputed, we believe the overall patterns we saw in this study are valid, and we will watch for confirmation of our findings in subsequent usability studies.

Data Collection

We used different methods to collect data during the tests. Carolyn Snyder took notes on a laptop PC. Rolf Molich and Sofie Scheutz wrote their notes by hand and transcribed them after the test. Rolf and Sofie suspected that the presence of a laptop in the test room can be distracting, although they hadn't tested that theory yet. Carolyn likes using a laptop because she can type much faster than she writes and thus gather more data. As the sole note-taker in her tests, Carolyn felt that this advantage outweighed the possibility that users would be distracted by the sound of her typing. None of the 39 users she tested showed any overt reaction to her laptop.

Tip: If you type continuously, users tend to ignore the sound of the keyboard because it becomes part of the background noise. Intermittent typing is much more likely to alert the user that he or she has just "done something," and thus is more distracting. With some practice, it is possible to type one's observations and thoughts on an ongoing basis without a great deal of conscious attention. (Allow 15 minutes after each test session to correct your notes and make sure they are readable.)

Post-Test Questionnaires

We used a post-test questionnaire to capture quantifiable feedback about the site, products, and optionally, the test process (see the Site Feedback Questionnaire at the end of this chapter). Questionnaires are difficult to write well. The questions must be neutrally phrased. The rating scale must have non-prejudicial endpoints (not "good" and "bad," for example). Even though we design these questionnaires to elicit honest feedback about the participants' experiences, the results of the questionnaire often conflicted with what happened during the test. These discrepancies can be attributed to various factors, such as when users:

- Want to say nice things about the site or product tested or want to please the test administrator.
- Blame themselves for the difficulty they encountered.
- Forget or misunderstand the question in relation to the experience of the site.

Unfortunately, we discovered some problems with the questionnaire. For example, when we asked users to rate "Completing the order form" (from "very unsatisfied" to "very satisfied"), one user indicated that the order form was satisfactory even though she'd gotten stuck and needed help from the facilitator to proceed. Upon further questioning, she explained that she didn't think the order form as a whole was bad because she'd only had trouble with the e-mail address. In other words, her answer was based on the *proportion* of confusing fields rather than the *severity* of her confusion with one field. Her logic was unflawed but her standards were quite different than ours. After finding several other instances in which users interpreted a question in a way that we didn't intend, we decided not to analyze the questionnaire data we had collected.

Data Analysis

The method we used to organize our data could be used in smaller usability studies. After each test, we put our observations into a table with one row per usability issue. The table columns included the site, observation ID, screenshot reference (when we had one), user number, task number, problem description, and observation category (classification of problem type).

By using a table format, we were able to sort the observations by various factors such as site or problem classification. (You can create sortable tables in many word processors or spreadsheets.) In this manner, we were able to manage the hundreds of pages of observations we collected during our study.

Example (slightly simplified and edited for clarity) of a test session observation table

Site	ID	Associated Screenshot	User	Task #	Problem Description	Observation Category
Se	3179	se-c-compare3	29	2	"If I wanted to get back to that main site. I guess I'd go here. Not really clear how I'd get back." (A few pages later, she finds the logo link.)	Navigation
Se	3180		29	3	From tools, types "microwave oven" into search. Gets nothing. "This reminds me of looking under the Yellow Pages. You're looking under lawyers and it's attorneys. I think I'm in the tool thing. I have to get out of the tool thing." (Note that there is no search facility for appliances.)	Search
Se	3181		29	3	On appliances page. Goes to cooking. Gets 113. Picks Panasonic. It narrows to 6. "It went from over 100 to 6. It narrowed my choices." (She gets how this works.)	Category Pages
Se	3182	Se-c-microwave-compare4	29	3	"This is interesting, I've not seen a compare list like this." Clicks compare with three microwaves selected. "How can you compare when it doesn't all fit on the screen? It's a good comparison, except I'd like it to fit on the screen. I don't understand why they'd need to keep this [the list at the right] out here."	Category Pages
Se	3183	Similar to se-c-details	29	3	Clicks one microwave for $139. Clicks to view more details. "Oh, I'll say. This almost looks like too much. Although, styling, door handle, easy to open. … I almost think this is too much. But I suppose this is kind of a substitute for actually seeing it. It has a steamed fruit pudding sensor" (she seems amused by this).	Product Pages

The US team and the Danish team produced one table each. We sorted the two tables by problem classification and used the sorted tables to organize our findings for the chapters. The uniform reporting format ensured that each author could easily manage data other team members had gathered.

Defining Success and Failure

After the tests were complete, we had many long discussions about what to consider a "success" or a "failure." ("Failure" always means a failure of the site, not the user.) A task success was relatively easy to define: The user was able to locate and order an item or find information that satisfied our task instructions.

When it came to defining a task failure we kept discovering gray areas. For instance: A user completed a purchase on Peet's but said she wouldn't return because the prices were too high. Should that be counted a success or a failure?

We finally realized much of our disagreement stemmed from our different ideas about what we were trying to measure, and why. Finally, we defined two failure categories: "task failures" and "sales catastrophes." These failure definitions overlap quite a bit (that's why it took us a while to realize the nature of our disagreement), but they are distinct in their purpose.

Even given the detailed failure definitions we ultimately formulated, it wasn't always easy to determine the difference between a task failure and a sales catastrophe. Reasonable people may disagree with our definitions and how we classified some of those gray-area incidents.

Task Failures

Task failure is a usability metric that answers the question: When people tried to accomplish a task we asked them to do, did they succeed or fail at completing the task?

Anyone who is directly involved in the design of a website must pay attention to task failures. These failures involve features of the site the designer can correct or improve. For example:

- Tune the search engine so users can find products more easily.

- Provide better instructions on choosing a password.

- Reveal shipping costs before users have to submit personal information.

Criteria for Task Failures

Task failures can take many forms, including:

- **Substantive assistance** – If the facilitator had to provide substantive assistance or encouragement, we took careful notes and decided whether the user would have been able to get past the problem without our help. For example, we assisted a couple of users who could not determine how to get into Gevalia's catalog. We counted these as failures even when the user went on to complete the rest of the task as instructed.

- **User on the wrong path** – Our users spent about 40 minutes on each site they tested. If time ran out when the user was on a significantly wrong path to task completion, we counted it as a failure. For example, when time ran out, one user on 1800flowers believed she had to register before purchasing something, which was not true or even possible. We had a reasonable expectation this user was eventually going to get stuck. Previous research has indicated that the longer users work on a task, the less likely they are to succeed. When the user was on the right path when time ran out, we gave the site the benefit of the doubt and counted the task a success.

- **Solving the problem by non-site means** – Sometimes a user assumed the only way to complete the task would be to call, e-mail, or fax the company rather than using the site. Some users had this reaction as soon as they read the task: "Oh, I'd just call them." In these cases we asked the user to attempt the task anyway. We counted the task a failure only if the user was unable to find the answer on the website.

- **Significant unanswered questions** – We counted a failure when the user had unanswered questions of significant magnitude to prevent a purchase. For example, one user on Jcrew wasn't sure why the site was charging him sales tax. He said he wouldn't have proceeded with the purchase until this issue was resolved.

- **Anticipated fulfillment problem** – Sometimes users completed the order form and believed all was well, but we observed a problem that would have led to disappointment. For example, some users ordered an item without ever realizing that the site would not ship to Denmark. Another user thought he had ordered a blue shirt when he had actually ordered a green one. Some users, however, spotted a problem with a task, such as, "This task is unsolvable because the website does not ship to Denmark." When this was true, we counted a success.

- **User-defined task variations** – When a user voluntarily made the task more complicated and then couldn't accomplish the task, we counted it as a failure. We counted such incidents as failures because they represented something the user would have attempted normally. For instance, one user decided she wanted to ship items to multiple addresses on 1800flowers. She wanted to order something for herself at the same time she was working on the assigned task of sending a gift. Although the site did support multiple shipping addresses, the user couldn't figure out how to send to multiple addresses. We counted this as a failure.

Most of these criteria have subjective aspects, and we probably could have applied other criteria as well. The way we measured task failures in this study is not the only way to count failures. The best way to measure success or failure of any e-commerce site depends on the:

- **Business goals of the site** – Because we were not working with the designers in this study, we did not know the specific business goals of the sites we tested.

- **Purpose of the usability study** – We were studying a broad range of issues that affect people buying products online.

- **Audience who will read the results of the study** – Our audience is diverse.

We would like to have clearly defined the criteria for success and failure before conducting the tests. Unique cases always arise during testing, but the more clear these criteria are beforehand, the easier it is to record, count, and report the results.

Sales Catastrophes

We attempted to assess not only why users got stuck on a task but also which aspects of their experience were sufficiently negative to drive them away from the site or to discourage them from returning. These we called "sales catastrophes." Sales catastrophes overlap with task failures, but generally they are more serious because they are a better proxy for lost sales.

Task failures are caused by factors under the control of the site designer. *Sales catastrophes* are broader in scope and sometimes can't be solved by the site designer alone. For example, unreasonable shipping charges can provoke users to leave a site. Sales catastrophes represent areas of concern not just to site designers but also to those who are responsible for pricing, policies, sales fulfillment, and other non-design aspects of an e-commerce enterprise.

Criteria for Sales Catastrophes

We counted as a sales catastrophe any task in which the user:

- **Was not able to complete a purchase.** (This aspect overlaps with the task failure metric.)

- **Refused to proceed or indicated they were proceeding only to please us.** Reasons why users refused to continue included reluctance to give out personal information, misunderstanding something on the site, or feeling that the site was too slow.

- **Gave a reason why he or she would have left the site and / or not returned to the site.** Our test introduction included the following request:

  It's not unusual for people to look on a website but not find something they're interested in. If you get to a point where you'd give up in real life, please let me know. I may ask you to continue for a few minutes past that point if you're willing, but one of the things we're researching is what causes people to leave websites without buying anything. So please let me know immediately if you have an inclination to leave the site.

  We made exceptions to this rule when users expressed disinterest in a site's content during their initial exploration. We didn't penalize a site by recording a sales catastrophe when the user wanted to leave the site due to a simple lack of interest.

Quite a few people made statements such as, "If I were doing this in real life, I'd leave this site and go to the mall instead." It's always risky to assume that people will behave exactly the same way when involved in self-motivated tasks and unobserved. We did discover many things that potentially cause users to leave e-commerce sites without making a purchase, however.

As with task failures, counting a sales catastrophe was often a subjective decision. We have no way of knowing whether users will return to a site or not — no matter what they said during the test. Even so, we recommend that site developers and designers take users' statements of intent seriously. At the very least, when conducting usability tests of their own, designers and developers should take a close look at those site features that seem to have a strong negative effect on users.

Examples of Task Failures and Sales Catastrophes

- **A user completed the task on BasketHaus but said he wouldn't buy from this site because he couldn't determine exactly what he would get or how much the shipping cost would be.** We counted this as both a task failure and a sales catastrophe. It's a task failure because the user had questions significant enough to prevent him from buying the item. By definition, anything that prevents a purchase counts as a sales catastrophe.

- **The user found suitable coffee on Peet's and completed the order form. She said, however, that she wouldn't return to the site.** "It was pricey. … four times what I'd pay in the grocery store. Plus, I'd pay shipping. I don't pay shipping to anybody." We counted this test as a sales catastrophe but *not* a task failure. The user successfully completed the mechanics of the task, including the order form. This test qualified as a sales catastrophe, though, because the user stated clearly that the pricing and shipping costs were unacceptable to her.

Testing Websites: A Cautionary Tale

As mentioned in the Checkout & Registration chapter, while testing one of the sites (which shall remain nameless, because it wasn't entirely the company's fault), a user had reached the order form. She filled out her first and last name, using the Tab key to move between fields. When she tabbed from the last name field, the cursor moved to the URL location field. The user typed the first two digits of the street address before noticing that the numbers weren't going into the address field. She used the mouse to place the cursor in the address field and continued completing the form. Several fields later, she hit the Enter key. This action activated the URL for that two-digit number, which went to ... a page that made two grown women blush!

The test facilitator, Carolyn Snyder, was able to reconstruct the user's actions and carefully explained to her how it happened. Carolyn told the user that what she had seen was totally inadvertent and had nothing to do with the site she'd been testing or the purpose of the study. Fortunately, the user accepted the explanation and didn't seem too traumatized by the experience. On her way out the door, the user said she had never believed people who claimed they got to pornography sites by accident. Now she knows.

As Jakob Nielsen commented when he heard the story, "This is an issue that never came up in the old days of usability testing the installation procedures for Unix!" On the Web today, you are only a hyperlink away from an embarrassing or stressful incident. From a legal perspective, even an accidental display of pornography creates the potential for liability if it causes the user distress. Earlier in the study, a different user came to the test session without having signed her consent form. She wanted to be sure we would not ask her to visit any websites with sexual content. We assured her we would not.

This episode underscores the need to have users sign a comprehensive informed consent agreement when testing websites. The consent form should state that the study facilitators are not responsible for the pages that the user visits during the test, or for the content of sites other than the ones they are testing. (In our case, we weren't even responsible for the sites we tested.) This incident has taught us all to keep an eye on the URL field. Carolyn believes that she might have been able to stop the download in time if she'd looked at the URL field to see what page was taking so long to load.

Participant Screening Questionnaire

We gave this questionnaire to the US market research firm that recruited users. DialogDesign used a variation of this questionnaire, as noted below.

1. Do you have access to the Internet during your non-work hours? (Must say yes.)

2. How often do you use the Internet? (Most participants should access it at least a few times per week. Daily is good.)

3. How long have you had access to the Internet? (We don't want more than a few people with less than three months of experience.)

4. What kinds of things do you use the Internet for? (Must answer one or more of the following: shopping, looking up information, news / weather, research for school or work.)

5. Have you ever bought something online or shopped without buying? (They don't necessarily have to have bought, but we don't want more than a few people who've never shopped online before.)

6. Gender: (About equal mix of men and women.)

7. Age: (About evenly distributed among people in their 20s, 30s, 40s, and 50s. Youngest age is 18. No upper age limit.)

8. Occupation: We want people who have disposable income, ideally people who are employed. (We do not want full-time students, retirees, unemployed, and homemakers to be over-represented, so no more than one or two of each.)

9. Do you know any computer programming languages, or have you ever created a Web page? (We want to screen out people who have technical proficiency with the Internet or website development.)

In screening participants, DialogDesign asked a few additional questions to weed out people who didn't know enough to qualify — or who knew too much:

- "What does the Back button do?"
- "How would you locate all occurrences of the word 'toaster' on a long Web page?"
- "How do you stop an animation?"

Consent Form (USA)

Informed Consent

Study Administrator is:　　　　　　　Participant is:

Name

Address

Introduction

You have been scheduled to participate in a research study about online shopping. Our purpose in conducting this study is to understand what makes some websites easier to use than others. The results of this study will be published in professional reports to help website developers create more user-friendly sites. Please keep in mind that this is a test of websites; we are not testing you!

Please bring the completed background questionnaire with you to the study. In the session, we'll ask you to visit some websites and shop for various things. You will not be required to actually buy anything or to enter any personal or credit card information online. (Any such information that you voluntarily choose to enter online is your responsibility.)

All information we collect concerning your participation in the session is confidential. We will not videotape or audiotape the session. We will use the information for statistical and summary purposes only and will make certain that your name is not associated with your records.

To the best of our knowledge, there are no physical or psychological risks associated with participating in this study. During the session, the study administrator will assist you and answer any questions. You may take short breaks as needed and may stop your participation in the study at any time. Participants who complete the 2-hour session will receive a cash payment of $80.

Statement of Informed Consent

I have read the description of the study and of my rights as a participant. I agree to participate in the study.

Signature _____

Date _____

Pre-Test Questionnaire

Online Shopping
User Id:
Date:

Background Questionnaire

This information will be kept strictly confidential.

1. Your age: 16 – 20   21 – 25   26 – 30   31 – 35
              36 – 40   41 – 45   46 – 50   over 50

2. Gender: Male   Female

3. Occupation:

    _____

4. Where do you access the Internet?   home   work   both

5. About how long have you been using the Internet?

    _____

6. Who is your Internet Service Provider at home (if known)?

    _____

7. What do you use the Internet for?

    _____

    _____

    _____

8. Which search engines (if any) do you typically use?

    _____

9. What (if anything) have you purchased online?

    _____

10. Please list any sites you use often and / or that you think are
    especially useful:

    For work? _____

    For home / personal use? _____

Site Feedback Questionnaire

Online Shopping
User Id:
Date:

Please rate your satisfaction with these aspects of the site you have just finished working with by circling the appropriate *number*. As you evaluate other sites, you may come back and change ratings you have already made for this site.

		Very Unsatisfied	Very Satisfied
1.	Getting to the right part of the site		3 2 1 0 1 2 3
2.	Quality of information about individual products		3 2 1 0 1 2 3
3.	Ease of reading the text		3 2 1 0 1 2 3
4.	Site's search facility (if used)		3 2 1 0 1 2 3
5.	Appearance of site, including colors and graphics		3 2 1 0 1 2 3
6.	Speed of pages displaying		3 2 1 0 1 2 3
7.	Fun, entertainment value		3 2 1 0 1 2 3
8.	Completing the order form		3 2 1 0 1 2 3
9.	Quality of information about ordering and delivery		3 2 1 0 1 2 3
10.	Use my credit card and personal information		3 2 1 0 1 2 3
11.	Overall shopping experience		3 2 1 0 1 2 3

12. **How sure are you that you found the best product based on what you were asked to do?**

Not at all sure   3 2 1 0 1 2 3   Very confident

13. **Were all your questions answered?**

No, none of them   3 2 1 0 1 2 3   Yes, completely

14. **Do you feel that this site:**

Only wants my money   3 2 1 0 1 2 3   Cares about my satisfaction as a customer

15. **How relevant are the products on this site to you?**

I can't even imagine shopping for products like this.   3 2 1 0 1 2 3   I love these kinds of products and shop for them all the time.

16. **How likely are you to return to this site on your own?**

No way   3 2 1 0 1 2 3   I'll probably return the next time I sit down at my own computer.

Tasks

For the Danish tests, the tasks were translated into Danish. The translated questions are not included in this chapter.

Task 1

For each site, Task 1 encouraged the user to explore the website freely for 2–3 minutes. The facilitator then asked the user:

- What does this site offer?
- Who is it for?
- Does it appear that this site would have products that you might want or need?

Tasks 2 (Specific Task), 3 (Open Task), and 4 (Customer Service or Information-Seeking Task) for each site are described below:

Audio and Video Sites			
	A. Reel	**B. TowerRecords**	**C. CustomDisc**
Specific Task	Order the following video for yourself: *One Flew Over the Cuckoo's Nest*.	Order the following video for yourself: Disney's *Fantasia*.	One of your friends was born in 1956. Make a CD that contains hits from that year.
Open Task	A friend gave you a $30 gift certificate for Reel.com. Buy one video according to your preferences.	Who directed the movie *Paths of Glory*? Order a video of your choice by that director.	Order a CD with your favorite music.
Customer Service or Information-Seeking Task	You have now received the Cuckoo's Nest video. Unfortunately, the day after you received it from reel.com your mother gave you exactly the same video. Can you get your money back from Reel.com?	Buy a gift certificate for $50. Have it sent to: Carolyn Snyder 55 Main St., #7 Salem, NH 03079.	Is it possible to cancel an order after you have submitted it?

	A. NorwaySweaters	B. Jcrew	C. Boo
Specific Task	Please buy a blue sweater, size Large, for your aunt and include a message to her.	For his birthday, you want to give your brother a pair of brown leather boots in size 10 (medium width). Please buy the boots and have them delivered to your brother. His address is: Bob Rice, 267 Wildwood Terrace, Naperville, IL 60565.	For a ski trip, you need very warm gloves. Please find the warmest gloves sold by this website and buy them.
Open Task	Please buy the sweater you would prefer to wear yourself.	Pretend that you have just moved from Florida to a cold climate and that you don't own any winter clothes. Please buy what you will need to be able to go for a walk in freezing temperatures.	Pretend that you have just moved from Florida to a cold climate and that you don't own any winter clothes. Please buy what you will need to be able to go for a walk in freezing temperatures.
Customer Service or Information-Seeking Task	Your aunt received the large blue sweater that you bought earlier. Upon trying it on, she discovered that she needs a size Medium instead. Are you allowed to return a purchase for this reason? Please find out exactly what you should do to exchange the sweater.	Is there a J. Crew shop in San Francisco? If so, what is the address?	Pretend that you have received the gloves that you were looking at earlier. While trying them on, you discover that you really need a different size. Are you allowed to return a purchase for this reason? If yes, please find out exactly what you should do to exchange the gloves.

Toy Sites

	A. SmarterKids	B. Disney	C. eToys
Specific Task	You want to get some software for your niece, who is 6. She is interested in science, especially space. Her mom says that she has the *Magic School Bus* CD on the human body and likes it. Your niece's name is Robin Rice and her address is 267 Wildwood Terrace, Naperville, IL 60565.	Your 6-year-old niece loves Winnie the Pooh. Find some sort of stuffed Pooh to send her. You can spend about $20. Your niece's name is Robin Rice and her address is 267 Wildwood Terrace, Naperville, IL 60565.	You want to get a gift for your 3-year-old nephew. He loves Hot Wheels cars and has several of them (the non-motorized kind), but he doesn't have anything to run them on. You need to keep the total cost of the gift under $20. Your nephew's name is Adam Rice and his address is 267 Wildwood Terrace, Naperville, IL 60565.
Open Task	Your 10-year-old nephew is getting only average grades in math. You want to get him something to help him develop his math skills. But if it isn't fun, he'll just ignore it.	Your niece and nephew (ages 6 and 3) love the Lion King and Toy Story videos. Send them something related to these videos as a gift. (And they don't always share well, so if it's not something they can enjoy together you might get two separate gifts.)	Your 2-year-old loves Barney and Thomas the Tank Engine. He loves unwrapping gifts, so you want to get him as many presents as you can, keeping the total less than $25.
Customer Service or Information-Seeking Task	You're not sure how the prices on this site compare to those at the toy store down the street. Will this site do anything if you can find a toy for less money than they're charging?	You bought your nephew a Baseball Pooh Mini Bean Bag, not realizing he already has one. You no longer have the original packaging — can you return it?	Your child's birthday is coming up and she has a long list of toys she wants. Several relatives will be getting something for her, and you want to avoid duplicates. Can this site help you manage this problem?

Flower Sites

	A. Iflorist	B. 1800flowers
Specific Task	Find some roses to send to your mother. Pick whatever color and arrangement you think she'd like, as long as you get at least a dozen.	Find some roses to send to your mother. Pick whatever color and arrangement you think she'd like, as long as you get at least a dozen.
Open Task	Your elderly aunt has just returned home after an operation. Send her something to cheer her up. Keep the total cost under $50. Her address is: Pearl Hanes 87 Brookwood Dr. Wheaton, IL 60187	Your elderly aunt has just returned home after an operation. Send her something to cheer her up. Keep the total cost under $50. Her address is: Pearl Hanes 87 Brookwood Dr. Wheaton, IL 60187
Customer Service or Information-Seeking Task	You're thinking of getting your significant other some flowers for Valentine's Day, but you tend to put things off until the last minute. How far ahead of time do you have to order the flowers to make sure they arrive in time?	You want to send flowers to someone who works from noon until 8 pm. Can you have the flowers sent to her home in the morning? If not, what should you do?

Food Sites

	A. Gevalia	B. Peet's	C. BasketHaus
Specific Task	A friend of yours has a different kind of coffee maker that you fill with hot water and push the plunger down (see picture). It makes great coffee so you want to get one for yourself.	A friend of yours has a different kind of coffee maker that you fill with hot water and push the plunger down (see picture). It makes great coffee so you want to get one for yourself.	Choose something with lots of candy and chocolate in it.
Open Task	Select several special coffees that you particularly enjoy and arrange for them to be delivered to your home on a regular basis. Decide if the delivery amount of coffee will be enough for your household.	Your manager at work would like you to order coffee for the office from time to time. There are 10 coffee drinkers. Decide what to buy and make this process as easy as possible for yourself.	Your best friends just bought a house. Choose something for a housewarming gift, buy it, and send a note with the gift.
Customer Service or Information-Seeking Task	You now have 20 extra pounds of coffee in your freezer. You want to make the deliveries less frequent or have less coffee delivered at a time. How can you best do this?	What if you hate the coffee you bought, after drinking some of it? Can you get a refund?	You need to know if you can get an order sent on your friend's birthday, which is 2 weeks from now. How can you do this?

Furniture Sites

	A. Furniture	B. Living	C. HermanMiller
Specific Task	Your uncle needs a suitable piece of furniture to store 20–30 bottles of wine in his dining room. The dining room is English Country style. Can you find something suitable for him?	Your aunt wants a rocking chair. Can you find something suitable for her?	You overheard a conversation between two co-workers about a product on this website. It seems to be a cleverly designed bag for a portable PC, which also functions as a desktop. Find out precisely what it is.
Open Task	You want a new table for six persons for your dining room. Find a table that suits your taste and order it.	Your two boys share a bedroom. They need a new bed. All the other kids on the road have beds in two levels, like berths in a ship. Find a bed that suits them and order it.	Your boss has given you permission to buy an office chair of your choice for your new home office. No price limit! Find a chair that suits you and order it.
Customer Service or Information-Seeking Task	Order their paper catalog.	Can you try out the furniture before you make your final decision?	Is it possible to cancel an order after you have submitted it?

Department Store Sites

	A. Nordstrom	B. Sears	C. Wal-Mart
Specific Task	Order a Lego watch for your niece, who is 10 years old.	Order a cordless power drill, approximately 10V.	Find their cheapest toaster and order it.
Open Task	You just got a new job. To celebrate your new job, your rich aunt gave you a $200 gift certificate from Nordstrom. Order something that suits your taste to remind you of the event.	Your old microwave oven just went on strike. The repairman says it will cost you more than the price of a new one to repair it. Select a new micro-wave oven that best fits your needs and order it.	One of your friends has a son. You have been invited to his 1 year birthday. Find a suitable car seat for the baby and order it.
Customer Service or Information-Seeking Task	Can you get your money back if you are dissatisfied with the product you ordered after you receive it?	Is it possible to cancel an order after you have submitted it?	Two days after you bought the car seat, you found exactly the same seat $10 cheaper in a local store. Can you get the $10 difference refunded?

References

Adams, Anne and Martina Angela Sasse. December 1999. Users Are Not The Enemy. *Communications of the ACM*. Pages 41–46.
This is an excellent article about motivating users to create secure passwords.

Apple Computer. 1993. *Macintosh Human Interface Guidelines.*
Addison–Wesley.
ISBN 0201622165

Cheskin and Studio Archetype. 1999. *E-Commerce Trust.*
http://www.sapient.com/cheskin

This is a user study of Web trust. The key finding was that trust is a long-term proposition that builds slowly as people use a site, get good results, and don't feel let down or cheated. In other words, true trust comes from a company's actual behavior towards customers over an extended set of encounters. The methodology has a few weaknesses. Most quotes were from super-users, not regular folks. Also, users were asked to view sites rather than buy things from the sites. Nonetheless, the main results are credible and match earlier studies.

Del Galdo, E.M. and Jakob Nielsen (eds.). 1996. *International User Interfaces.*
New York, NY: John Wiley & Sons.
ISBN: 0471149659
http://www.useit.com/papers/international_usetest.html

This book is a collection of chapters on topics dealing with usability engineering, culture and design, international differences in software user training, case studies on international user interface design, and the design of multilingual documents. Examples of Arabic, Chinese, Japanese, and European designs are shown. An excerpt from Jakob Nielsen's chapter on international usability engineering in this book is available from the URL cited.

Designing More Usable Web Sites
http://www.trace.wisc.edu/world/web

Trace Research and Development Center's comprehensive site is dedicated to accessibility tools and information.

Dumas, Joseph S. and Janice C. Redish. 1999. *A Practical Guide to Usability Testing.* (rev. ed.) Intellect.
ISBN 1-84150-020-8
http://www.intellectbooks.com/authors/dumas/practic.htm

From the publisher: "In this volume, the authors begin by defining usability, advocating and explaining the methods of usability engineering and reviewing many techniques for assessing and assuring usability throughout the development process. ... It discusses the full range of testing options from quick studies with a few subjects to more formal tests with carefully designed controls. ... Included are forms to use or modify to conduct a usability test, as well as layouts of existing labs that will help the reader build his or her own."

Earth Calendar
http://www.earthcalendar.net

A resource site for culture-linked holidays around the world. Site information is not always current.

Egger, F.N. and B. de Groot. 2000. Developing a Model of Trust for Electronic Commerce: An Application to a Permissive Marketing Web Site. *Poster Proceedings of the 9th International World Wide Web Conference — Amsterdam, The Netherlands.* Reston, VA: Foretec Seminars Inc. Pages 92–93. ISBN 1-930792-01-8
http://www.ipo.tue.nl/homepages/fegger/WWW9.htm

This is an interesting model of trust and an application of the model. The model has four main components: pre-interactional filters (factors affecting trust before the site is accessed); interface properties; informational content (competence, risk); and relationship management (all aspects of customer service).

Fogg, B.J. and Jonathan Marshall, et al. 2000. Elements that Affect Web Credibility: Early Results from a Self-Report Study. *CHI 2000 Extended Abstracts.* ACM Press. Pages 287–288.
http://www.webcredibility.org

The authors conducted an online survey about Web credibility. The self-report study was carried out in the US and in Finland, and it included more than 1,400 participants. People reported that website credibility increased when the site conveyed a real-world presence, was easy to use, and was updated often. People reported that a website lost credibility when it had errors, technical problems, or distracting advertisements.

Forms in HTML Documents
http://www.w3.org/TR/REC-html40/interact/forms.html

This site is the definitive reference for HTML 4.01. This page explains the controls, form elements and attributes. Of particular interest is "17.11 Giving focus to an element," which explains keyboard access to form elements and how to set options for particular fields to a default or keyboard shortcut.

Godin, Seth. 1999. *Permission Marketing.* Simon & Schuster.
ISBN 0-684-85636-0

Godin says the more messages are shoved at us, the more we ignore them. His solution is to allow customers to choose the messages they receive, so they will be less likely to screen them out.

Hoffman, Donna L., Thomas Novak, and Marcos Peralta. April 1999. Building Consumer Trust Online. *Communications of the ACM.* Pages 80–85.

The paper discusses the conflicting interests for consumers and commercial website providers. The paper was based on consumer responses to two biannual surveys:

- The spring "1997 Nielsen Media Research / CommerceNet Internet Demographics Study" (1,555 Web users). Note: This survey was carried out by Nielsen Media Research (www.nielsenmedia.com), not by Jakob Nielsen (www.useit.com).
- The "1997 Georgia Tech GVU 7th WWW User Survey" (14,014 self-selected Web users).

Hurst, Mark. September 1999. Holiday '99 E-Commerce. *CreativeGood.*
http://www.creativegood.com

This 75-page report focuses on the customer experience of 10 e-commerce websites in August 1999. Mark Hurst tested each of the 10 sites in 45 user tests in which he watched "average" online shoppers attempt to find and buy items they wanted. The tested websites were Avon, Beyond, Buybooks, Disney, eToys, Godiva, LLBean, PETsMART, Sharperimage, and Wal-Mart.

The main findings are in the areas of customer experience, home pages, branding, categories, and search. The eight-page section on search corroborates some of the findings in the Search chapter.

Intercultural Issues. ACM SIGCHI.
http://www.acm.org/sigchi/intercultural

This website has an extensive number of links to useful resources such as books, companies that develop software for intercultural / multilingual markets, newsgroups, standards, and translation. The website also contains links to articles about more specific issues such as character sets, date format, online dictionaries for different languages, examples of systems that have been internationalized or localized, and usability issues.

Jarvenpaa, Sirkka L. and Noam Tractinsky, et al. December 1999. Consumer Trust in an Internet Store: A Cross-Cultural Validation. Electronic Commerce and the Web. *Journal of Computer-Mediated Communication.*
http://www.ascusc.org/jcmc/vol5/issue2/jarvenpaa.html

This study is a cross-cultural validation of an Internet consumer trust model. The paper focuses on the consumer's initial development of trust in a commercial online store. The validation was carried out in Australia, Israel, and Finland by 100–200 participants in each country. To give an example, this is one of the seven hypotheses tested — and validated — in this study: The store's perceived reputation is positively associated with a consumer's trust in an Internet store.

Jerome, Marty. December 2000. E-Commerce Showdown. *Ziff Davis Smart Business for the New Economy.* Pages 104–119.

Lerner, Michael. September 1999. *Building Worldwide Web Sites.*
http://www-4.ibm.com/software/developer/library/web-localization.html

A short and interesting summary of the author's localization experiences. Author's summary: "Playing in the global economy means preparing Web sites that speak to customers and communities all over the world. Find out ways to convert your Web sites to reach other cultures effectively, starting with language translation. But don't just translate — localize your site. With ten tips for localizing without tears."

Marcus, Aaron and Emilie West Gould. July 2000. Crosscurrents — Cultural Dimensions and Global Web User-Interface Design. *interactions.* ACM (Association for Computing Machinery). Pages 32–46.

"Companies that want to do international business on the Web must consider the impact of culture on the understanding and use of Web-based communication, content, and tools." The article contains an interesting discussion of dimensions of culture. The practical examples are few and their relation to the text is not always clear. The article ends with a good list of resources.

Microsoft. September 1999. Localization. *Microsoft Windows User Experience.* Microsoft Press. Pages 494–509.
ISBN: 0735605661

Microsoft is one of the most experienced and authoritative companies in the world regarding localization. Read what they have to say about text, layout, graphics, keyboards, character sets, formats, and so forth. Even though the section is written for Windows designers, it contains much valuable information for Web designers.

Nancy Hoft Consulting
http://world-ready.com/r_intl.htm

Excellent resource site for English as a Second Language and cultural differences worldwide.

Molich, Rolf, Nigel Bevan, Ian Curson, Scott Butler, Erika Kindlund, Dana Miller, and Jurek Kirakowski. June 1998. *Comparative Usability Evaluation (CUE) Tests.*
http://www.dialogdesign.dk/cue.html

CUE-2 is a comparative usability test of the popular www.hotmail.com website. Nine teams have simultaneously usability tested this website. Their reports are available from this URL, along with overall findings about the study.

Nielsen, Jakob. February 18, 2001. Success Rate: The Simplest Usability Metric. *Jakob Nielsen's Alertbox.*
http://www.useit.com/alertbox/20010218.html

Nielsen, Jakob. 2000. *Designing Web Usability: The Practice of Simplicity.* New Riders. Translated into 13 additional languages. For international titles and ISBN numbers, see http://www.useit.com/jakob/webusability
ISBN 1-56205-810-X

This book explains how to design for the user and avoid common mistakes in every major aspect of Web development today.

Nielsen, Jakob. March 19, 2000. Why You Only Need to Test With 5 Users. *Jakob Nielsen's Alertbox.*
http://www.useit.com/alertbox/20000319.html

"Elaborate usability tests are a waste of resources. The best results come from testing no more than 5 users and running as many small tests as you can afford."

Nielsen, Jakob. 1999. Trust or Bust: Communicating Trustworthiness in Web Design. *Jakob Nielsen's Alertbox.*
http://www.useit.com/alertbox/990307.html

"True trust comes from a company's actual behavior towards customers experienced over an extended set of encounters." The article explains how websites communicate trust and why e-mail addresses must be used sensitively.

Nielsen, Jakob. 1994. *Usability Engineering.* Cambridge MA: Academic Press, Inc.
ISBN: 0-12-518405-0

This book surveys the different methods and explains when to use each in the design process.

Nielsen, Jakob. 1993. *Usability Engineering.* AP Professional.
ISBN 0-12518-406-9

Nielsen, Jakob and Thomas K. Landauer. 1993. A mathematical model of the finding of usability problems. *Proceedings of ACM INTERCHI '93 Conference*, **Amsterdam, The Netherlands.** Pages 206–213.

Nielsen Norman Group's Scorecard service.
Nielsen Norman Group can deliver a scorecard that measures your site's compliance with the e-commerce design guidelines in this book.
http://www.nngroup.com/services/scorecard

Nua Internet Surveys
http://www.nua.ie

Rehman, Aamir. October 2000. Holiday 2000 E-Commerce.
Creative Good.
http://www.creativegood.com

SDL International, Article Section
http://www.sdlintl.com/articles/nav/main.htm

SDL International is a globalization solutions provider. Their article section contains interesting articles on localization and related issues, for example, "How to Internationalize Your Web Site and Make It Localizable" and "SDL — Tips for Web Site Localization." Access to some of the articles requires registration, which is uncomplicated and free.

Rubin, Jeffrey. 1994. *Handbook of Usability Testing: How to Plan, Design, and Conduct Effective Tests.* John Wiley & Sons.
ISBN 0-471-59403-2

A step-by-step practical guide to usability testing, including templates, models, tables, test plans, and other indispensable tools.

Souza, Randy K. October 2000. The Best of Retail Site Design.
The Forrester Report.
http://www.forrester.com/ER/Baseline/QuickView/0,1338,10003,FF.html

Spool, Jared M., Tara Scanlon, Will Schroeder, Carolyn Snyder, and Terri DeAngelo. 1998. *Web Site Usability: A Designer's Guide.* Morgan Kaufman.
ISBN 1-55860-569-X

This 156-page classic describes what happened when users attempted to find information on eight information-rich websites in late 1996. The tested websites were Edmund's, Hewlett Packard, WebSaver, Travelocity, Inc.com, C|net, Fidelity, and Disney. The main findings are in the areas of navigation, links, search, readability, and graphic design. Although this book is based on usability studies conducted in 1996, most of its findings still hold true. It describes problems with comparing products on websites, including sites that cause "pogo-sticking."

Underhill, Paco. 1999. *Why We Buy: The Science of Shopping.* Simon & Schuster.
ISBN 0-684-84913-5

Underhill has spent decades hiding behind potted palms in stores, watching how customers' buying patterns were affected by the layout of the store and merchandise. In essence, he was testing stores for usability long before usability testing was commonplace. The book includes a chapter on e-commerce, but it's sketchy, as Underhill tries to extrapolate his extensive knowledge of physical stores to websites. The true value of this book is its message that you learn fascinating things when you watch people shop.

Web Accessibility Initiative
http://www.w3.org/WAI

Web Content Accessibility Guidelines Working Group
http://www.w3.org/WAI/GL

Web Content Accessibility Guidelines – most recent version
http://www.w3.org/TR/WAI-WEBCONTENT

The three URLs above point to the authoritative reference materials for Web accessibility. Most, if not all, of the major accessibility resources can be found through these pages.

Weinman, Lynda. 1999. *Designing Web Graphics.3.* New Riders Publishing. ISBN: 1562059491

The classic reference, updated. It focuses on image and software issues for the Web, including color considerations, image editing, image formats, and which tools do what. The original edition made some hotly debated usage recommendations, but most of the theory seems to be sound, and it remains the most popular tutorial on its subject.

Worldwide Holiday and Festival Site
http://www.holidayfestival.com

This website is a resource for religious and national holidays worldwide. Some information is free.

Wright, Patricia. 1983. Manual Dexterity — A User-Oriented Approach to Creating Computer Documentation. *Human Factors in Computing Systems. Special Issue of the SIGCHI Bulletin.* Conference on Human Factors in Computing Systems. New York: Association for Computing Machinery (ACM). Reprinted in **Baecker, R. A. and W. A. S. Buxton (eds.). 1987. *Readings in Human-Computer Interaction: A Multidisciplinary Approach.*** Los Altos, CA: Morgan Kauffman.

The search model used in the Search chapter was inspired by the FLUID model for user documentation. The FLUID model consists of the following steps:

1. Formulate the problem.
2. Locate the proper place in the documentation.
3. Understand the message.
4. Implement the solution.
5. Determine whether the problem has been solved.

The paper both describes the model and uses the model to derive a number of practical actions that a documentation writer should take to write more usable documentation.

About the Authors

The entire team planned the studies and evaluated the results. The studies were conducted and observed by Rolf Molich and Sofie Scheutz (Denmark), and Carolyn Snyder (New Hampshire). Although each report has a primary author, reports were extensively reviewed by all members of the team. We are also indebted to Tom Durkin for editorial assistance, Steven Thomas for design, and Shuli Gilutz for research.

Nielsen Norman Group

48921 Warm Springs Blvd.
Fremont, CA 94539, USA
www.nngroup.com

Jakob Nielsen <nielsen@nngroup.com>
Susan Farrell <farrell@nngroup.com>

Jakob Nielsen, Ph.D., is principal of Nielsen Norman Group. His latest book, *Designing Web Usability: The Practice of Simplicity*, has sold a quarter million copies in 13 languages. In its review, *Business Week* said that the book "should [...] be read by any executive with responsibility for managing online operations." *NewMedia* magazine called it "the most important book of the year." Nielsen's *Alertbox* column has been published on the Web since 1995 and has more than 200,000 readers (www.useit.com/alertbox). Dr. Nielsen has been called: "the world's leading expert on Web usability" (*U.S. News & World Report*), "the next best thing to a true time machine" (*USA Today*), "the reigning guru of Web usability" (*FORTUNE*), "the smartest person on the Web" (*ZDNet*), "eminent Web usability guru" (*CNN*), "the usability Pope" (*Wirtschaftswoche Magazine*, Germany), and "the patron saint of ordinary computer users" (*Dr. Dobb's Journal*).

Susan Farrell has been a Web developer since 1993. Before joining Nielsen Norman Group as a user experience specialist in 1999, she worked in Human Computer Interaction at Sun Microsystems and in Customer Service Tools Research and Development at Silicon Graphics.

DialogDesign

Skovkrogen 3
DK-3660 Stenlose, Denmark
www.dialogdesign.dk

Rolf Molich <molich@dialogdesign.dk>
Sofie Scheutz <sofie.scheutz@dialogdesign.dk>

Rolf Molich is an independent usability consultant with more than 25 years of experience in the software industry. He has been working in usability since 1984. Before starting DialogDesign in 1997, Rolf Molich worked in the Methodology department of various Danish companies. He is the author of *Usable Computer Systems* (available in Danish only). He and Jakob Nielsen invented the heuristic inspection method.

Sofie Scheutz is a usability consultant for DialogDesign where she has been employed since January 1999, when she completed her master's degree in Rhetoric.

Snyder Consulting

88 Brookwood Drive
Salem, NH 03079, USA
www.snyderconsulting.net

Carolyn Snyder <snyder3961@mediaone.net>

Carolyn Snyder is an independent usability consultant with more than 17 years of experience in the software industry. Before starting Snyder Consulting in March 1999, Carolyn was a principal consultant at User Interface Engineering. Carolyn is co-author of *Web Site Usability: A Designer's Guide*.

Summary of Recommendations for Designers

Selling Strategies

Trust

Category Pages

Search

Index

A

abandoned shopping carts, 4, 8
About Us. *See* company information
accessibility, 262
ad blindness, 53
address book, 258
address forms, 254, 255
  errors made, 261
  international, 312, 317
  layout for international users, 292
  multiple recipients, 258
  showing examples, 314
  alphabetical order, 130
ALT text, 206
Amazon.com
  login form, 286
analyzing data, 349
animated assistant, 64
asterisks
  required fields, 265
autofill, 260
availability
  definition, 34
  sales catastrophes, 39
availability, 218
  methods of showing, 219

B

B2B guidelines, 20
Back button, 32, 241
  losing cart information, 225
benefits, 27, 29
bias, 347
billing address
  forms, 254
brand names, 82
browsers, 342
browsing
  multiple windows, 12
  parallel, 3
buttons
  multiple button confusion, 233
Buy button, 50, 231
  placement, 232
  problems finding it, 231

C

case sensitivity in search, 171

checkout
  step diagrams, 245
checkout process, 287
cleanup between users, 342
clearance, 39
collecting data, 348
color
  name problems, 221
  showing available, 222
  showing product, 221
company information
  what to include, 78–79
comparison shopping, 147
confirmation e-mail, 271, 342
consent form, 356
consider offering, 53
continue shopping button, 240
conversion rate, 2
cookies, 342
cost of usability, 22
costs
  show all, 215
credit cards
  accept a variety, 49
cultural differences, 320
cultural issues, 336
currency, 214
currency converter, 302
cursor placement, 171
custom search result pages, 161
customer
  needs, 3
  service representatives, 39
  expectations, 43

D

Danish tests, 346
data
  analysis, 349
  collection, 348
default
  changed without notice, 43
defaults
  most recent choice, 227
definition of shopping, 5
delivery
  showing delivery information, 217
  options, 251

delivery area
  problems finding, 293
delivery information
  additional, 45
  large, perishable items, 253
delivery time, 43
  definition, 34
  customer expectations, 44
  sales catastrophes, 43
demographics of participants, 333
design guidelines
  developing, 5
disclaimers
  didn't help, 223
discount usability testing, 235, 330
don't substitute cleverness for helpfulness, 64
download time
  perceived, 130
  costs some users money, 322
downloads, 203
drop-down menu, 258

E

e-mail address, 100
  two-piece form, 261
  providing. *See* personal information
e-mail confirmation, 271
e-mail newsletters. *See* newsletters
email accounts for testing, 342
empty shopping cart, 232
  encouraging additional, 55
English As a Second Language, 307
Enter / Return key, 171, 262
error messages, 92
  constructing, 263
  in search results, 185
error recovery, 263
estimate, 44
example observation table, 350
examples
  on forms, 314
external links
  must be useful, 298
eye tracker, 235

F

facilitating usability tests, 345
failure
  definition, 351
  examples, 353

sales catastrophes, 352
  task, 351
false personal information, 345
feedback
  shopping cart, 234
feedback form, 39
form
  tools, 255
form elements, 93
  preserve information, 95
forms
  entry errors, 261
  international, 258
  losing data, 260
Furniture Finder, 141. *See also* winnowing

G

gift
  certificates, 67
  confirm delivery, 71
  registry, 67
  wrapping, 69
grouping by visual similarity, 132
guarantee, 82, 97, 216
guideline compliance
  by design aspect, 18
  by size of site, 17
guidelines
  B2B, 20
  company-specific, 21
  compliance with, 16
  development costs, 21
  development methodology, 21
  multiple levels of, 20
  review, 19

H

help, 255
helping users, 347
hints, 280
holidays
  international mistakes, 322
hybrid stores, 71

I

images
  dark-colored products, 136
  high-quality, 29
  missing, 91
  noticeable, 231

order summary, 266
ordering
  alternative methods, 106
other e-commerce studies, 7

P

password
  creating, 275
  explaining, 278
  hints, 280
  inventing, 279
  secret question, 280
payment
  alternatives, 49
  forms, 268
  options, 49
personal information
  appropriate use, 98
  asking for, 254
  phone numbers, 99
  re-using, 260
  reluctant to enter, 98
  Social Security number, 99
  someone else's, 100
phone numbers, 99
pilot tests, 343
plug-ins, 203
policies, 26, 97, 216
  customer satisfaction, 46
  links to, 46
  testing, 98
pre-ordering, 42
pre-test documents, 334
price
  click for, email for, 30
  hidden, 29
  justify odd, 85
  perceived value, 27
  sales catastrophes, 27
  show currency, 214
  show total, 30
  where to show, 214
privacy policy, 46, 97, 255, 275.
product
  options, 220
  comparisons, 147
    See also comparison shopping
  descriptions for international users, 307
  out-of-stock, 39
product images, 206

alternative views, 211
  buying decisions, 208
  color options, 222
  enlarged, 209
product information
  layering, 200
product listings
  show 2–3 pages, 14
product options
  when there is only one choice, 227
  when to specify, 225
  where to show them, 228
product pages
  details users wanted, 197
  examples, 194
production process, 29
prototyping
  rapid, 235

Q

queries
  most unique word, 168
  multiple-word, 168
  no one used quotes, 168
questionnaire
  post-test, 348
  pre-test, 357
  screening, 355
  site feedback, 358

R

rapid prototyping, 235
ratings, 201
RealPlayer, 203
recruitment of users, 333
registration
  allow customers to cancel, 104, 105
  approaches, 272
  do not require, 272
  incentive, 104, 105
  incentives, 274
  make it optional, 104, 105
  optional, 273
  why it fails, 271
Remove button, 242
reputation
  ranking, 83
required fields
  asterisks, 265
Return key, 262